BASIC MATHEMATICS FOR ADMINISTRATION

BASIC MATHEMATICS

FOR ADMINISTRATION

F. PARKER FOWLER, JR.

**Assistant Professor of
Business Administration
Colorado State University**

E. W. SANDBERG

**Associate Professor of
Business Administration
Colorado State University**

JOHN WILEY & SONS, INC. NEW YORK • LONDON

Second Printing, April 1963

Library of Congress Catalog Card Number: 62-15189

Printed in the United States of America

TO GRETCHEN AND PHYLLIS

Preface

This book is the result of almost four years of study and experiment at Colorado State University, where, as in many universities, the program in business administration has expanded at a phenomenal rate. At the same time, recent developments in the subject matter of administration, understandable and teachable at the undergraduate level, have required changes in the curriculum, which included the development of a mathematics course at the freshman level to prepare students for these studies. Many constraints upon the project existed: our students were generally poorly prepared in mathematics, many submitting the minimum requirement of one year of high school algebra; thus the course had to be rudimentary, although not necessarily remedial. To serve its purpose properly, it had to be extensive, covering many subjects in mathematics rather than delving intensively into a few. The amount of time which the student could allocate to mathematics courses was a further consideration, and thus the course had to be of a terminal nature.

Within these constraints, we have experienced an unexpected degree of success, in terms of both the students' achievement and their willingness (we are much too modest to say eagerness!) to tackle what for the most part was new to them. Many of their reactions, criticisms, and suggestions are incorporated in this book, which, like any of its type, could continue to so benefit if it were not for publication deadlines.

A noticeable difference between this book and a standard mathematics textbook is the absence of theorems and their proofs. We feel that the study of mathematics by rigorous proofs of theorems, although necessary to the mathematician, is not only unnecessary for the level of understanding and operational competence we wish to attain, but also prejudicial to its attainment. Thus we have attempted to explain the mathematical reasoning behind certain concepts in an intuitive, discursive fashion, sketching mathematical proofs in our lectures when it seemed advisable. Although we have not held our students responsible for the development of the mathematical ideas, we do hold them responsible for understanding the abstractions with which they work, and for interpreting results. In short, our concern is not with the internal development of the mathematics, but with its ability to handle certain types of problems. (Of course, students who desire to go further in mathematics are encouraged to follow the regular curriculum of the mathematics department.)

The development of our course and book could not have been possible without the encouragement and cooperation of many people, notable among whom is Professor M. L. Madison, Head of the Department of Mathematics at Colorado State University. It requires a very special type of person to allow interlopers to roam at will within his province of responsibility, not to mention encouraging them to do so. Professor Madison's sympathy with our point of view and his appreciation of our goals, even in the face of violence done to his discipline, are deeply appreciated. Our thanks also go to Professor Walter C. Butler of the Department of Mathematics, Colorado State University, for assistance in the early development of the course, and to Professors Franklin A. Graybill and Ervin R. Deal, both of the Department of Mathematics, Colorado State University, for reading the manuscript. Any errors of commission or omission are of course ours, since these adept people also displayed heroic self-control concerning our methods and substance. Mrs. Mary Jane Butler Dodson, always cheerful, did yeoman's work, typing the book manuscript accurately and with consummate speed. And to Mrs. Wilda Christensen and Mrs. Lois Stroh goes our gratitude for all their work in getting the course underway and producing the original manuscripts. Graduate students Donald K. Olsen, Alan C. Utter, and Joel R. Manzolillo did a fine job in tutorial sessions and contributed materially by their suggestions.

F. P. Fowler, Jr.
E. W. Sandberg

Fort Collins, Colorado
March, 1962

Foreword to the Student

Good old Charlie Brown and Lucy, characters in the "Peanuts" comic strip, were discussing academic affairs one day.

LUCY: How are you doing in school these days, Charlie Brown?

CHARLIE BROWN: Oh, fairly well, I guess . . . I'm having most of my trouble in arithmetic.

LUCY: I should think you'd like arithmetic. It's a very precise subject.

CHARLIE BROWN: That's just the trouble. I'm at my best in something where the answers are mostly a matter of opinion!*

There is little doubt that Charlie Brown's attitude is shared by most students, for the study of mathematics seems to require an inordinate amount of work. In addition, much of mathematics appears to be of little use to the student planning a career in other than engineering or "scientific" fields. As to the former criticism, we can only pass along the true but hardly satisfying bromide that anything worthwhile requires hard work. However, we should like to express some "Charlie

*Peanuts, copyright 1959, by United Feature Syndicate, Inc.

Brown"opinions on the usefulness of mathematics to the student of administration.

Only a few years ago the standard image of the successful administrator or manager was that of the fellow who rose to a position of leadership by dint of early rising, thrift, aggressiveness, and luck, among other virtues extolled by people like Benjamin Franklin. This man's training consisted almost entirely of on-the-job experience, and often his success was measured not by any new ideas he produced, but by how well he emulated his teachers. It does not seem strange that nothing but personal criteria for success should have evolved from such a system; thus, early collegiate schools of commerce concerned themselves with the technical details of business processes, such as accounting, legal instruments, and office skills.

As national and international markets for raw materials and finished goods and the money capital necessary for production and distribution matured in the first half of this century, schools of commerce broadened their offerings to include descriptions of the manner in which these markets, and the resulting institutions, both public and private, had developed. The stereotype of the administrator of that era was the business tycoon, the exploiter who apparently cared little for the means by which he attained his somewhat questionable goals.

Some thirty years ago, there were people who began to detect another fundamental change in the nature of the administrator: he was developing into a hired professional. He was skilled in getting things done in order to reach prescribed goals, and his primary equipment was the ability to make decisions toward that end. The beginning of the last half of this century marks the emergence of the *executive*, whose responsibility in the increasingly complex world of administration is not primarily *to do* but *to decide*. Even the smallest businesses today find this distinction important. We find the traditional school of commerce becoming a college of administration, whose graduates not only enjoy the collected experience of the past, as reflected in institutional developments, but more importantly have been exposed to the science of decision-making. It would of course be fatuous to say that man has begun to make decisions only in the past decade; we are talking not about a new phenomenon, but about a new emphasis which is the result of changes in the way man goes about his affairs.

We do not propose these remarks as the result of any kind of clairvoyance; the evidence that these changes have taken place is readily at hand. Have you ever seen the comic strip "Buck Rogers in the 25th Century?" Some twenty years ago it dealt with space ships, satellites, moon voyages, and other fanciful dreams; its only error appears now to have been in the title. At the present rate of change in the nature of our institutions and technology, it is even more important that the student be equipped to analyze and decide, for this function of man will never be outdated.

The course in which this book is used is only designed to lay the groundwork for your future studies in administration. As we shall point out, the study of decision-making requires a more precise and powerful language than English, and the purpose of this book is to present the necessary fundamentals of a language that can improve your ability to understand the decision processes you will study later, and accordingly can improve your ability to contribute both to society and to yourself.

Contents

Administration
Chapter 1 ——————— and
Mathematics

1.1 Introduction

How many widgets should we carry in inventory? ... What is the best sales promotion program for July? ... Should we meet union demands for a higher wage? ... What strategy should we employ to counteract fierce competitive pressure? ... How many minutes should we allow for employee coffee breaks? ... What monetary policy should be followed next quarter? ... What is the cheapest routing for this carload? ...

Such questions are the grist of the administrative mill and represent the types of problems faced by the administrator. By administrator we mean a person whose function it is to make decisions, i.e., to choose from among alternative courses of action that set of alternatives which will result in the attainment of certain specified goals. The decision process consists of searching for goals and alternative means for their attainment, evaluating the "payoff" that would result from the choice of any of the alternatives, and defining rules for choosing alternatives. In any industrial or institutional organization, no matter what its size, it is possible to identify the administrator (or executive or manager) because this is precisely his function: to decide, rather than to do. Obviously, every one of us is a decision maker. In enterprise directed to the attainment of goals, however, it is possible to distinguish the

1

administrator in terms of the nature of decisions which he must make, a clue to which is given at the beginning of this section.

No one would disagree that the world of business has changed radically since the advent of mechanization marked by the Industrial Revolution. Changes of perhaps even greater importance to the student of administration today are those which have ensued since World War II; we take for granted the assembly line and the monster integrated factory, as well as the big merchandising outlets and financial institutions. These outward appearances are startling, but even more startling are the subtle but sweeping changes that have been made in the administration of such enterprises. It stands to reason that the highly sophisticated business society in which we live today cannot be run by methods of a century ago, or even those in vogue twenty-five years ago. The development and implementation of the modern high-speed computer and data-processor have not only changed the means by which businesses are operated, but more importantly, they have caused the administrator to re-evaluate the total decision-making process. With the so-called "brains" available, it is reasonable that the wise administrator should search for further uses of this potential which, as a human being, he realizes he could not possibly possess. Thus, not only methods but total concepts of the administration of enterprises, whether public or private, have changed and continue to change at a rapid rate. The administrator of tomorrow, whether in big business or small, must not only understand these changes but must also be capable of turning them to his own use.

It is not our purpose here to explain in depth the nature of the "new" science of decision-making, but to point out the importance of mathematics in the study of this science. We hope that the student is sufficiently motivated in his desire to learn something about administration to take as "given" the definition of an administrator noted above. Considered in this light, mathematics is important to the administrator for reasons far more subtle than the obvious benefits to be gained from improving one's ability to perform arithmetic or "plug" numbers into some algebraic expression. The remainder of this chapter will be used to introduce these subtleties in terms of communication, with the hope that the student will be better able to comprehend both the art and the science of administration.

1.2 Communication

Communication is very "big" nowadays. We can hardly find an area of human endeavor in which communication is not recognized as one of the most important elements, if not *the* most important. Only a little speculation upon life and nature is required to illustrate the extent to which modern man is enmeshed in and constrained by this concept. As narrow examples, consider the billions of telephone calls made each year, or the millions of tons of newsprint, or the tremendous amount of mail handled by the post office. These are called "narrow" examples because they illustrate only one kind of communication— "people to people." We shall see that communication applies in other instances, too.

We should here make clear what we mean by this word communication since there are undoubtedly many ways in which we could construe the term. We shall mean the conception, coding, transmission, reception, decoding, and understanding of an *idea*, as it is communicated between two points, not necessarily persons. If we can effectively transfer an idea from one point to another, through a communications network, then we can say that communication has been established, and our system of communication is effective. There are semantic (word meaning) difficulties here, since some people consider that they either have communication, or they have not, purely on the basis of correct understanding of the original idea transmitted.

"When they said *brains*, I thought they said *trains*, and I told them I didn't want any." Here the original idea, brains, was misunderstood, and thus some would say that communication did not exist. Rather than going so far as this, however, we shall say that communication is established if the system or network within which ideas flow is established, i.e., that ideas could get through as originally intended if it were not for failures in certain parts of the system. Defining communication in this way allows us to speak of idea flows in relative terms, i.e., perfect or imperfect, or good or bad, etc. In our example above, we would say that communication is imperfect because of a defect in coding, transmission, reception, or decoding, or perhaps all four. Notice, however, that the error was not made at the very ends of the line. The conception of brains as a part of the original personal endowment was properly formulated; the receiver knew what the system was trying to communicate and also knew that he must make a decision among the alternatives offered to him. He understood, but the content of the message, the idea, had been garbled elsewhere in the system.

The system itself was operative, however, and we therefore say that communication existed, no matter how poor the result. Thus, communication exists if the system exists; however, if the intended idea is misunderstood, communication can be described as imperfect.

We have detailed our explanation of the communication phenomenon in order to emphasize the concept of a *system*, containing a number of parts each of which must operate properly if the original reason for setting up the system is to be satisfied. A new science, called *cybernetics*, has emerged in the last few years to deal with systems generally, and the importance of findings in this area cannot be overlooked by the modern administrator.

1.3   People to people

As has been pointed out, our most common notion of communication is the flow of ideas among people. For instance, our purpose in this chapter is to communicate to the reader an idea about communication itself. We have attempted this ambitious feat through the transmission device of the textbook, coded in the English language. Let us see what could happen to our system that might result in poor communication:

(*a*) *Conception:* The notion of communication is faultily conceived by the authors. (This is of course impossible by the definition of an author!)

(*b*) *Coding:* Here is a real stumbling block. The authors assume that the reader understands the English language, *as the authors understand it.* If the text were originally coded in gothic German, certainly the system would break down immediately when used in the United States. English is very often a poor code, because it is, among other things, ambiguous, as we shall see when we study logic.

(*c*) *Transmission:* Many people have an aversion to reading, and most people have an aversion to reading textbooks. On the other hand, most people do not mind reading the "funnies" or comic books, or looking at pictures, especially when the pictures move, as on television. Recognizing the aversion to textbooks, we wonder why this relatively ineffective transmission system is chosen to present so many important ideas. It is like using carrier pigeons or smoke signals to arrange a Saturday night date. There is no doubt that we could put together a "spectacular" in any number of academic areas, thereby overcoming this transmission problem, *if we had the money.* The cost of your textbook, however, is diminutive when compared with the cost of a television show, and it is doubtful that commercials, which pay the cost of the television show, would go over very well in the classroom.

(*d*) *Reception:* By reception we mean the simple physical fact of being in a position to receive the idea transmitted, as in having the radio or television tuned to the proper station, or even turned on. This element is important, for it appears that the human mind can assimilate only one idea at a time, being tuned out to any other ideas arriving simultaneously. How many times have you had to re-read something merely because you were not "concentrating" upon the subject initially? Another idea occupied your thoughts, and, although you went through the motions of reading, nothing registered. We hope, then, that as you read this book, you will be "tuned in," for, failing this, you will cause the system to break down.

(*e*) *Decoding:* Decoding is the counterpart to coding, and the student must be able to "break" the code used in the text. Once again, failure to understand the elements of the code (English words), causes the system to fail. Our "trains-brains" problem probably arises here. Since the words *sound* alike they were assumed to *be* alike (although it is also likely that the receptor was probably not very well tuned in). Thus the words or symbols used to transmit the original idea must be capable of being decoded, i.e., must mean the same thing to the receiver that they meant to the transmitter.

(*f*) *Understanding:* We know least about this process, although it appears that the receiver must have some reference to the transmitted idea stored somewhere in his brain, so that he might compare the new idea with a similar old idea and thus have some basis for action or reaction. Our unlucky friend did not need any trains; had he perceived the proper symbol, his answer would most likely have been different. Thus our system is also likely to break down at the very end, because the person to whom the idea was transmitted could make no "sense" of it, even though the other elements of the system operated very well.

The description above of the workings of a communication system and the difficulties which can be encountered therein should have an immediately apparent use in the determination of the cause of breakdown in any such system. Since the failure of any component of the system will cause the entire system to fail, it is quite important that we be able to identify the defective element correctly, and then take steps to improve the performance of that element.

The element of communications systems of greatest importance to us at the present time deals with the language used in the system, or the problems of encoding and decoding.   People communicate according to a learned language, and we know that the level of learning of all languages varies from person to person, whether he is learning his mother tongue or a foreign tongue.   The problems of international communication are great enough to have fostered a number of plans for a world language, "Esperanto" being one of them.   Any one language, however carefully it was originally devised, can be shown to have inconsistencies and ambiguities which render it a very imperfect element in communications.   Our own English language is one of the worst offenders.

Perhaps the most important characteristics of a language are its *precision* and its *power*.   By precision we mean the ability of the language to express exactly what the nature of any idea is; that the language has a "word" which describes perfectly some aspect of the idea which we wish to convey, and that this "word" may have no other meaning which may confuse the idea (unambiguous).   In addition, a precise language should also be succinct, i.e., be able to express our exact thought without a great deal of verbiage.   How often have you had to call something a thingamabob or whatchamacallit, or use such words as kind of or sort of, leaving your listener to fill in the blanks and hoping that his mental image of your idea is the same as yours?   On the other hand, you have undoubtedly been exposed to the professor who thinks and speaks in polysyllables, words which you not only have never heard, but do not even know how to spell, in order to look up their meanings.   We note here that these things called words are really only *symbols* for ideas, and, since we have just mentioned spelling, we should also note that it is necessary that encoding into words be done properly by spelling properly (trains-brains could have been a spelling error.)   Consider the Chinese, with some 450 one-syllable symbols and 30,000 unique words, the next time you are feeling bad about your inability to spell properly!

The English language is notorious for its imprecision.   Consider such prosaic words as *table* and *chair*, which have different meanings depending upon whether they are used as nouns or verbs.   Check the dictionary to see how "precisely" any word may be used.   We are all but defied to find a unique meaning for any given word.   Usually there are numerous meanings for any word, listed in order of preferred usage. Certainly these meanings are seldom the opposite of one another, but it is true that they are often sufficiently different to confuse the meaning intended, *except in context*.   We know that we usually expect our listener to condition the words which we use by the general nature of the subject about which we are talking, and thus a discussion of parliamentary procedure will produce a different image of the word chair from the one we have if we are looking for some place to rest our bones. The word-symbol then takes on meaning according to how it fits the subject, and it is important for the student to realize that this is true in most languages.

The second most important part of a language is its *power*, by which we mean the efficiency with which the language can be used to convert any idea into transmittable form. "A picture is worth 10,000 words," suggests that certain things can be handled only very inefficiently by word-symbols, i.e., that many symbols are required to transmit a certain total idea. Music is another medium of communication where word-symbols are insufficient to the task of transmitting ideas. Practically everyone enjoys music, yet relatively few people understand the written symbols from which the musician plays. (*Exercise:* Try to describe in words how to sing the first four bars of "Three Blind Mice," to someone who does not know what tune you are thinking of.) Telegraphy is a good example of what was once considered a powerful communication device, merely because the transmitting mechanism was so much superior to any previously known mechanism. The language used in this system, although precise, is very inefficient since each letter itself requires coding. A statement written in Morse code requires a tremendous number of symbols to communicate only a very few ideas. Finally, consider how often your tone of voice, expression, gestures, etc., play *the* important part in your daily communication with others, mostly because the English language word-symbols for many things are not sufficiently powerful to handle your message.

Once again, then, the precision and power of a language in which ideas can be expressed represent the important characteristics of that language; and the context, or subject area, within which the language is to be used becomes an important conditioning factor in the effectiveness of communication through the medium of that language.

1.3 Exercises

1.3.1 Analyze the following situations and indicate which aspect(s) of communications is(are) faulty:

(a) In order to complete the project on schedule, the job superintendent finds it necessary to work both Saturday and Sunday of the coming weekend. He stops a passing worker and says, "Tell the men you see that we have to work this weekend." Only part of the crew checks in Saturday morning.

(b) A graduate of Colorado State University in Civil Engineering is on his first job in Central Mexico. He did not take Spanish in school, and most of these people do not read or write English. He has found that his orders to his native work force are carried out in a haphazard manner, if at all.

(c) A large corporation has several departments, each being more or less independent. When a sale is made, a sales invoice is prepared in triplicate. One copy of the invoice is sent to the Accounts Receivable section and then forwarded to the Inventory Record clerk in the Purchasing Department. A large sale of a particular item completely depleted the stock of that item; the copy of the sales invoice was lost in the Accounts Receivable section; and thus the firm found itself unable to fill orders for that item for a protracted period of time, even though company records showed stock on hand.

(d) A massive, 150-foot tree falls to earth somewhere in Colorado's mountains, 50 miles from the nearest human being. No one heard it fall, and therefore we must assume that it made no noise.

(e) The personnel office wishes to reduce turnover to help control increasing recruiting and selection expenses. The office finds that company accidents have contributed to the high turnover rates. The safety engineer is called in and told to institute a comprehensive safety program to prevent further accidents. Many of his safety devices slow up production. The shop foreman's instructions are to increase production wherever possible. The safety engineer has been unable to convince the shop foreman of the benefit of installing any equipment which might reduce output.

1.3.2 Very often we must rely on the context of a sentence to interpret the meaning of a particular word known to have two or more meanings. List five words that pose this difficulty.

1.3.3 Often, in speaking or writing, we are faced with a situation where several different words would serve equally well to convey an idea. List five English words with five or more synonyms. (List synonyms as well.)

1.3.4 Describe the communication symbols which can be used between people to replace, supplement, or complement words.

1.4 People to things and vice versa

Many students will have wondered what all this has to do with mathematics, although it is hoped that many will be able to guess correctly what lies ahead. For mathematics is obviously a language; it satisfies the requirements of power and precision imposed upon any language within the context of its use. It turns out that mathematics is more than this, however, as we shall discuss later. For the time being, let us explore its nature as a communication device.

People constantly communicate with "things," by transmitting ideas through action into some accomplishment. The operation of a business is uniquely tied to the concept of an idea being converted into money through the complex transmitter of the business organization. The consumer himself converts ideas of need into satisfaction of that need. If the need is an economic one, we notice that his criterion of satisfaction is *value*, usually measured in monetary terms, as in the example above. Economic ideas, however, need not be limited to monetary terms. Relative satisfaction gained from one type of work as compared to another is not always determined by the size of salary earned. Other factors such as status and security may condition our evaluation of a job. Notice that even here we must have some concept of measurement, although not an absolute measurement such as that provided by measurement in money terms. In such a case we are said to *order* our preferences, ranking them in order of their ability to satisfy our needs. Such English word-symbols as "better" or "worse" imply that such an ordering has taken place, thus the term *ordinal* which connotes the ordering of something into "first," "second," etc. Ordinal ranking leaves something to be desired in a communications system since it is not precise; it does not specify "how much" better or worse one thing is than another. We know, however, that it is not always possible to be precise in measuring, and ordinal ranking may be very important if the alternative is no communication at all.

The last sentence implies what we wish to note about the communication of Things to People: just as conversations between people are seldom one-sided (except as between husband and wife), i.e., ideas flow in both directions, so the communication between people and things is bilateral. The sculptor imposes his ideas upon the block of stone, which behaves in a certain way under the blows of his hammer and chisel, reshaping and reforming the original idea of the sculptor. The businessman directs his enterprise by imposing his decisions upon the organization. As the organization responds, its behavior can be measured (for instance, by accounting techniques), and such information flows back to the decision maker to reshape his original ideas. Communications systems in business are highly complex, yet the importance of understanding them is recognized by every businessman. The languages of business, already alluded to as having something to do with money-number-symbols, are nonetheless poorly understood in practice, a condition about which this book purports to do something.

Without spending much time with the idea, the student might consider the nature of communication between and among "things." Such natural phenomena as the seasons, or meteorological arrangements, offer some tempting areas of speculation. The current development of automation, narrowly construed here as the automatic control of machines by other machines, is another case in point.

1.4 Exercise

1.4.1 With respect to communication between people and things, describe the information flow between: (**a**) typist and typewriter; (**b**) driver and automobile; (**c**) lathe operator and lathe.

1.5 Relationships

At the moment of birth (and, some psychologists speculate, even before that) human beings begin to learn. Until the brain matures to some extent, this learning takes place almost completely through experience: the small child touches a hot match, and learns the word-symbol "hot," which henceforth he associates with pain. It is undoubtedly true that experience is our best teacher throughout life; yet our lifetime is too limited to allow for direct experience with all possible things. Through communication, one man's experience and the ideas he has drawn from that experience may be transmitted to others, to become a part of their fund of knowledge without their actually having experienced the substance of the idea themselves. Once the small child has learned the meaning of the word "hot," it is no longer necessary for him to experience all those circumstances where the result might be a burning sensation, because he can be told that the stove is "hot," the cigarette is "hot," and eventually he will be able to inform his parents, turning the tables on them, that his bath water is too "hot."

The essence of such learning is the understanding of *relationships:* the small child relates pain to the match, the stove, the cigarette, and to the bath water.   As he becomes more intelligent, however, he realizes that these things may not always be hot, although the concept of heat and its source will be unknown to him for quite a while, as is shown by the number of houses burned down each year by children playing with matches.   The adult understands that matches are hot only when put to their use of producing heat; that the important relationship is not between matches themselves and pain, but heat and pain.   Once the concept of heat generation is understood, this concept can be *related* to any source of heat, i.e., that anything producing heat may become hot, and produce pain if we are curious enough to test our understanding of the relationship.

Please note here the importance of such an idea.   If we are going to expand our understanding of the world in which we live, it becomes necessary to be able to construct relationships among things, so that by knowing the nature or behavior of certain basic phenomena it is possible to *generalize* about the nature or behavior of related phenomena.   A statement concerning the nature and behavior of some phenomenon is called a *theory*, which relates the elements of the phenomenon in such a way that its behavior is known and/or can be predicted.   The modern practice of medicine, for instance, is based on the theory that disease is caused by germs, and that to stamp out a disease the offending germ must be discovered, isolated, and killed.   Not all medical scientists agree with the germ theory; some current research indicates that germs only cause disease under conditions of "tension," and that perhaps if the profession were to concentrate on "killing" tension rather than germs, the germs would be rendered harmless.

The important part of any theory is the strength of the relationship which it purports to be true.   If there were only a weak relationship between germs and disease, a theory based on this relationship would undoubtedly be a poor theory.   Obviously we have been discussing cause and effect relationships; our good theory would state that, given the cause, the effect will be known.   We know, however, that the mere presence of germs is not always sufficient to cause disease, and, on the other hand, disease may persist in the absence of germs, at least the type of germs of which we are aware.   Thus the cancer problem: the disease persists, yet we have not found the germ which causes it.   Most cancer research, however, is oriented to the discovery of the offending germ, in accordance with our theory of medicine.

When we attempt to apply this theory to disease in individuals, we find that there are differences in the response to an invasion of germs which appear to be caused by some built-in resistance of individuals to the disease.   Thus two individuals may not experience the same reaction to a given dose of germs, and the cause and effect relationship must be conditioned by another factor, resistance to disease. Here we introduce the concept of a *variable;* some people are more resistant than others, and the degree of this resistance will determine their susceptibility to disease, given a certain dose of germs. Thus the effect of germs *varies* with an individual's resistance (among other things, of course), and resistance is called a variable, as it can take on a broad range of values, from high to low. In our simplified example, the student will recognize the elements of a theory, or cause and effect relationship, including the notion of variable elements, which will condition the ultimate effect.

We have brought up the discussion of relationships in connection with ideas of communication because there are strong ties between the two concepts. A theory is of course an idea which must be communicated to and from the thing that the theory attempts to explain, in terms of the relationships discovered. Whether or not a theory, or a statement of truth, can be discovered at all depends to a great extent upon the language with which we hope to explore those variables and the relationships among them which provide us with a correct statement. As in any communication system, we must again emphasize, language is only *one* of the necessary elements. Like a powerful tool which may be useless in the hands of an idiot, however, it can provide for optimum communication only if the remainder of the system is capable of using it.

Areas of theoretical exploration that are hampered by the absence of a language powerful and precise enough to make possible the accurate description and prediction of the behavior of phenomena are thus unlikely to develop meaningful statements concerning the nature of the world. It should be your purpose in the study of administration to learn the nature of the process of decision-making by learning the relationships in and among many complex variables. Our English language is wholly unsuited to this purpose in many instances, and thus if we are to develop a more than superficial understanding of the complicated process of administration, we must equip ourselves with a more powerful tool.

We have perhaps belabored the idea of communication in the preceding pages, but, as mentioned in the first section, the primary purpose of this text is to develop in the student an awareness of mathematical language in terms of its power to handle certain types of communication problems in a precise way. The eclectic concept of communication is highly useful to the administrator in the solution of his decision problems. Therefore, where we deal strictly with mathematical ideas, apparently unconnected to the solution of technical problems, the student should remember that he is learning the mathematical language as a communication tool to assist him in problem solving. Learning the language is the primary goal; knowing how to apply it, however important, must be secondary except to the extent that this knowledge motivates learning.

1.5 Exercise

1.5.1 Construct a very small practical theory concerning the nature and behavior of something (or anything!) which you have observed or experienced. Express your theory in English, limiting yourself to a relationship of a very few variables. Indicate how you might use this theory to predict, and state how exact you expect such a prediction to be.

Some
Chapter 2 —— Elementary
Ideas

2.1 Symbols

No matter what tongue is spoken or language is written by the people of the modern world, all peoples share to a great extent a common understanding of most things, abstract or concrete. For instance, such ideas as love, motherhood, morality, money, chair, brains, and trains would not be unknown in foreign lands as ideas. However, the word-symbols used in the English language to describe these ideas would be meaningless to most foreign people who had not studied our language, just as their symbols for these ideas are meaningless to us. Although the Russians have undoubtedly "decoded" most scientific articles written in the English language (and those in every other language, too), we have availed ourselves of only a small proportion of the available literature published in the Russian language. Until such information is translated into symbols that our scientists can understand, it will be unknown to us.

"Let X equal the number of peanuts which the elephant can gather in his trunk ... ." Remember how difficult such a concept has been in the past? "Let Mary be the name of that very interesting female ... ." Do you find this statement as confusing or difficult as the previous one? Most likely not. Yet they are exactly the same kind of thing—the assignment of a symbol to represent something, in

14

order to simplify consideration of it. Students often have difficulty with algebra because they do not realize that the symbols must *mean* something. "*X* plus *Y* minus *Z* equals *C*" is itself a meaningless statement, but if we let *X* equal beginning inventory, *Y* equal purchases, and *Z* equal ending inventory, then *C* has meaning; it is what we call "cost of goods sold" in accounting parlance. Please note that our symbolic statement required more than an understanding of those things for which *X*, *Y*, and *Z* stand; the connectives "plus," "minus," and "equals" are symbols also, whether written out or expressed in their short form, and thus *their* meaning must be understood as well. (Interestingly enough, the basic arithmetic symbols $(+, -, =)$ are almost universally understood!)

Generally then, we see that symbols are merely a convenient shorthand for ideas; that symbols themselves are void of any meaning unless meaning is imparted to them by the communicators of ideas. Modern abstract art is often meaningless to anyone but the artist (and sometimes we wonder about the meanings of his own work to him!) because the symbols are peculiar to his own purpose. Color, on the other hand, is usually recognizable to all, and many modern works are held forth as valid communications by transmitting a mood through the use of color, which we recognize to be a coding device different from that of form. Colors may be mixed and blended in myriad ways, to express myriad ideas. Thus we are introduced to an important attribute of any *symbol system:* the symbols must have some correspondence, i.e., be related so as to be capable of "mixing" or "blending" in some sense. As the color "black" is the "opposite" of the color "white," the symbol "$+$" is the "opposite" of the symbol "$-$," and thus the system of connective symbols which we use in arithmetic has this property of correspondence. The student should recognize that all of our arithmetic connectives are derived from the basic concepts of addition and opposites—multiplication is purely repetitive addition, division is repetitive subtraction. The property of correspondence, while important, should not be considered very startling.

It is important for the student to realize at this point the arbitrariness of symbols and systems of symbols. "A rose by any other name . . . ." We construct such systems to suit our convenience; once a symbol has been established as having certain meaning, it becomes grossly inconvenient to change that meaning. Consider the semantic difficulties of the English language, which is in a constant state of change as old words assimilate new meanings (as in Beatnik argot) and new words are coined (e.g., hot rod). The languages of mathematics, however, are quite specific on this semantic point: once we define the meaning of a symbol, it is not possible to change that meaning wherever the symbol is used in its original context. Thus, if C is the "cost of goods sold," we realize that although C may have any one of a host of dollar *values*, any one of them still represents the dollar "cost of goods sold."

Another term for the assignment of symbols and meanings is called *notation*. You will find that not all authors use the same notation for the same idea. Unfortunately, in some areas such as statistics, you must carefully understand the notation used in each instance of study or application, because the general application of statistics to a wide variety of problems is relatively new and the language itself has not been standardized on a national or international basis. Although such a condition is odious to the student, we realize that it arises from the development of new ideas and applications from many independent sources, which itself is a healthy condition.

2.1   Exercise

2.1.1   Review the following and note for each the common symbols used and the meaning of each symbol: (**a**) road map; (**b**) weather map; (**c**) football referee's signals.

2.2   Numbers and counting

By the time a student enters college, he is so familiar with *numbers* that he takes them completely for granted. It is obvious to most students that our number system is probably due to the physiological fact that human beings have ten fingers, conveniently placed in such a way that they can be used for enumerating the occurrence of something. (*Exercise:* How many months are there from March to October? You will probably *count* them on your fingers!) Such a process is called *quantification*, and we generally believe that any idea which can be quantified, that is, expressed in numerical form, can be communicated with a great deal more power and precision than those ideas which are not capable of such description, and which may only be *qualified*. If the local Chevrolet dealer were to send in an order for "some convertibles, a few red and a few blue, and a bunch of station wagons," the roof would probably fall on him, because such an order is imprecise in a situation where an exact number or quantity is necessary. On the other hand, were you to describe a friend as "25 blonde, 300 poise, $4\frac{1}{4}$ blue eyes, etc.," your listeners would have a difficult time understanding exactly the nature of these *qualities*. How smart are you? To answer such a question, you might quote your Intelligence Quotient (IQ), which represents an attempt to quantify brain power. Some distinct problems of measurement are implied in such things as the IQ. However, if we know something about the general *standard* against which the IQ is measured, we have a much better idea of any individual's brain power when measured against this standard than we would have if we had to use such qualifying terms as "very bright," "exceptionally dumb," "smart," "stupid," or other word-symbols. Obviously, such non-quantitative statements require that the receiver impose his own idea of the meaning of the word-symbol, which may not be the same as the meaning assigned when such an idea was originally transmitted. Thus a communication in numerical form may be much more efficient than the same communication transmitted in another medium, such as the English language.

Why? Because we all understand the meaning of number-symbols, or numerals. A 2 is a 2 is a 2 ... eins, zwei, drei; uno, due, tre; un, deux, trois; one, two, three; in four languages the word-symbols are different, but the numerals are the same: 1, 2, 3. More important, however, is the fact that the ten characters of the decimal system are universally understood to exhaust the possible number of symbols available for the quantification of ideas by this system. The number 7,983,752,006,341 is a very "large" number, yet we observe that it is composed of only ten symbols; how the symbols are positioned of course plays the important part in numbering.

The word *decimal* comes from a Latin word meaning "tenth": the decimal numbering system has ten basic symbols, 0 through 9. Note that the number 10 itself is a composite of two of the basic symbols; there is no basic symbol for the number 10. Counting is accomplished by placing in *one-to-one correspondence* the items to be counted and the accepted basic and composite symbols in their proper order. Every student knows how to count, of course; of interest to us now is not the method but the language. We note that when limited to ten basic symbols, *positioning* of these symbols relative to each other determines the "size" of a number greater than 9. In Fig. 2.2.1 we have placed some of the decimal counting symbols in their usual order. (The three vertical dots, which also may be written horizontally, are called an *ellipsis* and indicate that something has been left

Fig. 2.2.1

out, of the same nature and following the same pattern as the data presented.) When we have counted up to 9, we must start over, in a sense; the next larger integer is indicated by a composite of the two "smallest" numerals. Although the resulting numeral, 10, is made up of small elements, its size or *order of magnitude* is indicated by the *number* of elements. The efficiency of our counting system is thus manifested in the fact that we utilize *all* possible arrangements of the number-symbols, with the exception of insignificant zeroes, and when these possibilities have been exhausted we merely increase the order of magnitude, thereby expanding the possible number of arrangements.

It is important to realize that the decimal system to which we have been exposed for so long is only one of a number of possible systems of numbering, and thus counting. Human beings find it simple to communicate ideas of quantity in the decimal system because they are trained at an early age to do so, mostly by memorizing tables. Many communicators, however, find our ten-symbol method very inefficient, and thus they communicate in other, different systems, with names such as *binary*, *biquinary*, and *octal*. One of these systems, the binary system, is important enough that we shall spend some time examining it.

Just as the decimal system has ten symbols, the binary system has two symbols: 0 and 1. The rule for expanding the size of a number is the same, however; when we run out of combinations of symbols, we increase the order of magnitude of the number. This is illustrated in Fig. 2.2.2, which shows some binary equivalents of decimal numbers. We note that there is no unique symbol corresponding to the number 2; upon counting to 1, we have exhausted the symbol possibilities, and must therefore shift to the next order of magnitude. The *base* of the binary number system is 2—we would expect the number 2 to have something to do with this system! This relationship can best be explained by reference to Fig. 2.2.3, which portrays the equivalence among powers of 2 and decimal and binary numbers. Note that each time that the exponent of 2 increases, the order of magnitude of the binary number increases and the exponent in fact indicates the number of zeros in the binary number. Any decimal system number has a binary equivalent; there are means for finding these equivalents, which we shall not explore since the detail is beyond our purpose at present.

Arithmetic is performed in the binary mode by exactly the same rules that are used in decimal arithmetic. Since there are fewer symbols in the binary system, the "carry" operation must be performed more often. Notice that just as it is necessary to perform the "carry" operation in decimal arithmetic when we exceed the permissible number of

Decimal	Binary
0	0
1	1
2	10
3	11
4	100
5	101
6	110
7	111
8	1000
9	1001
10	1010
11	1011
12	1100
13	1101
14	1110
15	1111
16	10000
17	10001
.	.
.	.
.	.
100	1100100
101	1100101
102	1100110

2^n	Decimal	Binary
0	0	0
2^0	1	1
2^1	2	10
2^2	4	100
2^3	8	1000
2^4	16	10000
2^5	32	100000
2^6	64	1000000
2^7	128	10000000
2^8	256	100000000
2^9	512	1000000000
2^{10}	1024	10000000000
2^{11}	2048	100000000000
2^{12}	4096	1000000000000
2^{13}	8192	10000000000000
2^{14}	16384	100000000000000
2^{15}	32768	1000000000000000
2^{16}	65536	10000000000000000
2^{17}	131072	100000000000000000
2^{18}	262144	1000000000000000000
2^{19}	524288	10000000000000000000
2^{20}	1048576	100000000000000000000

Fig. 2.2.2. Some binary and decimal equivalents.

Fig. 2.2.3. A table of 2^n, showing binary and decimal equivalents.

symbols, we must "carry" in binary when we have exhausted the symbol supply, i.e., gone "beyond" the symbol "1." Examine carefully the equivalent operations in binary and decimal arithmetic shown below.

Binary	Decimal	Binary	Decimal
1	1	100	4
+ 1	+1	− 11	−3
10	2	1	1
10	2		
× 10	×2	110	6
100	4	10⟌1100	2⟌12

The student will notice how cumbersome such a system appears to be, but his reaction is merely that of a person highly trained in the manipulation of a relatively complex set of symbols. Ask a child in the third grade to multiply 9 by 7, and you may recall that such a simple product was not always simple. Had our ancestors chosen to count on their ears, eyes, knees, or whatnot, there is no doubt that today we might be using the binary system rather than our finger-developed decimal system.

Our purpose in exposing the student to additional ideas of number systems and counting is not to confuse him with what may seem to be unnecessary details in light of his already developed sophistication in the use of the decimal number system. Rather, we wish to show that a language which is usually taken for granted as "true" because we were "born" with it, or for some other reason, is really "true" only because it is convenient to make it "true." Our conventional system does not preclude, however, the development of another system which is a more efficient communication device in a given situation. Let us briefly recall here that a prime purpose of mathematics is to provide an efficient, precise, and powerful language with which we may communicate *with* problems.

2.3   Measurement and decision-making

How many cars should be ordered for next month's sales? What wage should be paid to the Plant Investment Clerk? Should a certain product be bought or made in our plant? What sort of man should be chosen to "manage" Department A? How large should the operating budget of a government agency be? These are the types of business-like decisions faced continually by administrators in government as well as business organizations.

As a social and economic system matures, the decisions which must be made to ensure continued vitality and to foster new growth become more and more complex. New methods of analysis are now being utilized to communicate with and solve these increasingly complex problems of our system. While these new techniques are for the most part mathematical in nature and require the availability of quantified information, the need for accurate *measurement* of appropriate data is not a new decision-making requirement. (As an example, consider the frontier merchant who *measured* the indebtedness of his customers in his books of account.)

Measurement is the process of establishing the *relative* or *absolute* amount of a given quality that an item possesses, or in other words, the quantification of a given quality, against some established standard. It is the existence of a well-defined and generally understood number system which makes quantification meaningful. For example, we might consider the measurement of the weight of different objects. Obviously the quality we wish to measure is weight, and we have found it convenient to measure this quality by counting the number of pounds or kilograms representing the mass of an object. Although in the United States we measure weight in pounds, measurement of weight would be just as meaningful by any standard of measure, as long as we understood the standard being used. As another example, business firms find it very important to measure profits. In this sense profits are the "quality" and the established standard of measure for profits in the United States is the dollar. We should note that the measure of profits would be no less meaningful if it were made in beads, shells, or whatnot—provided we used beads, shells, or whatnot as a standard of measure.

The critical problems in measurement are the *qualitative* classification of items according to identifiable characteristics, and the *quantification* of the "amount" of the characteristic present in the items. It is important for us to realize that measurement is itself a decision problem involving quality identification, selection of measurement standards, selection of measurement methods, and the selection of a proper symbol system for communication. In addition, before measurement is undertaken a decision maker must have already decided why measurement is necessary, how it will be used, the level of accuracy necessary, and, of course, what phenomena of his world will be measured. In working with the exercises to which we will be exposed, we will assume that all these other problems of measurement have been satisfactorily solved. However, in the application of mathematical techniques to the solution of problems in real life, these considerations must be brought into the solution of any given problem.

While we will not concern ourselves directly with the problems of qualification and quantification, these problems cannot be taken lightly by the student of administration. Although the bulk of our work will assume data that satisfy our concept of quantifiability, and thus there is the implication that such data are precise and accurate, the reader should not be deluded into thinking that problems which cannot be so quantified must necessarily be examined in the light of "vague" data. This warning is given because the qualification of phenomena is really the significant first step to understanding.

2.4   Quantification and qualification

From our discussion above, the concept of quantification of ideas and the ability of mathematics to deal with this concept should be clear. Whether or not the student can handle problems in mathematics competently is quite immaterial at this point.   Only the most naive college student does not understand that problems which are stated in quantitative terms, i.e., in numbers, can often be solved with such mathematical techniques as arithmetic, algebra, geometry, or trigonometry.   It should be pointed out, however, that it is equally naive to believe that the quantification of an idea is *sufficient* to provide a means for problem solution by mathematical techniques.   Quantification is a *necessary* condition if we are to apply such mathematical techniques successfully, but it does not guarantee that a technique exists for solving problems merely because our problems can be stated numerically.   We cannot emphasize too strongly this basic truth.   Improperly conceived or untrue ideas cannot be corrected merely by casting them in mathematical terms, no matter how powerful the mathematical language or technique used for communication.   In addition, many mathematical techniques are still in the process of development themselves.   Thus quantification may fail us on two counts: (1) the idea or problem which we wish to solve may not lend itself to meaningful quantification, and (2) a mathematical technique may not exist for solving the problem even if the data are capable of quantification.

Many ideas which do not lend themselves to quantification in the sense discussed above, i.e., the measurement of data in some absolute sense, are capable of another type of enumeration on a more conceptual or abstract level.   For instance, we can count exactly the number of players on the football field, the number of passes completed and intercepted, and the number of shirts ruined on a muddy afternoon.   If we were asked, however, to state exactly the amount of football skill possessed by each individual player, we would find that the best we could do would be to say: "Jake is better than Joe; Bill passes better than Abe, although Abe is a better kicker; etc."   The concept of quantification is present, but the means of measurement are not, at least in any absolute sense.   There are exactly six more men on a football squad than there are on a basketball team.   How precisely, however, can you measure the degree of difficulty of the two sports in order to compare them on the basis of necessary expertise, rather than on the basis of the size of the squad?   We can count the number of men on the squads by placing each man in one-to-one correspondence with our counting symbols; on the other hand, we have no such exact standard for measuring difficulty. Such measurement may be performed only by relating one game to the other in terms of some criterion indicating greater or lesser difficulty. This kind of measurement is called *ranking*, as opposed to counting; we also speak of *ordering*, in the sense of ordering along a scale from high to low, rich to poor, etc. Such ordering results in different number-symbols than we use in counting, and these number-symbols are called *ordinal* numbers, in contrast to the *cardinal* numbers which we use in counting. First, second, twenty-fifth, etc., are ordinal numbers, or ranks.

The problems of measurement in ordinal or cardinal numbers are extremely important to students of business administration or the other social sciences, because so many of the phenomena which we should like to understand cannot be quantified cardinally, but can only be ordered. This is especially true in the area of the behavioral sciences, where the actions and emotions of people comprise our subject matter. What is a "normal" individual? Can one be twice as normal as another? Obviously, we have no standard by which we can measure even so overworked an idea as normalcy, although it is true that we make interpersonal comparisons between individuals every day. The problem of quantifying data thus boils down to whether we have an absolute, or at least an accepted, standard against which we may measure, or whether measurement can only be accomplished on a relative basis. The mathematical techniques that we shall explore require that we be able to measure cardinally if we are to arrive at valid solutions; arithmetic, for instance, does not tell us what to expect of the sum of first plus third, although the first-grader can sum one and three. On the other hand, we should never dismiss mathematics as a possible means of solving a problem merely because at first blush the data do not appear to meet our requirements of quantifiability. Indeed, much insight has been gained into many problems by casting them in mathematical terms, even though measured data could not be made available.

A fair question at this point might be asked concerning the qualification of ideas, and how mathematics can help us solve problems or communicate ideas that are qualified to some extent by statements whose relationship to the original communication cannot be quantified. We have already taken the English language to task for its ambiguities and redundancies in communicating ideas (see Section 1.3); our word-symbol language can be analyzed by mathematical methods to determine the real meaning of statements made in it. Such analysis deals with the connectives, which we use to tie ideas together (*and, or, if*, etc.), whether expressed or merely implied in English communication. In the next chapter we shall see that some applications of simple arithmetic can be used to assist in the analysis of statements and arguments, in an area of study called *symbolic logic*. Some of the ideas of symbolic logic are then carried further, into a study of *Boolean algebra*, in which we wish to examine the assignment of a certain quality to objects.

2.4   Exercise

2.4.1   Analyze the items listed below, noting for each how you would measure it, and stating why you chose such a system of measurement:

(a) Sales   (b) Fatigue
(c) Morale   (d) Age
(e) Worker performance   (f) Intelligence.

Chapter **3** ———————— # Logic

3.1   Introduction

Almost every day in our communication with other people we run across statements made in support of or as conclusions to some argument, to which our reaction is something like this: "that is not logical," or "it does not follow," or "your argument isn't valid." More often than not, such a reaction is improper. Few people have sufficient understanding of logic to imply anything at all about the logic of others. For logic is the science of the *form* of propositions and arguments; it is not easy, although it is highly intuitive. Usually our disagreements with others are based upon meaning or fact, and not really upon the way in which the argument is made. Thus, it is incorrect to take our antagonists to task for faulty logic when more properly *our* view of *their* facts is at fault.

The examination of statements and arguments can be simplified by the use of *symbolic logic*, a language for communicating with such problems. Although we shall not proceed very deeply into the subject, we shall develop some basic ideas which we feel have salutary motivating and conditioning effects for our work in mathematics, as well as immediate benefits in terms of elementary logic itself. In addition, we shall show how a simple arithmetic can be developed into a useful algebra for solving a class of problems in logic.

3.2   Statements

Up until this point we have been more or less inexplicit about exactly what we mean by "ideas," although we have used the term extensively in our discussion of communication. We shall consider here those ideas that are expressed in the English language, and expressed by what we call *statements* or *propositions*. Whether or not these are statements of fact or statements of opinion does not concern us at the moment; what is important is that an idea expressed as a statement appears in English as a sentence, or as a part thereof. We state that a sentence can have only one of two possible values; it is either true or false. The student will recognize that any simple statement can be verified; i.e., we can determine (by observation, for instance) whether the idea contained in the statement is true. If it is not true, then it is false.

A *simple statement* is an English sentence containing one subject, one verb, and one object or modifier, such as: "College is difficult." "A centerfielder must have a good arm." "Advertising promotes sales." Each of these sentences is said, then, to convey an idea by means of a declarative statement. A *compound statement*, on the other hand, is a statement which contains, for example two subjects, or three objects, or two verbs, or any number of such combinations. Examples are: "College is difficult or fun." "Centerfielders, rightfielders, and leftfielders must have good arms." "Advertising and customer service promote sales but increase costs." Each of these is also an idea, but a more complicated idea than those expressed by simple statements. We note that compound statements are formed by using *connectives*, such as *and, or, but, if . . . then,* and *either . . . or.* The effect of each of the connectives upon the idea transmitted in a compound statement is really what we wish to determine. We will take the connectives up in turn.

Many ideas require more than one statement or sentence to describe them fully, and, since any of these simple statements may be either true or false, the ultimate truth of an idea that is expressed in a number of statements depends upon the truth of the individual statements in some unique manner. This, then, is the substance of logic: the examination of complex ideas to determine their validity or internal consistency.

Let us examine some simple sentences: A. "I am bored." B. "I must stay awake during the lecture." C. "To be caught napping is not a humiliating experience for me." D. "I am sensitive to humiliation." Notice that no matter how many words are used, there is but one idea asserted in each of the sentences.

Recall that we have stated that such sentences can have only one of two values: they can be either true or false. Each of the statements above can be "turned around" to reflect an opposite meaning by negating it, thus: $\bar{A}$. "I am not bored." $\bar{B}$. "I may sleep during the lecture." $\bar{C}$. "To be caught napping is a humiliating experience for me." $\tilde{D}$. "I am insensitive to humiliation." We see that it is not necessary to use the exact symbol "not" to negate an idea, for "to sleep" is *not* "to stay awake," "sensitive" and "insensitive" have opposite meaning, etc.

Let us construct a compound statement of these simple statements: "I am bored and may sleep during the lecture, but to be caught napping is a humiliating experience for me and I am particularly sensitive to humiliation." Thus we have constructed a rather complex idea from quite simple ideas, and have made what we call a compound statement. Although it was technically easy to negate the simple statements comprising the compound statement, we notice that expressing the opposite of the compound statement is not necessarily accomplished by negating all of the simple statements comprising it. (Re-read the sentence as if each element were negated; is the meaning clear?) Since the ultimate truth or falsity of any idea is determined by the system that describes the effect of changing the *truth values*, i.e., truth or falsity, of the elements of the idea, it is important that we understand this system.

It would be very difficult to analyze the truth values mentioned if we were required to consider each sentence in its English language format, i.e., strung out in words. In "communicating" with this problem then, we must have a more powerful language with which to work, and this is the language of *symbolic logic*. The language consists of symbols of two types: a set of symbols which stand for simple declarative sentences, and another set of symbols which stand for the connectives that we use to combine the simple sentences. One additional symbol, the *negation* symbol, completes this language. The symbols which stand for our simple sentences are called *variables*, since any sentence can be either true or false. We usually use alphabetic letters to symbolize these sentences. Looking back, we find that the simple sentences on page 26 have already been assigned symbols in the process of setting them down. Thus we let A stand for the statement, "I am bored," B for "I must stay awake during the lecture," etc.

When we negate the original idea or sentence, we do not change the sentence symbol itself, but merely indicate that its meaning has been "reversed" by superimposing another symbol, "$\sim$," above the original symbol; thus, $\tilde{A}$ means "I am not bored." It is extremely important at this point that the student understand that we had not determined whether any of these statements was true or false, only that they were opposite statements. If A is false, then "I am not bored" is a true statement, and likewise, if $\tilde{A}$ is false, then "I am bored" is a true statement. We can illustrate this in a table, called a *truth table*, which describes the relationship between a sentence and its opposite depend-

$$A \quad \tilde{A}$$

| T | F |
| F | T |

Fig. 3.2.1

ing upon the truth or falsity of the original sentence (see Fig. 3.2.1). The meaning of the $\sim$ symbol is thus made clear and unambiguous; it serves to give an opposite meaning to any statement, and it is generally read "not."

3.2 Exercises

3.2.1 This is a simple exercise in breaking down compound statements into their elements, and assigning a symbol to the resulting simple statements, thus:

"The shipment was to have been made by rail or truck."
A. The shipment was to have been made by rail.
B. The shipment was to have been made by truck.

(a) Joe plans to date Mary and Genevieve.
(b) The delay was caused by neither operator error nor machine breakdown.
(c) Frivolous and capricious behavior may be fun but it is not considered very adult.

3.2.2 Negate each of the compound statements above, noting carefully the distinction between negating the elements and achieving the opposite meaning of the compound sentence.

3.2.3 Your plant superintendent reports that morale in the plant is low and productivity is high. Determine the truth values of the following statements, that is, whether they are true or false:

(a) Morale is high and productivity is high.
(b) It is not true that morale is high and productivity is high.
(c) Morale and productivity are low.
(d) Morale is not high and productivity is not low.
(e) It is not true that morale is not low and productivity is not high.

3.3 Conjunction

Negation changes the meaning of a sentence but does not make it a compound sentence. We shall now construct some compound sentences using symbols. Let A be the statement "We have a good football team," and B be the statement "We don't lose many games." If we know that both of these statements are true simultaneously, we express this idea as "We have a good football team *and* we don't lose many games." In symbols, we write $A \land B$, the symbol "$\land$" meaning that both A and B are true at the same time. This symbol is the *conjunctive*, and we speak of the conjunction of A and B. Such a conjunction is a *sentence;* it is either true or false depending upon the truth values of its elements. By intuition, the student can see that this compound sentence can only be true if both elements are true. We can construct a truth table to define the conjunction, as is shown in

A	B	$A \land B$
T	T	T
T	F	F
F	T	F
F	F	F

Fig. 3.3.1

Fig. 3.3.1. *Note carefully:* it is not important that the *facts* stated in the truth table be intuitively true; whenever we make something true by definition, we create what is called an *axiom*, a fact that is true because we define it to be true. Fortunately, this axiom and those to follow do agree with our intuition of what we mean by "true" and "false" statements. We read the conjunction symbol as "and."

3.3 Exercises

Example. Construct a truth table to analyze the following compound statement. Under what conditions is the statement true (i.e., what truth values of the elements of the sentence render the sentence true)?

$A \land B$. *Mathematics and English are difficult subjects.*

A. Mathematics is a difficult subject.

B. English is a difficult subject.

A	B	$A \wedge B$
T	T	?
T	F	?
F	T	?
F	F	?

Fig. 3.3.2

We recall that any one sentence can have two possible truth values, true or false. When we combine two sentences, there are four possible combinations of truth values: both true, A true and B false, A false and B true, or both false. Each of these four possible combinations must be analyzed to determine its effect upon the truth value of the compound statement. The conjunction of A and B is defined in Fig. 3.3.1. The table indicates therefore that the statement, "Mathematics and English are difficult subjects," is true only if both of the statements are true simultaneously.

3.3.1 Construct truth tables for the following sentences, and indicate the conditions under which the statements are true.

(a) The city of Denver has professional football and baseball teams.

(b) Industrial goods markets and the stock market are in a slump.

(c) I like brains, trains, and planes. (*Note:* Three simple sentences combined result in eight possible T-F possibilities.)

(d) It is not true that she is dumb and not blonde. [*Hint:* find $\tilde{B}$; then $(A \wedge \tilde{B})$; then find $\overline{(A \wedge \tilde{B})}$.]

(e) It is not raining but the sun is not shining. (*Note:* We shall consider the connective *but* to be also a conjunctive.)

(f) $\tilde{A} \wedge \tilde{B}$ (*Hint:* Find $\tilde{A}$ first; then $\tilde{B}$; then $\tilde{A} \wedge \tilde{B}$.)

(g) $P \wedge (\tilde{Q} \wedge \tilde{R})$ [*Hint:* Find $(\tilde{Q} \wedge \tilde{R})$; then find $P \wedge (\tilde{Q} \wedge \tilde{R})$.]

(h) $\overline{(A \wedge B)}$ [*Hint:* Find $A \wedge B$; then find $\overline{(A \wedge B)}$.].

3.3.2 Consider a simple electrical circuit containing a light bulb, a power source, and two switches, as portrayed in Fig. 3.3.3. Each of the switches, P and Q, can be either on (T) or off (F). Show by means of a truth table the conditions under which the bulb will light up.

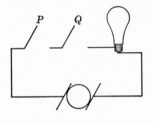

Fig. 3.3.3

3.4 Inclusive disjunction

Often a total idea will be expressed by a combination of elements all of which we do not require to be true in order that the compound statement be true. "Jake plays tackle" and "Jake plays fullback" can be combined into one sentence "Jake plays tackle *or* fullback," meaning that Jake is so versatile that he can play either position, and not one to the exclusion of the other. Such a connective is called a *disjunction*, and, since either possibility is *included* in our meaning, we call such a case of "and/or" *inclusive disjunction*. Inclusive disjunction is represented by the symbol " ∨ " and is defined by the truth table in Fig. 3.4.1.

A	B	$A \lor B$
T	T	T
T	F	T
F	T	T
F	F	F

Fig. 3.4.1

Thus, the compound statement of two sentences inclusively disjoined is false only if both of the statements are false. (Test this one intuitively.) Read " ∨ " as "or."

3.4 Exercises

3.4.1 Construct truth tables for the following statements, and indicate the conditions under which the statements are true.

(a) The personnel department has advertised for a good receptionist or a good typist.

(b) Some quarterbacks are good at stumbling or fumbling.
(c) $\tilde{A} \lor \tilde{B}$ (Compare with Exercise 3.3.1h.)
(d) $\overline{\tilde{A} \lor B}$

(e) $\overline{(A \lor B)}$ (Compare with Exercise 3.3.1f.)
(f) $(A \lor B) \land \tilde{A}$ (*Hint:* Solve for statement within parentheses first.).

3.4.2 Consider another simple electrical circuit containing a light bulb, a power source, and two switches, as portrayed in Fig. 3.4.2. Each of the switches, P and Q, can be either on (T) or off (F). Show by means of a truth table the conditions under which the bulb will light up.

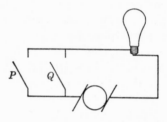

Fig. 3.4.2

3.5   Exclusive disjunction

The word "or" is also used in another sense with a decidedly different meaning. During any given play of a football game, "Jake can play tackle *or* fullback" but not both, no matter how versatile or quick he might be. If this is the meaning of the sentence, then we should undoubtedly say "either . . . or, but not both." Such a connective is called *exclusive disjunction*, because the truth of one of the elements

A	B	$A \underline{\lor} B$
T	T	F
T	F	T
F	T	T
F	F	F

Fig. 3.5.1

excludes the possibility that the other can be true. The symbol for exclusive disjunction is "$\underline{\vee}$," read "either . . . or," and the truth table for this connective is displayed in Fig. 3.5.1.

3.5 Exercise

3.5.1 Construct truth tables for the following statements, indicating under which conditions the statements are true. Where the statement is given in English, read carefully in order to determine which connective applies.

(a) The professor is a teacher or an advisor.
(b) She is either blonde or brunette.
(c) The machine can be operated manually or automatically.
(d) The traffic signal is red, green, or yellow.
(e) He has neither brains nor ambition, but his father has influence.
(f) $A \underline{\vee} \bar{B}$
(g) $(A \wedge B) \vee C$
(h) $(A \vee C) \wedge (B \vee C)$
(i) $A \wedge (B \vee C)$
(j) $(A \wedge B) \vee (A \wedge C)$.

3.6 Conditional

The world about us is very "iffy"; very seldom can we be completely certain about the truth of anything. Usually we must constrain our ideas about the world within certain conditions. Such conditions are usually expressed in terms of an "if" clause, such as, "If I get my degree I shall get a good job." Connecting two ideas together in such a way that one of them is conditional upon the other is achieved through use of the *conditional* connective "$\Rightarrow$." Thus a conditional statement $A \Rightarrow B$ is read in any one of a number of ways: "If A then B," or "A implies B," or "B is conditional upon A," etc. The truth table of the conditional is defined in Fig. 3.6.1; the student must ponder this table since the truth value of the conditional is not so intuitive as that of the other connectives. We shall be able to show more powerfully (in Chapter 4) the reason why this truth table suits our purpose; let it stand by definition for the time being. The important thing for the student to understand about the conditional is that *in logic*, there is no *causal* relationship intended between the elements conditionally connected. It is convenient for us to set down an unambiguous system,

A	B	$A \Rightarrow B$
T	T	T
T	F	F
F	T	T
F	F	T

Fig. 3.6.1

i.e., one which is precise in its meaning and use.   To introduce causation into our system would complicate it unnecessarily.   In our example above, for instance, there is a strong notion implied that college degrees have something to do with jobs.   Although there is an observable real-life relationship between these two ideas, logic does not recognize such cause and effect.   Our symbolic logic system, which is unemotional and indifferent to the substance of our ideas, reflects only what we wish it to reflect, and it is convenient in most instances for this connective to have the meaning shown in the truth table.

Our last connective is used when we wish to convey the idea that something is true "if and only if" something else is true; likewise that something is false "if and only if" something else is false.   The *biconditional* is true if both elements have the same truth value, i.e., both true or both false; otherwise the compound statement is false. The truth table defining this connective, written "$\Leftrightarrow$" and read "if and only if," is shown in Fig. 3.6.2.   An example of the biconditional is: "One of the presidential candidates will become president if and only if he does not drop dead before his inauguration."   Living through inauguration for the winning candidate is thus *logically equivalent* to becoming president.

A	B	$A \Leftrightarrow B$
T	T	T
T	F	F
F	T	F
F	F	T

Fig. 3.6.2

3.6   Exercise

3.6.1   Construct truth tables to determine the conditions under which the following statements are true:

(a) I will watch the game on television if it rains this afternoon.
(b) Only if the Yankees win the league pennant will I attend the World Series.
(c) Her roommate will date a freshman only if he is tall and has a convertible.
(d) $(A \wedge B) \Rightarrow A$
(e) $A \Leftrightarrow \tilde{B}$.

3.7   Operational symbols

It has been necessary up to this point for the student to refer to the truth table for a given connective in order to determine the truth value for the compound statement in which it is used. There is a much simpler system which makes use of the student's ability to perform arithmetic, and which considerably reduces the time necessary for working out the table. The table below shows the correspondence between the connective symbols which we have used in logic, and the familiar arithmetic symbols.

Connective	Meaning	Operational Symbol	Meaning
$\sim$	Negation	$-$	Opposite
$\wedge$	Conjunction	$\times$	Multiplication
$\vee$	Inclusive disjunction	$\oplus$	Addition (except $1 + 1 = 1$)
$\underline{\vee}$	Exclusive disjunction	$+$	Addition; ignore carry
$\Rightarrow$	Conditional	$\leq$	Less than or equal to
$\Leftrightarrow$	Biconditional	$=$	Equal

Most students will recognize the truth of the statement: "$2 \times 2 = 4$." Not so easily recognized is the truth of the statement: "If A is true and B is true, then $A \wedge B$ is true." It does not even help much to shorten the statement by inserting the truth values of A and B: "$T \wedge T = T$," because the student has performed such manipulations only with numbers in the past. If we are to make use of the correspondence between symbolic logic connectives and arithmetic symbols, we must find a

A	B	$\tilde{A}$ (Opp. A)	$A \wedge B$ ($A \times B$)	$A \vee B$ ($A \oplus B$)	$A \underline{\vee} B$ ($A + B$)	$A \Rightarrow B$ ($A \leq B$)	$A \Leftrightarrow B$ ($A = B$)
T 1	T 1	F 0	T 1	T 1	F 0	T 1	T 1
T 1	F 0	F 0	F 0	T 1	T 1	F 0	F 0
F 0	T 1	T 1	F 0	T 1	T 1	T 1	F 0
F 0	F 0	T 1	F 0	F 0	F 0	T 1	T 1

Fig. 3.7.1

number-symbol system which means something to the student already. The binary system comes to our aid at this point. If for the symbol "T" we use instead the symbol "1," and for "F," "0," we can reconstruct our truth tables in a system which is operational in known terms, i.e., the arithmetic manipulation of numbers according to known rules (with one exception). The table in Fig. 3.7.1 indicates this correspondence, and the student should verify that the correspondence is complete. Inclusive and exclusive disjunction differ only when both elements are true, and therefore we will use a different symbol, "$\oplus$," for inclusive disjunction, to indicate that $1 \oplus 1 = 1$. For exclusive disjunction when both elements are true, we note that we disregard carry, so that $1 + 1 = 0$ (rather than $1 + 1 = 10$), since we are allowed only one symbol for the truth value of the compound statement (i.e., true or false, since true-false has no meaning).

3.7   Exercise

3.7.1   Construct truth tables using (1, 0) for (T, F) and using the operational symbols.

(a) $\tilde{A}$
(b) $A \wedge B$
(c) $A \vee B$
(d) $A \underline{\vee} B$
(e) $A \Rightarrow B$
(f) $A \Leftrightarrow B$

(g) $\overline{(A \ \underline{\vee} \ B)}$

(h) $[(A \ \vee \ B) \Rightarrow B] \Leftrightarrow (A \Rightarrow B)$.

3.8 Arguments

An argument is an idea in which a statement, called a *conclusion*, is supported by and follows from other statements, called *premises*. One of the prime purposes of logic is to determine whether or not arguments are valid; the student has undoubtedly heard such phrases as "his argument doesn't hold water; it's shot full of holes; etc." A valid argument, in logic, is one which is true no matter what the truth values of the premises are. The argument itself consists of the compound statement: "The conjunction of the premises implies the conclusion," or, in symbolics, if A, B, and C are premises and P is the conclusion, the argument has the symbolic form $[(A \wedge B \wedge C) \Rightarrow P]$. If this statement is true no matter what the truth values of A, B, and C (i.e., the column containing the truth values of this statement has no "F" (or "0")), the statement is called a *tautology*, and the argument which it represents is said to be valid. It is helpful in checking arguments to write them in a way that facilitates analysis, as shown below:

		Symbolic
Premises:	I. If our football team shows no improvement, we shall win no prizes.	$A \Rightarrow B$
	II. Our football team shows no improvement.	A
Conclusion:	We shall win no prizes.	B

This argument is valid if the statement "the conjunction of the premises implies the conclusion" is a tautology, i.e., if $[(A \Rightarrow B) \wedge A] \Rightarrow B$ is true no matter what the truth values of A and B are. Let us examine this argument for its validity using a truth table, in Fig. 3.8.1.

A	B	$A \Rightarrow B$ $\leq$	$(A \Rightarrow B) \wedge A$ $\times$	$[(A \Rightarrow B) \wedge A] \Rightarrow B$ $\leq$
1	1	1	1	1
1	0	0	0	1
0	1	1	0	1
0	0	1	0	1

Fig. 3.8.1

Logical validity, then, is determined by the form of the argument rather than the truth values of the elements.

3.8   Exercise

3.8.1   Put the following arguments into symbolic form, showing premises and conclusion. Test the arguments for validity in truth tables using operational symbols.

(a) If the Yankees win the league pennant, I shall attend the World Series. The Yankees will not win the pennant. Therefore, I shall not attend the World Series.

(b) If our football team does not improve we shall win no prizes. We shall win no prizes. Therefore, our football team will not improve.

(c) If our football team shows no improvement, we shall win no prizes. Our football team shows improvement. Therefore, we shall win no prizes.

(d) If the moon is made of green cheese, then blue is orange. If blue is orange, then $3 \times 7 = 23\frac{1}{2}$. The moon is made of green cheese. Therefore, $3 \times 7 = 23\frac{1}{2}$.

(e) If worms are not polka-dotted, then $1 + 1 = 2$. Worms are polka-dotted. Therefore, $1 + 1 = 11$.

3.9   Equivalent statements

Two statements are said to be *equivalent* if they have the same truth sets. In Exercises 3.4.1,*c* and *e*; 3.5.1,*g* and *h*, *i* and *j*; and 3.6.1,*d* and *e*; we notice that there are two sets of statements which are in fact the same, although they do not appear to be so. We do not propose to investigate this feature at this time, although it is an important and powerful idea in the study and application of logic. Such diverse areas as electrical switching circuits and voting coalitions can be explored and analyzed through the concept of equivalent statements. In addition, our next chapter will deal with the meaning of equivalence, but at this point the concept should be intuitively clear.

3.9   Exercise

3.9.1   Show that statements (*a*) and (*b*) are logically equivalent.

(a) $[(P \wedge \tilde{Q}) \vee (P \wedge R)] \Rightarrow Q \wedge R$
(b) $P \Rightarrow Q$.

Qualification

Chapter **4** ─────────── **and**

Quantification

4.1 Sets and subsets

In the study of logic, it was our practice to identify a simple statement, no matter how many words it contained, by a single symbol. Each statement contained some unique quality or characteristic of interest to us. We discovered that unique ideas could be combined into arguments that would have certain properties, such as validity, depending upon the manner in which the ideas were combined to *qualify* each other. If it were not for the ability to represent statements by a unique symbol, the mechanics of symbolic logic would be quite complicated. We again notice that each of these symbols is used to represent some quality, characteristic, or property.

Whenever we can classify or describe something by a characteristic or property, we say that the thing belongs to the *set* of all things having that property. A student in a college class belongs to the set of all students in that class; that class of students belongs to the set of all classes of students in their university; the University belongs to the set of all Universities in the state; etc. If we name the desired characteristic or property whose nature we wish to explore, it is then possible to examine all those things which might be of interest to us by including them in the set having the property, and, conversely, to exclude those that do not belong in our set. This concept of a set is not different

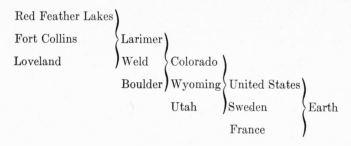

Fig. 4.1.1

from that implied when, for instance, we speak of the social set, meaning a group of people that is characterized by the property that each member recognizes the status of the other members by virtue of wealth, influence, etc. Each person in the set is called an *element* of the set, and smaller groups of persons in the set are called *subsets*, identifiable by some characteristic common to each of the elements of the subset.

We can illustrate the idea of a set and subset by examining the population of certain governmental or political units. In Fig. 4.1.1 we see that the communities of Red Feather Lakes, Fort Collins, and Loveland are sets: the elements (residents) of each of these groups have the distinct characteristic of living in the specified community. Note also that these three sets are subsets of the set of all people living in Larimer County; that the sets of the residents of Larimer, Weld, and Boulder counties are subsets of the set of all people living in the state of Colorado; that the residents of the states of Colorado, Wyoming, and Utah comprise subsets of the set of all people living in the United States; and that the people living in the United States comprise a subset of the set of all people living on Earth. To the limits of our current knowledge, the set of all people living on Earth is also the universal or complete set of "human" beings (people).

A geometric notion of sets, elements, and subsets may make the concept clearer. In Fig. 4.1.2 a rectangle illustrates a set (sometimes

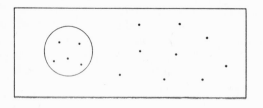

Fig. 4.1.2. A set, subset, and elements.

called a *space*), a circle within the rectangle illustrates a subset (sometimes called a *subspace*), and a number of *points* represent the elements of the set and subset. Since we shall use such pictures to assist us in understanding some of the concepts of set theory, we will use the words *set* and *space*, *subset* and *subspace*, and *element* and *point* synonymously.

In the process of classifying things into sets, it is convenient to use some additional concepts, which will assist in building the mathematical language of set theory. The set that includes all of the elements having a given characteristic is called the *universal set* of things having the given property. This set is also called, simply, the universe, and is usually represented by the rectangle illustrated in Fig. 4.1.2. The set that contains no elements is called the *empty* or *null* set. Symbols are conventionally used for these two sets, the capital Greek letter *omega* "Ω" standing for the universal set, and the special symbol "ϕ" for the null set. Other sets are usually symbolized by a capital letter of our alphabet, just as ideas conveyed in sentences were represented in symbolic logic.

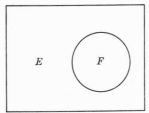

Fig. 4.1.3

At this point the student should understand that there is no conceptual difference between an English statement containing one idea, and the concept of a set, since both of these things describe some property or characteristic. The statement "All Frenchmen are Europeans" can also be interpreted as a compound statement of two simple ideas, "If one is a Frenchman, then he is a European," which we recognize as a conditional statement. Let us consider the universal set of all Europeans; a subset of this universe is the set of all Frenchmen. A diagram of this statement appears in Fig. 4.1.3. Think of all Frenchmen as being enclosed by the circle, and all Europeans enclosed by the rectangle. The statement $F \Rightarrow E$ is represented by the fact that if one is in the circle, he is also in the rectangle, although the converse is not necessarily true. Thus in terms of sets we can represent the meaning of the conditional in logic. We shall describe this relationship in terms of a set and subset.

The following basic definitions and system of notation will provide the necessary background for our subsequent study of the algebra of sets, called *Boolean* algebra:

(*a*) A *set* is a collection of individual elements that all have a specific characteristic (or property), which defines the set. To indicate that an element a belongs to a set A, or is contained in set A, we write: $a \in A$, which is read "a is an element of set A." We indicate a is not an element of set A by writing $a \notin A$.

(*b*) The set with no elements is called the *null* or *empty* set, and is indicated by the symbol "ϕ."

(*c*) The set A is a *subset* of set B if each element of A is also an element of B. To show that set A is a subset of B, we write $A \subseteq B$, read "A is a subset of B" or "A is contained in B." A *proper* subset is a set all of whose elements are contained in another set which, in addition, contains at least one element not in the subset. To indicate that A is a proper subset of B, we write $A \subset B$, read "A is a proper subset of B." Every set is of course a subset of itself, since the elements are identical.

(*d*) Two sets are said to be *equal* if, and only if, they contain the same elements. If two sets are equal, we notice they must necessarily have the same number of elements, but this is not a sufficient condition for equality; equal sets have exactly the same elements. If two sets, A and B, are equal we write $A = B$, and if we wish to indicate that sets A and B are *not* equal, we write $A \neq B$.

(*e*) The *complement* of a set is the set of elements in the universe that are not in the complemented set. If $A \subseteq \Omega$, the complement of A, written $\bar{A}$ and read "not A," is the set of elements in Ω which are not in A.

(*f*) A set may be described by enclosing in braces the characteristic or property common to all elements of the set; for example, $A = \{\text{All positive, odd numbered integers}\}$. The braces are used to indicate that A is a set, and that the characteristic noted describes each element of the set. A set may also be described by listing *all* the elements of the set, enclosing them in braces; for example, $A = \{1, 3, 5, 7, 9, \ldots\}$. (Recall that the ellipsis indicates an omission of elements which follow the pattern already established.)

Many of the properties of sets which we have just considered can be illustrated by means of a diagram called a *Venn diagram*. In fact we have already encountered members of this family of diagrams in Figs. 4.1.2 and 4.1.3. Very simply, a Venn diagram is a "picture" of the universal set and any subsets of interest. Consider the universe $\Omega = \{1, 2, 3, 4, 5, 6\}$ and subsets $A = \{1, 3, 5\}$, $B = \{2, 4, 6\}$,

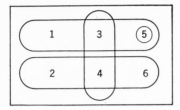

$$\Omega = \{1, 2, 3, 4, 5, 6\}$$
$$A = \{1, 3, 5\}$$
$$B = \{2, 4, 6\}$$
$$C = \{3, 4\}$$
$$D = \{5\}$$

Fig. 4.1.4

$C = \{3, 4\}$, and $D = \{5\}$ where the integers one through six comprise the elements of the various sets.

Figure 4.1.4 illustrates the universe Ω and its various subsets. In this figure we note the element indicated by the symbol "3" is common to set A and set C, i.e., $3 \in A$ and $3 \in C$. We note also that $D \subset A$, $4 \in B$ and $4 \in C$, $\tilde{A} = \{2, 4, 6\}$, $\tilde{A} = B$, $A \neq B$, etc. Although A and B have the same number of elements, $A \neq B$, for equivalence requires, as we recall, that the sets have the same elements. However, the reader could construct a set $E = \{5, 3, 1\}$ so that $A = E$. The order in which the elements appear in a set is of no consequence at this time.

4.1 Exercises

4.1.1. If $A \subseteq B$ and $B \subseteq A$, then A and B must be equivalent. Illustrate this statement by Venn diagrams.

4.1.2 If $A \subset B$ and $B \subset C$, then $A \subset C$. Illustrate by Venn diagrams.

4.2 Intersection

The *intersection* of two sets is another set which contains those elements common to both sets. Thus, the intersection of the set A and the set B is the set $A \cap B$ which is read, "A intersection B." In Fig. 4.2.1 this concept is illustrated by means of a Venn diagram. If A is the set of all students registered in the Department of Business Administration, and B is the set of all students enrolled in freshman English, then $A \cap B$ is the set of all Business students in freshman English. The rectangle describing the universal set might be thought of as the set of all students in the university. The student will notice the exact

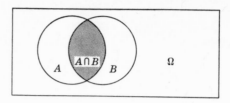

Fig. 4.2.1.   Intersection.

correspondence of this notion of intersection with that of conjunction in the previous chapter. The statement "I am in freshman English *and* in the Department of Business Administration" is a conjoint statement, and can be represented exactly in set theory by the intersection of the two sets described in Fig. 4.2.1. In addition, the truth value of this compound sentence can be determined from the diagram. A student, in order to satisfy the sentence, must be in set A *and* set B simultaneously. The concept of "true-false" takes on a new meaning in terms of "in-out," i.e., either in the set or out of it. Verify this by referring back to Fig. 3.3.1.

4.2   Exercises

4.2.1   Assume that Joe is a four letter man by virtue of his being on the football team, track team, basketball team, and baseball team. Let Ω be the set of all athletes in the university, and P, Q, R, and S be the sets containing the players on each of the teams. Draw a Venn diagram of this situation, indicating the set containing Joe by shading it. How would you write this set using the set notation?

4.2.2   Draw Venn diagrams representing the following sets. Shade that part of the diagram corresponding to the set.

(a) $P \cap Q$ (b) $\tilde{P} \cap Q$

(c) $P \cap \tilde{Q}$ (d) $\tilde{P} \cap \tilde{Q}$.

4.3   Union

The *union* of sets A and B is the set of all elements in A *or* in B. The union of set A and set B is written $A \cup B$ and is read, "A union B." The word "or" used in the definition should be taken in the inclusive sense as in the inclusive disjunction, and is interpreted to

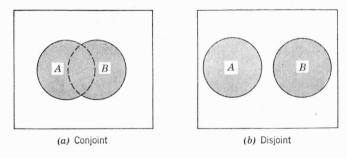

(a) Conjoint   (b) Disjoint

Fig. 4.3.1. Union.

mean "*A and/or B.*" In Fig. 4.3.1 the union of set A and set B is represented by two Venn diagrams. Two diagrams are necessary since two sets may or may not intersect; if two sets have an intersection, they are said to be *conjoint* (Fig. 4.3.1*a*); if they do not, they are said to be *disjoint* (Fig. 4.3.1*b*). The shaded parts of the diagrams indicate the union of set A and set B.

The student should keep in mind two important facts: the intersection, the union, and the complement (defined in Section 4.1) are all sets in their own right; and up to this point we have considered only whether elements are members of a set, *not* the *number* of elements in a set.

4.3 Exercises

4.3.1 If A is true, then $\tilde{A}$ is false. If $a \in A$, then $a \notin \tilde{A}$; stated differently, if it is true that a is an element of A, then it is not true that a is an element of $\tilde{A}$. Illustrate this idea by a Venn diagram.

4.3.2 "*a* is an element of $A \cup B$." This may be considered to be a compound statement, the truth of which depends upon the truth of its elements. Construct a truth table to determine the conditions under which the statement is true. Illustrate by Venn diagrams.

4.3.3 Consider the universe $\Omega = \{-5, -4, -3, -2, -1, 0, 1, 2, 3, 4, 5\}$, and the sets $A = \{-5, -4, -3, -2, -1\}$, $B = \{1, 2, 3, 4, 5\}$, $C = \{$all odd integers in $\Omega\}$, $D = \{$all integers in Ω not odd$\}$. Determine the elements of the sets required below, illustrating by Venn diagram. (0 is neither odd nor even.)

Example. $C = \{-5, -3, -1, 1, 3, 5\}$

-4	-2	0	2	4	$\leftarrow$ Ω
-5	-3	-1	1	3	5 C

(a) $\tilde{A} \cup \tilde{B}$ (b) $\tilde{A} \cap \tilde{B}$

(c) $C \cap D$ (d) $C \cup D$

(e) $A \cap C$ (f) $B \cap C \cap D$

(g) $\tilde{B} \cup (C \cap D)$ (h) $\overline{(A \cap B)}$

(i) $\overline{(A \cup B)}$ (j) $\overline{(A \cap \tilde{D})}$.

4.4   Boolean algebra

The manipulations upon sets that we have performed in the previous sections comprise the operational parts of what is known as Boolean algebra, named after George Boole, who was the first to consider sets and sentences and their correspondence in terms of an algebra. Besides their usefulness in logic and fundamental mathematics, these concepts have broad application in such diverse areas as electronic engineering and administrative decision theory, through such techniques as "NOR" logic and probability theory. In fact, such wide use is being made of set theory and Boolean algebra in communicating new findings in management science through the various professional journals that it is all but a requirement that the student of administration understand and be able to use this language.

Comprising any algebra, or "symbol language," is a set of laws and definitions of permissible operations. Each of the laws of Boolean algebra (listed below) is stated as an equivalence, which in this case can be proved either by drawing a Venn diagram or by considering the given set relationship as statements, the equivalence of which can be proved by showing that they have the same truth sets. The names of the laws are also given, since it will be useful to refer to them later. As far as we are concerned here, these names need no further discussion, but are defined by the sense of the operation named. (After all, why do you call a chair a chair?)

The Idempotent Laws: $A \cap A = A$

$A \cup A = A$

The Commutative Laws: $A \cap B = B \cap A$

$A \cup B = B \cup A$

The Associative Laws: $A \cap (B \cap C) = (A \cap B) \cap C$
$A \cup (B \cup C) = (A \cup B) \cup C$
The Distributive Laws: $A \cap (B \cup C) = (A \cap B) \cup (A \cap C)$
$A \cup (B \cap C) = (A \cup B) \cap (A \cup C)$
Operations with the Universal Set: $A \cap \Omega = A$
$A \cup \Omega = \Omega$
Operations with the Empty Set: $A \cap \phi = \phi$
$A \cup \phi = A$
Laws of Complements: $\tilde{\tilde{A}} = A$
$A \cup \tilde{A} = \Omega$
$A \cap \tilde{A} = \phi$
$\tilde{\Omega} = \phi$
DeMorgan's Theorems: $\widetilde{(A \cap B)} = \tilde{A} \cup \tilde{B}$
$\widetilde{(A \cup B)} = \tilde{A} \cap \tilde{B}$

4.4 Exercise

4.4.1 Either by Venn diagramming or with truth tables, prove the equivalence of each of the laws stated in this section.

4.5 Open sentences

In our study of logic we dealt with sentences which conveyed complete ideas through the medium of the syntax of the English language, i.e., subject, verb, predicate, arranged in the proper order. "Jacques is a Frenchman" conveys the idea, as we have seen in set theory, that Jacques is an element of the set of all Frenchmen. Now there are undoubtedly many more people who satisfy this idea of being French; we could surely find that Raoul is also French, as is Marie, et al. Very often we would like to describe a certain characteristic, and then explore the world to find those elements which have the characteristic. In doing this, we might ask the question, "What are the names of those things which have the required characteristic?" In looking for Frenchmen, we would ask, "Who are those people that are Frenchmen?" Our statement is: "_____is a Frenchman," and we want to find the set of those people who, listed as the subject of this sentence, make it true. To avoid possible confusion in the use of "blanks" we adopt a convenient symbol to represent the elements in our set. For example, we might now change our basic sentence to read "x is a Frenchman."

To specify the set of all possible Frenchmen we write "$X = \{x|x$ is a Frenchman\}," which is read "X is the set of elements x, such that x is a Frenchman." The vertical bar "$|$" is read "such that," and the braces indicate that our statement defines the set X. Such a sentence is called an *open sentence*, and the concept of open sentences.is useful throughout mathematics. It is important for us to realize at this time that x is merely a symbol representing an element of set X, and any other symbol could be used as effectively.

An open sentence is a statement defining a set, and specifying those elements of the universe which are contained in the set. The *solution set* of an open sentence is a "list" of elements that satisfy the open sentence; i.e., that are elements of the set defined by the open sentence.

Consider the open sentence, $X = \{x|x$ is an integer\}, whose solution set is found by answering the question, "what are all of the elements of the set X such that each element is an integer?" We see that x can take on a number of "values" in making the sentence true, and that we can insert a great number of "values" which render the sentence false. Therefore, x is called a *variable*, because it stands for the name of things, and can take on all sorts of names. Whether or not any given name will be included in the list of those things satisfying the sentence (the solution set), is determined by whether or not it has the characteristic required. Very often we will restrict the things which we can insert as values of the variable; i.e., we may define a set of *possible* things to test for their ability to satisfy the sentence. We say, then, that these values are restricted to a *domain*. Associated with every variable is the domain of that variable, being the set of all possible names of things that might be inserted as a value of the variable. Note carefully that the domain does not define the solution set, which is defined only by the open sentence, but merely states what values of the variable can even be considered as possible elements of the solution set. In our original example, if the domain of x is the set of all males, then Jacques and Raoul could be two elements of the set of all Frenchmen, but Marie could not.

In problems of administration, we usually deal in real things, such as people, money, and machines, so that the domain of many variables must not only be restricted to real numbers in which we quantify these things, but also to the set of positive numbers, since there is little meaning associated with negative people (except in a personality sense), money, or machines.

The concepts of open sentences, solution sets, variables, and the domain of a variable are extremely important and the reader must understand them completely.

4.5 Exercises

4.5.1 Let x be a variable whose domain is the set $\Omega = \{-5, -4,$ $-3, -2, -1, 0, 1, 2, 3, 4, 5\}$. List the elements of the following sets:

(a) $\{x \mid x$ is a positive number$\}$
(b) $\{x \mid (x$ is negative$) \vee (x$ is odd$)\}$
(c) $\{x \mid x$ is greater than 5$\}$
(d) $\{x \mid (x$ is greater than or equal to 4$) \vee (x$ is smaller than or equal to $-4)\}$
(e) $\{x \mid x$ is at least as great as $-2\}$
(f) $\{x \mid 2x = -4\}$
(g) $\{x \mid 2x = 3\}$
(h) $\{x \mid (x + 2 = 0) \wedge (x$ is positive$)\}$
(i) $\{x \mid x$ is positive$\} \cap \{x \mid x$ is negative$\}$ (*Hint:* Remember that the intersection of two sets is also a set!)
(j) $\{x \mid x$ is positive$\} \cup \{x \mid x$ is negative$\}$.

4.6 Quantification: counting and partitioning

Previously we have studiously avoided any consideration of the *number* of elements in any given set, our interest having been centered only upon those elements included in the set or excluded from it. Having thus developed methods for describing a set, specifying its elements, and manipulating sets by Boolean algebra, we now come to the matter of quantification, by which we mean counting the number of elements in a set. The reader may recognize that quantification is only a special case of qualification, which we have studied in some detail up to this point. We qualified a sentence, for instance, by negating it or by stating that it would be true only if something else were true. The statement "Seventy million Frenchmen can't be wrong" is qualified by the number of Frenchmen, as well as by stating a certain characteristic of Frenchmen. (We might ask whether sixty-nine or seventy-one million Frenchmen could be wrong.)

In inductive reasoning, for example, we attempt to prove the veracity (truthfulness) of a statement by the number of true elements we observe in the workings of the theory that supports the statement. If we were to draw the conclusion that the set of all blondes is a proper subset of the set of all dumb people (i.e., that all blondes are dumb) merely from a solitary experience with one blonde (a set of observations containing only one element), our conclusion would not be very tenable. Such a statement could not be verified unless we were to examine all blondes (the domain of the variable being the set of all blondes) and find that every one of them satisfied the sentence, i.e., belonged to the solution set. Such phrases as " . . . the preponderance of evidence . . . " imply that because certain truth cannot be found, it is necessary to tot up the number of elements in a given set and also those not in the set (but still in the domain of the variable) and strike some kind of balance in which the set containing the greater number of elements has the greater "weight."

Very often we should like to know whether the characteristic of some set is related to the characteristic of some other set (see Section 2.4), and we hypothesize that if the number of elements in one of the sets is the same as the number of elements in the other, the characteristics must be related. Such an hypothesis can obviously be true only if all of the elements of each of the sets have been examined. Since this is usually impractical, if not impossible, we depend upon the *theory of statistics* to tell us how bad our guesses are when we try to draw inferences merely from counting. With these short-comings it is more often true than not that our determination of relationships must depend upon counting only *some* elements of sets, and then making educated guesses concerning the relationships involved.

One system which facilitates such counting is called *partitioning*, which means dividing sets into various subsets having characteristics which we wish to examine. Partitioning may be accomplished, when the problem is not very large, by making a table in such a manner that the entries in the table provide a cross-classification of the various characteristics under examination. A table provides what is called a twofold classification, in that one characteristic, with its associated subsets, is placed at the top of the table, and the other with its subsets along the side. There are thus two dimensions to a twofold classification or partition; if we were to have three major characteristics, we would need some sort of box in which to make entries in three dimensions. Partitioning is possible in as many dimensions as we have characteristics to study, but the method becomes considerably more complex than that employed by tabulation.

Let us consider the application of partitioning techniques to a decision problem of a hypothetical automobile manufacturing firm. Suppose the vice president in charge of sales must decide what advertising media to utilize to promote sales of the types of cars this firm produces. In developing his magazine advertising budget, he realizes that the type of reader of a given magazine (e.g., women read *Mademoiselle*)

Ownership		By Sex of Owner		Total
		Set A: Male	Set B: Female	
By Car Type	Set C: Sedan	250	50	300
	Set D: Convertible	50	70	120
	Set E: Station wagon	150	30	180
	Total	450	150	600

Fig. 4.6.1

determines the probable market for a product advertised in that magazine. Therefore, he decides to divide his magazine advertising budget between "men's magazines" and "women's magazines" on the basis of the ratio between male and female ownership registrations for cars sold during the last twelve months in the United States, and to feature in each magazine the type of automobile its readers seem to favor. To develop the necessary information he analyzes the statistics on car registrations, partitioning the universe of all cars sold into subsets defined by the sex of the registered owner and the types of cars purchased, as detailed in Fig. 4.6.1. (Registrations of cars which are co-owned are not included.)

The hypothetical figures (thousands of units) shown in Fig. 4.6.1 are the *number* of elements in each of the various subsets. For example, the number of women who are registered car owners is determined, *first* by defining the set B = {Female Car Owners}, and *second* by enumerating the elements of the set. We denote the number of elements in set B by nB and our table shows that $nB = 150$. In similar fashion we see that $nC = 300$, and $nD = 120$. To find the number of women who are registered owners of convertibles we must first define this set, which we find to be the intersection of set B and set D, and then find $n(B \cap D)$. Note that $(nB \cap nD)$ is meaningless.

Having completed the analysis of automobile registrations, as summarized in Fig. 4.6.1, the firm's vice president is ready to apply his decision rule to the allocation of magazine advertising funds. In the absence of other criteria he would allocate three quarters of the funds to advertising in men's magazines, in which "sedan" copy would be featured. Similarly, women's magazines would receive one quarter of the budget, with "convertibles" receiving a relative emphasis.

Two additional important concepts are illustrated in the example we have just discussed; one involves the idea of *mutually exclusive* subsets, and the other *collectively exhaustive* subsets. Two subsets are said to be *mutually exclusive* if the set formed by the intersection of the subsets is empty. In the example the set of male owners obviously does not contain any elements from the set of female owners, and vice versa (e.g., $A \cap B = \phi$). Two or more subsets of a given universe are said to be *collectively exhaustive* if every element of that universe is contained in the union of the subsets (e.g., $A \cup B = \Omega$). The concepts of mutually exclusive and collectively exhaustive subsets are extremely important to the administrator in analyzing decision alternatives. In the study of decision-making, considerable emphasis is placed on the development of alternative courses of action which are mutually exclusive and which collectively exhaust decision alternatives. Although our decision maker in this example appears to have oversimplified his budget allocation problem, we should note that his method is straightforward and allows a solution to be reached. For what good is realized by complicating a decision problem to the point where no solution is possible, although some solution is required? Thus we see that basic principles are useful in problem solving, even if the result of their application is only a rough approximation of the truly optimum solution.

We recall that a necessary condition for the equivalence of sets was that they contain the same number of elements, but that this was not a sufficient condition. To illustrate this, we can see in the table that the set of female sedan owners has the same number of elements as the set of male convertible owners, but they are not equivalent.

4.6   Exercise

4.6.1   Refer to Fig. 4.6.1. If the domain of x is the set of all auto drivers, how many elements are there in each of the following sets? Use Boolean algebra to reduce the statements to their least complicated equivalent, and then "count."

(a) $\{x | x \in (A \cap C)\}$

(b) $\{x | x \in [(B \cup A) \cap (B \cup E)]\}$

(c) $\{x | x \in (D \cup \tilde{E})\}$

(d) $\{x | x \in [B \cup (A \cap E)]\}$

(e) $\{x | x \notin [(B \cap C) \cup (A \cap D)]\}$

(f) $\{x | x \in B\} \cap \{x | x \text{ is the set of all truck drivers}\}$.

Chapter 5

Some Properties of Numbers

5.1 What is a number?

In our earlier discussion of number symbols and numbering systems, certain concepts were ignored on the basis of the fact that the college student has already studied sufficient mathematics to understand such notions as a negative number. As has been our purpose in the foregoing sections of the text, we do not only wish to lean upon what the student already knows, but to exploit and strengthen this knowledge by pointing out its original source. Therefore we shall discuss some very basic notions concerning numbers and the manner in which they may be used in quantitative analysis.

What is a number? Since we all have a strong intuitive idea about the answer to this question, it seems almost silly to ask it! Yet, like many simple concepts, it is really quite difficult to find a definition which satisfies everyone, especially mathematicians and philosophers. Perhaps more importantly, the philosopher's definition is probably unsatisfactory to most laymen, since it appears to be circular, i.e., the word *number* is used to define itself. This definition is: a *number* is anything that is the number of some set. Whether this is circular or not depends of course upon what one means by the "number of some set." We shall not pursue the logic of this expression, but merely

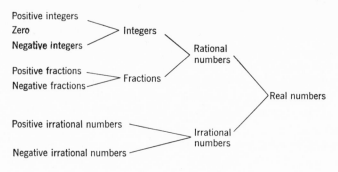

Fig. 5.1.1

recall from the previous chapter that it is possible and useful to count the elements in a finite set; the result is a number. The fact that numbers are used for counting provides another logical difficulty, but we shall ignore this problem and go on to describe various kinds of numbers.

Since there are various kinds of numbers, it is useful to consider their classification in terms of sets. The simplest set of numbers is the set of all positive *integers* or "whole" numbers, represented by our counting symbols. Another "simple" set is the set of all negative integers; this set is not so intuitive as the set of positive integers is. We shall discuss the idea of negative numbers in the following section. One more set makes up this simplest of classifications; it is the set containing only the number zero. These three sets are mutually exclusive, and they collectively exhaust the set of all integers. In other words, they are each proper subsets of the set of all integers, the characteristic setting them apart from each other being the *sign* of the elements in each set. (Zero has no sign, which will be discussed shortly.) In Fig. 5.1.1 this set-subset relationship is illustrated, as are the sets comprising the other kinds of numbers.

The union of the set of all integers with the set of all fractions is the set of *rational* numbers. A *fraction* is the quotient of two integers, a/b, where b is not 1, 0, or -1. There are numbers which cannot be represented as the quotient of integers (as described above), such as the number whose symbol is π. Such a number is called *irrational*, and it is represented in decimal form by a non-repeating decimal: $\pi = 3.14159+$. It can be proved that any decimal fraction which repeats itself in a given pattern (as the process of finding the quotient is carried out at length) is a rational number. This characteristic is useful for distinguishing between rational and irrational decimal numbers.

Finally, the sets of rational and irrational numbers are subsets of the set of all *real* numbers. The set of all real numbers is a subset of the set of all *complex* numbers, etc. We shall deal in this text only with real numbers, and therefore our illustration stops at this point. It should be realized, however, that numbers and number systems are a creation of man, as is mathematics itself, and that therefore new sets of numbers having certain characteristics may be developed any time our familiar tools fail to do a given job.

5.1 Exercise

5.1.1 Draw Venn diagrams, labeling each set, of Fig. 5.1.1

5.2 Directed numbers

Consider Fig. 5.2.1 in which a line has been divided into equal segments, and an object (▼) is at rest at one of the dividing points. We shall call each of the segments a unit. Our object can only be moved back and forth along this line, no other movement being possible. We are told to move the object five units to the right; this quantity of movement is the *positive directed number* "+5." We move the object three units to the left; this quantity of movement is the *negative directed number* "−3." We notice then that whether a number is positive or negative depends upon the "direction" moved. The position at which the object rests is as yet unnamed, although if we are to be able to communicate this position to anyone, we must obviously have a name for the position. Let us define another number, called the *origin*, and symbolize it by "0." If our object initially rests at position "0," and then we move it +5, i.e., five units to the right, we say that it comes to rest in position +5. We name this position in accordance with the number of units it is away from the origin, and give it its sign in accordance with the direction from zero.

Fig. 5.2.1

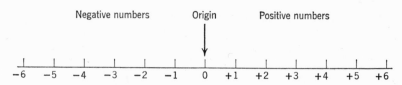

Fig. 5.2.2. "The number line."

An object which rests on the right side of the origin (zero) is in a positive position, while an object at rest on the left side is in a negative position. This position, or location, is indicated, then, by (1) the number of units from the origin and (2) the direction from the origin. The origin itself, although it has a unique location, obviously has no direction, and thus the number zero has *no sign:* by convention, positive numbers are shown without sign, however. In Fig. 5.2.2 we establish the *number line* in accordance with the above. This line has the property that every real number lies upon it, assuming it possible to extend the line indefinitely in both directions. Thus, every point on the line (which is, of course, a collection of points) is, in a geometrical sense, a real number.

Although this is a simple concept, there are many phenomena which behave along a line, as does our object in Fig. 5.2.1. Such behavior is called one-dimensional, and is characterized by movement "up" or "down," "in" or "out," "back" or "forth," etc. A thermometer, a speedometer, and an altimeter are all examples of devices used to measure such behavior. A clock, on the other hand, is not a good example because clocks in effect only measure in terms of positive directed numbers, since we cannot turn back time in the real world.

5.2 Exercise

5.2.1 Given the set, $\Omega = \{-4, -3, -2, -1, 0, 1, 2, 3, 4\}$:

(a) Draw a Venn diagram noting the following proper subsets: $A = \{$all positive directed numbers$\}$; $B = \{$all negative directed numbers$\}$; $C = \{0\}$.

(b) Determine the elements of these sets: (1) $A \cup B$; (2) $\overline{A \cap B \cap C}$; (3) $A \cup B \cup C$.

(c) Of what significance is your answer to question $b(2)$?

5.3   Opposite numbers

"What goes up, must come down" is an old "saw" which has been disproved since Sputnik I went into orbit, yet the idea helps us to define what we mean by an *opposite* number.   If we toss a rock 10 feet into the air, it will fall 10 feet back to our hand; the magnitude of the movement up is the same as the magnitude of movement down.   Yet these numbers are not the same, unless we are not interested in direction.   If we let $+10$ be the magnitude "up" and the number -10 be the magnitude "down," then we have sufficiently described these movements, both as to magnitude (10) and direction ($+$ or $-$).   Such pairs of numbers are called opposite numbers.   We may define the opposite of a number as that number which must be added to the given number to produce zero; or state that two directed numbers are opposite directed numbers if their sum is zero.   (Could any other pair of directed numbers satisfy this requirement?)

The concept of directed numbers has been introduced only to indicate how the conventional positive and negative numbers "got that way."   However, this concept is also useful in performing arithmetic with positive and negative numbers.   If our object had been moved $+5$ and then -3, we see that it would come to rest at location $+2$, and we have therefore defined, in a very unrigorous fashion, the difference between two numbers, which is indeed the sum of a positive number and a negative number.   The student will recognize this as the algebraic identity "$x - y = x + (-y)$."   This identity expresses the idea that there is basically no operational difference between the use of the symbols "$+$" and "$-$" in arithmetic, and their use in assigning a direction to a number.   The arithmetic statement "$2 + (-3)$" is the same as "$2 - (+3)$"; any confusion which arises can be handled by using parentheses to indicate the desired meaning.   The pitfall here is the student's reluctance to realize that when we let x be a directed number, x can be positive, or negative, or zero, i.e., the number can be an element of the set of all positive directed numbers, the set of all negative directed numbers, or the set containing the number zero.

5.3   Exercise

5.3.1   Show the opposite numbers for the following directed numbers:

(a) 1   (b) 12
(c) -7 (d) -5.3147
(e) 0   (f) $\frac{1}{2}$.

5.4   Absolute value

It is often true that we are not interested in the direction of movement of a phenomenon, but only in the magnitude of the movement.
For instance, an airplane trip from Denver to Chicago covers some
1000 miles, the return trip requiring the same.   Although it is true
that in some sense we went "out" 1000 miles and came "back" 1000
miles, the total distance traveled is 2000 miles, not zero miles.   We
can see that if we consider the directed numbers corresponding to the
above trip, we end our trip at the origin, because the directed numbers
are opposites.   If we are concerned, however, not with where we are
after making this trip, but how far we have traveled, it is obvious that
we must ignore the direction of the numbers and consider only their
magnitude.

Such a consideration is based on the concept of *absolute value*, which
can be defined as the magnitude of a number without regard to its sign.
Very simply, the absolute value of a number x, written $|x|$, is always
positive (except for the number zero which has no sign at all).   A
more rigorous way of stating this is: if x is a positive directed number,
then $|x| = x$; if x is a negative directed number, then $|x| = -x$; and
$|0| = 0$.   The student should realize that every directed number really
determines a pair of numbers; the given number and its opposite.
Thus the absolute value of a directed number is the same as the positive
number of the pair.

5.5   Ordering directed numbers

Even though the concept of absolute value is useful, we realize that
the direction of a number can be as important as the magnitude of the
number, and, in fact, sometimes more important.   Often, for instance,
it makes little difference if a business of a given size loses x dollars or
y dollars, where y is greater than x, if the loss of x dollars is sufficient
to cause the demise of the business.   The concept of direction is equally
applicable to the circumstance of an airplane pilot who cannot main-
tain the minimum flying speed required to stay airborne: *any* speed less
than the critical or stalling speed will make the aircraft merely a large
piece of complex junk hurtling through the air, no longer an example of
man's ingenuity in overcoming the force of gravity.   Thus we introduce the concept of *ordering* numbers, by which we mean comparing

them according to their magnitude and direction (or sign). For instance, the number 3 is larger than the number 2, -100 is smaller than 25, -2 is greater than -5. As we examine the number line in Fig. 5.2.2, we see that any number to the right of any other number is greater than the number to its left.

Thus we may define "greater than" and "less than" as follows: if x and y are directed numbers, then x *is greater than* y if $x - y$ is a positive directed number. We write "greater than" by using the symbol "$>$," and "less than" by the symbol "$<$." We have ordered two directed numbers when we have stated that one is larger or smaller than the other.

We recall that the set of all numbers can be divided into three subsets: the set of all positive directed numbers, the set of all negative directed numbers, and the set containing the number zero. If a directed number x is not greater than another directed number y, we note that x could belong to either of two possible sets: the set of numbers less than y, or the set containing that one number equal to y. We refer to the definition of ordering given above, and write it in symbolic terms: $(x - y) \in \{$positive directed numbers$\} \Rightarrow (x > y)$. But if $(x - y) \notin \{$positive directed numbers$\}$, there are two alternatives: either $(x - y) \in \{$negative directed numbers$\}$ or $(x - y) \in \{0\}$. In words then, statements such as "not less than," "not greater than," "at least," "at most," imply that one of the directed numbers could be *equal* to the other as well as being less than or greater than it is. This idea is expressed by the symbols "$\leq$" and "$\geq$," the first being read "less than or equal to," or "not greater than," or "at most," and the second being read "greater than or equal to," or "not less than," or "at least." Some of the properties of ordered numbers are shown in symbolic form below; the student should test each of these properties by referring to the number line (Fig. 5.2.2) and substituting various values for the variables.

If x, y, and z are directed numbers, then

(a) If x is positive, then $x > 0$; if x is negative, then $0 > x$.

(b) If x is negative, then $x < 0$.

(c) If $x > y$ and $y > z$, then $x > z$.

(d) If $x > y$, then $(x + z) > (y + z)$.

(e) If $x > y$ and $z > 0$, then $xz > yz$.

(f) Only one of the following conditions can be true: $x > y$ or $x < y$ or $x = y$.

(g) If $x > y$, then $-x < -y$.

5.5   Exercises

5.5.1   Note whether the following statements are true or false:

(a) $+7 > +5$

(b) $-1 > -12$

(c) $0 > +3$

(d) $+1 < -5$

(e) $+4 > +7$

(f) $-4 > -7$

(g) $-5 > 0$

(h) $\frac{1}{2} > -\frac{3}{4}$.

5.5.2   Find the absolute values for the following directed numbers:

(a) $+6$

(b) -6

(c) $+3$

(d) $-\frac{1}{2}$

(e) 0

(f) $+4$.

5.5.3   Indicate whether the following statements are true or false:

(a) $|1 + 7| > |+3|$

(b) $+5 > |-5|$

(c) $0 > |-3|$

(d) $|-3| \leq |+3|$

(e) $-6 > |-1|$

(f) $\frac{1}{2} \geq |-\frac{1}{2}|$.

5.5.4   Translate the following symbolic sentences into English:

(a) $(x - y) \in \{\text{negative directed numbers}\} \Rightarrow (x < y)$

(b) $(x > y) \Rightarrow (x + 2) > (y + 2)$

(c) $(x > y) \land (y > 2) \Rightarrow (x > 2)$

(d) $(x > y) \land (z > 0) \Rightarrow (xz > yz)$

(e) $(x > y) \land (z \leq 0) \Rightarrow ([xz \leq yz] \lor [(xz < yz) \underline{\lor} (xz = yz = 0)])$.

Equations, Relations, and Functions

Chapter **6**

6.1 Equalities and equations

Equalities are not new to the collegiate student; he has used them for many years both academically and in his daily life. This fact has allowed us to use equalities heretofore without any further description of them. Our purpose at the moment is to retrace some of our steps, making explicit some of the concepts of equalities and equations which we will apply in studying relations and functions.

The *equality* $a = b$ can be taken to mean that a and b are two names for the same object or thing. If an equality is true for all values of the variables for which each member of the equality is defined, then we call it an *identical equality*, or simply an *identity*. If the equality is true for some but not all of the values which the variable (or variables) may assume, then it is called a *conditional equality*, or simply an *equation*. The difference between an identity and an equation can be shown in terms of the solution sets of each:

Identity: The solution set of the identity $x^2 - 9 = (x + 3)(x - 3)$ is the set of all real numbers.
Equation: The solution set of the equation $2x + 7 = 11$ is the set containing the number 2.

An equation is an open sentence whose verb is "equals." The

student will recognize $2x - 3 = 5$ as an equation, the solution to which is 4.   Why?   Because if we "plug in" the number 4, i.e., substitute it for x in the equation, we find that the equation is "satisfied," by which we mean that the two "sides" of the equation are equal, or names of the same object.   There is nothing wrong with this interpretation of an equation at all, except that it is very mechanical and provides little intuition by itself.   Equations can be better understood by thinking of them as open sentences such as those we studied in Chapter 4.   Our equation above can be expressed as the open sentence $\{x|2x - 3 = 5\}$. Knowing some characteristics of sets and sentences, we recognize that, as a set, this sentence can be rewritten in terms of the elements of the solution set: $\{4\}$.

At this point it should be very clear why we bothered to discuss logic preliminary to the mathematics itself.   In symbolic logic, we worked with simple statements which could take on the values true or false. Depending upon the truth values of the simple statements, the compound statements and arguments, which were constructed by means of logical connectives, could be analyzed to determine the values of their truth sets.

Corresponding to the simple statements are the number-variable combinations which we call equations; the only difference is that where previously our statements could take on only the values true or false, a variable in an equation can take on any of the values specified in the domain of the variable.   In effect, the domain of a statement contains only the values T or F.   Whether or not a statement is indeed true or false is a matter of fact to be determined by observation in the world; logic does not attempt to prove the veracity of a given assertion, but merely provides the scheme by which we may analyze combinations of statements to find, under given true-false conditions of the simple statements, the true or false condition of the combination.   The algebra by which we manipulate equations has exactly the same characteristic: "$2 \times 4 = 8$" is a true statement only because we have chosen to make it true by our definitions of numbers and arithmetic operations. On the other hand, consider the statement $\{x|2x - 1 = 3\}$.   Is this statement true or false?   Obviously, this is a nonsensical question; mathematics does not give us any means of determining the truth or falsity of this statement any more than logic tells us whether the statement "It is raining" is true or false.

The important thing implied by an open sentence, such as $\{x|2x - 1 = 3\}$, is that there may be some number (or numbers) which, when substituted for x, will *make* this a true statement, and, perhaps, a host of numbers which will make it false.   Algebra provides the means for finding the "true" values of the variable, by following certain permissible manipulations of the statement, just as Boolean algebra allowed us to manipulate statements in a truth table. An equation is thus but an assertion about the behavior of some variable; whether the assertion is true or false can only be determined by observing the real world and the behavior of the phenomenon itself which the assertion describes.

Consider this example. The corner grocery asserts in a sign in the window that bananas are $0.05 per pound. Since this is a very good price for bananas, and you have $0.25 in your pocket, you decide to buy 5 pounds of bananas, under the assertion that, where x is the number of pounds of bananas, $\{x|0.05x = 0.25\}$. Now you put 5 pounds of bananas in a sack and take them to the checkout stand; the checker rings up $1.05. You call his attention to the sign in the window, and he says, "Yes. The first pound costs only a nickel, but each additional pound costs a quarter!" Disregarding the fact that you will probably take your banana business elsewhere in the future, we notice that there was nothing at all wrong with your mathematics; the problem arose because your assertion about the world of bananas and the price behavior thereof was *false*. The language of mathematics, like the language of logic, provides a precise and powerful way to conceptualize and "solve" problems; however, the original assertion about the nature of a problem is a matter of fact, not of logical or mathematical method. Human ingenuity will always be required to formulate "correct" assertions; no amount of mathematics will ever replace judgment, although it is certainly an important means by which this power can be improved.

Our notation for the open sentence is quite involved, and therefore we will not always write an equation as an open sentence; the reader, however, should always be able to express an equation in terms of an open sentence. Indeed, this notation, which appears all but trivial when we consider equations in only one variable, becomes all important when our equations include many variables, such as in our study of linear algebra and linear programming.

There are certain mathematical operations which can be performed on an equality without changing its solution set, and although all of us have been exposed to these fundamental operations before, a review at this time may be useful. Given an equality $a = b$:

(*a*) The same constant or variable c may be *added* to both members of the equality; i.e., $a + c = b + c$.

(*b*) The same constant or variable c may be *subtracted* from both members of the equality; i.e., $a - c = b - c$.

(*c*) Each member of the equality may be *multiplied* by the same non-zero constant c; i.e., $ca = cb$.

(*d*) Each member of the equality may be *divided* by the same non-zero constant c; i.e., $a/c = b/c$.

It is often useful to multiply or divide both members of an equality by an expression containing the variables involved in the equality. Although such an operation may be algebraically feasible, it must be remembered that the solution set of the equality may be changed, either by introducing extraneous elements into the set, or by losing some of the members of the original solution set.

6.1 Exercise

6.1.1 If the domain of the variable x is the set of all real numbers, the domain of the variable y is the set of all integers, and the domain of the variable z is the set of all positive real numbers, restate the following equations as open sentences and list the elements in their solution sets.

(a) $2x + 3 = -4$
(b) $2y + 3 = -4$
(c) $2z + 3 = -4$
(d) $-3x - 4 = 1.5x + 2$
(e) $x - 4 = 0$
(f) $x + 4 = 0$
(g) $x^2 - 4 = 0$
(h) $y^2 - 4 = 0$
(i) $z^2 - 4 = 0$
(j) $x^2 + 4 = 0$.

6.2 Inequalities

Our study of ordered numbers in Chapter 5 introduced the concept of the domain over which a variable could take on various values, and implied the notion of a limit or limits to this domain. Paralleling the concept of an equality we have the concept of an inequality. An *absolute inequality* is an inequality that holds for all values of the variables concerned for which the members of the inequality are defined, e.g., $x + 1 > x$. A *conditional inequality* or *inequation* is an inequality which does not hold for all values of the variables concerned, e.g., $x > 2$. A statement such as $\{x|x > 2\}$ is thus an *inequation*. As in the section above, it implies the question, "What values of x, given the domain of x, make this a true statement?" An inequation may therefore be considered to be an open sentence whose verb is symbolized by $<$, $>$, $\leq$, or $\geq$.

The fundamental operations which can be performed on an equality without changing its solution set can also be performed on an inequality without changing the solution set of the inequality, except as noted below. If $a > b$, then:

(a) The same constant or variable c may be *added* to both members of the inequality; i.e., $a + c > b + c$.

(b) The same constant or variable c may be *subtracted* from both members of the inequality; i.e., $a - c > b - c$.

(c) Each member of the inequality may be *multiplied* by the same positive constant c; i.e., $ca > cb$, $(c > 0)$.

(d) Each member of the inequality may be *divided* by the same positive constant c; i.e., $a/c > b/c$, $(c > 0)$.

Note that in (c) and (d) above, the constant c was restricted to the set of positive numbers. If c is negative, then the inequality is reversed, in order that the solution set of the original inequality not be changed. Thus:

(e) Each member of the inequality may be multiplied by the same negative constant c, reversing the direction of the inequality; i.e., $ca < cb$, $(c < 0)$.

(f) Each member of the inequality may be divided by the same negative constant c, reversing the direction of the inequality; i.e., $a/c < b/c$, $(c < 0)$.

Multiplying or dividing both members of an inequality by an expression containing one of the variables in the inequality is subject to the same limitations imposed upon these operations when applied to equalities, i.e., the solution set may be changed. If an inequality is multiplied or divided through by zero the statement is without meaning. Division by zero is, in fact, not a defined operation in arithmetic, because the result cannot be defined to be a number.

Where the solution set of an equation in one variable is a set of one unique value (or unique values in certain cases; see Exercise 6.1.1, e and g), the solution set of an inequation usually contains many and sometimes infinitely many values which make the statement true. The open sentence $\{x|x > 2\}$, where the domain of x is the set of all real numbers, has the solution set {all real numbers greater than 2}. There is no upper limit to the value of x in this set; we could fill in elements of this set for a lifetime and not even begin to fill the set with all of its elements. Therefore, the solution set to this sentence contains all real numbers larger than 2. Such a set is called an *infinite* set. Since the listing of all the elements of an infinite set is impossible, the ellipsis (i.e., three dots) may be employed to indicate the omitted items in a patterned list of elements. For instance, if the domain of x is the set of all positive integers (an infinite set), then $\{x|x > 2\} = \{3, 4, 5, \ldots\}$. However, it is generally considered more desirable to describe an infinite set by defining the characteristics which specify the set. Thus, in our example above, the solution set would be {all positive integers greater than 2}.

A *finite* set is a set whose elements may be ordered and counted to the *last* element. The reader should not get the idea that a finite set contains only a small number of elements, for there are a number of finite sets which have a very large number of elements; for example, the set of all human beings on earth, the set of all fish in the seas, or the set of all grains of sand on the earth. Obviously, such "large" finite sets do not lend themselves to description by element listing (extension), and, like infinite sets, are best specified by the definition of set characteristics (intension). These concepts are of fundamental importance to the administrator and we will deal interchangeably with finite and infinite sets as we develop our understanding of analytical techniques.

We have previously mentioned "infinity" as if the term had been properly defined elsewhere. We could of course spend a great deal of time philosophizing about the true meaning of the word or idea, but we shall content ourselves in the hope that the student already has an intuitive notion about the meaning of infinity, and merely point out some important properties of this idea. In the first place, it must be realized that infinity is a mathematical or philosophical *abstraction* from reality; our real world has no physical counterpart of infinity, except in terms of time, which is itself an abstraction. Since to quantify behavior by counting it is necessary to place our counting symbols in one-to-one correspondence with the "real" things which we wish to count, and since infinity has no real counterpart, it is obvious that there can be no number which would represent the size of this "quantity." Infinity is thus *not* a number; it cannot be manipulated arithmetically or algebraically as are numbers.

Since from our study of the number line we realize that numbers grow infinitely in both the positive and negative directions, we adopt the convention of using a sign with the infinity symbol. Thus "$+ \infty$" represents positive infinity and "$- \infty$" represents negative infinity. For the sake of simplicity, we do use the symbol in much the same way as we use numbers, however. For example, the solution set of the open sentence $\{x|x > 2\}$ can be written $\{2 < x < \infty\}$; and

$$\{x|x \leq -5\} = \{-\infty < x \leq -5\}$$

Note that we may never write $x = \infty$ or $x \leq -\infty$, for instance; for x, a variable, is only a place-holder for numbers, and ∞ is not a number.

A statement such as $\{a < x < b\}$, where a and b are real numbers, defines an *interval*, which is a particular kind of set whose elements are restricted by certain limits. An interval can be expressed as a compound sentence; for instance, $\{-2 < x < 2\}$ can be written $\{x | (x > -2) \wedge (x < 2)\}$. (We must be very careful with the direction of the symbols $<$ and $>$, that we do not construct nonsense sentences such as $\{5 > x > 10\}$). Intervals constructed with $<$ and $>$ are called *open intervals;* they do not include their end points, e.g., $\{-2, 2\} \nsubseteq \{-2 < x < 2\}$.

The interval $\{-2 \leq x \leq 2\}$ is called a *closed interval;* we notice that this set includes its end points, i.e., -2 and 2 are elements of this interval. Since we have spoken of "open" and "closed" intervals, we will define as "ajar" an interval which is "half open" or "half closed," such as $\{-2 \leq x < 2\}$.

The concept of an interval, and the inequation whose solution set it describes, are important because many of the practical problems which we shall solve later deal with intervals. As an example, consider the size, in terms of units produced, of a manufacturing plant; it cannot be less than zero, but there are practical limitations on the number of units which can be produced.

6.2 Exercises

6.2.1 If the domain of the variable x is the set of all real numbers, the domain of the variable y is the set of all integers, and the domain of the variable z is the set of all positive real numbers, restate the following inequalities as open sentences and solve them.

(a) $2x + 3 < -4$ (b) $2y + 3 > -4$
(c) $2z + 3 < -4$ (d) $x^2 + 4 > 0$
(e) $y^2 > 3$ (f) $3 > x > 1$
(g) $5 > y > 9$ (h) $-5 > z > -9$.

6.2.2 Which of the following statements are true?

(a) $-4 < 0$ (b) $-3 > -4$
(c) $x \geq x$ (d) $5 \geq 3$
(e) $2x > x$ (f) $1 - [-(-1)] \neq 0$
(g) $6 < -1$ (h) $2 - (-2) > 1$.

6.2.3   Restate the following statements as inequations.

(a) The inventory value of item x must not exceed \$12,000.
(b) We will hire not less than 12 new men, nor more than 15.
(c) Total costs must be kept below 90 per cent of total revenue.

6.2.4   Give the solution sets for the following open sentences.

(a) $\{x| \ |x| = +2\}$ \qquad\qquad (b) $\{x| \ |x| < 1\}$
(c) $\{x| \ |x| + 2 > 1\}$ \qquad\quad (d) $\{x| \ |x| > 1\}$
(e) $\{x| \ |x| \geq 2\}$ \qquad\qquad (f) $\{x| \ |x| \leq -4\}$.

6.3   Graphing: one variable

Just as Venn diagrams were of assistance in visualizing the elements of sets and subsets, graphs of equalities and inequalities assist in visualizing their solution sets.   The *graph* of an equality or inequality in one variable is the *locus* of points along the number line which satisfy the equality or inequality, i.e., make its open sentence true.   The number associated with the locus (location) of the point or points is called the *coordinate* of the point.   In Fig. 6.3.1 is the graph of the equation $x - 4 = 0$; the solution set of this equation contains one element: $\{4\}$. (The graph of this set is the *point* on the number line; the circle is used merely to identify it.)   Figure 6.3.2 shows the graph of the equation $x^2 - 4 = 0$, the solution set of which contains two elements: $\{2, -2\}$. In Fig. 6.3.3 is the graph of the equation $|x| - 1 = 0$, the solution set of which is $\{-1, 1\}$.

The concept of the domain of the variable x can also be expressed clearly by graphing.   If the domain is the set of all real numbers, then we see that any point on the real number line is admissible in a solution

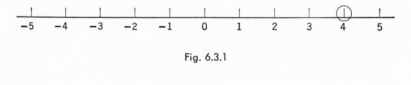

Fig. 6.3.1

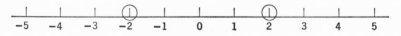

Fig. 6.3.2

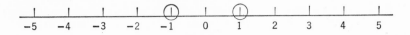

Fig. 6.3.3

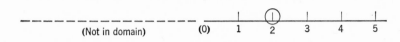

(Not in domain)   (0)   1   2   3   4   5

Fig. 6.3.4

set. If the domain is the set of all positive real numbers, then the point having coordinate zero and all those points which are negative are excluded from a solution set. If this were the case, the solution set of the equation graphed in Fig. 6.3.2 would be {2}, rather than {−2, 2}, since, as shown in Fig. 6.3.4, the domain of the variable does not include the number −2. If the domain of any given variable is not specified, the student should understand the domain to be the set of all real numbers; however, if it is specified, then it must be taken into account.

The graph of an inequation is more interesting than the graph of an equation, since the solution set of the inequation must usually be defined over an interval, i.e., over a *set* of points. In graphing, the student must take pains to note whether he is dealing with an open interval, a closed interval, or an interval "ajar," since these considerations will affect the correctness of the graph. Consider Fig. 6.3.5, which is the graph of the inequation $x > -2$. The solution set of the sentence $\{x|x > -2\}$ is the open interval $\{-2 < x < \infty\}$. Note the convention we use to indicate that the point whose coordinate is (-2) is not in the interval: a symbol that looks like an arrowhead, the tip of which rests at the point not included. The graph of the rest of the interval is indicated by drawing a line on either side of the number line above and below those points included in the interval. If the interval includes an end point, we indicate this by turning the arrowhead

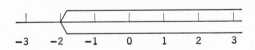

Fig. 6.3.5

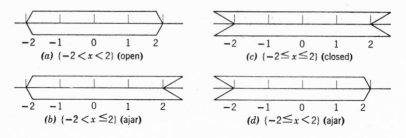

Fig. 6.3.6

around so that it points in the direction of the interval, instead of away from it as for an open interval. Various intervals are graphed in Fig. 6.3.6 as illustrations.

6.3 Exercises

6.3.1 Find the solution sets for the following open sentences and graph them:

(a) $\{x | x + 1 = 5\}$ (b) $\{x | x + 1 = 1\}$

(c) $\{x | x - 3 < 0\}$ (d) $\{x | x - 2 > 0\}$

(e) $\{x | x^2 = 9\}$ (f) $\{x | 2x^2 - 4 = 4\}$

(g) $\{x | \ |x| = 4\}$ (h) $\{x | x \geq 3\}$.

6.3.2 Graph the following intervals:

(a) $\{7 > x > 2\}$ (b) $\{4 < x \leq 9\}$

(c) $\{0 \geq x \geq -3\}$ (d) $\{7 \geq x > 3\}$

(e) $\{1.5 < x < \infty\}$ (f) $\{-\infty < x \leq 0\}$.

6.4   Ordered pairs and rectangular coordinates

In our discussion of directed numbers we used the example of moving an object back and forth along a line, and called such movement "one-dimensional." We located the place where the object came to rest by noting the name of this point, which had some "value" on the number line. Now consider the problem of identifying the location of an object, such as a chessman, which can move in two "dimensions," i.e., up and down as well as back and forth, upon a plane or flat surface.

In a city laid out in square blocks, we could direct a stranger to the intersection of any two streets merely by telling him to go "so many blocks this way, then so many blocks that way" from the point at which such conversation took place. If we were in Fort Collins and giving the same sort of directions for locating a given point in Denver, we would need some reference point in Denver, from which we could reckon direction and magnitude. A simple system is in effect in most cities which informs the questioner immediately of the location of some desired spot: an "address" which gives the direction and magnitude of some location from a given reference point. In Fort Collins, this reference point is the intersection of College and Mountain Avenues. *Direction* from this reference point is indicated by naming streets East, West, South, or North; *magnitude* is indicated by numbering each block by the hundred's digit, or digits, of a three- or four-digit code, the ten's and one's digit identifying given locations within a block. The address "500 West Mountain" is thus a location in the fifth block west of College on Mountain. This system is not complete, however, since the names of streets, including Mountain or College, give no clue as to their relative position: "1218 West Oak Street" is a location in the twelfth block west of College Avenue (the North-South reference line), but there is no clue as to how far north or south of the East-West reference line (Mountain Avenue) Oak street lies.

Mormon-settled communities in Utah and elsewhere follow a much more practical numbering system which identifies exactly any location when the reference point is known, although perhaps something is lost in the name of practicality when we live on West Twenty-first Street South rather than on East Plum Street. In many older cities, especially in foreign lands, no system whatever exists for numbering blocks, and the taxi business can thrive at the expense of the stranger to the city.

In mathematics we do not have such a problem, however. The concept of the one-dimensional number line can easily be extended to two dimensions, by merely erecting a perpendicular to our original number line at its origin, and numbering this perpendicular in exactly the same fashion, except that the positive values are above the horizontal line on the perpendicular, and the negative values below it. The origins of both number lines coincide. These lines have names. The horizontal line is called the axis of abscissas and is often referred to as the *x axis;* the vertical line is called the axis of ordinates, and is often referred to as the *y axis*. These two lines lie in a plane, and any point on this plane can be located by referring to the numbers on the axes (pronounced ax-ees). These axes provide a number line reference system called a *rectangular coordinate system.*

A point in the plane is located by first measuring the shortest distance from the point to the y axis. This distance, which is called the *abscissa* of the point, will be a positive directed number if the point lies to the right of the y axis and a negative directed number if the point lies to the left of the y axis. The abscissa of a point can be conveniently read off the x axis, hence its name: *the axis of abscissas*. Having located the abscissa of a point, the *ordinate* of a point can be similarly identified by measuring the shortest distance from the point to the x axis, the ordinate being a positive directed number if the point is above the x axis and a negative directed number if below. The ordinate of a point can be conveniently read off the y axis, hence its name: *the axis of ordinates*. In this fashion the abscissa and ordinate of any point located on the plane of our rectangular coordinate system can be established. To locate a point in the plane, given the abscissa and ordinate, the procedure is reversed.

In Fig. 6.4.1, a number of points have been identified by their coordinates, which are called *ordered pairs* of directed numbers. They are said to be *ordered* because it makes considerable difference which number appears first within the parentheses if we are to have a consistent rule for finding locations. Our convention is that the first number of the pair (the one on the left) indicates the location relative to the axis of abscissas, while the second indicates the location relative to the axis of ordinates. If we let X be the domain of all values located on the x axis, then we say that x is any value in this domain. We have a different name for the set of all admissible values along the axis of ordinates: this set is called the *range*. It performs exactly the same function as does the domain. We may let Y be the set of all admissible

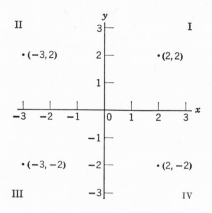

Fig. 6.4.1

values along the axis of ordinates, i.e., the range, such that y is any value in this range. Then the point (x, y) is any point on the plane such that x is an element of X and y is an element of Y.

We now define a new set, called the *Cartesian product* of X and Y, which defines the whole *space* in which an ordered pair (x, y) may lie. The Cartesian product is written $X \times Y$, and is read "X on Y." The student should recognize that it is necessary to define this space, since X only defines the domain of x along the x axis, and Y the range of y along the y axis; since any point (x, y) may lie on or off the axes, we must know what constitutes the admissible space in which (x, y) may be located. As an example, if the domain of x is $X = \{1, 2, 3\}$ and the range of y is $Y = \{1, 2, 3\}$, then

$$X \times Y = \{(1, 1), (1, 2), (1, 3), (2, 1), (2, 2), (2, 3), (3, 1), (3, 2), (3, 3)\}.$$

(The student should recognize here the exact correspondence between points in a space and elements in a set.) We may now write an open sentence in two variables, such as $\{(x, y) | (x \in X) \wedge (y \in Y)\}$. The solution set of this sentence turns out to be $X \times Y$. If X and Y are defined as above, and we ask $\{(x, y) | x = y\}$ the solution set is $\{1, 1)$, $(2, 2), (3, 3)\}$, since these are the only admissible elements which make the open sentence true.

Since the axes divide the space into four parts, or *quadrants*, we name each of these quadrants for purposes of quick identification. In Fig. 6.4.1 each of the quadrants is identified by a Roman numeral. The reader should note the characteristics of each quadrant:

$$\begin{aligned}
&\textit{Quadrant} &&\text{I}: &&x \geq 0 \text{ and } y \geq 0 \\
&\textit{Quadrant} &&\text{II}: &&x \leq 0 \text{ and } y \geq 0 \\
&\textit{Quadrant} &&\text{III}: &&x \leq 0 \text{ and } y \leq 0 \\
&\textit{Quadrant} &&\text{IV}: &&x \geq 0 \text{ and } y \leq 0
\end{aligned}$$

Note that the point $(0, 0)$, i.e., the origin, is common to all quadrants.

6.4 Exercise

6.4.1 Given the sets: $\Omega = \{-5, -4, -3, -2, -1, 0, 1, 2, 3, 4, 5\}$, $A = \{x | x < 0\}$, $B = \{-1, 0, 1\}$, $C = \{x | x > 0\}$, and $D = \{-5, -3, 0, 3, 5\}$; graph the following sets of ordered pairs:

(a) $A \times B$

(b) $B \times C$

(c) $C \times D$

(d) $C \times A$

(e) $A \times D$

(f) $A \times A$

(g) $B \times D$

(h) $C \times C$

(i) $B \times A$

(j) $D \times D$.

6.5   Graphing two variables

The domain and range of the space described in Section 6.4 were limited in order to restrict the number of elements in the set strictly for ease in spelling them out.   If the domain and range each consisted of the set of all real numbers, then the resulting set of all admissible points would be infinitely large.   This would still be true if the domain and range were restricted to the set of all non-negative numbers, for instance (why?).   In the former case, any point in our map of coordinates (Fig. 6.4.1) would be admissible; in the latter, only those in the first quadrant.

Consider an example in which the domain and range of x and y respectively is the set of all real numbers, which will henceforth be the case unless specified differently.   We ask for $\{(x, y)|x - y = 0\}$; a little thought will develop the fact that the solution set to this open sentence contains an infinite number of elements, some of which are $(5, 5)$, $(-5, -5)$, $(0, 0)$, $(\frac{1}{2}, \frac{1}{2})$, and $(378.943, 378.943)$.   Since it is impossible to list all of the elements in this set, it is difficult to communicate this solution to someone who does not understand something about infinite sets; however, by graphing this set, we can show much more intuitively and powerfully what we mean by a solution to the sentence.   As the reader graphs a few of the ordered pairs which satisfy the sentence, he should begin to notice that they all lie in a straight line, and by induction he would assume that the solution set for this sentence consists of the infinite number of points which lie along this line.   He would be correct; and we shall study later how to recognize some of these lines without having to plot them.

6.5   Exercise

6.5.1   Given the domain and range as the set of all real numbers, graph the solution sets of the following open sentences, choosing by trial and error enough points satisfying the sentences to get a good idea of the behavior of the graph.

(a) $\{(x, y)|x + y = 0\}$
(b) $\{(x, y)|2x - 3y = 6\}$
(c) $\{(x, y)|y = x^2\}$
(d) $\{(x, y)|y = |x|\}$

(e) $\{(x, y)|(x < 5) \wedge (y > -3)\}$

(f) $\{(x, y)|x^2 + y^2 \leq 4\}$

(g) $\{(x, y)|[(2 \leq x \leq 5) \wedge (2 \leq y \leq 5)]\}$

(h) $\{(x, y)|(x + y = 0) \wedge (x - y) = 0\}$

(i) $\{(x, y)|(x + y = 0) \vee (x - y = 0)\}.$

6.6   Relationships revisited

A *relationship* between two phenomena exists when the nature or behavior of one of them has unique correspondence with the nature or behavior of the other. The study of set theory provides us a tool for a more rigorous definition. If we can list the various elements of, or take measurements upon the behavior of, two phenomena, and find that the two sets of elements both make up a description of one of the phenomena, then a relationship between the two exists when we may place the elements of one of the sets in correspondence with the elements of the other set. In Fig. 6.6.1 this idea is expressed in a diagram of two sets, A and B. For every element a in A, there is a corresponding element b in B.

As a "real" example, consider that the heat of a stove can be measured by a thermometer, so that the set of all elements describing the nature of heat can be expressed in terms of degrees registered on the measuring instrument. Now consider the phenomenon of pain. Measuring pain is not quite so easy, but, depending upon the strength of the stimulus causing it, we can say that pain has varying degrees of intensity. One possible way of measuring its intensity would be to

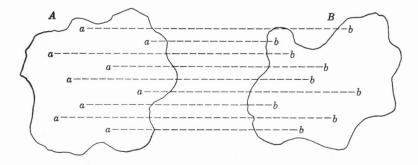

Fig. 6.6.1

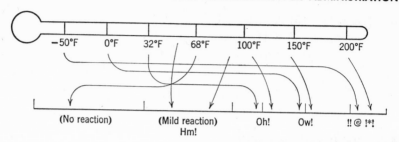

Fig. 6.6.2

record the intensity of the noise created by some luckless human being who is exposed to varying intensities of the stimulus. If this stimulus were heat, we could build a relationship by noting the behavior of the noise level with changes in the behavior of the stimulus. For each level of heat, we would probably find a corresponding value of the noise level; i.e., for each element in the behavioral set of the heat phenomenon we would find a corresponding element or elements in the behavioral set of the pain phenomenon. This relationship is diagrammed in Fig. 6.6.2. Here we note that more intense pain may be caused by either high temperatures or low temperatures, i.e., a given element in the pain set may be associated with more than one element in the heat set. Such a relationship is not uncommon.

The potential value of understanding relationships should be very obvious at this point. As illustrated in Chapter 2, once a child understands the basic relationship between heat and pain, he is able to make several important decisions for his own physical well-being. Of equal importance is the fact that he is able to discard false relationships, which might have persisted without this information (e.g., a fear that stoves whether hot or cold, or matches whether lighted or not, cause pain). Our ability to develop meaningful relationships and apply them in the decision-making process, and our ability to identify and discard meaningless relationships, are among the most important factors determining success in administration, if not, in fact, in all decision-making experiences of life.

The heat–pain relationship is a cause and effect system. Having experienced this relationship himself, it is obvious to the student that it is the heat which causes the pain. If we touch a hot stove, the nerve ends in our fingers carry the panic signal to our brain, "heat—it causes pain," and our brain issues instructions for our fingers to withdraw.

It is also obvious that we are here talking about the relationship between two variable phenomena; i.e., they exist in life, even for the same person, in varying degrees. It is important to note that although they exist in different degrees, the system of their relationship never changes; i.e., heat causes pain and not the reverse, and for every degree of heat there is some corresponding degree of pain. In describing any cause and effect relationship we call the causal variable (heat) the *independent variable,* in that its value will affect the related variable (pain), which is known as the *dependent variable.*

It must be remembered that not all relationships involve a cause and effect system. For example, it has been observed that there is a correspondence between the periods of increased storm activity on the sun and depression tendencies in our economy. In spite of the observation of these phenomena, the validity of a cause and effect hypothesis has not been proved. We question whether such upsets occurring on the sun should so uniquely upset our economic system; nevertheless we continue to study such relationships. In describing this relationship, we relate the condition of our economy to the condition of the sun; therefore, the storm activity is considered the independent variable, and the condition of our economy the dependent variable.

The student will be exposed to a great many relationships where no cause and effect exists directly between the variables considered. In such cases, the variables being considered may be causally related to a third variable. For example, we observe that there is a relationship between the number of new cars sold and the number of refrigerators sold. This correspondence, while interesting, does not involve a cause and effect relationship, for this would require that the dependent variable (sale of refrigerators) would change if and only if the independent variable (sale of cars) changed. Examining the correspondence between them, it becomes apparent that both are related to, among other things, income and population. It is important that we analyze any observed relationships to establish the system of relationship present. A logical analysis will eliminate from consideration specious relationships, and will tend to direct our attention to basic systems, where cause and effect relationships do exist. We do not say that an appliance dealer should not be interested in the relationship between cars and refrigerators sold, if indeed one exists, for it is often valuable to study phenomena that have similar patterns of variation; but he must not believe that the sale of cars causes the sale of refrigerators, or he may find the administration of an applicance business a rather unhappy career.

6.6   Exercises

6.6.1   Analyze the following relationships common to business operations and determine for each whether the relationship involves a cause
and effect system: if so, why; if not, why not?

(a) Quantity sold and selling price
(b) Quantity purchased and cost price
(c) Age and skill
(d) Income and education level
(e) Income and output (Look at this relationship from the standpoint
     both of the *firm* and of the *individual*.)

6.6.2   List three relationships which you have observed in your
daily life.   Diagram each relationship showing the system of correspondence between the variables, as in Figs. 6.6.1 and 6.6.2, and explain
the basis on which the variables in each relationship are related (i.e.,
cause and effect, etc.).

6.7   Relations

We have discussed the meaning of relationships in broad, intuitive
terms, and now wish to formalize the concept mathematically.   A
mathematical relationship is called, simply, a *relation*, and is defined as
any subset of $X \times Y$, where X and Y are sets.   We recall from Section

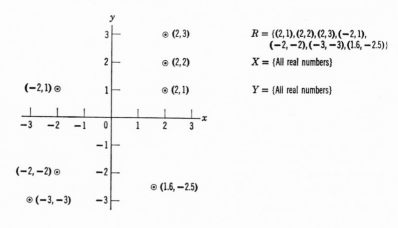

Fig. 6.7.1

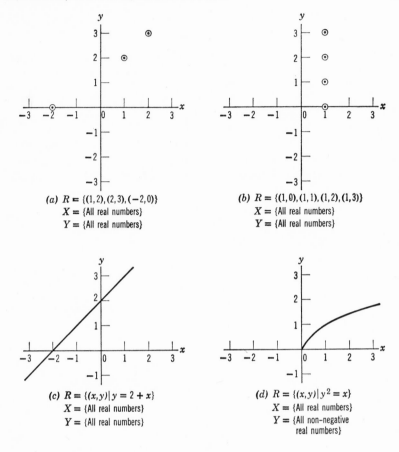

(a) $R = \{(1,2),(2,3),(-2,0)\}$
$X = \{$All real numbers$\}$
$Y = \{$All real numbers$\}$

(b) $R = \{(1,0),(1,1),(1,2),(1,3)\}$
$X = \{$All real numbers$\}$
$Y = \{$All real numbers$\}$

(c) $R = \{(x,y)\,|\,y = 2 + x\}$
$X = \{$All real numbers$\}$
$Y = \{$All real numbers$\}$

(d) $R = \{(x,y)\,|\,y^2 = x\}$
$X = \{$All real numbers$\}$
$Y = \{$All non–negative
real numbers$\}$

Fig. 6.7.2

6.4 the definition of $X \times Y$ as a Cartesian product, which is the set of all ordered pairs of numbers (x, y) such that x is an element of X and y is an element of Y. Thus, any subset of $X \times Y$, such as $\{(x_1, y_1), (x_1, y_2), (x_{32}, y_{43})\}$ is a relation in $X \times Y$. If X is a set such that x (a value on the x axis) is an element of X, and if Y is a set such that y (any value on the y axis) is an element of Y, then X is called the *domain* of the variable x, and Y the *range* of the variable y, as previously explained. If both X and Y are the set of all real numbers, then we can see from Fig. 6.7.1 that $X \times Y$ defines the whole space of points (x, y) in which we might define some relation of X to Y.

At this point it is important for the student to recall that x and y are merely convenient symbols chosen to represent the variables under consideration. Although we generally identify the domain, independent variable, and axis of abscissas by the symbol x, and the range, dependent variable, and axis of ordinates by y, any symbols could be used, and many will be encountered by the reader.

A number of points are plotted in Fig. 6.7.1 which represent a relation in $X \times Y$; this relation is spelled out by listing the ordered pairs (x, y) which satisfy the relation. Once again, we notice that a relation is a *set;* it is a set of ordered pairs, within a given range and domain, that satisfies the relation stipulated. In Fig. 6.7.2 there are plotted some additional relations using number symbols to define points; i.e., those ordered pairs of numbers which are elements of the set satisfying the relation R.

The ordered pairs graphed in Fig. 6.7.2c represent only a small number of the elements of the solution set satisfying the relation $R = \{(x, y)|y = 2 + x\}$. As a matter of fact, the solution set of this relation is an infinite set of ordered pairs. The graph shows some of these ordered pairs; obviously, limitations of space prevent drawing this graph throughout its indefinitely great range and domain. Note that the same holds true for 6.7.2d, even though the range is limited to non-negative real numbers, since this is also an infinite set. Thus a relation, being a set, can be specified by *extension*, i.e., listing all of the elements in the set, or by *intension*, i.e., stating the characteristic common to all elements in the set, usually by an equation or inequality.

6.7   Exercise

6.7.1 Let X be the set $\{-2, -1, 0, 1, 2, 3, 4, 5\}$ and Y the set $\{$all real numbers$\}$. Graph the following relations, giving the domain and range of each of the relations.

(a) $R = \{(x, y)|x = y\}$

(b) $R = \{(x, y)|x = 2y\}$

(c) $R = \{(x, y)|x^2 + y^2 = 1\}$

(d) $R = \{(x, y)|x > y\}$

(e) $R = \{(1, 0), (2, 0), (3, 1), (3, 2), (4, 3), (4, -3)\}$

(f) $R = \{(3, 1), (3, 2), (3, 1), (3, 0), (3, -1), (3, -2)\}$

(g) $R = \{(x, y)|(x + y = 2) \wedge (x > -1)\}$

(h) $R = \{(x, y)|(x + y = 3) \wedge (x \geq 0) \wedge (y \geq 2)\}$

(i) $R = \{(x, y)|(2x + 2) > y\}$.

6.8   Functions

A *function* is a special type of *relation* which has the characteristic that with *each* value in the domain, there is associated *one and only one* (unique) value in the range.   Examine the examples *a*, *c*, and *d* in Fig. 6.7.2 and note that this requirement is met, whereas in *b* it is not. Each of these four examples displays a relation; only *a*, *c*, and *d* display functions.   We will be concerned with functions throughout the remainder of this text, because of the unique characteristic of this type of relation.   Figure 6.6.1 we now recognize as the pictorial representation of a function in terms of sets.

The study of functions is of unusual importance in administration because of the function's characteristic of relating a value in the domain to a unique value in the range.   Relations are important also, but one or two or many values in the range can be associated by a relation with any value in the domain.   We see, then, that the determination of the existence of a relation which is not a function does not provide us with nearly so powerful a tool as that provided by the knowledge that phenomena are functionally related.   An example of this follows.   (As mentioned earlier, administration implies the making of decisions, i.e., choosing, from a number of available alternatives, that one course of action that appears to have the best chance of providing us with what we seek.)

Let us take revenue as our example.   If we analyze the development of revenue from sales we see that one determinant of how much revenue we will receive is the price of our product (among a number of determinants which we shall disregard for the moment).   If we give our product away free we shall obviously receive no revenue; on the other hand, if we price it too high, we shall likely not sell any of it, again receiving no revenue.   Somewhere between the high price and no price must be a price at which we can realize the most revenue.   The student should notice that we have described a relationship between revenue and price, and should also notice that revenue *depends* upon price.   Assuming that we have some discretion as to how we price our product, we call price the *independent* variable, and revenue the *dependent* variable.

In this highly simplified statement in which we consider only price and revenue, our decision problem is to determine what price gives us the most desirable revenue level.   Through market research or other means we might hope to determine what the relation looks like, i.e., to find the set of ordered pairs of price and revenue values which will describe the alternatives available to us. Two of the ordered pairs we already know: $(0, 0)$ and $(h, 0)$, where h is that high price at which no one will buy our product. The first of the ordered pairs above, then, describes the fact that when our price is zero, we receive zero revenue; the second states that when our price is too high, we also receive no revenue. Let us pick a price, p, somewhere between zero and h, and examine our revenue, r. If there is only one value of r for each value of p, then we have found a *function* relating them, and our decision is relatively simple. We price our product so that r is greater at that price than at any other price. Now, if instead of finding only one value of r for each value of p, we should find a number of values for r, we could only state that a relation existed. Our decision would not be determined (since different revenues would be determined by one price), and we would not know which of the revenue figures to expect.

If, having found a relationship between two variables, we can determine that a mathematical relationship and finally a functional relationship (function) describes the correspondence between them, we have gone a long way in solving what might otherwise be an extremely complicated decision problem.

So far we have said nothing about the mathematical description of a function, except to imply in the example above that if we can list the elements of the set of ordered pairs which defines the function, we are able to define the function sufficiently. If, in our example above, we were selling lemonade and we found the following set of ordered pairs of price and revenue to exist, then this set would define the function of price (in cents) to revenue: $\{(0,0), (1, 15), (2, 20), (3, 15), (4, 8), (5, 0)\}$. Note that although for each value of p there is but one value of r, the reverse is not true, and need not be true so long as we do not try to define the function of r to p.

In previous illustrations we have noted that functions could be specified by listing the elements of a set, in which case the graph of the function consisted of isolated points in the rectangular coordinate system; or by stating an equation whose solution set graphed as a line. Although neither a sufficient nor rigorous distinction of terms, we may think of illustrations of the first type as describing *discrete* functions, and illustrations of the second type as describing *continuous* functions. A simple way to consider this distinction, which is quite important in mathematics, is that if the graph of a function can be drawn without lifting the pencil from the paper, the function is continuous. We shall have more to say about continuity later; it suffices at the moment to realize that this property of functions must be considered, because otherwise we might develop misleading ideas about behavior. For instance, our lemonade-selling decisions should be made on the basis of the known correspondence established by the discrete function given. If we were to price a glass of lemonade at a penny and a half, our function does not tell us what to expect about the behavior of revenue at this price. Now we might assume that revenue at this price will be between fifteen and twenty cents, a very tenable assumption, but not one which is given by the function. If we assume that the function is continuous, as in Fig. 6.8.2, then we will make our decisions on the basis of a relationship whose graph looks like the inverted bowl illustrated. This is only an assumption, however; the graph of the known relationship is that of the discrete function given, as in Fig. 6.8.1.

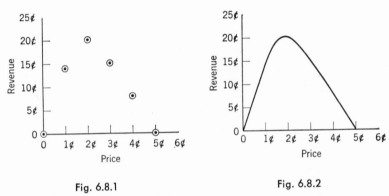

Fig. 6.8.1   Fig. 6.8.2

Surprisingly few relationships in administration are continuous; however, in order to perform much of the mathematical analysis upon discrete behavioral patterns which we observe, we must assume them to be continuous. Therefore the assumption must be well understood. Although this is a very sketchy description of continuity, it will serve our purpose until we take up the subject later in the text.

Additional important properties of functions will be discussed later, and we will close this introduction with some remarks concerning notation, i.e., symbolism, used in conjunction with functions. Consider the equation $y = 3x - 2$, which, we have previously noted, satisfies the definition of a function. We say that y is a function of x, of $y = f(x)$, the symbol f implying that, if we are given a value of x, the functional relationship existing between y and x tells us the unique value of y associated with that value of x. Thus "$f(x)$," read "f of x," is a new type of symbol; one does not multiply f times x, nor perform any other algebraic type of operation within the symbol. The symbol simply stands for the fact that some function whose independent variable is x can be defined. The expression $y = 3x - 2$ is not a function, but merely an equation which describes the functional relationship between y and x, and therefore we will often write $f(x) = 3x - 2$, since we have defined that $y = f(x)$.

Each element in the set of ordered pairs which also defines the function can be written $(x, f(x))$ in lieu of (x, y). The change is a practical one. It simplifies the determination of those elements (ordered pairs) which are in the set describing the function. For instance, using $f(x) = 3x - 2$, if we wish to know the value of the function when x has the value 2, we write $f(2) = 3(2) - 2 = 4$, so that the ordered pair comprising this element in the function is $(2, 4)$. Similarly, $f(-3) = 3(-3) - 2 = -11$; the ordered pair is $(-3, -11)$: $f(\frac{1}{2}) = 3(\frac{1}{2}) - 2 = -\frac{1}{2}$; the element is $(\frac{1}{2}, -\frac{1}{2})$. Finally, if we recast all that has been said here in the question, "what are the ordered pairs of numbers (elements) of the set satisfying the equation $f(x) = 3x - 2$," and write the sentence $\{(x, f(x))|f(x) = 3x - 2\}$, we realize that the list of elements contains all those ordered pairs of numbers having the form $(x, 3x - 2)$, where x can be any number in the domain of the variable x.

6.8   Exercise

6.8.1   Graph the following functions.

(a) $y = f(x)$; $\{(x, f(x))|f(x) = x + 3\}$

(b) $y = f(x)$; $\{(x, f(x))|f(x) = 3x - 1\}$, Show: $f(-1), f(0), f(1), f(2),$ $f(2.3)$

(c) $y = f(x)$; $\{(x, f(x))|f(x) = x^2 + 2\}$, Show: $f(-2),\ f(-1),\ f(0),$ $f(\frac{1}{2}), f(1), f(2)$

(d) $y = f(x)$; $\{(x, f(x))|f(x) = x + 2\} \cap \{$All positive integers$\}$

(e) $y = f(x)$; $\{(x, f(x))|f(x) = x - 1\} \cap \{-2 \leq x \leq 3\}$

(f) $y = f(x)$; $\{(-2, -2),\ (-1, -1),\ (0, 0),\ (1, 1),\ (2, 2)\}$

(g) $y = f(x)$; $\{(-2, 5),\ (-1, 2),\ (0, 1),\ (1, 2),\ (2, 5)\}$.

Chapter 7

Linear Systems

7.1 The algebra of straight lines

In Section 6.5 the student was required to plot various sets of ordered pairs of numbers, some of which, when graphed, described straight lines. Straight lines were also graphed from the solution sets of various types of relations in Section 6.7. Finally, we noticed that many functions turned out to be definable in terms of straight lines. This has not occurred by accident; the straight line as the locus of points satisfying some given requirement (or, in set terms, the graph of a set of ordered pairs which lie along a straight line), is an extremely important mathematical property, which we use a great deal in defining many relationships in administration. Before discussing the uses of straight lines, we wish to develop some of their properties.

We should recognize that straight lines are not limited to two dimensions. If we pull taut a string reaching from one corner of a room to the opposite, diagonal corner, then the string will define a straight line in three dimensional space. If we could define four, five, six, or n dimensions, we would still find that it would be possible to conceive of a straight line in these dimensions of space. However, since most of our work and analysis must be done with pencil and paper, or chalk and blackboard, and since what we have to say about lines in two dimensions (two-space) applies with equal force and consequence in n dimensions (n-space), we shall limit ourselves at present to the properties of lines which we can draw on paper or on the blackboard, i.e., in a *plane*. Many of these concepts should be familiar to the student from his previous work in plane geometry, although this is not required for

85

an understanding of the concept, since we have already developed all of the necessary fundamentals in this text.

We have seen that the solution set of any equation in two variables traces out a set of points (a graph), curved or straight, in the space described by the range and domain of the variables. In other words, if X is the domain of the variable x and Y is the range of the variable y, then the Cartesian product $X \times Y$ defines the space in which we may graph any relation involving x and y. If such a relation can be defined by the set $\{(x, y) | y = a + bx\}$, where a and b are some real number constants, then the relation is said to be linear and its solution set can be graphed as a straight line.

Let us examine the relation $R = \{(x, y) | y = a + bx\}$, whose solution set consists of the ordered pairs of numbers $(x_1, y_1), (x_2, y_2)$, etc. Given the value x_1, to find the associated value y_1 we multiply x_1 by b and add a to the result. To find the value y_2 we multiply x_2 by b and add a to the result. To find that value of y associated with any value of x, we multiply the value of x by b and add a. We notice again that this relation is also a function, since the rule operates in such a way that only one value of y will be selected for each value of x. This idea is illustrated schematically in Fig. 7.1.1; the correspondence between the set X and the set Y is defined by the rule $y = a + bx$. The important attribute of this kind of function is that within each ordered pair (x, y) in the solution set, the values of x and y differ by some constant amount, specified by a and b. The word *linear* derives from the geometric consequence of this feature: the graph of a linear function is a straight line.

Now by a combination of these facts and some elements of plane geometry we can further describe a linear function in terms of its

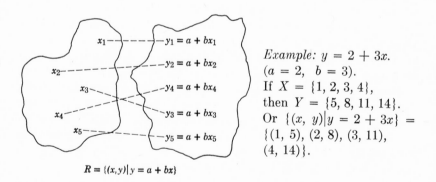

$R = \{(x,y) | y = a + bx\}$

Example: $y = 2 + 3x$.
$(a = 2, \ b = 3)$.
If $X = \{1, 2, 3, 4\}$,
then $Y = \{5, 8, 11, 14\}$.
Or $\{(x, y) | y = 2 + 3x\} = \{(1, 5), (2, 8), (3, 11), (4, 14)\}$.

Fig. 7.1.1

graph.   When the set X and the set Y (each the set of all real numbers) are graphed along the axis of abscissas and the axis of ordinates respectively, a linear function $y = f(x) = a + bx$ in $X \times Y$ graphs as a straight line.   The constants a and b have names associated with this graph: a is called the y *intercept* and b is called the *slope*.   The y intercept (or, simply, the intercept) is that value on the axis of ordinates, i.e., the y axis, where the line intersects the axis.   We note that every linear function *must* intersect the y axis, and in only *one* point; and that a vertical line is not the graph of a function, but the graph of a relation. The point where the straight line intersects the y axis has x coordinate of zero, i.e., the coordinates of the intercept are $(0, a)$.   When x is zero, the value of y becomes $y = a + b(0) = a$.   Thus we can quickly locate one point on the line, the intercept, by examination of the equation of the line.

Intersecting the y axis does not, of course, make the graph of a straight line unique, since graphs of non-linear curves may also cross the y axis.   The distinguishing feature of the linear function is the constant rate at which y changes with respect to changes in x as shown by the ordered pairs in the solution set of the equation describing the line in Fig. 7.1.1.   This constant rate of change is indicated by b, as previously described in the correspondence between the sets X and Y.   In geometrical terms, b is the *slope* of the line, i.e., the ratio of the change in y to the change in x, as measured by directed segments along the respective axes.   If (x_1, y_1) and (x_2, y_2) are *any* two points on a given straight line, then the slope of the line is $b = (y_2 - y_1)/(x_2 - x_1)$. Note that the expression $y_2 - y_1$, a *change* in y, is a directed number, as is $x_2 - x_1$, which is the corresponding *change* in x.   This is illustrated in Fig. 7.1.2a.   The change in x is always measured in the positive direction, i.e., $x_2 > x_1$; we then note whether y increases or decreases in value as x becomes larger.   If y increases in value under these conditions, then the sign of the change in y is positive and the slope of the line is positive, and we see that a positive slope indicates that the line slopes upward and to the right as in Fig. 7.1.2b.   If y decreases in value as x increases in value, then the sign of the change in y is negative, the slope is negative, and the line slopes downward to the right as in Fig. 7.1.2c.

The determination of the slope of a line is shown in Fig. 7.1.2.   In (b) the change in x, for instance, from 2 to 3, is 1, from left to right; the corresponding change in y is from 1 to 2, reading up, or a directed distance of $+1$; the slope of this line is therefore $1/1$ or 1.   In (c) the change in x, as measured from 0 to 2, is 2; the corresponding change in y is from 1 to 0, downward, or a directed distance of -1; the slope is therefore

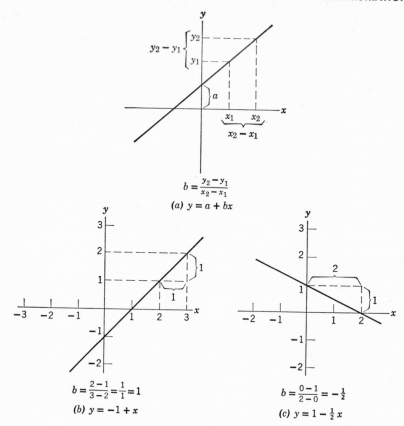

Fig. 7.1.2

$-\frac{1}{2}$. The student should verify for himself this salient feature of straight lines; *the slope of any given straight line is the same no matter where it is measured along the line.* In Fig. 7.1.2*b* we could measure the directed distance along the *x* axis from 1 to 3, or $+2$, and the corresponding directed distance along the *y* axis from 0 to 2, or $+2$, and the slope $b = +2/+2$ would still be 1 as we determined previously. It is often more convenient to measure the slope by means of a triangle whose length measured along the *x* axis is one unit, since the ratio will then consist of the corresponding directed distance along the *y* axis divided by 1, and thus the slope is just that distance measured along the *y* axis.

Suppose that we are told that a certain linear function has slope $b = -4$, and passes through the point $(-1, 8)$. What is the equation of the line? Since the function is linear, we know that it has the standard form $y = a + bx$; we know b, and we also know that $(-1, 8)$ lies upon the line, i.e., that $x = -1$ and $y = 8$ satisfies the equation. We therefore "plug" these values into the equation: $8 = a + (-4)(-1)$; $8 = a + 4$; $a = 4$. The intercept is thus 4, and the equation of the line is $y = 4 - 4x$. Thus we can find the equation of the line describing a linear function if we know (1) one point on the line and the slope of the line, or (2) two points on the line; we note that the intercept, of course, defines a point on the line.

Any linear equation in two variables can be expressed in standard form by following the rules given previously for the algebraic manipulation of equations. For instance, if we are told that a certain linear function $f(x)$ is defined by the equation $8x + 2y - 4 = 0$, we convert this equation to standard form by subtracting $8x$ from, and adding 4 to, both sides of the equation, and then dividing both sides by 2. The result, $y = 2 - 4x$, is an equation in standard form, and we may immediately find $a = 2$, $b = -4$. These values, of course, are not readily evident when the equation is not in standard form.

7.1 Exercises

7.1.1 Determine the intercept (a) and slope (b) of the following linear equations, and graph each:

(a) $y = 3 + x$ (b) $y = 1 + 3x$
(c) $y = -4 + x$ (d) $y = 1 - 3x$
(e) $y = -2 - x$ (f) $y - x - 3 = 0$
(g) $x = y + 4$ (h) $5 = 2y + 2x$
(i) $2x - 3y + 2 = 0$ (j) $\frac{2}{3}y = \frac{1}{2}x - \frac{1}{2}$.

7.1.2 Given the following sets of ordered pairs, graph the straight line they determine, noting for each the slope and intercept. Identify those lines which are not graphs of functions.

(a) $\{(0, 0), (2, 4)\}$ (b) $\{(1, 1), (-2, -2)\}$
(c) $\{(0, 3), (0, -2)\}$ (d) $\{(-2, 2), (2, 2)\}$
(e) $\{(3, 1), (1, -3)\}$ (f) $\{(2, 0), (5, 0)\}$
(g) $\{(4, -4), (-4, 4)\}$ (h) $\{(2, 4), (1, 1)\}$.

7.1.3 Given the following information about some linear functions, find the equation describing them.

(a) $a = 32; b = -10$ (b) $a = 0; b = 6$
(c) $a = 28,965; b = 0$ (d) $a = 14; \{(5, 3)\}$
(e) $\{(9, 17)\}; b = 1\frac{7}{9}$ (f) $\{(9, 17)\}; b = -1\frac{7}{9}$.

7.1.4 Graph the following sets: (a) $\{(x, y) | x = 0\}$; (b) $\{(x, y) | y = 0\}$.

7.1.5   Find the solution set of $\{(x, y)|(x = 2) \wedge (y = 3)\}$ by graphing the lines $x = 2$ and $y = 3$.

7.2   Linear functions of one variable

The relation defined by the set $\{(x, y)|y = a + bx\}$, a linear function of the variable x, can be rewritten $\{(x, f(x))|f(x) = a + bx\}$.   Every straight line can be defined by such a set, with the exception of a vertical line, which is defined by the relation $\{(x, y)|x =$ any constant$\}$.   A function in one variable is sometimes called a function of one *argument*, the argument being the value of the independent variable x.   Rather than use the word "argument," however, we shall usually use the terminology "independent variable" when referring to x, and "dependent variable" when referring to y or $f(x)$.

The slope of a function is an extremely important concept because it tells us an important fact about the functional relationship between the variables: the rate of change of y with respect to x.   The idea of rate of change can be seen in many phenomena which we observe every day. In driving an automobile, for instance, we are concerned (we hope!) with such things as how "fast" we can stop in an emergency, i.e., the rate of decrease in our speed when we slam on the brakes.   Some drivers enjoy testing their automobiles for acceleration, i.e., how "fast" they can reach a certain speed, at every opportunity.   The businessman is interested in how "fast" profits are increasing or decreasing. In each of these cases, what concerns us is not where we are at any given time, but the rate at which we are changing our position.

Linear functions have the unique characteristic of defining a relationship between the variables in which the rate of change of the dependent variable with respect to the independent variable is *constant;* i.e., the slope is constant.   We have already observed this fact in connection with determining the slope of a straight line (Section 7.1), in seeing that the slope is the same no matter where measured.

Many illustrations from life are available to describe such a relationship.   One illustration is the price for filling the gas tank of an automobile: 1 gallon of gas costs \$0.38; 2 gallons cost \$0.76; 3 gallons, \$1.14; 10 gallons, \$3.80; etc.   Hourly workers are paid according to a similar schedule; if the rate of pay is \$1.25 per hour, then 8 hours work will provide a gross pay of \$10, and 40 hours work will gross \$50.   If we drive along the highway at a *constant* speed of 60 mph, then in 1 hour we will travel 60 miles; in $2\frac{1}{2}$ hours we will go 150 miles, etc.   In Fig. 7.2.1 each of these examples is graphed to show its linearity, and

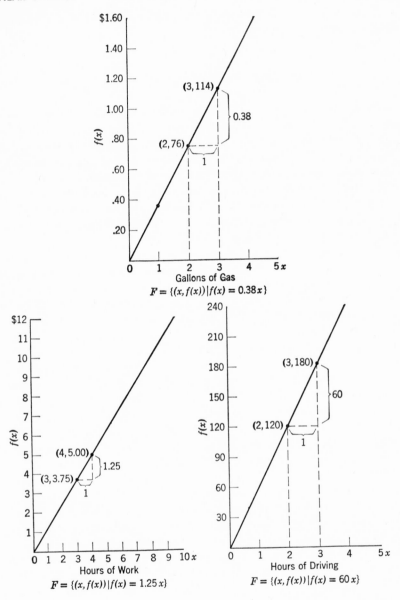

Fig. 7.2.1

we note that each of these is a function whose graph is a straight line of constant slope: total price of gas is a function of gallons purchased, and the slope is the price per gallon; gross pay is a function of hours worked, and the slope is the rate of pay; distance traveled is a function of time, and the slope is the speed. The student should attempt to describe for himself other functions of this nature, such as the varying number of bricks used in a wall of constant width but varying height.

We note in Fig. 7.2.1 that each of the graphs passes through the origin, and in addition, that the values of x are limited to the set of all non-negative real numbers, which is usually true of real-life situations since real objects or quantities cannot be "negative." Not all such functions must pass through the origin, however. Consider the consumer who wants to purchase something at a discount house, and who is required to buy a membership for \$1 before he is allowed to make a purchase, perhaps of gasoline at a price of \$0.38 per gallon. No matter what his gas bill is, his total bill is increased by \$1, as shown in Fig. 7.2.2a; we see that the graph no longer passes through the origin, but passes through the intercept at $f(x) = \$1$. A bureaucrat in Texas was recently criticized for requiring his employees to contribute \$5 per month to a flower fund, actually a campaign fund, which he used to help keep himself in office. Consider an employee of his making

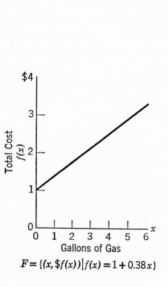

$$F = \{(x, \$f(x)) \mid f(x) = 1 + 0.38x\}$$

Fig. 7.2.2 (a)

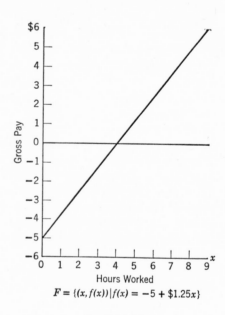

$$F = \{(x, f(x)) \mid f(x) = -5 + \$1.25x\}$$

Fig. 7.2.2 (b)

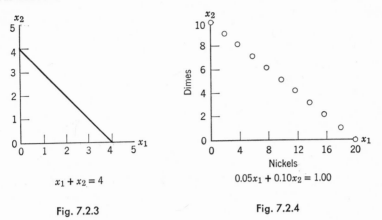

$$x_1 + x_2 = 4$$

Fig. 7.2.3

$$0.05x_1 + 0.10x_2 = 1.00$$

Fig. 7.2.4

$1.25 per hour, who now must contribute $5 per month no matter how many hours he might work during a given month. The graph of this situation is shown in Fig. 7.2.2b where the $5 deduction is represented by a negative intercept of $5, indicating that he must work 4 hours before he begins to net anything at all from this employer.

Sometimes we cannot say explicitly that one of our variables is independent and the other is dependent, although we know that they are related, and that a value assigned to one of them forces a value to be assigned to the other. Such a function is called an *implicit* function, whereas most of the functions with which we have worked heretofore are called *explicit* functions. In the explicit function the dependency relationship is indicated by placing the dependent variable on the left side of the defining equation and the independent variable or variables on the right side. Conventionally, implicit functions are written with all of the variables on the left side of the equation, for instance, $x_1 + x_2 = 4$. If we let the axis of abscissas be the x_1 axis and the axis of ordinates be the x_2 axis, then we can graph this equation, as in Fig. 7.2.3, and we see that this implicit function graphs as a straight line. Consider the following example of an implicit function: suppose we wish to change a dollar bill into coins, and we restrict ourselves to nickels and dimes. If we let x_1 be the number of nickels we get in change, and x_2 the number of dimes, then the implicit function $\$0.05x_1 + \$0.10x_2 = \$1$ describes the combinations of nickels and dimes which we could get in change. Note that there are only eleven elements in the set of ordered pairs (x_1, x_2) that satisfy this function: $\{(0, 10), (2, 9), (4, 8), \ldots, (20, 0)\}$. (The student should list all of them.) This function is graphed in Fig. 7.2.4.

7.2 Exercises

Each of the following word problems describes a linear relationship between two variables, x and y. Analyze each problem, graph the relationship, state the relationship as a linear equation, and note the slope and intercept of the straight line so determined.

7.2.1 A group of high school students was given a physical examination and their weight and height were compared. One student was 60 inches tall and weighed 120 pounds, another was 72 inches tall and weighed 144 pounds. These students were representative of a linear relationship between height and weight found for all students examined. In your analysis use x to symbolize height and y to symbolize weight.

7.2.2 If it costs a firm $10 to produce a single unit of an item, and $100 to produce 100 units of the item, analyze the equation describing the linear relationship between the cost of production (y) and the quantity produced (x).

7.2.3 If it costs $6 in brokerage fees to purchase $100 worth of securities and $30 in brokerage fees to purchase $1000 worth of securities, analyze the equation describing the linear relationship between brokerage fees (y) and total value of securities purchased (x).

7.2.4 You are an automobile dealer who handles two different models of automobiles. You have $20,000 to invest in an inventory of these automobiles. One model costs $2000 per unit, the other costs $2500 per unit. State the implicit function which relates the number of cars of one model and the number of cars of the other model that you may stock if you wish to invest your entire $20,000. Use x_1 and x_2 for the variables.

7.2.5 A dump truck can carry 5 tons of material. Gravel weighs 1000 pounds per cubic yard and sand weighs 1500 pounds per cubic yard. If you do not care if the sand and gravel become mixed in transit, state the implicit function which relates the cubic yards of gravel and sand which can be hauled in one truck load (quantity of sand $= x_1$; quantity of gravel $= x_2$).

7.3 Simultaneous linear systems in two variables

Consider the following problem which is faced by every businessman (whether he knows it or not). One measure of success in a business (among other things) is the ability to make a profit by earning more total revenue through the selling of goods than must be paid out through the total cost of buying or manufacturing them. If it costs more to produce and sell products than we can earn by selling them, then we sustain a loss, and businesses cannot sustain losses over very long periods of time without eventually going out of business. Thus we may measure dollar profit by taking the difference between total revenue and total cost, or Profit $= TR - TC$. We should immediately notice two things. We would expect our total revenue to increase as the number of goods we sold increased. We expect our total costs to increase likewise. If total revenue increases faster than total costs, there must be some point at which we can expect to start earning money, and this point is called the breakeven point; it is at that point that our total revenue equals total cost, and it is extremely important to the businessman to know where this point is in his own operation.

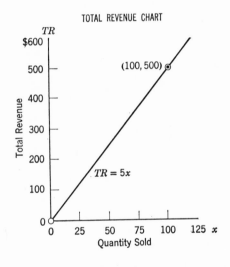

Fig. 7.3.1

We have indicated that the amount of total revenue will depend upon the quantity of goods sold, so that $TR = f$(quantity of goods sold). Letting x be this quantity, we can simplify this expression to $TR = f(x)$. Suppose that we have a business and have priced our product at \$5 each; if we sell none of our product, then we shall receive no revenue; if we sell 100 units, then we shall earn \$500 in total revenue. We thus have two points, (0, \$0) and (100, \$500) on the graph of the function of TR and x. Assuming that this function is linear, we can then draw in the straight line connecting these points, and determine the equation of this line: $TR = \$5x$, as shown in Fig. 7.3.1. Suppose that there are certain costs associated with selling our product that persist whether or not we sell anything, such as rent, insurance, and salaries, and that these amount to $100 for a given time period, and that it costs us $3 to make each unit of our product. The total cost graph appears in Fig. 7.3.2. We have assumed that total costs are also linear with respect to the quantity made available for sale, and have drawn a straight line connecting two points which we know to lie upon this line: (0, $100), since we must pay $100 even if we sell nothing, and (100, $400), which states that if we sell 100 units, then the total cost is equal to the $100 which we cannot avoid plus the cost of 100 units at $3 each. The equation of this cost function is thus $TC = \$100 + \$3x$.

We now ask the question: "How many units must we sell in order to break even?" If we combine the two graphs which we have already

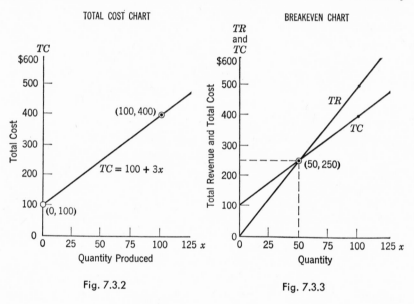

TOTAL COST CHART   BREAKEVEN CHART

Fig. 7.3.2   Fig. 7.3.3

drawn, which is possible since they have the same units along the axis of abscissas (quantity) and along the axis of ordinates (dollars), we have what is called a *breakeven chart*, and the breakeven point is evident as that point where the lines intersect. Two straight lines can intersect in only one point if they do not have the same slope; this point has the coordinates (50, $250). The breakeven point tells us that if we sell 50 units, then total revenue equals total cost equals $250; our profit is zero and we neither make nor lose money. If we sell more than 50 units, we earn a profit; if we sell less than 50, we suffer a loss. Our problem has been oversimplified in many ways, but the technique of breakeven analysis is no different from that described.

Let us consider the mathematics of this technique. We know that the locus of points describing a line can also be interpreted as a set of ordered pairs. The graph of our total revenue function thus satisfies the statement $\{(x, TR)|TR = \$5x\}$. The set satisfying this sentence is $\{(0, \$0) \ldots (50, \$250) \ldots (100, \$500) \ldots\}$ (we have left out all but three of the infinite set of ordered pairs of values that make the statement true). Likewise, our cost function can be expressed as $\{(x, TC)|TC = \$100 + \$3x\}$, and the solution set is $\{(0, \$100) \ldots (50, \$250) \ldots (100, \$400) \ldots\}$. The *intersection* of these two sets is the set containing elements common to both sets, and we see that there is but one element common to both sets, the ordered pair (50, $250). Algebraically, since we wish to find that point where $TC = TR$, we set $\$100 + \$3x = \$5x$, and solve for x; $x = 50$, and we substitute 50 for x in one of the equations to determine the associated cost or revenue: $TC = \$100 + \$3(50) = \$250$.

The two functions with which we have been concerned comprise what is called a system. Since the functions are linear, we speak of them as a *linear system*. The solution to such a system is determined by finding those unique values that, when substituted in the equations comprising the system, make each equation true simultaneously. As the ordered pair (50, $250) makes both of the equations in our system above true at the same time, it is the solution of the given system of linear equations. It is very important that the student understand that the solution to a simultaneous system of linear equations is the coordinates of the point of intersection of the lines describing the system graphically, or, in set terminology, that set comprised of the one ordered n-tuple of numbers which is the intersection of the solution sets of the given functions.

It is of course possible to graph the equations involved in a simultaneous system carefully, and find the coordinates of the intersection by inspection, i.e., by locating them on the graph. This is a relatively poor method as far as accuracy is concerned, and we should prefer to determine this intersection as exactly as possible, using the algebraic technique of *substitution*, as we have done in the example above. For example, if $y = 3 - x$ and $y = -2 + 3x$, then we can substitute for y in the second equation the equivalent expression $3 - x$, so that we develop $3 - x = -2 + 3x$; adding x and $+2$ to both sides, $5 = 4x$; and $x = \frac{5}{4}$. Then $y = 3 - (\frac{5}{4}) = \frac{7}{4}$, and the solution is then $(\frac{5}{4}, \frac{7}{4})$. The student should verify that this ordered pair does satisfy each of the equations in the system.

Although the method of substitution provides us with the solution set rather handily when we deal with two variables, it becomes rather unwieldy in larger systems. For this reason we will use a different solution method for solving simultaneous systems, called *elimination*. (Mathematically, the methods are really equivalent, although we will not explore this fact.) The procedure is as follows: the equations are written down so that their equivalent parts correspond vertically. Using the equations of the example above, we write:

$$y = \quad 3 - \quad x$$
$$y = -2 + 3x.$$

Now we wish to eliminate one of the variables by subtracting one of the equations from the other; we shall eliminate y since it requires no change in the equations as they stand:

$$y = \quad 3 - \quad x$$
$$y = -2 + 3x$$
$$\overline{0 = \quad 5 - 4x.}$$

We then solve for x, which we again find to be $5/4$, and substitute this value back into one of the equations to find the associated value of y, as we did when solving by substitution.

Suppose that we are given a system of implicit linear equations such as shown in Fig. 7.3.4; note the procedure followed to arrive at the solution. We choose the variable to be eliminated and then multiply through one of the equations by some number, to eliminate the variable by "subtracting" one equation from the other. (It is often easier to multiply by a number chosen so that the signs of the variable that we wish to eliminate are opposite, and then *add* the equations together.)

Given:

$$x_1 + \quad 2x_2 = \quad 5 \qquad \text{I}$$
$$-3x_1 + \quad 3x_2 = \quad 3 \qquad \text{II}$$

Step 1. Multiply I through by 3.
Step 2. Add I to II.
Step 3. Solve for x_2.
Step 4. Substitute $x_2 = 2$ in I.
          Solve for x_1.

$$3x_1 + \quad 6x_2 = 15 \qquad 3 \times \text{I}$$
$$-3x_1 + \quad 3x_2 = \quad 3 \qquad \text{II}$$
$$\overline{\qquad\qquad 9x_2 = 18}$$
$$x_2 = \quad 2$$
$$x_1 + 2(2) = \quad 5$$
$$x_1 + \quad 4 \quad = \quad 5$$
$$x_1 = \quad 1$$

Check: I

$$1 + 2(2) \overset{?}{=} 5$$
$$1 + 4 \overset{?}{=} 5$$
$$5 = 5$$

II

$$-3(1) + 3(2) \overset{?}{=} 3$$
$$-3 + 6 \overset{?}{=} 3$$
$$3 = 3$$

Solution: (1, 2).

Fig. 7.3.4

The example in Fig. 7.3.4 illustrates but one of many possible ways in which the system might be solved. By inspection, one should determine what multiplier is required to provide the simplest and most direct elimination of one of the variables. Although we shall study still another technique in the next chapter, the method of elimination works for systems of any size, and should be well mastered.

7.3 Exercises

7.3.1 Graph the following pairs of straight line equations, and find their simultaneous solution by *elimination*. *Check* each solution.

(a) $x + y = 3$
$x - y = 3$

(b) $3x + 2y = 0$
$x - 3y = 2$

(c) $y = 5 - x$
$2y + 2x = 4$

(d) $x + y - 3 = 0$
$3x + y - 5 = 0$

(e) $2x - y + 4 = 0$
$2x = 4y$

(f) $x - y + 2 = 0$
$2y = 4 + 2x$

7.3.2 Solve the following:

(a) $\{(x, y)|(2x + y = 2) \wedge (y = 1 + x)\}$
(b) $\{(x, y)|(x - y + 4 = 0) \wedge (x + y + 4 = 0)\}$
(c) $\{(x, y)|(3x + 2y = 2) \wedge (y = 1 - 1.5x)\}$
(d) $\{(x, y)|(x = 2y) \wedge (y + 0.5x = 0)\}$.

7.3.3 Analyze the following word problems. Set up the applicable straight line equations, graph the equations, and solve the equations simultaneously.

(a) An employer pays his employees on a piece work basis, $0.25 for each unit produced. However, he also has an agreement with the union that he will pay his employees a minimum wage of $12 per day. By separate agreement with the union a policy has been established to terminate the employment of any employee whose average piece work production falls below the minimum daily wage requirement. How much must an employee produce to keep his job?

(b) What if the minimum wage in 7.3.3a were $15 a day?

(c) Company A sells product H at $25 per unit; the production cost of H is $1000 for 25 units and $2000 for 100 units. If both revenue and cost are linear functions at what quantity of production and sales will total revenue equal total costs?

(d) At what production and sales level in Exercise 7.3.3c will profits equal $2000?

7.4   Degenerate systems

We have defined the meaning of a linear system in two variables as a set of linear equations upon which we can perform certain operations in order to arrive at a suitable "solution." In particular, we have dealt with linear systems which have only two linear equations, and we have searched for the intersection of these two linear equations, which we have defined to be the simultaneous solution set of the system. If we had a system in two variables which contained more than two equations, say three, then we would graph three lines, and search for a solution in terms of the intersection of all three. We should realize that such a circumstance would result in a maximum of *three* points of intersection of two lines at a time, and a possible minimum of none, but only *one* intersection of all three lines. Likewise, as the number of equations is increased in two-space, the possible number of intersections grows, depending upon whether or not all of the lines have different slopes, whether some of them are parallel, or whether some of them coincide. We shall not describe all of the possible types of combinations nor their mathematics, but shall dispatch this subject with a brief comment concerning *degeneracy*. Degeneracy exists when no solution to a system can be found, or when an infinity of solutions exists. Whenever either of these situations occurs the system is said to be degenerate.

In linear systems of two equations in two variables there are three possibilities regarding a solution, which we know to be the intersection of the graphs of the equations: if the two lines intersect, the solution is determined; if the two lines are parallel, no solution exists; and if the two lines coincide, there is an infinite number of solutions. In the last two cases the system is said to be degenerate, and the equations are called *inconsistent* and *dependent*, respectively. In the first case, the equations are said to be *independent*. Two linear equations in two variables are inconsistent if they have the same slope but different intercepts (parallelism). They are dependent if one of them is a multiple of the other (coincidence), i.e., if by multiplying one of the equations through by some number, we can develop the other equation. Note that the second condition also describes a circumstance where the lines have the same slope; indeed, they are the same line.

7.4   Exercises

7.4.1   Graph the following straight line equations, and find their simultaneous solution or solutions.   Note for each system of equations the equations that are dependent or inconsistent.

(a) $x + y = 3$
$\quad\;\; x - y = 3$
$\quad\quad\;\; y = 2x$

(b) $y = 5 - x$
$\quad\; 2y = 1 + 2x$

(c) $x - y - 2 = 0$
$\quad\; 2y = 4 + 2x$
$\quad\; 3x = 3y - 6$

(d) $\quad\quad\; y = 2x$
$\quad\; y - 2x = 5$
$\quad\; 2y - 3 = 4x$

(e) $y - x = 3$
$\quad\; 2y = 3 - 2x$
$\quad\; y + x = 3$

(f) $y = 3x - 3$
$\quad\; 2y - 6x = 0$
$\quad\; y - 3 = -2x.$

7.5   Linear systems in n variables

We can observe that straight lines exist in three dimensions as well as two, as is shown by the clothesline in the backyard.   Just as any point on a line in two-space could be located by its distance from the axes expressed as an ordered pair of numbers, any point on a line in three-space can be expressed as an ordered *triple* of numbers, each number of which represents the distance of the point from one of the three basic axes of three-space.   In general, a point in n-space can be represented by an ordered *n-tuple* of numbers.

We can thus conceive of a system of linear equations in any dimension, and define a solution to such a system as the ordered n-tuple of numbers which makes all of the equations in the system true simultaneously.   We note that such a system cannot be written in the general explicit form of the two-space system, $y = a + bx$, but is written in the implicit form

$$ax + by + cz + \cdots = k,$$

where a, b, c, etc., and k are constants and x, y, z, etc., are variables. If not degenerate, a system of three linear equations in three variables, four equations in four variables, ... , n equations in n variables, has a unique solution consisting of an ordered n-tuple of numbers $(x, y, z, \ldots)$ which makes all of the equations in the system true at the same time.

The method of solution of such systems is similar to the method used to solve equations simultaneously in two-space, although graphing is not satisfactory since only two axes can be accurately represented in a plane (on a sheet of paper). The method is as follows:

Given:

$$x + 2y + z = 3 \quad \text{I}$$
$$2x - y - z = -1 \quad \text{II}$$
$$-x + y - 2z = -3 \quad \text{III}$$

Step I. Make two equations in two variables by combining two pairs of equations in such a way that one of the variables is eliminated from both equations.

Add I to III

$$x + 2y + z = 3$$
$$-x + y - 2z = -3$$
$$\overline{\quad 3y - z = 0}$$

Multiply I by -2 and add to II

$$-2x - 4y - 2z = -6$$
$$2x - y - z = -1$$
$$\overline{\quad - 5y - 3z = -7}$$

Step II. Solve the two resulting equations simultaneously.

$$3y - z = 0$$
$$-5y - 3z = -7$$

Multiply by -3 and add:
$$- 9y + 3z = 0$$
$$- 5y - 3z = -7$$
$$\overline{-14y \qquad = -7}$$
$$y \qquad = \tfrac{1}{2}$$

Step III. Substitute $y = \tfrac{1}{2}$ in one of the equations developed in Step I to find z.

$$-9(\tfrac{1}{2}) + 3z = 0$$
$$3z = \tfrac{9}{2}$$
$$z = \tfrac{3}{2}$$

Step IV. Substitute $y = \tfrac{1}{2}$ and $z = \tfrac{3}{2}$ in one of the original equations to find x.

$$x + 2(\tfrac{1}{2}) + (\tfrac{3}{2}) = 3$$
$$x = 3 - \tfrac{5}{2}$$
$$x = \tfrac{1}{2} \qquad \textit{Solution: } (\tfrac{1}{2}, \tfrac{1}{2}, \tfrac{3}{2}).$$

Check: The student should substitute the values of (x, y, z) into the original equations to make sure that the system is satisfied, i.e., all of the equations are true at $(\tfrac{1}{2}, \tfrac{1}{2}, \tfrac{3}{2})$.

7.5 Exercises

7.5.1 Solve simultaneously the following systems of linear equations in three unknowns.

(a) $\begin{aligned} x + y \quad\quad &= 5 \\ x + \quad\quad z &= 2 \\ y + z &= 1 \end{aligned}$

(b) $\begin{aligned} 2x + 3y - z &= 5 \\ x - y + z &= 1 \\ 4x + 3y - 2z &= 1 \end{aligned}$

(c) $\begin{aligned} x + y \quad\quad &= -3 \\ 4x - 3y + 2z &= 1 \\ 2x + 3y + 2z &= -1 \end{aligned}$

(d) $\begin{aligned} 4x - 2y + 2z &= 3 \\ 8x + 4y - 4z &= 2 \\ x + 3y - z &= 2. \end{aligned}$

7.5.2 Analyze the following word problems developing the appropriate linear equations. Solve the equations for the unknowns.

(a) A man deposits a total of $10,000 in x, y and z amounts in three banks. The interest rate paid by the banks is 4, 5, and 6 per cent respectively. The annual income from deposits x and y is $230, and from x and z is $380. How much was deposited in each bank?

(b) The total take-home pay of three machine operators (x, y, z) of the ABC Company is $210 for one week. The sum of the take-home pay of x and z is $140, and x takes home $20 more than y. Find the take-home pay of each of the employees.

The Algebra
Chapter 8 ——— of Vectors
and Matrices

8.1 Vectors

In the solution of simultaneous linear systems we have noted the importance of the concept of an ordered pair of numbers as the solution of a two-space system, and an ordered triple of numbers in a three-space solution. We emphasize this concept: a solution to such a system consists of a set of *numerical values* having the unique property of making all of the equations in the system true at the same time. In a solution set, moreover, the order in which the values are set down has one-to-one correspondence with the predetermined set of unknowns whose values we wish to discover.

A *vector* is a set consisting of an *ordered n-tuple of numbers;* we see then that our solution set above is a vector. If the elements in any list of a set have corresponding numerical values, we can associate a vector of these values with the set. For instance, if we were to list the towns of Fort Collins, Loveland, Boulder, and Denver, then we could define the vector of the population of these towns as (25,000, 10,000, 37,000, 470,000). Whenever we can represent the behavior of elements of some system in terms of vectors, we may take advantage of a set of laws or rules for operating upon vectors, i.e., an algebra of vectors, which vastly simplifies the work of analysis. The laws of vectors and matrices (a matrix is a combination of vectors) are basic to

104

recent advances in varied areas, from national economic planning to automatic direction and control of industrial firms.

In our study of vectors and matrices we shall omit a great deal of the mathematical reasoning behind the concept (for instance, the geometry of vectors) since it adds little for our immediate use. In addition, we shall proceed through the algebra in a fashion slightly different from that used previously, since the various laws and rules are quite simple and intuitive. The student is urged to consider each section carefully, understanding one section fully before progressing to the next.

A *column vector* is an ordered collection or set of numbers written in a column, i.e., vertically, and enclosed in parentheses:

$$\begin{pmatrix} 0.10 \\ 0.06 \end{pmatrix}; \begin{pmatrix} 2 \\ 4 \end{pmatrix}; \begin{pmatrix} 1 \\ 0 \\ -1 \end{pmatrix}; \begin{pmatrix} \frac{2}{3} \\ -\frac{1}{4} \\ 19\frac{9}{20} \end{pmatrix}; \begin{pmatrix} 105 \\ 3217 \\ -564 \end{pmatrix}; u = \begin{pmatrix} u_1 \\ u_2 \\ u_3 \\ \cdot \\ \cdot \\ \cdot \\ u_m \end{pmatrix}.$$

An important characteristic of a column vector is the number of elements in the set comprising the vector, called *components*. One may describe a column vector by saying, " ... a two-component column vector" (as in the two left-hand illustrations), " ... a three-component column vector" (as in the next three examples), or "an m-component column vector" (as in the right-hand example). Note that this last vector can be also indicated by the single symbol "u," whose components are the m symbols $u_1, u_2, u_3, \ldots, u_m$. Thus a vector is symbolized by a lower case letter of the alphabet, without a subscript. The components of the vector are symbolized by the same letter, but they are identified by a subscript, a numeral, which indicates their position in the ordered set, i.e., in the vector. When we wish to refer to some unspecified component of a column vector, we speak of the "ith" component (pronounced "eye-th"). Therefore, where u might be a column vector, then u_i ($i = 1, 2, 3, \ldots, m$) represents any component of the vector u. The subscript i is called an *index*, and is used to indicate the component to which we refer. Thus if we specified a column vector whose components were u_i, $i = 1, 2, 3$, then we know that

$$u = \begin{pmatrix} u_1 \\ u_2 \\ u_3 \end{pmatrix}.$$

A *row vector* is analogous to a column vector in all respects except that it is written in a row, i.e., horizontally, and the components are separated by commas:

$$(1, 3); (-14, 56, 32); (0.006, -1.3); v = (v_1, v_2, \ldots, v_n).$$

Note that the row vector v has n components, rather than m as in the column vector u above. This is a convention that will assist us later; we will see shortly that in working with vectors, $m = n$ is a necessary condition for many operations. We will often refer to the "jth" component of an n-component row vector, $j = 1, 2, 3, \ldots, n$. The subscript j thus serves the same purpose for the row vector as the subscript i for the column vector: it is an index for some unspecified component of the row vector.

We define the *zero vector* to be the vector all of whose components are zero. We shall let the lower-case letter o represent the zero row or column vector:

$$o = (0, 0, \ldots, 0); o = \begin{pmatrix} 0 \\ 0 \\ \cdot \\ \cdot \\ \cdot \\ 0 \end{pmatrix}.$$

8.1   Exercise

8.1.1   Identify the following vectors by their type (row or column) and the number of components:

(a) $p = (1, 2)$　　　　　　　　　　(b) $q = (5, 9)$

(c) $r = \begin{pmatrix} 1 \\ 2 \end{pmatrix}$　　　　　　　　　(d) $s = \begin{pmatrix} 5 \\ 9 \end{pmatrix}$

(e) $t = (1, 2, 3, 4)$　　　　　　　(f) $u = (0)$

(g) $v = (1, 0, 0)$　　　　　　　　(h) $w = \begin{pmatrix} 1 \\ 0 \\ 0 \end{pmatrix}$

(i) $x = (4, 3, 2, 1)$　　　　　　　(j) $y = \begin{pmatrix} 0 \\ 0 \\ 1 \end{pmatrix}$

(k) $z = \begin{pmatrix} 0 \\ 0 \\ 0 \end{pmatrix}.$

8.2 The algebra of vectors

Vectors may be combined and otherwise operated upon according to the following rules, each of which will be identified by a number to facilitate reference in the exercises to follow.

Rule 8.2.1: Two vectors are said to be equal if and only if:
(a) *They are both column vectors or both row vectors, and*
(b) *Corresponding components are equal.*

We notice that as a consequence of Rule 8.2.1(b), two vectors are equal only if they have the same *number* of elements. Although this condition is *necessary* for equivalence, it is not *sufficient*, since corresponding elements must also be equal. Under no condition can a row vector be equal to a column vector. If $p = (1, 3)$, $q = \begin{pmatrix} 1 \\ 3 \end{pmatrix}$, $r = (1, 3)$,

$s = \begin{pmatrix} 3 \\ 1 \end{pmatrix}$, $t = \begin{pmatrix} 1 \\ 3 \\ 4 \end{pmatrix}$, $u = \begin{pmatrix} 1 \\ 3 \end{pmatrix}$, then $p = r$, and $q = u$, but $p \neq q$, $q \neq s$,

$q \neq t$, $s \neq u$, etc.

To multiply a vector by a number, we multiply each of the components of the vector by the number. In vector algebra this multiplier is called a *scalar*. As we shall see, there is a difference between multiplying a vector by a scalar and multiplying two vectors; since "numbers" are involved in either case, it is important to be able to distinguish which operation we are performing. Again, a vector is an ordered set of numbers; a scalar is a single number, which we will represent symbolically by the lower-case Greek letters α, β, γ, etc.

Rule 8.2.2: The product of a vector and a scalar is a vector whose components are found by multiplying each of the components of the vector by the scalar.

Thus, if $u = (1, 2)$, then $2u = (2, 4)$, $(\frac{3}{2})u = (\frac{3}{2}, 3)$, and $-u = (-1, -2)$; if $v = \begin{pmatrix} -1 \\ 4 \end{pmatrix}$, then $2v = \begin{pmatrix} -2 \\ 8 \end{pmatrix}$, $(\frac{1}{2})v = \begin{pmatrix} -\frac{1}{2} \\ 2 \end{pmatrix}$, and $-v = \begin{pmatrix} 1 \\ -4 \end{pmatrix}$, etc. Since a scalar may be negative as well as positive, we note that multiplication by a negative scalar changes the sign of each component except, of course, for those components which are zero.

Rule 8.2.3: The addition or subtraction of two vectors is defined if and only if:
(a) They are both row or both column vectors, and
(b) They have the same number of components.

To add two vectors meeting these qualifications, add corresponding elements, so that the sum of two n-component vectors is also an n-component vector, and likewise for subtracting one vector from another. Thus, if $u = (1, 3)$, $v = (2, 1)$, $x = \begin{pmatrix} 3 \\ 2 \\ 1 \end{pmatrix}$, $y = \begin{pmatrix} 1 \\ 2 \\ 3 \end{pmatrix}$, and $z = (1, 2, 3)$, then:

$$u + v = (1, 3) + (2, 1) = (1 + 2, 3 + 1) = (3, 4),$$

and $\quad u - v = (1, 3) - (2, 1) = (1 - 2, 3 - 1) = (-1, 2);$

$$x + y = \begin{pmatrix} 3 \\ 2 \\ 1 \end{pmatrix} + \begin{pmatrix} 1 \\ 2 \\ 3 \end{pmatrix} = \begin{pmatrix} 3 + 1 \\ 2 + 2 \\ 1 + 3 \end{pmatrix} = \begin{pmatrix} 4 \\ 4 \\ 4 \end{pmatrix},$$

and $\quad x - y = \begin{pmatrix} 3 \\ 2 \\ 1 \end{pmatrix} - \begin{pmatrix} 1 \\ 2 \\ 3 \end{pmatrix} = \begin{pmatrix} 3 - 1 \\ 2 - 2 \\ 1 - 3 \end{pmatrix} = \begin{pmatrix} 2 \\ 0 \\ -2 \end{pmatrix};$

but $u + z$, $v - x$, etc., are not defined.

Generally, then, if u is an n-component row vector, and v is an n-component row vector, $u + v = (u_1 + v_1, u_2 + v_2, \ldots, u_n + v_n)$ (subtraction is performed in the same way, except that the signs are changed), and similarly for column vectors:

$$x + y = \begin{pmatrix} x_1 + y_1 \\ x_2 + y_2 \\ \cdot \\ \cdot \\ \cdot \\ x_m + y_m \end{pmatrix}.$$

Rule 8.2.4: The product of two vectors is defined if and only if:
(a) One of the vectors is a row vector and the other a column vector, and
(b) Each vector has the same number of components ($n = m$), and
(c) The row vector is written first.

The product will be the sum of the arithmetic products of the corresponding elements; or, if u is an n-component row vector, v is an m-component column vector, and $m = n$, then:

$$u \cdot v = (u_1, u_2, \ldots, u_n) \begin{pmatrix} v_1 \\ v_2 \\ \cdot \\ \cdot \\ \cdot \\ v_m \end{pmatrix} = u_1 v_1 + u_2 v_2 + \ldots + u_n v_m.$$

Examples:
$$(3, 1, 4) \begin{pmatrix} 1 \\ 2 \\ -3 \end{pmatrix} = (3 \times 1) + (1 \times 2) + [4 \times (-3)]$$
$$= 3 + 2 - 12 = -7$$
$$(1, 0) \begin{pmatrix} 0 \\ 1 \end{pmatrix} = (1 \times 0) + (0 \times 1) = 0 + 0 = 0.$$

Note that the result of "multiplying" vectors is a scalar, i.e., a number; this kind of multiplication is sometimes called the "inner product," and sometimes the "dot product."

8.2 Exercises

8.2.1 Refer to Exercise 8.1.1, and correct the following statements if necessary, stating your reason for the change.

(a) $p = r$ (b) $q = s$
(c) $p = q$ (d) $t = x$
(e) $u = u$ (f) $u = v$
(g) $w = y$ (h) $w = z$
(i) $u = z$.

8.2.2 Compute the quantities below for the following vectors:

$$r = \begin{pmatrix} 1 \\ 0 \\ 1 \end{pmatrix}, \qquad s = \begin{pmatrix} -2 \\ 4 \\ 1 \end{pmatrix}, \qquad t = \begin{pmatrix} 0 \\ 1 \\ 0 \end{pmatrix},$$

$$u = (1, 0, 1), \quad v = (-2, 4, 1), \text{ and } w = (0, 1, 0).$$

(a) $3r$ (b) $-3r$
(c) $-2r + 3t$ (d) $u + v - w$
(e) $(1/2)w - v + 3u$ (f) $r + t$
(g) $u + w$ (h) $t + u$
(i) $3r - 2w$.

8.2.3 Show that if u is any vector, $u + o = u$.

8.2.4 Show that if x and y are both n-component row or column vectors, then $x + 0y = x$.

8.2.5 (a) If $\begin{pmatrix} 3 \\ 1 \\ 2 \end{pmatrix} - \begin{pmatrix} q_1 \\ q_2 \\ q_3 \end{pmatrix} = \begin{pmatrix} -1 \\ 0 \\ 0 \end{pmatrix}$, find q.

(b) If $3 \begin{pmatrix} p_1 \\ p_2 \\ p_3 \\ p_4 \end{pmatrix} = \begin{pmatrix} 3 \\ 6 \\ 9 \\ 12 \end{pmatrix}$, find p.

8.2.6 Given the following vectors, compute the quantities below:

$$a = (4, 3, -2), \ b = (1, 0, -1), \ c = \begin{pmatrix} 0 \\ 1 \\ 0 \end{pmatrix}, \text{ and } d = \begin{pmatrix} -2 \\ 2 \\ -2 \end{pmatrix}.$$

(a) $(a \cdot c) + (b \cdot d)$ (b) $(-2a + b) \cdot (4c - d)$
(c) $(b \cdot c)a$ (d) $(a \cdot c)b$
(e) $(b \cdot d)[(a + b) \cdot (c - d)]$ (f) $(c \cdot d) + (a \cdot b)$.

8.2.7 Three service station operators, A, B, and C are engaged in a competitive sales campaign. In one particular day A sold 2 tires, 1 battery, 12 quarts of oil, 1 set of tire chains, and 1000 gallons of gas; B sold 1 tire, 14 quarts of oil, and 1200 gallons of gasoline; and C sold 3 tires, 2 batteries, 16 quarts of oil, and 1400 gallons of gasoline.

(a) Write the sales of A, B, and C as row vectors. (*Note:* Since we desire to compare their sales, make each vector contain 5 components, representing no sales by "0.") (Sales vector for $A = a$; for $B = b$; for $C = c$.)
(b) By means of vector addition compute the total number of each item sold by the operators.
(c) A, B, and C used the same price schedule, selling tires for $20 each, batteries for $15 each, oil for $0.50 a quart, tire chains for $6 a set, and gasoline for $0.35 a gallon. Make a column vector of these prices, and compute for each operator the value of his day's sales (price vector $= p$).
(d) Compute the total value of the sales by all operators, indicating the vector notation used.

8.2.8 A broker sold one of his customers 100 shares of stock A, 200 shares of stock B, 150 shares of C, and 25 shares of D. The stocks cost $5, $6, $9, and $4.50 respectively.

(a) Set the problem up in vector notation, and by vector multiplication find the total cost of all stocks sold to this customer.

8.3 Matrices

A rectangular array of numbers enclosed in parentheses is called a *matrix*. These are some examples of matrices:

$$(a) \begin{pmatrix} 1 \\ 0 \end{pmatrix} \qquad (b) \begin{pmatrix} 1 & 2 \\ 3 & 4 \end{pmatrix}$$

$$(c) \begin{pmatrix} 0 & 1 & 0 \\ 3 & 5 & -2 \\ -4 & 0 & 1 \end{pmatrix} \qquad (d) \begin{pmatrix} 5 & 2 \\ 41 & 1 \\ 22 & -3 \\ 3 & 22 \\ 9 & 3 \end{pmatrix} \qquad (e) \begin{pmatrix} 1 & 5 & 9 & 7 \\ 2 & 4 & 3 & 9 \end{pmatrix}$$

$$(f) \qquad X = \begin{pmatrix} x_{11} & x_{12} & \dots & x_{1n} \\ x_{21} & x_{22} & \dots & x_{2n} \\ \cdot & \cdot & & \cdot \\ \cdot & \cdot & & \cdot \\ \cdot & \cdot & & \cdot \\ x_{m1} & x_{m2} & \dots & x_{mn} \end{pmatrix} = ((x_{ij}))$$

A matrix is described by the number of rows and columns in it, by stating first the number of rows and then the number of columns, connecting the number of rows and columns by the word "by". Illustration (a) above is a 2×1 matrix, read "two by one." This is also known as the *order* of the matrix; we note that the order of a matrix gives both its "size" and its "shape." The order of each of the other matrices illustrated is, in alphabetic order: $2 \times 2, 3 \times 3, 5 \times 2, 2 \times 4$, and $m \times n$. It is of course obvious that a matrix is a combination of vectors; in fact, a $1 \times n$ matrix is a row vector, and an $m \times 1$ matrix is a column vector. A matrix in which $m = n$ is called a *square* matrix, as in *b* and *c* above.

The numbers comprising the matrix are called *elements*, or *entries*. The position of each element in a matrix is identified by the row and column in which it is located, in that order, as illustrated in *f*. Note the similarity between the matrix notation and the vector notation. There are m elements in a column, and any element in a column may be specified by the subscript i; there are n elements in a row, and any element may be specified by the subscript j. Thus any element in the matrix may be specified by the notation x_{ij}, making sure that we follow the convention of stating the number of the row first.

Rather than spelling out all of the elements in a given matrix, it is usually more convenient to adopt a symbol for the matrix. We shall therefore use a capital letter to stand for a matrix, and where the values of the elements are not specified, as in f, we shall use the capital letter corresponding to the lower-case letter used in the body of the matrix. Another means of symbolizing a matrix is illustrated in f, although we shall not use that notation, since the double parentheses are perhaps awkward. Our notational scheme is as follows: a capital letter represents a matrix, a lower-case letter with two subscripts represents an element in a matrix, a lower-case letter with one subscript represents a component of a vector, and a lower-case letter with no subscript represents a vector, although it is true that a vector is a matrix.

8.3 Exercise

8.3.1 State the order of the following matrices:

(a) $A = (a_1, a_2, a_3, \ldots, a_n)$

(b) $\begin{pmatrix} 0 & 0 \\ 0 & 0 \\ 0 & 0 \end{pmatrix}$

(c) $\begin{pmatrix} 1 & -5 & 4 & 3 & 2 \\ 2 & 4 & -1 & 3 & 1 \end{pmatrix}$

(d) $\begin{pmatrix} 3 & 4 & 7 \\ 2 & 1 & 3 \\ 4 & 2 & 1 \end{pmatrix}$

(e) $\begin{bmatrix} 1 & 0 & 0 & 0 & 0 \\ 0 & 1 & 0 & 0 & 0 \\ 0 & 0 & 1 & 0 & 0 \\ 0 & 0 & 0 & 1 & 0 \\ 0 & 0 & 0 & 0 & 1 \end{bmatrix}.$

8.4   The algebra of matrices

Matrix algebra is similar in many respects to the algebra of vectors, as we would expect. Rules for operations will be given, to correspond with the rules stated in Section 8.2.

Rule 8.4.1: *Two matrices are said to be equal if and only if corresponding elements are equal.*

Obviously, in order for two matrices to be equal they must be of the same order.

Rule 8.4.2: *The product of a matrix and a scalar is a matrix whose elements are found by multiplying each element in the matrix by the scalar.*

Multiplication of a matrix by a scalar is thus the same as multiplying a vector by a scalar, as shown by the following illustrations.

$$\text{If } A = \begin{pmatrix} a_{11} & a_{12} & a_{13} \\ a_{21} & a_{22} & a_{23} \\ a_{31} & a_{32} & a_{33} \end{pmatrix}, \text{ then } \alpha A = \begin{pmatrix} \alpha a_{11} & \alpha a_{12} & \alpha a_{13} \\ \alpha a_{21} & \alpha a_{22} & \alpha a_{23} \\ \alpha a_{31} & \alpha a_{32} & \alpha a_{33} \end{pmatrix}.$$

$$\text{If } B = \begin{pmatrix} \tfrac{1}{2} & 3 \\ 2 & -\tfrac{1}{4} \end{pmatrix}, \ -4B = \begin{pmatrix} -2 & -12 \\ -8 & 1 \end{pmatrix}; \text{ and } 0B = \begin{pmatrix} 0 & 0 \\ 0 & 0 \end{pmatrix}.$$

Note that when a matrix is multiplied by the scalar zero, the result is a matrix all of whose elements are zero; it is called the *zero matrix*.

Rule 8.4.3: *The addition or subtraction of two matrices is defined if and only if they are of the same order.*

To add or subtract matrices of the same order, corresponding elements are added or subtracted; the resulting matrix is of the same order as the matrices operated upon.   Thus:

$$U + V = \begin{pmatrix} 3 & 1 & 2 \\ 2 & 3 & 2 \\ 1 & 3 & 1 \end{pmatrix} + \begin{pmatrix} 1 & 2 & -3 \\ -2 & 4 & -6 \\ -1 & -5 & 2 \end{pmatrix}$$

$$= \begin{pmatrix} 3+1 & 1+2 & 2-3 \\ 2-2 & 3+4 & 2-6 \\ 1-1 & 3-5 & 1+2 \end{pmatrix} = \begin{pmatrix} 4 & 3 & -1 \\ 0 & 7 & -4 \\ 0 & -2 & 3 \end{pmatrix}.$$

Rule 8.4.4: *The product XY of two matrices is defined if and only if the number of columns in X is the same as the number of rows in Y.*

Thus if X is of order $m \times p$, and Y is of order $p \times n$, then X may be multiplied *on* Y; the result will be an $m \times n$ matrix.   Notice that we describe the process of multiplying XY by saying "X on Y," first to indicate that this is a different kind of multiplication, and second to define the fact that X is to be multiplied on Y, and not vice versa.   For matrices do not generally *commute* in multiplication, i.e., $XY \neq YX$, except in certain special cases.   Note that this differs from traditional algebra, where generally $ab = ba$.   Rule 8.4.4 must be read quite literally: the number of columns in the matrix on the "left" must be the same as the number of rows in the matrix on the "right."

The process of multiplying matrices is best explained by symbols: suppose we wish to multiply X, an $m \times k$ matrix, on Y, a $k \times n$ matrix.   The product, which we shall call Z, is defined, since Rule 8.4.4

is satisfied, and Z will be of order $m \times n$. Our problem is to find each element of Z, or z_{ij}. Each z_{ij} will be the inner product of the ith row and the jth column of X and Y respectively.

Let us illustrate this by an example:

$$XY = \begin{pmatrix} 1 & 4 \\ -2 & 3 \end{pmatrix} \begin{pmatrix} -1 & 2 & 3 \\ 3 & 1 & -1 \end{pmatrix} = \begin{pmatrix} -1+12 & 2+4 & 3-4 \\ 2+9 & -4+3 & -6-3 \end{pmatrix}$$

$$= \begin{pmatrix} 11 & 6 & -1 \\ 11 & -1 & -9 \end{pmatrix} = Z.$$

The element z_{11} is the inner product of the first row of X on the first column of Y: $(1, 4)\begin{pmatrix} -1 \\ 3 \end{pmatrix} = -1 + 12 = 11$. The element of Z in the second row and third column, z_{23}, is the inner product of the second row of X on the third column of Y: $(-2, 3)\begin{pmatrix} 3 \\ -1 \end{pmatrix} = (-6) + (-3) = -9$, etc. Thus one in effect uses the rows of the matrix on the left, and the columns of the matrix on the right; the student should therefore recognize that XY would be equal to YX only in very special cases.

As a means of avoiding error, it is recommended that the product matrix, i.e., Z, be set up with blanks for its elements before the multiplication is begun. In this way the student can assure himself that the multiplication is defined, and also keep track of his progress. To fill in a blank, i.e., find the value of an element, one merely needs to identify its row and column, and then take the inner product of the corresponding row of the left matrix and the corresponding column of the right matrix.

8.4 Exercises

8.4.1 Add the following matrices:

(a) $\begin{pmatrix} 3 & 1 & 2 \\ 4 & 2 & 7 \\ 1 & 5 & 2 \end{pmatrix} + \begin{pmatrix} 2 & -1 & 1 \\ -2 & 1 & -3 \\ 3 & -1 & 2 \end{pmatrix}$

(b) $\begin{pmatrix} 2 & 3 & -2 \\ 3 & 1 & 1 \\ 4 & 7 & -3 \\ 5 & 2 & -1 \end{pmatrix} + \begin{pmatrix} 1 & 2 & 3 \\ -2 & 2 & -2 \\ -1 & -4 & 1 \\ -4 & 2 & 2 \end{pmatrix}$

(c) $\begin{pmatrix} 3 & 4 & 5 \\ 1 & -1 & 3 \end{pmatrix} + \begin{pmatrix} 3 & 1 & -2 \\ 2 & 2 & -1 \end{pmatrix}$

(d)
$$\begin{pmatrix} 3 & 2 \\ 4 & -1 \\ 3 & 1 \\ -2 & 2 \end{pmatrix} + \begin{pmatrix} 3 & 4 & -1 & 1 \\ 2 & -1 & 2 & 2 \end{pmatrix}.$$

8.4.2 Subtract the matrices given in Exercise 8.4.1a, b, c, and d.

8.4.3 Perform the indicated operations on the following matrices:

(a) $(3, 3)\begin{pmatrix} 4 \\ 5 \end{pmatrix}$

(b) $\begin{pmatrix} 4 & -1 \\ 2 & 3 \end{pmatrix}\begin{pmatrix} 2 & 1 \\ 3 & -1 \end{pmatrix}$

(c) $\begin{pmatrix} 4 & 2 & -1 \\ 3 & -2 & 2 \end{pmatrix}\begin{pmatrix} 3 & 6 \\ 4 & 2 \\ 5 & -1 \end{pmatrix}$

(d) $-2\begin{pmatrix} 3 & 1 & 4 \\ 2 & -1 & -5 \end{pmatrix}$

(e) $\begin{pmatrix} 4 & 3 \\ 2 & 1 \end{pmatrix}\begin{pmatrix} 1 & 0 \\ 0 & 1 \end{pmatrix}$

(f) $\begin{bmatrix} 2 & 1 & -1 \\ 3 & 2 & -2 \\ 4 & 1 & 4 \\ 1 & -3 & 1 \\ -2 & 2 & 2 \end{bmatrix}\begin{pmatrix} 4 \\ 2 \\ 1 \end{pmatrix}$

(g) $\begin{pmatrix} 2 & 3 & 1 \\ -2 & 2 & 2 \end{pmatrix}\begin{pmatrix} 3 & -2 & 3 & -1 \\ 2 & 1 & 4 & 2 \\ 1 & -1 & 2 & 1 \end{pmatrix}$

(h) $3\begin{pmatrix} 2 & -1 & -1 \\ 3 & -1 & 2 \end{pmatrix}.$

8.5 The inverse matrix

We have defined the *zero matrix*, which, added to another matrix, gives a sum identical to the latter matrix. The zero matrix is called the *identity element in addition;* the word identity stems from the fact that the result of adding the zero matrix to a matrix is identically that matrix. In traditional algebra, the number 0 is the identity element in addition; thus we see exact correspondence in this respect between matrix algebra and the algebra we have learned previously.

In traditional algebra we define the identity element in multiplication to be the number 1, i.e., any number multiplied by the number 1 is that number, so that $1a = a$. In matrix algebra, the corresponding *identity element in multiplication* is called the *identity matrix*, symbolized by the capital letter I. Unlike the zero matrix, which can have *any* order, the identity matrix is a square matrix ($m = n$). Associated with every square matrix A is its identity matrix I, such that $AI = IA = A$. We note that the identity matrix commutes with its associated matrix in multiplication, an exception to the general rule. Some examples of identity matrices follow; we note their chief characteristic.

Along the *main diagonal* each element is 1:

$$\begin{pmatrix} 1 & 0 \\ 0 & 1 \end{pmatrix}; \begin{pmatrix} 1 & 0 & 0 \\ 0 & 1 & 0 \\ 0 & 0 & 1 \end{pmatrix}; \text{ and } \begin{pmatrix} 1 & 0 & 0 & \cdots & 0 \\ 0 & 1 & 0 & \cdots & 0 \\ 0 & 0 & 1 & \cdots & 0 \\ \cdot & \cdot & \cdot & \cdots & \cdot \\ \cdot & \cdot & \cdot & \cdots & \cdot \\ \cdot & \cdot & \cdot & \cdots & \cdot \\ 0 & 0 & 0 & \cdots & 1 \end{pmatrix};$$

everywhere else in the matrix the elements are 0. That is, $x_{ij} = 1$ when $i = j$; $x_{ij} = 0$ when $i \neq j$. If A is some given matrix, then $AI = A$:

$$AI = \begin{pmatrix} 4 & -7 \\ -9 & 3 \end{pmatrix} \begin{pmatrix} 1 & 0 \\ 0 & 1 \end{pmatrix}$$

$$= \begin{pmatrix} (\ 4)(1) + (-7)(0) & (\ 4)(0) + (-7)(1) \\ (-9)(1) + (\ 3)(0) & (-9)(0) + (\ 3)(1) \end{pmatrix} = \begin{pmatrix} 4 & -7 \\ -9 & 3 \end{pmatrix}$$

We have now learned to add, subtract, and multiply matrices of different types; we note that nothing has been said about the process of division, with respect to either matrix or vector algebra. Division is a very useful arithmetic tool, and we should believe it an oversight to ignore it where matrices are concerned. Although division as we know it is not defined in matrix algebra, we do have a process which performs ostensibly the same function. Consider the algebraic equation $ax = b$. To solve this expression for x, we divide both sides of the equation by $a(a \neq 0)$: $x = b/a$. Another way to solve this equation for x is to multiply both sides by the reciprocal of a (which can be written a^{-1}): $(a^{-1})ax = a^{-1}b$; $x = a^{-1}b$. This result follows from the fact that $a^{-1}a = (1/a)a = 1$.

Given a square *non-singular* matrix A, a unique matrix A^{-1}, such that $AA^{-1} = I$, exists, and it is called the *inverse matrix*. (The relationship of A and A^{-1} is, obviously, similar to that of a and a^{-1}.) The word non-singular, for our purposes, means that A does in fact have an inverse, for there are many matrices which do not have inverses. As another exception to the general rule, a matrix commutes with its inverse in multiplication, i.e., $AA^{-1} = A^{-1}A = I$. We should not confuse the inverse matrix with the algebraic reciprocal of a number; although they perform the same function, the similarity stops there, and we have drawn the parallel between traditional algebra and matrix algebra merely to clarify the concept. There are a number of ways to find the inverse of a given matrix. Although the processes are tedious, we shall explore one of them, since the inverse matrix is highly useful.

The method which we shall employ to find the inverse matrix makes use of the *partitioning* of a matrix, by which we mean the separation of a matrix into parts, indicated by a vertical line drawn between certain columns of the matrix. (Matrices may be partitioned by horizontal lines as well.) Examples:

$$(A|B) = \begin{pmatrix} 3 & 4 & 9 & 1 & -1 \\ 2 & -1 & 6 & 3 & 2 \\ 4 & 3 & -7 & -5 & 4 \end{pmatrix}; (C|I) = \begin{pmatrix} -4 & 3 & 1 & 0 \\ 2 & -8 & 0 & 1 \end{pmatrix}.$$

The substance of our method for inverting a matrix can be understood by following this argument: given a partitioned matrix such as that to the right above, $(C|I)$, we note that if both partitions are multiplied by the inverse of C, the result will give a new partitioned matrix, the left side of which will be the identity matrix, and the right side of which will be the inverse matrix. Symbolically:

$$(C|I) \to (C^{-1}C|C^{-1}I) = (I|C^{-1}).$$

The arrow indicates that we perform a *linear transformation* on the partitioned matrix $(C|I)$ to develop the matrix $(I|C^{-1})$; these two matrices are obviously not equal. The linear transform of a matrix is the result of performing certain *row and column* operations upon it; we shall not attempt to define the rationale for these operations, but merely state them and illustrate how they may be used to transform a matrix. We shall refer to this method as the *Gaussian*, or *Gauss'*, method of matrix inversion.

Allowable operations can be stated as: (1) Any row may be multiplied through by a number, and (2) Any row may be added to or subtracted from another row.

Let us illustrate the above, remembering that our goal is to transform a partitioned matrix whose left side is some given matrix and whose right side is the associated identity matrix, into a new partitioned matrix whose left side is the identity matrix, and whose right side is the inverse of the given matrix, i.e., $(C|I) \to (I|C^{-1})$.

Problem: given $C = \begin{pmatrix} 1 & 3 \\ -1 & 2 \end{pmatrix}$, find C^{-1}. We restate this problem as:

$$\text{Transform } \begin{pmatrix} 1 & 3 & 1 & 0 \\ -1 & 2 & 0 & 1 \end{pmatrix} \text{ into } \begin{pmatrix} 1 & 0 \\ 0 & 1 \end{pmatrix} C^{-1} .$$

Step 1: Add row I to row II, to get a zero in the lower left corner.

$$\begin{pmatrix} 1 & 3 & 1 & 0 \\ -1 & 2 & 0 & 1 \end{pmatrix} \xrightarrow{\text{II+I}} \begin{pmatrix} 1 & 3 & 1 & 0 \\ -1+1 & 2+3 & 0+1 & 1+0 \end{pmatrix}$$

$$= \begin{pmatrix} 1 & 3 & 1 & 0 \\ 0 & 5 & 1 & 1 \end{pmatrix}.$$

Note that we have not transformed row I and therefore it does not change. Now we wish to replace the 5 in the second row, second column, by a 1.

Step 2: Divide row II by 5 (i.e., multiply by $\frac{1}{5}$).

$$\begin{pmatrix} 1 & 3 & | & 1 & 0 \\ 0 & 5 & | & 1 & 1 \end{pmatrix} \xrightarrow{(\frac{1}{5}) \text{ II}} \begin{pmatrix} 1 & 3 & | & 1 & 0 \\ 0 & \frac{5}{5} & | & \frac{1}{5} & \frac{1}{5} \end{pmatrix} = \begin{pmatrix} 1 & 3 & | & 1 & 0 \\ 0 & 1 & | & \frac{1}{5} & \frac{1}{5} \end{pmatrix}.$$

Once again, we have not transformed row I and therefore it remains unchanged. Now we need only to change the 3 in the first row, second column, into 0.

Step 3: Subtract from row I three times row II.

$$\begin{pmatrix} 1 & 3 & | & 1 & 0 \\ 0 & 1 & | & \frac{1}{5} & \frac{1}{5} \end{pmatrix} \xrightarrow{\text{I} - (3)\text{II}} \begin{pmatrix} 1 - (3)0 & 3 - (3)1 & | & 1 - (3)\frac{1}{5} & 0 - (3)\frac{1}{5} \\ 0 & 1 & | & \frac{1}{5} & \frac{1}{5} \end{pmatrix}$$

$$= \begin{pmatrix} 1 & 0 & | & \frac{2}{5} & -\frac{3}{5} \\ 0 & 1 & | & \frac{1}{5} & \frac{1}{5} \end{pmatrix}; \text{ thus } C^{-1} = \begin{pmatrix} \frac{2}{5} & -\frac{3}{5} \\ \frac{1}{5} & \frac{1}{5} \end{pmatrix}.$$

The student should verify that $CC^{-1} = I$ for this example. The tedium of these operations requires that great care be taken to assure accuracy of arithmetic in adding, etc., for one mistake will result in developing an incorrect inverse. Of course, the result should always be checked.

A general rule of procedure is to start in the "northwest corner" (upper left-hand corner) of the partitioned matrix, transforming that element into a 1; then proceed down the first column, transforming the matrix to develop zeroes elsewhere in that column. Generally, the fewest steps in the transformation will be required by next transforming the second row to develop its main diagonal element ($x_{22} = 1$), and then transforming the rest of the second column, *below* the main diagonal, into zeroes. About halfway through the process, then, the main diagonal will have been transformed into 1's and all elements below it into 0's. We then start in the "southeast corner," or lower right-hand corner, and work back. A little practice will develop sufficient skill in determining which element should be subsequently transformed to reduce the total number of steps required.

8.5 Exercise

8.5.1 Find the inverses of the following matrices, if they exist.

(a) $\begin{pmatrix} 2 & 1 \\ 3 & 4 \end{pmatrix}$
(b) $\begin{pmatrix} 1 & -5 \\ -1 & 3 \end{pmatrix}$

(c) $\begin{pmatrix} -1 & 3 \\ 2 & -6 \end{pmatrix}$

(d) $\begin{pmatrix} 1 & 2 & -1 \\ -3 & 1 & -1 \\ 4 & 2 & 2 \end{pmatrix}$

(e) $\begin{pmatrix} 3 & -1 & 2 \\ 1 & 2 & 1 \\ 1 & 1 & -1 \end{pmatrix}$

(f) $\begin{pmatrix} -2 & 2 & 1 \\ -3 & -1 & -1 \\ 1 & 2 & 2 \end{pmatrix}$.

8.6 Axioms for matrix algebra

All of the operations, definitions, and properties described above pertaining to the algebra of matrices satisfy the set of axioms given below. We have used a similar set of axioms in the study of set theory; the student will notice that the names of the axioms or "laws" are for the most part identical. We recall that an axiom is a statement which is true by definition, and represents the starting point for constructing an algebra. Since we have already described the operations of matrix algebra, these axioms should serve to reinforce the student's understanding of these operations. It is not necessary that the axioms be memorized. However, they must be meaningful to the student, and he is encouraged to learn the names of these laws, as they are basic to most systems of mathematics.

Axiom 8.6.1: *The Associative Laws*

$$(A + B) + C = A + (B + C)$$
$$A(BC) = (AB)C$$

Assuming that A, B, and C are of such order that they can be combined by addition and multiplication, it makes no difference which we combine first. These laws do not give license to change the arrangement of the matrices, however.

Axiom 8.6.2: *The Commutative Law*

$$A + B = B + A$$

Assuming again that A and B are of the same order, it makes no difference how we arrange them for addition. Combined with Axiom 8.6.1, we see that the process of adding matrices is indifferent to the arrangement of the matrices. This is generally untrue, of course, in the multiplication of matrices; thus the commutative law is silent on this point.

Axiom 8.6.3: *The Distributive Laws*

$$(\alpha + \beta)A = \alpha A + \beta A$$
$$\alpha(A + B) = \alpha A + \alpha B$$
$$C(A + B) = (CA) + (CB)$$
$$\alpha(AB) = (\alpha A)B = A(\alpha B)$$

These laws define equivalent operations for multiplying matrices by scalars and/or multiplying a matrix on the sum of two matrices. Note that we never change the arrangement defining the multiplication of two matrices (except as allowed below).

Axiom 8.6.4: *The Identity Laws*

$$A + O = A$$
$$AI = IA = A$$

This axiom defines the identity elements in addition and multiplication, i.e., the zero matrix and the identity matrix. Note that the second law provides an exception to the non-comutativity of matrices in multiplication.

Axiom 8.6.5: *The Inverse Laws*

$$A + (-A) = O$$
$$AA^{-1} = A^{-1}A = I$$

The first law merely states that if there is a matrix A, we can define a matrix $-A$ such that their sum is the zero matrix. The second law follows the argument given previously concerning the inverse matrix, and also provides an exception to the commutative law. This law of course assumes that A does have an inverse A^{-1}.

As mentioned previously, a matrix which has no inverse is said to be *singular*. All non-square matrices are singular, for they do not have identity matrices, a necessary and sufficient condition for the existence of the inverse. This does not mean that all square matrices have inverses, however; for example, see Exercise 8.5.1c. Note that if the first row is multiplied by -2, it is then identical to the second row. It is thus impossible to find an inverse matrix in this example by row operations, since the ensuing subtraction will generate a row of zeros without developing the 1 on the main diagonal. In such a matrix, the rows are said to be *linear combinations* of each other, or to be *linearly dependent*. This condition exists whenever we may combine rows by the allowable operations (i.e., multiplying a row by a number, or adding rows together) to generate one of the original rows in the system from other rows. Conversely, in a *non*-singular matrix, the rows are *linearly independent*, and row operations will generate the desired identity or inverse matrices. In the next section, where matrix methods are used to solve simultaneous systems of equations, the correspondence between singular matrices and degenerate linear systems should become clear.

8.6 Exercises

8.6.1 Show that each of the axioms holds for the following matrices and scalars:

$$A = \begin{pmatrix} -4 & 3 \\ 2 & -5 \end{pmatrix}; B = \begin{pmatrix} 2 & -9 \\ 9 & 16 \end{pmatrix}; C = \begin{pmatrix} 1 & -4 \\ 3 & 1 \end{pmatrix}; \alpha = 2; \beta = -3.$$

(Of course, the matrices A, B, and C used in the axioms represent any matrices whose order allows the operation called for, and similarly for the scalars.)

8.7 Solution of simultaneous systems by matrix methods

One of the most useful applications of matrix algebra is in the solution of simultaneous systems, especially when there are many equations in many unknowns (variables). The technique is tedious when performed by hand, but it provides a simple solution method for high-speed digital computing equipment, and a very handy notation for dealing with problems of administration which can be set up in matrix form. Follow carefully the following argument, checking each step to make sure that its development is understood: suppose we are told to find the solution of the linear system

$$3x_1 + 2x_2 = 4$$
$$2x_1 - x_2 = -1.$$

Now the solution to this system is the ordered pair of numbers x_1 and x_2, which we write as a column vector $\begin{pmatrix} x_1 \\ x_2 \end{pmatrix}$, or simply the vector x. If the coefficients of x_1 and x_2 are written as the matrix A, and the right-hand side of the system is written as the column vector b, then we see that this linear system can be written as the matrix equation $Ax = b$:

$$A = \begin{pmatrix} 3 & 2 \\ 2 & -1 \end{pmatrix}; \; x = \begin{pmatrix} x_1 \\ x_2 \end{pmatrix}; \; b = \begin{pmatrix} 4 \\ -1 \end{pmatrix}; \begin{pmatrix} 3 & 2 \\ 2 & -1 \end{pmatrix}\begin{pmatrix} x_1 \\ x_2 \end{pmatrix} = \begin{pmatrix} 4 \\ -1 \end{pmatrix}.$$

The student should perform the matrix multiplication indicated to show that $Ax = b$ is indeed the original system.

Now A and b are known in this equation; we must somehow solve this equation for the vector x, whose values will provide us with the solution to the system. If our equation were a simple algebraic one, we would solve for x by dividing both sides of the equation by A; however, we have not defined the operation of matrix division, which, indeed, does not exist. But all is not lost; we recall the properties of the inverse matrix, such that any matrix when multiplied by its inverse produces the identity matrix, and in turn, any matrix multiplied by the identity matrix provides the original matrix as a result of the multiplication. We solve this matrix equation by applying the axioms given in Section 8.6, first multiplying both sides of the equation by the inverse of A:

$$A^{-1}(Ax) = A^{-1}b; \text{ by the Associative Law,}$$

$$(A^{-1}A)x = A^{-1}b; \text{ by the Inverse Law,}$$

$$Ix = A^{-1}b; \text{ and thus by the Identity Law,}$$

$$x = A^{-1}b.$$

The solution vector for any simultaneous system can therefore be found (if it exists) by (1) inverting the matrix of coefficients A, and (2) multiplying this inverse A^{-1} on the right-hand side vector b.

For our example above, we invert A:

$$A^{-1} = \begin{pmatrix} \frac{1}{7} & \frac{2}{7} \\ \frac{2}{7} & -\frac{3}{7} \end{pmatrix}.$$

We multiply on b:

$$\begin{pmatrix} \frac{1}{7} & \frac{2}{7} \\ \frac{2}{7} & -\frac{3}{7} \end{pmatrix}\begin{pmatrix} 4 \\ -1 \end{pmatrix} = \begin{pmatrix} (\frac{4}{7}) - (\frac{2}{7}) \\ (\frac{8}{7}) + (\frac{3}{7}) \end{pmatrix} = \begin{pmatrix} \frac{2}{7} \\ 1\frac{4}{7} \end{pmatrix} = x.$$

This can be verified by substituting in the original matrix equation.

In the example above we assume that the inverse of the matrix had been found, presumably by the Gaussian method. It is possible, by the same method, to develop the solution vector along with the inverse. Indeed, this method provides the means for finding the solution vector without having to find the inverse at all. Let us see how this is done. If we write a partitioned matrix of part of our original system as

$(A|I|b)$, then multiply each of the partitions by the inverse of A, we develop the partitioned matrix $(A^{-1}A|A^{-1}I|A^{-1}b)$. But $A^{-1}A = I$, and $A^{-1}I = A^{-1}$, and $A^{-1}b = x$, which we found above. Therefore we have transformed $(A|I|b)$ into $(I|A^{-1}|x)$. The method of row and column operations is merely extended to include the added partition b, which is transformed into x, the desired solution vector.

Finally, we see that it is not necessary to find the inverse of A in the transformation process, since we can check the solution equally well by proving that $Ax = b$. That is, if we transform $(A|b)$ into $(I|x)$, we find the solution vector x without finding A^{-1}. Let us apply this method to our problem, remembering that the steps followed are arbitrary, and in this instance we perform more operations than are necessary merely to reduce the number of fractions in the transformations. *Example:*

$$(A|b) = \begin{pmatrix} 3 & 2 & 4 \\ 2 & -1 & -1 \end{pmatrix} \xrightarrow[\substack{(2)\text{I}\\(3)\text{II}}]{} \begin{pmatrix} 6 & 4 & 8 \\ 6 & -3 & -3 \end{pmatrix} \xrightarrow[\text{II}-\text{I}]{} \begin{pmatrix} 6 & 4 & 8 \\ 0 & -7 & -11 \end{pmatrix}$$

$$\xrightarrow[\substack{(\frac{1}{6})\text{I}\\(-\frac{1}{7})\text{II}}]{} \begin{pmatrix} 1 & \frac{2}{3} & \frac{4}{3} \\ 0 & 1 & 1\frac{4}{7} \end{pmatrix} \xrightarrow[]{\text{I}-(\frac{2}{3})\text{II}} \begin{pmatrix} 1 & 0 & \frac{2}{7} \\ 0 & 1 & 1\frac{4}{7} \end{pmatrix} = (I|x).$$

8.7 Exercises

8.7.1 Set up the following linear systems in partitioned matrix form $(A|I|b)$ and develop the *inverse matrix* and the *solution vector*. Check the inverse matrix by multiplying it on the matrix of coefficients; and check the solution vector to make sure that it satisfies the original system, i.e., that $Ax = b$.

(a) $\quad x_1 + 2x_2 = 3$
$\quad\quad 2x_1 \quad\; x_2 = 1$

(b) $\; -3x_1 + 2x_2 = -2$
$\quad\quad\; x_1 - \; x_2 = \frac{5}{6}$

(c) $\; x_1 \quad\quad = 1$
$\quad\quad x_2 \quad = 2$
$\quad\quad\quad\; x_3 = 3.$

8.7.2 Solve the following systems by transforming $(A|b) \to (I|x)$. Check solution by showing that $Ax = b$.

(a) $\; -x_1 + \; x_2 - \; x_3 = 0$
$\quad\quad 2x_1 - \; x_2 + 2x_3 = 0$
$\quad\quad 2x_1 - 2x_2 + \; x_3 = 0$

(b) $\; x_1 + x_2 \quad\quad = 3$
$\quad\quad\quad\; x_2 + x_3 = 5$
$\quad\; x_1 \quad\quad + x_3 = 4.$

8.7.3 As a small bakery operator whose output consists solely of pies, cakes, rolls, and cookies, you realize that you have not used your raw materials inventory properly because a lot of it has spoiled before it could be used. Therefore, you would like to know what combination of pies (x_1), cakes (x_2), rolls (x_3), and cookies (x_4), you should bake in order to use up your available inventory of materials. This inventory consists of milk, flour, sugar, and shortening; the following things are known about the baking process and the inventory:

YOUR BAKERY—SCHEDULE OF INPUTS PER UNIT OF OUTPUT

Outputs \\ Inputs	Pies	Cakes	Rolls	Cookies	Total Inventory Available for Use
Milk	0.25 qt.	0.15 qt.	0.25 qt.	0.10 qt.	11 qt.
Flour	0.5 lb.	0.5 lb.	2.0 lb.	1.0 lb.	55 lb.
Sugar	0.5 lb.	0.5 lb.	0.5 lb.	0.5 lb.	30 lb.
Shortening	0.25 lb.	0.25 lb.	0.25 lb.	0.5 lb.	20 lb.

(a) Construct the linear system expressing the above problem.
(b) Construct the partitioned matrix $(A|I|b)$.
(c) Transform the matrix to develop the inverse of A and the solution vector.
(d) Check both the inverse matrix and solution vector.

Chapter 9 ——————— Linear Programming

9.1 Concepts and assumptions

One of the most important elements of the economic process is the conversion of resources from one form to another. The conversion of iron ore into steel and steel into automobiles, of crude oil into gasoline, of raw chemicals into myriad products for both producers and consumers, of goods in a warehouse into goods on a retailer's shelves, of unproductive labor into productive labor, of savings into useful, productive capital; all of these are examples of conversion. It is not surprising to find that practically every economic unit in an advanced industrial society is faced with decisions concerning the "best" way to effect such conversions. The industrial decision maker will find many resources available to him, in varying amounts and at varying costs and with varying efficiencies in terms of their ability to accomplish a given task. There are various ways in which these resources can be combined into potentially many products, and these outputs are assigned varying values in the market place. The task of determining which products should be produced, which processes should be used to produce them, and which resources should be combined in the processes chosen, can be quite formidable when one is searching for the one "best" way to accomplish the task. For instance, a manufacturer who produces only three products, using four machines on which each of these products may be made, and using any or all of five raw materials, finds that there is a minimum of sixty decision alternatives available to him (3 × 4 × 5), assuming that he will produce only one of the products.   Should the manufacturer decide to produce more than one product, then the number of decision alternatives could conceivably become very large indeed.   Under certain assumptions (linearity), such problems can be solved by the method of *linear programming*.

The decisions surrounding this general and complex problem are made within the framework of what is called "input-output" analysis in Economic Theory, economics itself being the science of the allocation of scarce resources towards the satisfaction of man's unlimited wants. The individual businessman takes it upon himself to try to satisfy some of these wants, and to do so in such a way as to be paid for his effort. This payment we call *profit*, and for the moment we will consider it to be the sole motivating force, the primary and only objective of the decision maker.   Our astute businessman will make decisions concerning the resources which he uses, and the manner in which he uses them, in such a way as to make the most possible profit, i.e., maximize profit. Since profit is the difference between cost and revenue (see Section 7.3), the businessman may maximize this difference by minimizing costs and maximizing revenue; as to the latter, however, the businessman very seldom knows exactly how many of a given product he will sell and generally has only limited control of this factor.   However, the number of items to be produced or stocked for sale is determined by him alone, and thus the total cost of producing the items, within certain given limits, will be determined by him.   These production decisions are motivated by the desire to minimize costs, and thus a very common linear programming problem is one that provides a solution which minimizes cost, assuming that there are minimum limits to how many of the items must be produced.   (The total cost will be zero when none at all are produced, barring the presence of fixed costs; but we must remember that the purpose of economic endeavor is to realize a profit, which requires that we have something to sell.)

A suitable definition of linear programming for our purposes is the maximization or minimization of a *linear objective function* subject to *linear constraints*.   In other words, if we have a problem the solution to which can be stated as the maximum or minimum of the sum of a number of variables which are related linearly, and where combinations of these variables are restricted within a range of given values according to a linear relationship, then this solution can be found by linear programming techniques.   An example will assist in making the terminology clear.

As a builder of houses, you realize a profit of $800 per house on each frame house which you sell, $1000 on a concrete block house, and $1200 on a brick house, these being the only types which you build.   Your objective is to make as much money as possible on all of the homes which you build. Thus we can state your objective function mathematically:

$$\pi = f(x_1, x_2, x_3) = \$800x_1 + \$1000x_2 + \$1200x_3,$$

where x_1 is the number of frame houses which you build, x_2 the number of concrete block houses, and x_3 the number of brick houses. We note that this is a linear function, and that if the number of houses to be built were respectively two, three, and one, our profit would be $\$800(2) + \$1000(3) + \$1200(1) = \$5800$. This function as it stands will of course be maximized by building an infinite number of houses, but since our resources are limited, and in addition have differing costs, we realize that there must be some finite solution (x_1, x_2, x_3) such that no other solution gives a greater value for the objective function and that satisfies the constraints imposed upon the resources.

Let us examine what we mean by *constraints* upon a problem. It is not generally considered feasible to build a frame house completely out of wood, nor is it feasible to build a brick house completely of bricks. Each of the products which we plan to produce "competes" with the other products for each of the available resources; the *substitutability* of these resources in the production of our various products is one of the salient features of linear programming, since it provides us with alternative uses concerning which we must make our decisions. Were this not the case, i.e., if the frame house required only lumber, the brick house only bricks, etc., the problem would become trivial: the decision would be to make as many of each house as one had resources available. However, since lumber (for instance) is required in each of the houses, we must make judicious use of it by assuring that it is applied where it will return the greatest profit.

An additional constraint common to all linear programming problems is that the variables themselves must not be negative, i.e., take on negative values. Since we shall be dealing with problems similar to those faced in real life, this constraint should appear to be neither arbitrary nor confining; it is difficult to conceive of "negative" houses, for instance.

Finally, we should understand the meaning of *linearity* as it applies to the linear programming problem. We *assume* that the relationships existing among all of the variables in our problem are *linear*. It has already been pointed out that the objective function is linear; we must also set up the constraints on the problem as a linear system. We shall reserve discussion of the method of doing this for the example in Section 9.2.

Before we look at the example, however, let us reiterate the important elements of a linear programming problem, so that what we are looking for and the conditions under which we can find "it" by linear programming techniques will be well understood. The solution to a linear programming problem consists of the *set* of numerical values (each value corresponding to one of the outputs or inputs with which we are concerned) that maximizes or minimizes our objective function. (This set is a vector, as the student may have already noticed.) In plain terms, we are looking for "how many" of each of our possible outputs we should produce in order to make the most money, or suffer the least cost. In addition, the resources to be used in our production process can be used in different ways among the products, and these resources are in limited supply. Finally, the relationships among the variables, both in the objective function and in the system of constraints, are stated in linear form.

9.1   Exercise

9.1.1   List, in addition to those examples given in the text, five examples of conversion of inputs into outputs through some *production, marketing, financial,* or *organizational* process. Try to think of a real-life situation for each of the four areas, within your understanding of these terms. Also state how you think decisions are made concerning the inputs used, the nature of the process itself, and the type or number of outputs to be realized from the process.

9.2   A tabular solution technique

Let us continue the example of our building contractor, making the simplification that we will build only frame houses (x_1) or brick houses (x_2), and assume that our main purpose in being in business is to maximize profit. Our objective function is therefore

$$\pi = f(x_1, x_2) = \$800x_1 + \$1200x_2.$$

Suppose that we must build at least three frame houses and two brick houses in the area being developed; these constraints can be written $x_1 \geq 3$ and $x_2 \geq 2$. If this were all the houses which we built, our profit would be

$$\pi = \$800(3) + \$1200(2) = \$4800,$$

where the solution vector could be written: $\begin{pmatrix} 3 \\ 2 \end{pmatrix}$. We write the solution vector as a column vector for reasons that will become clear later; note that this follows our usual procedure as established in Chapter 8.

The upper limits to the number of houses which can be built are established by the resources available for making each of the types of houses; we shall assume that the relevant resources are cement, construction lumber, finishing lumber, man-hours, and bricks. The table (Fig. 9.2.1) indicates how much of each of these resources is required by *one* of each type of house, and also how much of each resource is available for use. The first line of the table, for instance, indicates that a frame house requires 20 bags of cement, a brick house 35 bags, and that we have 280 bags of cement available. From this table it is now possible to construct our system of constraints, each of which will be a linear inequation, since we may use *not more than* the amount available, although it is not necessary to use *exactly* the amount available. Thus the cement constraint has the form $20x_1 + 35x_2 \leq 280$.

Resource	House Type		Amount Available
	Frame	Brick	
I. Cement (bags)	20	35	280
II. Construction Lumber (bd. ft.)	6,000	5,000	60,000
III. Finish Lumber (bd. ft.)	1,000	500	9,000
IV. Man-hours	500	500	6,000
V. Bricks	0	4,000	24,000

Fig. 9.2.1. All figures are hypothetical.

Let us take note of some of the ways in which we can solve our problem if we consider only this one restriction. If we produce no brick houses, then we have sufficient cement for 14 frame houses; if we produce no frame houses, then we have enough cement for 8 brick houses. Since our problem requires that we build at least 3 frame and 2 brick houses, we should like to know whether we have sufficient cement for this combination. Three frame houses will require 60 bags, and 2 brick houses will require 70 bags, for a total requirement of 130 bags; we thus have sufficient cement for the minimum output required.

We can now write this linear programming problem in *standard form*, showing first the objective function and then listing the constraints within which we must search for the optimum ("best") solution:

Maximize: $\pi = \$800x_1 + \$1200x_2$

Subject to:
$$
\begin{array}{rlrcr}
\text{I} & 20x_1 + & 35x_2 & \leq & 280 \\
\text{II} & 6{,}000x_1 + & 5{,}000x_2 & \leq & 60{,}000 \\
\text{III} & 1{,}000x_1 + & 500x_2 & \leq & 9{,}000 \\
\text{IV} & 500x_1 + & 500x_2 & \leq & 6{,}000 \\
\text{V} & & 4{,}000x_2 & \leq & 24{,}000 \\
\text{VI} & x_1 & & \geq & 3 \\
\text{VII} & & x_2 & \geq & 2.
\end{array}
$$

This simple problem in two variables can be solved by a simple although tedious numerical process, i.e., by trial and error; we shall first use this method since many of the concepts discussed should become clear through this basic technique.

We recall that our problem is a decision problem: we are faced with a number of alternatives (combinations of frame and brick houses), one (or some) of which will result in the optimum solution in terms of maximizing profit. Let us therefore construct another table (Fig. 9.2.2) which will show these alternatives and the result of choosing one of the possible combinations available to us. Along the top of the table appear the alternative quantities (x_1) of frame houses; along the side are the alternatives (x_2) of brick houses. Note that only "whole" houses are considered; an unfinished or "fractional" house is assumed to be not saleable. Entered in the body of the table are the *payoffs* in terms of profit which will be realized by choosing a given combination as indicated by the intersection of a row and a column. Our minimum solution $\binom{3}{2}$ is thus found in the upper left-hand corner of the table: $4800. We do not show any alternative combinations less than the minimum since they are not *admissible;* we are constrained to produce

x_2 \ x_1	3	4	5	6	7	8
2	4,800	5,600	6,400	7,200	8,000	8,800
3	6,000	6,800	7,600	8,400	9,200	10,000
4	7,200	8,000	8,800	9,600	10,400	11,200
5	8,400	9,200	10,000	10,800	11,600	12,400
6	9,600	10,400	11,200	12,000	12,800	13,600

Fig. 9.2.2

at least this many, if we are to produce any at all. The table is truncated at the upper ends as well, for the following reasons: if we produce 2 brick houses, we must use 1000 board feet of finish lumber in their construction, leaving 8000 board feet available for frame house construction. Since each frame house requires 1000 board feet of this resource, and we have already committed ourselves to the 2 brick houses, we can build a maximum of 8 frame houses. To build any more frame houses would result in an *unfeasible* solution to the problem, since we would necessarily violate one or more of the constraints. A *feasible* solution is one that satisfies all the constraints.

Since there are only 24,000 bricks available and each brick house requires 4000 bricks, we also see that we are constrained to a maximum of 6 brick houses. If we build these 6 brick houses, we want to know if there are sufficient other resources available as well (since the 6 brick houses will also use cement, lumber, and man-hours) to build the minimum required number of frame houses i.e., 3. To determine whether $\binom{3}{6}$ is a *feasible* solution, i.e., whether it satisfies all of the constraints, we must test these values in the system of constraints to be sure that none of the constraints is violated. Try $x_1 = 3$, $x_2 = 6$:

$$
\begin{aligned}
\text{I} \qquad 20\,(3) + 36\,(6) &\overset{?}{\lessgtr} 280 \\
60 + 210 &\overset{?}{\leq} 280 \\
270 &< 280;\ \text{OK}
\end{aligned}
$$

$$
\begin{aligned}
\text{II} \qquad 6000\,(3) + 5000\,(6) &\overset{?}{\lessgtr} 60{,}000 \\
18{,}000 + 30{,}000 &\overset{?}{\leq} 60{,}000 \\
48{,}000 &< 60{,}000;\ \text{OK}
\end{aligned}
$$

$$
\begin{aligned}
\text{III} \qquad 1000\,(3) + 500\,(6) &\overset{?}{\lessgtr} 9000 \\
3000 + 3000 &\overset{?}{\leq} 9000 \\
6000 &< 9000;\ \text{OK}
\end{aligned}
$$

$$
\begin{aligned}
\text{IV} \qquad 500\,(3) + 500\,(6) &\overset{?}{\lessgtr} 6000 \\
1500 + 3000 &\overset{?}{\leq} 6000 \\
4500 &< 6000;\ \text{OK}
\end{aligned}
$$

$$
\begin{aligned}
\text{V} \qquad 4000\,(6) &\overset{?}{\leq} 24{,}000 \\
24{,}000 &\equiv 24{,}000;\ \text{OK}
\end{aligned}
$$

$$
\begin{aligned}
\text{VI} \qquad 3 &\overset{?}{\geq} 3; \\
3 &\equiv 3;\ \text{OK}
\end{aligned}
$$

$$
\begin{aligned}
\text{VII} \qquad 6 &\overset{?}{\geq} 2 \\
6 &> 2;\ \text{OK}.
\end{aligned}
$$

Every constraint is satisfied by the solution $\binom{3}{6}$, and it is therefore *feasible.* In addition, we know that $\binom{3}{5}$, $\binom{3}{4}$, $\binom{3}{3}$, and $\binom{3}{2}$ must be feasible, since they will each require less of our resources than $\binom{3}{6}$, and thus they must necessarily satisfy the constraints, too. However, since these solutions necessarily result in lower profit (see Fig. 9.2.2) they cannot possibly be optimum, and we therefore ignore them. We now wish to know whether or not $\binom{3}{6}$ is the best possible combination. This alternative would result in a profit of $9600, but as we scan Fig. 9.2.2 we notice higher profit opportunities of which we might avail ourselves, *if* they are feasible. We should note here that the *intuitive* (or "seat-of-the-pants") solution would be to build as many brick houses as possible, i.e., 6, since they return the higher profit per house, and then build frame houses with whatever resources are left over. However, we shall see that this intuitive solution is not the optimum.

Let us try $\binom{4}{6}$, for which we would make $10,400. As we look back at our first trial and error operation, we notice that there is considerable slack in each of the resources except cement. Our solution $\binom{3}{6}$ used all but 10 bags of cement; if we were to add another frame house, which requires 20 additional bags of cement, we would need 290 bags, thus violating that constraint. Therefore, $\binom{4}{6}$ is not feasible, nor are any of the other combinations using 6 brick houses.

Since $\binom{4}{5}$ would result in a lower profit than $\binom{3}{6}$, we will not bother to test it for feasibility (although it is feasible and the student should verify that fact). Let us examine $\binom{5}{5}$, which would result in a profit of $10,000; this combination requires 275 bags of cement, 5500 board feet of construction lumber, 7500 board feet of finish lumber, 5000 man-hours, and 20,000 bricks; all of the constraints are satisfied, including the minimum output required. Therefore $\binom{5}{5}$ is the best solution so far, since it results in a profit $400 greater than $\binom{3}{6}$. Now $\binom{6}{5}$ is even better; but we note that once again the cement constraint would be violated, and therefore $\binom{6}{5}$ and all of the alternatives to the right in that row in Fig. 9.2.2 must be excluded as not feasible. Further examination shows that $\binom{6}{4}$, $\binom{7}{3}$, and $\binom{8}{2}$ are feasible (the student should verify this), but the combinations to the right of each of these possibilities in the table are not feasible (verify this, also). Since each of these combinations results in a profit lower than that attainable by the solution $\binom{5}{5}$, we see that the objective function is maximized when we build 5 frame and 5 brick houses; therefore, this should be our decision.

The solutions $\binom{3}{6}$, $\binom{4}{5}$, $\binom{5}{5}$, $\binom{6}{4}$, $\binom{7}{3}$, and $\binom{8}{2}$ are called *boundary solutions*, since one or more of them may be the optimum solution; any combinations lying to the right of any of them in the same row are not feasible, and those lying to the left result in a lower profit. Therefore, once we establish the boundary solutions, we need only to choose that boundary solution which maximizes the objective function. Although there are 19 feasible solutions in this problem, only the 6 boundary solutions really need to be examined for optimality; therefore it usually saves time to determine the boundary of feasible solutions *before* the payoffs are calculated. The profit payoffs are then calculated only for the boundary solutions, since the other feasible solutions, known as *interior* feasible solutions, can never be optimum.

Although this technique is tedious, especially for a problem of a practical size, and impossible for a problem where the variables are continuous rather than discrete, the student should be able to develop a "feel" for the concept of substitutability of resources, as well as some of the nomenclature of linear programming, by working carefully through the example and the following exercises.

9.2 Exercises

9.2.1 Being careful to show all of your work, complete the example given in the text, by verifying that each of the combinations to the right of a boundary solution in the same row, or below the boundary solution in the same column, is not feasible. In addition, check an interior point (solution) to show that it cannot be optimum.

9.2.2 If the profit on each of the houses were $1000, find the optimum solution.

9.2.3 Note that in the original example, the combinations $\binom{3}{6}$ and $\binom{6}{4}$ result in the same profit payoff. In a real situation, if these were both optimum, which combination would you likely choose? (*Hint:* Consider man-hours.)

9.3 The graphic method for two-variable linear programming problems

A much more direct method than the tabular technique is available for problems involving only two variables. It is true that a problem in so few variables may be all but trivial in a real-life situation; yet the graphic solution technique serves to strengthen understanding of the basic linear programming concepts and in addition provides an even more intuitive insight into the power of linear programming itself.

Because the constraints upon a linear programming problem are usually expressed as linear inequations, the graphic method obviously requires us to understand how to graph a linear inequation. We recall that the solution set of an inequation in two variables is the set of ordered pairs satisfying the inequation, and that these pairs will graph as points in the solution space of the problem. This set will be similar to the interval representing the graph of an inequation in one variable (see Section 6.3) except that in two variables, this interval becomes a bounded "area" in the two-space plane defined by the range and domain. The method for graphing a linear inequation consists of two steps: (1) the step of converting the inequation to an equation, and drawing the graph of the equation, and (2) the step of observing whether the full solution set of the inequation, i.e., the points in the solution space, lie above or below (or to the right or left of) the graph of the equation.

The method is illustrated in Fig. 9.3.1*a* and *b*. In *a* we graph the linear inequation $2x + 3y \leq 18$; the corresponding linear equation in standard form is $y = 6 - \frac{2}{3}x$, which can be readily graphed. We then choose any point not on the line; if the coordinates of the point satisfy the inequation, then all of the points on the same side of the line as the point chosen will also satisfy the inequation. We indicate the graph of the inequation by drawing an arrow at a right angle to the line, pointing to the space containing the points in the solution set. For example, we choose the origin, (0, 0), and then test the inequation with these values: $2(0) + 3(0) \overset{?}{\leq} 18$; $0 < 18$. The origin is an element of the solution set of the inequation, and the *half-space* "below" the line (and including it) is the graph of the inequation. In *b*, we graph $y - 5x \geq 10$, the associated equation of which is $y = 10 + 5x$.

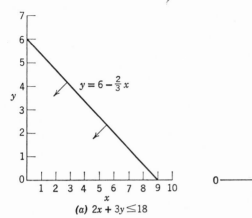

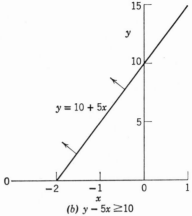

Fig. 9.3.1

Choosing the origin as our test point again: $0 - 5(0) \overset{?}{\geq} 10; 0 \not\geq 10;$ **the** origin is not an element of the solution set of the inequation, nor therefore are any points "below" (or to the right of) the line. The solution space of the inequation must therefore lie "above" or to the left of the line, and including the line, as indicated by the arrows.

We shall continue to use the example set forth in Section 9.2; let us graph the constraint upon the amount of cement available, the inequation for which is $20x_1 + 35x_2 \leq 280$. The first step is to determine the graph of $20x_1 + 35x_2 = 280$. Two of the points on this line are found where the line crosses the axes, and we find that when $x_1 = 0$, $x_2 = 8$, establishing the point $\begin{pmatrix} 0 \\ 8 \end{pmatrix}$. When $x_2 = 0$, $x_1 = 14$, establishing the point $\begin{pmatrix} 14 \\ 0 \end{pmatrix}$. These two points are plotted in Fig. 9.3.2, and the linear equation is graphed by a straight line drawn through them. (Note that we continue with the column vector notation as established in Section 9.2; previously we had designated a point in two-space by a row vector (x_1, x_2) rather than the column vector $\begin{pmatrix} x_1 \\ x_2 \end{pmatrix}$. This change is strictly a mechanical one in keeping with the algebra of vectors, and we shall see its importance in the next section.)

We know that it is not necessary to use all of the cement available, however; our constraint merely tells us that we may not use *more than* 280 bags. In Fig. 9.3.3 we reflect this fact by indicating all of those

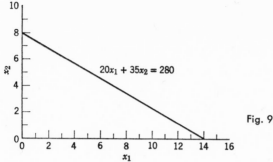

Fig. 9.3.2. x_1 = No. of frame houses
x_2 = No. of brick houses.

points which satisfy the inequation, which are all of the points on and below the line. Since it is not possible to build a negative number of houses, we have in addition restricted the graph to the first quadrant, i.e., $x_1 \geq 0$ and $x_2 \geq 0$. The student should now verify that any combination of houses $\begin{pmatrix} x_1 \\ x_2 \end{pmatrix}$ on the boundaries or within them in Fig. 9.3.3 can be built with the available cement (including unfinished or fractional houses). Our problem, however, requires that we build at least 3 frame houses, or $x_1 \geq 3$, and at least 2 brick houses, or $x_2 \geq 2$; these minimum constraints are shown in Fig. 9.3.4. Finally, we realize that an unfinished or partial house is not marketable (at least in this problem), and therefore we must restrict the range and domain of our variables to integers, indicated in Fig. 9.3.4 by the *points* encircled. Each of the points encircled now represents a feasible solution to the problem only with respect to the cement and minimum constraints; there are 23 of these points, as can be determined by counting them. Now suppose for a moment that these were the only

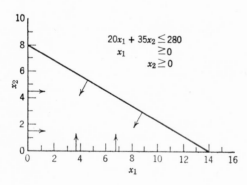

Fig. 9.3.3. x_1 = No. of frame houses
x_2 = No. of brick houses.

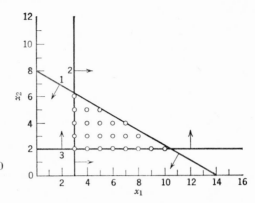

Fig. 9.3.4. (1) $20x_1 + 35x_2 \leq 280$
(2) $\quad x_1 \qquad \geq 3$
(3) $\qquad\qquad x_2 \geq 2$.

constraints upon the problem, and ignore the other constraints momentarily. The points which we have now found to satisfy these three constraints comprise what is called the *feasible solution space;* all we need to do now is to find that point or set of points which maximizes the objective function,

$$\pi = 800x_1 + 1200x_2.$$

This function determines a *family* of lines, since there are many lines (an indefinitely large number of them, in fact) which satisfy this expression.

In Fig. 9.3.5 some of these lines are plotted. We note that they all have the same slope, and that the equation defining each of them differs only by the amount of profit realized from producing any of the

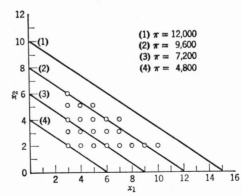

Fig. 9.3.5. Some members of the family of lines satisfying $\pi = 800x_1 + 1200x_2$.

combinations of houses, i.e., $\begin{pmatrix} x_1 \\ x_2 \end{pmatrix}$, lying upon the line. We note also that as the line is shifted out from the origin, profit increases. To maximize profit in the graphic sense, then, means that we wish to "push" the line representing the objective function as far out from the origin as possible, but still within the solution space. Since the boundary of the solution space is also in the space, it can be seen that our optimum solution will be found at the intersection of the boundary of the solution space and that graph of the objective function which is as

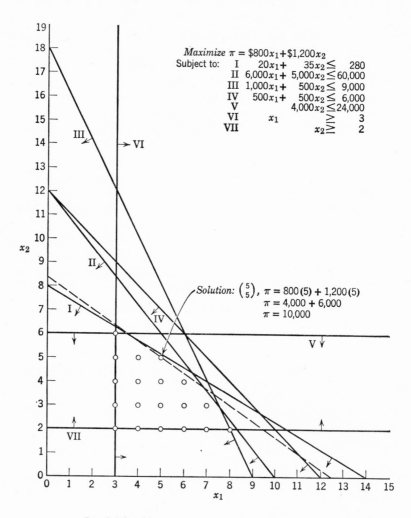

Maximize $\pi = \$800x_1 + \$1,200x_2$

Subject to:
I $20x_1 + 35x_2 \leq 280$
II $6,000x_1 + 5,000x_2 \leq 60,000$
III $1,000x_1 + 500x_2 \leq 9,000$
IV $500x_1 + 500x_2 \leq 6,000$
V $4,000x_2 \leq 24,000$
VI $x_1 \geq 3$
VII $x_2 \geq 2$

Solution: $\begin{pmatrix} 5 \\ 5 \end{pmatrix}$, $\pi = 800(5) + 1,200(5)$
$\pi = 4,000 + 6,000$
$\pi = 10,000$

Fig. 9.3.6. Linear programming graphic solution.

far out as the objective function can be "pushed" and still pass through a point in the solution space. In effect, as we move the objective function out in this truncated problem of few constraints, we see that there are *two* points through which the line passes, both providing the optimum solution: $\binom{10}{2}$ and $\binom{7}{4}$. Observing the cement constraint only and producing either 10 frame and 2 brick houses, or 7 frame and 4 brick houses (but no other combinations), we obtain an optimum profit of \$10,400.

The appearance of two (or more) optimum solutions should not be unexpected in the solution of linear programming problems, and in fact it is often a hoped-for result. For we have set up the maximization of profit as our sole decision criterion; but what if we really enjoyed building brick houses more than building frame houses? In this case, we may now add another decision criterion; our multiple solution allows us to attain two goals, profit maximization and "enjoyment" of our work, without sacrificing either! There is, of course, a limit to the number of such solutions in terms of practicality: our original purpose in casting our problems in linear programming terms is to make a relatively simple decision out of what may originally be an almost incomprehensible problem. If we have not appreciably reduced the number of decision alternatives in a problem through the application of a technique as arduous as the linear programming technique, then perhaps the technique should be critically reappraised.

Now let us add the other constraints on the problem, as shown in Fig. 9.3.6. We notice that the feasible solution space becomes more limited as the constraints are added, as we would expect, and that the total number of feasible solutions is reduced to nineteen! (Cf. Section 9.2.) Since $\binom{10}{2}$ and $\binom{7}{4}$ are solutions to the cement problem only, and are no longer in the solution space for the entire problem, we must shift the objective function back until it intersects the new point, or points, furthest out in the solution space. We find that this point is $\binom{5}{5}$, the same solution arrived at by the tabular technique.

9.3   Exercises

(*Note:* Problems 1–6 apply to the example in the text.)

9.3.1   If frame houses were equally as profitable as brick houses, what would be the optimum solution (i.e., what decision should be made)? Reconstruct the graphic solution as shown in Fig. 9.3.5 and show how you arrived at this answer. Draw in only the feasible solution space (its boundaries).

9.3.2 Under what conditions would the intuitive solution $\begin{pmatrix} 3 \\ 6 \end{pmatrix}$ be the optimum solution? Indicate this condition on your graph, and state your answer in terms of the slope of the profit function.

9.3.3 Under what conditions would the solution $\begin{pmatrix} 8 \\ 2 \end{pmatrix}$ be *unique* and optimum? Indicate graphically and in terms of the slope of the profit function.

9.3.4 What do you notice about the man-hour constraint? What would be the best decision if there were only 5000 man-hours available? 4000 man-hours available?

9.3.5 How much of each resource will be used by the optimum decision?

9.3.6 If we were allowed to build fractional houses, what would the solution be? Show graphically and determine algebraically by the Gaussian method. (The student should now notice why we write the solution vector as a column vector.)

9.3.7 As production superintendent of the Waukesha Widget Works, you face the problem of producing three products A, B, and C in such a way that production costs are minimized. Any of the products can be manufactured in either or both of two processes, I and II, but at different costs as measured by the time required in each process. (The processes are not sequential.)

Product	Process I	II	Minimum Required
A	10	6	10
B	5	5	20
C	3	15	15

Sales commitments require that certain minimum quantities of each of the products be produced. The rates of production and the minimum production requirements are illustrated in the table. In addition, only four hours of each process are available. Process I costs $2100 per hour and process II, $1800 per hour. Let x_1 be the number of hours of process I to be used, and x_2 be the number of hours of process II to be used. Find the least-cost process combination by the graphic method, solving algebraically for the optimum solution. (Use large scale graph paper and label all lines and relevant points carefully.)

9.3.8 How many of each of the products will be produced by this optimum decision?

9.3.9 What are the similarities and differences between the profit maximization problem and the cost minimization problem?

9.4 Solution concepts for n variables

Our discussion of solutions to linear programming problems has been necessarily restricted to decision alternatives in two variables by the relative lack of power of the solution techniques discussed. In order to expand the tabular method and the graphic method to three variables, we would need a three-way table for the former and a third axis for the latter; in either case the solution technique would become extremely unwieldy, and in any case the techniques cannot be extended to problems in more than three variables. The *concepts* developed, however, can be enlarged to cover problems in an indefinitely large number of variables, the restrictions upon this number being merely mechanical ones of digital computer capacity. To understand our two basic methods (and the student should have recognized that they are not really different), is thus to understand linear programming sufficiently to extend it to problems of a practical significance, in terms of the number of variables. We shall not take time here to develop the solution techniques for problems of higher order; indeed, since most practical problems require a computer for their solution, a brief drill in these rather tedious methods provides little, except perhaps a better understanding of the problem itself.

It is definitely important that the student be able to visualize the manner in which such solutions might be attained, since the form in which a problem might be presented to a computer for solution is the responsibility of the problem solver rather than the machine operator. So we shall explore the *form* of larger problems even though their *solution* is beyond the scope of this text. However, this does not mean that we should forget what we are looking for.

Referring back to Section 9.2, we find the contractor's problem written in a system of linear inequations, which we had to convert to equations before we could construct a graph. We know how to solve systems of linear equations, and thus it appears that this system must somehow be converted to a system of equations if we are to solve it algebraically. In fact, we can make this conversion quite easily by the mathematician's trick of introducing something into the problem, only to throw it out later. Consider constraint (I): $20x_1 + 35x_2 \leq 280$. Let us add to the left-hand side of this inequation a third variable x_3, which we shall call a *dummy* or *slack* variable (it "takes up the slack"), and to which we shall assign the unique positive value that makes this original inequation into an equation: $20x_1 + 35x_2 + x_3 = 280$.

Having made x_3 a part of our system of constraints, implying that we might produce some of this imaginary type of house, we must also include it in the objective function. However, should we arrive at a solution which included some value for x_3, it would be difficult to assess the amount of profit associated with producing that many imaginary houses! Therefore, instead of assigning a positive dollar profit to each unit of this non-existent product, we assign a very high cost to even the first unit of it; thus we can make sure that it will never be produced, since to produce it would result in utter failure to achieve our goal of profit maximization. Our objective function might be

$$\pi = 800x_1 + 1200x_2 - 5000x_3,$$

so that we would lose $5000 on each unit of x_3 produced. Since the loss to be suffered by producing any of the dummy commodity indicated by the slack variable x_3 can be arbitrarily determined by selection of a sufficiently negative value for the coefficient of the slack variable, we shall not bother to indicate how great a loss in dollars would be sustained, but merely let the letter M stand for this coefficient, understanding that M is such a large negative number, i.e., such a high cost, that we would never produce a commodity upon which we should have to pay such a high cost. It should appear obvious that a decision to produce any x_3 at all would be a very poor one, and our solution technique is set up so that this cannot happen.

Since there is "slack" in all of the constraints, we must obviously set up a slack variable for each of them, and we therefore arrive at a new formulation of our problem, as shown below. Variables x_8 and x_9 are called *artificial* variables; they are used to force x_1 and x_2 to take on values at least as great as 3 and 2 respectively. Although they are elements in the vector x, the profit associated with them is zero, and thus they do not appear in the objective function.

Maximize: $\pi = 800x_1 + 1200x_2 + Mx_3 + Mx_4 + Mx_5 + Mx_6 + Mx_7$

Subject to:

$$
\begin{aligned}
20x_1 + 35x_2 + x_3 &= 280 \\
6000x_1 + 5000x_2 + x_4 &= 60{,}000 \\
1000x_1 + 500x_2 + x_5 &= 9{,}000 \\
500x_1 + 500x_2 + x_6 &= 6{,}000 \\
4000x_2 + x_7 &= 24{,}000 \\
x_1 - x_8 &= 3 \\
x_2 - x_9 &= 2.
\end{aligned}
$$

We have now developed a system of seven linear equations in nine unknowns; and all x_i non-negative. Such a system has no unique solution, but an infinitely large number of solutions. However, the solution technique used to solve such a problem, by taking advantage of some of the concepts which we have already developed, reduces this number to a relatively small number of solutions, i.e., the infinitely large number of feasible solutions is reduced to a finite number of possible optimum (boundary) points, which may be examined for their optimality. This technique is called the *Simplex Method*, and forms the basis for the programs computers use to solve such problems.

Our system as it now stands is said to be *underdetermined*, as it does not contain sufficient information about the interrelationships among the nine variables to provide that unique set of values for them that will make all of the statements in the system true simultaneously. This is the usual form of the linear programming problem: the addition of the slack variables to the system results in a system containing more variables than information (in the form of equations) about them.

Although this system is underdetermined, we may still express it as a matrix, which shall be our final exercise in linear programming. Our first step is to set up the objective function in matrix form; the two matrices involved we find to be vectors as well. If we let x stand for the solution vector, and π for the profit vector, then we see that πx, the inner product of these two vectors, gives us the objective function, as follows (*Note: M* is a "large" negative number):

$$\pi x = (800, 1200, M, M, M, M, M, 0, 0) \begin{pmatrix} x_1 \\ x_2 \\ x_3 \\ x_4 \\ x_5 \\ x_6 \\ x_7 \\ x_8 \\ x_9 \end{pmatrix}$$

$$= 800x_1 + 1200x_2 + Mx_3 + Mx_4 + Mx_5 + Mx_6 + Mx_7.$$

Rather than writing out this long statement each time we wish to describe the objective function, we now merely write πx. If in similar fashion we write the matrix of coefficients of the variables in our system of constraints, we develop the following representation of the system of constraints:

$$
\begin{pmatrix}
20 & 35 & 1 & 0 & 0 & 0 & 0 & 0 & 0 \\
6000 & 5000 & 0 & 1 & 0 & 0 & 0 & 0 & 0 \\
1000 & 500 & 0 & 0 & 1 & 0 & 0 & 0 & 0 \\
500 & 500 & 0 & 0 & 0 & 1 & 0 & 0 & 0 \\
0 & 4000 & 0 & 0 & 0 & 0 & 1 & 0 & 0 \\
1 & 0 & 0 & 0 & 0 & 0 & 0 & -1 & 0 \\
0 & 1 & 0 & 0 & 0 & 0 & 0 & 0 & -1
\end{pmatrix}
\begin{pmatrix}
x_1 \\ x_2 \\ x_3 \\ x_4 \\ x_5 \\ x_6 \\ x_7 \\ x_8 \\ x_9
\end{pmatrix}
=
\begin{pmatrix}
280 \\ 60{,}000 \\ 9{,}000 \\ 6{,}000 \\ 24{,}000 \\ 3 \\ 2
\end{pmatrix}
.
$$

This is the matrix form of the expression $Ax = b$, where the order of the matrix of coefficients A is 7 by 9, the x vector is 9 by 1, and the right-hand side, or b vector, is 7 by 1. We see that the matrix multiplication indicated is allowable by the rules for multiplying two matrices, the product being exactly the system shown on page 142. The complete linear programming problem may then be stated in matrix form as follows:

> Maximize πx
> Subject to: $Ax = b$
> and $\quad x_i \geq 0, \quad i = 1, 2, 3, 4, 5, 6, 7, 8, 9.$

The last constraint, which states that only non-negative values of the variables are admissible, is unnecessary for x_1 and x_2 in this problem, since they are already required to be greater than 3 and 2 respectively by the problem. If x_3, however, were allowed to take on a negative value, then we see that building a negative number of our dummy houses would result in a contribution to profit, since we would multiply this negative number by the negative value M, resulting in a positive number, or dollar profit. This is of course senseless and violates our concept of the real world.

Since A is not a square matrix, it does not have an inverse, and the system cannot be solved by the matrix methods we have used previously. However, the solution technique is quite similar to that which we have used, since it consists of row and column operations upon a partitioning of this matrix. The Simplex algorithm, or solution technique, also provides rules for performing these operations which assure that each trial in the search for an optimum boundary point will improve the solution, and that as soon as the best solution is reached, certain things become evident which indicate that no further effort can improve the solution.

There are a number of other algorithms which apply to the solution of special types of linear programming problems. The student who is interested in following up on these algorithms as well as the Simplex technique is referred to these sources (there are many more):

Boulding, K. E. and W. A. Spivey, *Linear Programming and the Theory of the Firm;* The Macmillan Co., New York, 1960.

Churchman, C. W., R. L. Ackoff, and E. L. Arnoff, *Introduction to Operations Research;* John Wiley and Sons, Inc., New York, 1957.

Gale, David, *The Theory of Linear Economic Models*; McGraw-Hill, New York, 1960.

Gass, Saul I., *Linear Programming;* McGraw-Hill, New York, 1958.

Stockton, R. S., *Introduction to Linear Programming;* Allyn and Bacon, Boston, 1960.

New applications of the linear programming technique as a tool of administrative decision-making are being made daily, as understanding of the concept and method becomes more prevalent. For this powerful tool to be used, however, there must be a decision maker sufficiently familiar with his own decision problems *and* with this technique if the one is to serve the other.

9.4 Exercises

9.4.1 While examining the carton containing your breakfast cereal this morning, you reflected upon the fact that you were in the process of satisfying a number of the minimum daily requirements for certain elements believed necessary for the maintenance of good health. To satisfy the requirement for some of the other elements, however, you would have to eat a carload of the stuff. You then begin to wonder how cheaply you could feed yourself, satisfying all minimum daily requirements (M.D.R.) on a diet of milk, eggs, lettuce, and hamburger. Assume that there are only five relevant elements, and their nutritional values are as shown in the table, as well as the M.D.R. of each:

	Milk (qt.)	Eggs (ea.)	Lettuce (lb.)	Hamburger (lb.)	M.D.R.
Protein	34.2	6.1	5.4	100.0	70 grams
Calories	666.0	77.0	68.0	1654.0	3200 cal.
Vitamin A	1550.0	550.0	1470.0	0.0	5000 units
Vitamin B_1	0.35	0.05	0.20	0.35	1.6 mg.
Vitamin C	13.0	0.0	25.0	0.0	75 mg.

If milk costs 25 cents a quart, eggs 4 cents each, lettuce 10 cents a pound, and hamburger 50 cents a pound, set up this problem to find the least cost diet which satisfies the M.D.R. in the form shown on page 130, i.e., with constraints in the form of a system of linear inequalities. Complete the problem for solution by the Simplex technique by adding the proper slack variables and finally by showing the system in matrix form.

9.4.2 The manager of the rapid-transit system of a large city is faced with the problem of deciding how many buses to dispatch to critical areas of the city to handle rush-hour traffic. Many years ago, as the city began to expand, the company established two garages (in addition to the central garage) at outlying points, to reduce the distance that the buses had to travel to the critical areas. Recently, however, there have been many foul-ups as the dispatchers at the garages have assigned buses on an intuitive basis, so that there are insufficient buses when needed at certain points, while an oversupply exists elsewhere. In addition, costs of deadheading (running empty) have continued to increase as the problem has been attacked on a crisis basis. The manager would like to centralize the assignment decisions, but finds that he has neither the experience of the dispatchers nor modern training in administration. However, the manager does have some information as illustrated in our table. There are three garages, lettered A, B, and C, each housing the number of buses shown in the right margin. There are four critical areas, Q, R, S, and T, which on some given day require the number of buses shown at the bottom of the table. The entries in the body of the table are the distances from garage to critical area, e.g., from A to Q is 3 miles.

To ⟍ From	Q	R	S	T	Buses Available
A	3	5	1	1	50
B	5	9	2	5	20
C	2	2	6	6	30
Buses Required	20	20	20	40	100

No. of Buses Assigned	Q	R	S	T
A	x_{11}	x_{12}	x_{13}	x_{14}
B	x_{21}	x_{22}	x_{23}	x_{24}
C	x_{31}	x_{32}	x_{33}	x_{24}

Although there is a simple way to solve this problem by inspection, assume that the problem as stated is a simplification of the real problem, so that the linear programming technique must be applied. Set up the objective function and the constraints on the problem; convert to matrix form. Let the number of buses to be assigned from one garage to one destination be designated as in the statement to the right of the table, e.g., x_{11} is the number of buses assigned to Q from A; x_{34} is the number assigned from C to T. Assume that the cost of moving a bus from a garage to a destination is a linear function of the distance traveled, and thus the assignment should be made to minimize the total bus-miles traveled.

Having set up the linear programming formulation, try to solve the problem by inspection. Write your solution in the form of the solution vector for the linear programming problem above.

10 —— Probability

10.1　Certainty, risk, and uncertainty

In our study of linear programming, we assumed that all facts necessary to arrive at a decision were known.   Problem analysis and decision making where all facts are known is called *decision-making under conditions of certainty*.   However, an administrator's life is complicated by the fact that he is forced to make many decisions where all the facts are not specifically known.

Decision making under conditions *other than* certainty can be subdivided into two classes: *decision-making under conditions of risk* and *decision-making under conditions of uncertainty*.   When we speak of decision-making under conditions of risk, we refer to problem situations where the facts of the situation, and thus the outcome of any decision based upon these facts, are not known with certainty, but the likelihood of any given outcome is known.   The decision is "risky" because although we know the likelihood of any given outcome, that outcome is still not certain.   Decision-making under conditions of uncertainty prevails when the facts in a problem situation are not available, or when the likelihood of any given outcome is unknown.   It is vital that a decision maker know the condition under which he is making a decision; this knowledge is obviously fundamental to problem analysis. We shall devote our attention in this chapter to the study of decision-making under conditions of risk.   The mathematics of the study of decision-making under conditions of uncertainty is beyond the scope of this text.

Decision-making under conditions of risk requires a basic familiarity with *probability* concepts, concepts with which all of us are intuitively familiar, i.e., we "feel" that probability has something to do with the likelihood of occurrence of a chance event. We often hear and make statements such as, "It will probably rain today," "The Yankees are favored to win the pennant," or "The odds are against my passing this course." Such statements indicate that, based on (perhaps) prior experience or expert information, a decision has been made, or a conclusion reached, regarding the *likelihood* of some event occurring, out of a number of possible events which could occur.

Many administrative decisions are similarly made. Consider the inventory problem of a newsboy: each day he must decide upon the number of papers to order for the next day's sales. The product which he stocks is highly perishable, for the demand for a day-old paper is virtually zero. Assume, for a specific newsboy, the following facts: each paper costs him 5 cents, and sells for 10 cents; he has 10 regular customers; he is capable of carrying a maximum of 15 papers; and while he knows he has the potential of selling papers to people other than his regular customers, he does not know what the demand for these "irregular" sales will be. Therefore this young business administrator will make a "risky" decision if he decides to stock any more than 10 newspapers. The newsboy's decision requires a choice among several possible stocking alternatives, and each alternative holds the possibility of a certain level of profit—depending on the number of newspapers actually sold, the event which he must predict.

To analyze this or any decision problem, we must know the outcome resulting from the choice of any alternative or set of alternatives. Our analysis thus begins by developing in Fig. 10.1.1 a *payoff matrix*, which

PAYOFF MATRIX—NEWSBOY'S INVENTORY PROBLEM

Sales Demand		Stocking Alternatives—Number of Papers					
		10	11	12	13	14	15
	10	\$0.50	\$0.45	\$0.40	\$0.35	\$0.30	\$0.25
	11	0.50	0.55	0.50	0.45	0.40	0.35
Number of	12	0.50	0.55	0.60	0.55	0.50	0.45
Papers	13	0.50	0.55	0.60	0.65	0.60	0.55
	14	0.50	0.55	0.60	0.65	0.70	0.65
	15	0.50	0.55	0.60	0.65	0.70	0.75

Fig. 10.1.1

shows for each possible stocking alternative the profit associated with each possible level of sales demand.

The table indicates, for instance, that if he were to stock 12 papers but only sold the 10 to his regular customers, he would net $0.40; but if he sold all 12 papers, he would realize $0.60 profit. We note that the table excludes those "facts" which are known. To stock less than 10 papers when that many can be sold with certainty would be irrational, and 15 papers is the maximum which he can carry; therefore, no matter what the demand, he does not have the alternative of stocking more than 15 papers. With no more facts than those given, we also see that the newsboy has no reason to believe that he is more likely to sell one quantity of papers than another. Thus his problem as stated here is to make a decision under conditions of uncertainty, and one decision appears to be equally as good as another. We must realize that the only criterion by which any decision may be judged is whether or not the decision maximizes the possibility of attaining the desired goal *at the time that the decision is made.* To test a good decision by the criterion of how things turned out, having made the decision, is to beg the question; under such circumstances, no one would ever decide anything for fear of being wrong (although it is true that some administrators do exactly this!). Something other than the facts of the matter must be taken into account in such a situation: if the newsboy wishes to "play it safe," he might buy only 10 papers, thus guaranteeing himself a minimum of $0.50; or he might feel it important to be able to sell as many papers as possible as a matter of public relations, and thus might buy 15 papers merely to have them available, simultaneously maximizing his *potential* for gain, etc.

Unless our newsboy is brand-new on the job, however, he undoubtedly has additional information about his sales demand from his sales experience. He may have found, for instance, that he seldom sells less than 12 or more than 13 papers; his alternatives are thus reduced by this additional knowledge to a choice between 2, rather than among 6, alternatives. Finally, if he knew that he sold 12 papers twice as often as he sold 13, but he did not know on what day he would sell exactly 12 or 13, he would be in a position to make consistently good decisions, both before and after the fact. He would say to himself, "Today I shall most likely sell 12 papers," and thus would stock exactly 12. The key words in his statement are *most likely*, and this chapter will explore the *meaning* of this concept, how one can determine what *is* most likely, and how this concept can be *used* in making intelligent decisions. The basic tool is the notion of probability. In the next section we shall explore two different ideas about what it is.

10.1   Exercises

10.1.1.   Consider yourself the newsboy, and that you are starting your first day selling papers, with no previous experience. Your only information has already been tabulated in Fig. 10.1.1. How many papers would you stock? Defend your answer.

10.1.2   The addition of the knowledge that you will *most likely* sell a given number of papers does not rule out the possibility that you will not sell exactly that number; this is exactly the condition of risk. Why is the newsboy better off under a condition of risk than a condition of uncertainty?

10.2   Inductive and deductive reasoning

The newsboy problem illustrates a very common problem in administration: the necessity of converting a situation of uncertainty into a situation of risk. Such a conversion is not always possible, but the intelligent use of information may often provide us with sufficient basis for estimating the likelihood of some occurrence, and our decisions may be improved accordingly. One such source of information is the past history of the event or occurrence whose outcome we wish to predict. Hindsight, our ability to recognize and understand things that have happened in the past, provides us with such "history." The process of reasoning which leads us to expect things to occur in the future as they have in the past is called *a posteriori* reasoning, or *inductive* reasoning. If an event occurs over and over again in the same way, we are prone to believe that it must continue to do so. Some of our distant ancestors believed that the sun would rise each morning because, within their realm of experience, it had always done so. The history of the event led, *a posteriori*, to the expectation that the event would continue to occur.

Nowadays we would like to think that we are smarter, perhaps because we know the "real" reason why the sun rises each morning: we can not only define the solar system, but also actually state how the system operates. So long as the system is in balance, we know that the sun will "rise," and that the rising of the sun is an illusory phenomenon apparent only to a person standing at some point on earth more or less near the equator. To predict that the sun will rise is a matter not of past experience for most civilized people (although it is certainly taken for granted), but of an understanding, however meager, of the operation of our solar system. Reasoning from an understanding of the way in which a given system operates is called *a priori* or *deductive* reasoning. Our *hunches* are usually based upon some inexplicable personal theory about how a given system operates; without previous experience or hindsight we are often remarkably close to the actual outcome predicted *a priori*, by hunch.

It is seldom, in any decision situation, that we rely solely on hindsight or on hunch; we usually make our decisions by some combination of these two reasoning processes. There is a continuing, polemical argument among many scholars concerning the "usefulness" of *a posteriori* reasoning, sometimes called *empiricism*, and the "practicality" of *a priori* reasoning, which might be called *theoreticism*. Rather than join the argument, we should continue to use whatever information is available in the most intelligent manner.

What has this to do with probability, which deals in some way with the occurrence of some chance event? The process of reasoning either from historical data or from theoretical assumption very seldom results in a set of known facts and outcomes. Probability enters here as that measure of likelihood which we should like to establish for *any* facts or outcomes, no matter what reasoning process produced them. It is important that this idea be understood: the nature of probability itself is unaffected by the type of reasoning leading to the determination of any given probability. We shall assume henceforth that the student understands that probability is a *universal* concept, applicable in either inductive or deductive science. We shall see why this is true in the next section.

10.2 Exercises

For the following decision situations, state whether the facts and outcomes must be determined empirically or theoretically, i.e., whether the likelihood of occurrence of some event must be reached by inductive or deductive reasoning. Since the line between the two is seldom sharp or obvious, state your thoughts as to which is more likely (!), defending your answer.

10.2.1 Many civilizations have worshipped the sun as a god; to assure the successful arrival of the sun god each morning, human sacrifices and other rituals were performed.

10.2.2 The responsibility of the range safety officer at Cape Canaveral is to insure that a missile showing signs of improper performance does not become a menace to life and property. His job is to decide if and when a missile should be destroyed. Consider his circumstance when a new missile is being tested for the first time.

10.2.3 A farmer buys a certain brand of seed because it has a higher germination percentage than other brands which he has tried.

10.2.4 You are dealt a five-card poker hand containing a king, queen, jack, nine, and deuce. You do not know what the other players have, but you decide not to try to draw a ten in place of the deuce to fill out the straight (any five consecutive cards). Instead you discard the deuce and the nine, hoping to pair one of the high cards.

10.2.5 A quality control engineer must make sure that his product meets certain quality requirements, yet in the mass production system in effect he knows that many units do not measure up to standard. He must decide when to shut down the process for readjustment.

10.2.6 The small contractor bidding for a government contract knows that if his bid is too high for a certain job he will not get the work, yet if it is too low, he will realize no profit and there would be no point in doing the work. Yet he must decide a price at which to bid.

10.3 The concept of probability

In the previous section we briefly explored two basic notions surrounding the method of inquiry into the nature of phenomena which behave according to "chance." We have not, however, said anything about how chance behavior may be measured, for we must first examine and understand some of the basic concepts of probability theory. The student will notice that the theory of sets plays an important part in this examination.

Let us examine the behavior of some phenomenon by performing an experiment upon it. The first thing that we shall do is to make a list containing every possible outcome of the experiment. Remembering that we may specify a set by listing all of the elements in it, we see that this list of outcomes comprises a set, which we shall call the outcome set, or sample space, of the experiment. This leads to a definition:

Definition 10.3.1: The *outcome set* (*sample space*) of an experiment is a set having the characteristics that each element in the set is an outcome of the experiment, and each time the experiment is performed, one and only one of the elemental outcomes can result.

This definition does not tell us what specific elements to include in the outcome set of any particular experiment. However, we should undoubtedly construct the outcome set so that we can properly answer any question that might be asked concerning the outcome of the experiment. Analogous to the set concept (each outcome being an element of the outcome set) is the representation of each outcome as a point in the sample space. For each performance of the experiment, these points are mutually exclusive and collectively exhaustive by our definition of the sample space. We have thus described a universe, and we shall use the symbol Ω to stand for the outcome set or sample space. There is no restriction placed upon the number of points in the sample space by our definition; there could be none, one, two, or more, up to infinitely many. In most of our work we shall assume that the experiment has only a *finite* number of outcomes, and thus there will be a finite, or "countable," number of points in the sample space.

As an example of an experiment and its associated outcome set, let us consider the simple experiment of tossing a penny. What are the elementary outcomes of this experiment? Obviously, $\Omega = \{(H), (T)\}$, where H means heads and T means tails. If the experiment were to consist of tossing 2 pennies at the same time, then $\Omega = \{(H, H), (H, T), (T, H), (T, T)\}$.

Having specified the universal set of elementary outcomes, we may now ask some questions about events that ensue from performing the experiment. For instance, if 2 pennies are tossed, we might be curious about the event that one or more of them turned up tails. If we call this event A, then the event A can be represented as a subset of Ω such that the subset $A = \{(H, T), (T, H), (T, T)\}$; the event A will occur if any of the elementary outcomes in the subset occur. Likewise, if we should be curious about the event B that the coins matched, then this event could be represented by the subset $B = \{(H, H), (T, T)\}$; the event B would occur if either of the elementary outcomes in the set B occurred. How about the event C that one of the coins comes up heads and the other on edge? Obviously $C = \phi$, since there is no elementary outcome of this type specified in Ω; we remember that the empty set is a subset of every set. We may define what we mean by an event:

Definition 10.3.2: An *event* E is any *subset* of an outcome set Ω. The event E will occur if the result of the experiment is an element of the subset E.

We have discussed those outcome sets and subsets that are events, but have not yet mentioned probability itself. Probability is an abstract concept, not an observable thing or fact from real life. Therefore we must be careful in explaining this abstraction so that the student will understand that our definitions and some resulting theorems are derived strictly from a conceptual theory, and not from any observed or provable fact. Thus a probability does not arise from any real world experience, although we can tie the theory directly to such experience in order to make it useful. Let us do this in two steps: in the first step we shall examine the abstract concept of probability because it is basic to understanding an underlying assumption of practically all applied work, and in the second step we shall make another definition which renders the theory practical.

Consider an outcome space containing n outcomes, each of which we indicate by the letter "o," such that $\Omega = \{o_1, o_2, \ldots, o_n\}$. Any subset of Ω which contains but one outcome we shall call a *simple* event. There are thus n simple events, i.e., one-element subsets, in Ω.

Definition 10.3.3: A *probability* is a number which we assign to each simple event in an outcome set, called the probability of the event, and chosen so that the probability of each simple event is non-negative, and the sum of the probabilities assigned to all of the simple events is 1.

We indicate the probability of a simple event by writing $P(\{o_j\})$, read "the probability of the jth simple event." We may then write

$$P(\{o_1\}) + P(\{o_2\}) + \cdots + P(\{o_n\}) = 1.$$

From the definition it follows that a probability must be a number between zero and one inclusive.

Our theory says nothing at all about what numbers *should be* assigned to the simple events, but only what numbers *may be* assigned. Now this is the important part of step one of our explanation: the assignment of probabilities to simple events is *arbitrary* (within the constraints of Definition 10.3.3). For instance, in our example of flipping two pennies, we *could* assign probabilities in any of the three ways below. (The student should verify that these assignments

$P(H, H) = 1$	$P(H, H) = 0.1416$	$P(H, H) = 0.25$
$P(H, T) = 0$	$P(H, T) = 0.0004$	$P(H, T) = 0.25$
$P(T, H) = 0$	$P(T, H) = 0.8181$	$P(T, H) = 0.25$
$P(T, T) = 0$	$P(T, T) = 0.0399$	$P(T, T) = 0.25$
$\overline{1}$	$\overline{1.0000}$	$\overline{1.00}$

satisfy the definition.) Now it is our feeling about the real world that there is or should be some regularity in any system of chance, even if this regularity arises from complete ignorance. Only the assignment made in the right-hand column above really satisfies us as a realistic statement of what we expect when flipping two coins, and is indeed a definition of what we would call a "fair" game, or of "fair" coins.

In such a circumstance the simple events are said to be *equally likely*, which is a real world explanation of a completely arbitrary assignment of probabilities arising either from a feeling that there is no systematic reason why each of these outcomes should not be assigned the same probability, or from a condition of ignorance that dictates no better method.   If we are to choose a ball from an urn, a seed from a bin, or a person from a crowd, where some ball, seed, or person represents a simple event, and consider that the probability of this simple event is the same as the probability of any other simple event in the outcome set, then we have made the assumption of *equal likelihood*. We speak of such a selection procedure as being *random*.   This attribute of randomness of the simple events of an outcome set must thus be understood to be something imposed upon the experiment by the experimenter, and not something which arises systematically in the experiment itself, for the experimenter is the one who assigns the "primitive" probabilities to the simple events of the outcome set, whether by design or ignorance.   Since the word "random" is so often used nowadays, it is important to understand its true meaning in the probability sense, which is quite different from such popular meanings as "aimless," "haphazard," or "erratic."

The point made in the previous section concerning the indifference of probability theory to the method of inquiry, whether empirical or theoretical, is just the point made here: probability theory is silent upon the means by which primitive probabilities are assigned to simple events, and thus the theory has nothing to say about whether these probabilities are assigned *a priori* or *a posteriori*, as long as they satisfy the definition.

Having assigned probabilities to simple events in an outcome set, we may now ask questions about the probability of other events in the outcome space.   Any subset of the universal set, i.e., any event E, must contain no elements (the empty set), one element (a simple event), all of the elements (the universal set itself), or two or more elements (the union of simple events).   The following definitions, although axioms of our theory and thus indifferent to real world experience or test, should seem reasonable in the light of what has gone before.

Definition 10.3.4: The *probability* of the event E, written $P(E)$, where E is a subset of the outcome set, is the sum of the probabilities of the simple events whose union is the set E.

We defined earlier the event $A = \{(H, T), (T, H), (T, T)\}$.   Under the equal likelihood assumption,

$$P(A) = P(\{H, T\}) + P(\{T, H\}) + P(\{T, T\})$$
$$= 0.25 + 0.25 + 0.25 = 0.75.$$

(The student should compute this probability, using the other arbitrary assignments of primitive probabilities listed above.)

Definition 10.3.5: The *probability* of the empty set, $P(\phi)$, is zero.

We note that this is the only number assigned as a probability by definition in the theory.

Now we are ready to take step two, in which we shall develop the traditional, or what is sometimes called the *classical*, approach to finding the probability of an event. We shall see that this approach depends upon an understanding of the assumption of equal likelihood, as well as the other basic ideas of step one.

Suppose we were to observe an English class in which 30 students were enrolled. Let us define this class, i.e., the set of all students having the characteristic that they are enrolled in the English class, as the universal set, Ω. Our class contains 18 boys and 12 girls; let us define the subset A to be the set of all boys in Ω, and therefore the subset $\tilde{A}$ must be the set of all girls. The Venn diagram in Fig. 10.3.1 illustrates

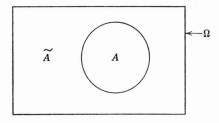

Fig. 10.3.1

the universal set and the subsets A and $\tilde{A}$. Let us now adopt a notation for the number of elements in a set: $n(A)$ is a symbol which means *the number of elements in the set* A. In this example, $n(A) = 18$, $n(\tilde{A}) = 12$, and $n(\Omega) = 30$.

Now consider this elementary problem: one person is absent from the class on a given day, and we are asked to guess whether the absentee is a boy or a girl. Having no more information than the fact that someone is absent, and with no predisposition to believe that the sex of a student has anything to do with absenteeism, we would guess that the absentee were a boy, simply because there are more "chances" for a boy to be absent than a girl. There are, in fact, 18 chances out of 30 that the absentee is a boy, while there are but 12 chances out of 30 that the absentee is a girl, i.e., the outcome of the "experiment" in which one of the students will be absent will be an element in either the set A or the set $\tilde{A}$. There are more points in A than in $\tilde{A}$, and thus if we choose a point *at random* it is more likely that the point will be in A than in $\tilde{A}$. Since an event *occurs* when the outcome is an element of the set described by the event, then we say that event A is more likely. How likely? To answer this question, we redefine probability in terms of events.

Definition 10.3.6: If in a universal set Ω each element is considered a simple event and each simple event is unique and equally likely to occur, and if in the universal set we can define a subset A of simple events, then the *probability* $P(A)$ that the event described by the characteristic of the subset will occur is

$$P(A) = \frac{n(A)}{n(\Omega)}.$$

where $n(A)$ is the number of elements in the subset and $n(\Omega)$ is the number of elements in the universal set.

In our example, we find the probability of the event that the absentee is a boy to be

$$P(A) = \frac{n(A)}{n(\Omega)} = \frac{18}{30} = \frac{6}{10} = 0.6.$$

The probability of the event that the absentee is not a boy is

$$P(\tilde{A}) = \frac{n(\tilde{A})}{n(\Omega)} = \frac{12}{30} = \frac{4}{10} = 0.4.$$

which is also the probability of the event that the absentee is a girl, since $\tilde{A}$ must be the set of all girls. The sets A and $\tilde{A}$ are thus disjoint; they have no elements in common. In addition, they exhaust the universe, since we usually consider only two sexes of people. These sets are then said to be mutually exclusive (disjoint), i.e., $(A \cap \tilde{A}) = \phi$, and collectively exhaustive, i.e., $(A \cup \tilde{A} = \Omega$. In terms of probabilities, we see that

$$P(A) + P(\tilde{A}) = 0.6 + 0.4 = 1.0.$$

The interpretation of this statement is that it is a sure thing that the absentee will be either a boy or a girl, i.e., $P(\Omega) = 1.0$. We also see that the probability that the absentee will be neither a boy nor a girl is zero, i.e., $P(\tilde{\Omega}) = 0$. Since $\tilde{\Omega} = \phi$, $P(\phi) = 0$, which we previously defined to be true.

It should be obvious that probability as defined above is indifferent to the reasoning leading to the assignment of events to sets; whether the number of elements in a given subset or universe is determined *a posteriori* or *a priori* does not affect the number expressing the likelihood of occurrence of some event.

10.3 Exercises

Analyze the following problem situations, illustrate each with a Venn Diagram, and compute the required probabilities. State any required assumptions.

10.3.1 You are given a standard deck of 52 cards which has been well-shuffled. Assume that the deck is placed face down on a table and you draw a card from the top. What is the probability that the card is:

(**a**) a heart?

(**b**) a red card?

(**c**) an ace?

(**d**) a face card?

(**e**) the nine of spades?

(**f**) smaller than a nine?

10.3.2

(**a**) What is the probability that a normal dime will turn up heads when tossed?

(**b**) What is the probability that a person will have February 28 as a a birthday? February 29?

(**c**) What is the probability that a two (two spots) will turn up when an ordinary six-sided die is thrown?

(**d**) Analyze problems *a, b,* and *c* of Exercise 10.3.2 and determine the probability that the event in consideration will *not* occur.

10.3.3 Assume that there are 40 employees in a small manufacturing plant, with the following known characteristics:

There are 30 women and 10 men.
There are 24 production department employees, 4 sales department employees, 10 accounting department employees, and 2 general executives.

What is the probability that:

(**a**) Any employee chosen at random will be a woman? a man?

(**b**) Any employee chosen at random will be a production department employee? a sales department employee? an accounting department employee?

(**c**) Any employee chosen at random will *not* be a production department employee?

(d) Any employee chosen at random will come from *either* the production department *or* the sales department? (Note the relationship to the probabilities for each separate event found in *b* above).

(e) If we knew that the two general executives were men, and that the remainder of the men worked in the production department, what would be the probability that any production department employee chosen at random would be a woman? If this were so, what would be the probability that any employee of the accounting department were a man? a woman?

10.4   Some additional probability properties

Many other questions than those simple ones already considered may be asked concerning the outcome of an experiment. For instance, if two events (subsets) have been described in the outcome space, we might wish to ask questions concerning the simultaneous occurrence of both, or perhaps the occurrence of either. The probabilities associated with such events can be determined from the definitions given previously. However, the algebra of sets can be used to simplify the determination of these probabilities, and we shall state three definitions in this section which are highly useful in finding such probabilities.

Definition 10.4.1: If event A and event B are disjoint subsets of Ω, i.e., A and B are mutually exclusive subsets in one outcome set, then the *probability* of the event A or the event B is the sum of the probability of A and the probability of B.

In the shorthand of set theory, if $A \cap B = \phi$, then $P(A \cup B) = P(A) + P(B)$. This situation is illustrated in Fig. 10.4.1. If $n(A) = 8$, $n(B) = 10$, and $n(\Omega) = 20$, then

$$P(A \cup B) = \frac{n(A)}{n(\Omega)} + \frac{n(B)}{n(\Omega)} = \frac{8}{20} + \frac{10}{20} = \frac{18}{20} = 0.9.$$

Definition 10.4.2: If event A and event B are conjoint subsets of Ω, i.e., their intersection is *not* empty, then the *probability* that both events will occur simultaneously, i.e., that the outcome will be in the intersection of A and B, is:

$$P(A \cap B) = \frac{n(A \cap B)}{n(\Omega)}.$$

The Venn diagram of Fig. 10.4.2 illustrates such a situation. If the intersection of A and B contained 2 elements, and the universe 20, then

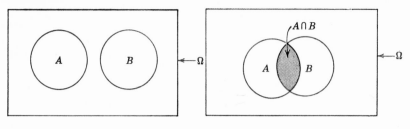

Fig. 10.4.1   Fig. 10.4.2

the probability that both event A *and* event B will occur simultaneously is $P(A \cap B) = \frac{2}{20} = 0.1$.

Definition 10.4.3: If event A and event B are conjoint subsets of Ω, then the *probability* that event A *or* event B will occur is the sum of the probabilities of each event less the probability that they will occur simultaneously.

Thus, if $A \cap B \neq \phi$, then

$$P(A \cap B) = P(A) + P(B) - P(A \cap B) = \frac{n(A) + n(B) - n(A \cap B)}{n(\Omega)}.$$

We must subtract $P(A \cap B)$ for the following reason: when we add the number of elements in A and the number of elements in B we have added the number of elements in their intersection twice. By the assumption of equally likely simple events, no element in a set can be counted more than once. But the elements in the intersection are counted once when we count the elements in A and again when we count the elements in B, and therefore we must exclude one of these countings, the result of which is exactly $n(A \cap B)$.

10.4   Exercises

Our figure represents the sort of wheel used for raffles, etc. It is delicately balanced so that each of the 12 numbers upon it is equally likely to be indicated by the pointer when it comes to rest after being spun around. The universe is obviously the set of possible outcomes: $\Omega = \{1, 2, 3, 4, 5, 6, 7, 8, 9, 10, 11, 12\}$.

Let A be the event that an odd number occurs on one spin.

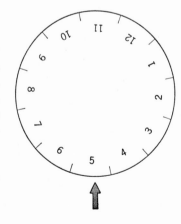

Let B be the event that an even number occurs on one spin.

Let C be the event that a number larger than 6 occurs on one spin.

Let D be the event that a number smaller than 7 occurs on one spin.

Compute the probabilities of the following events. Illustrate each with a Venn diagram, state the definition which applies, and write out in English the meaning of the question (Example: $P(A)$ = the probability of the event that an odd number occurs).

10.4.1 $P(A)$.	**10.4.2** $P(C)$.
10.4.3 $P(\Omega)$.	**10.4.4** $P(\phi)$.
10.4.5 $P(A \cup B)$.	**10.4.6** $P(C \cup D)$.
10.4.7 $P(A \cup \phi)$.	**10.4.8** $P(A \cup \tilde{C})$.
10.4.9 $P(A \cup D)$.	**10.4.10** $P(B \cup C)$.
10.4.11 $P(A \cap B \cap C)$.	**10.4.12** $P(A \cup C)$.
10.4.13 $P(B \cup D)$.	**10.4.14** $P(A \cup B \cup C)$.
10.4.15 $P(C \cap \tilde{D})$.	**10.4.16** $P(A \cap \tilde{C})$.

10.5   Joint, marginal, and conditional probability

To this point we have limited ourselves to consideration of the probability of an event (or events) which occurs on a single trial or experiment. We shall now expand our analysis to include events which occur over a number of trials, and thus develop some properties of the probability of *compound* events.

Consider for the moment a coin-tossing experiment of two trials; on the first toss we would expect to get "heads" with probability of $\frac{1}{2}$ and tails with a probability of $\frac{1}{2}$. On the second toss we would expect the same probabilities to apply since the events are independent of one another. (Events are independent when the occurrence of one has no effect upon the occurrence of any others. This statement will suffice for the moment; we shall re-examine the concept of independence after we have developed some better tools.) The "tree" diagram in Fig. 10.5.1 is a model of this experiment; it illustrates the probability of the various outcomes resulting from the experiment.

We should like to ask the question, "what is the probability of getting 'heads' on each of two successive trials, i.e., heads on each toss?" The probability of this event (two heads) is called the *joint probability* of a head on the first toss and a head on the second. We write $P(H_1, H_2)$ as this joint probability, where the subscript indicates the number of the toss. On the right in Fig. 10.5.1 are the joint

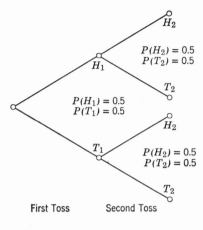

$P(H_1, H_2) = 0.5 \times 0.5 = 0.25$
$P(H_1, T_2) = 0.5 \times 0.5 = 0.25$
$P(T_1, H_2) = 0.5 \times 0.5 = 0.25$
$P(T_1, T_2) = 0.5 \times 0.5 = 0.25$

Fig. 10.5.1

probabilities associated with each of the outcomes of the experiment. There are four possible outcomes, each equally likely, and thus we would expect the probability of any of them to be 0.25. We note that if we asked for the probability that the outcome should be dissimilar, i.e., one head and one tail without regard for which happened first, the probability would be 0.5 (why?). We shall formalize the concept of joint probability by stating it as a definition.

Definition 10.5.1: The *joint probability* of two or more independent events is the product of the probabilities of the independent events.

Thus $P(A, B, C, \ldots) = P(A)P(B)P(C) \ldots$, where $A, B, C, \ldots$, are independent events.

Our examples and exercises heretofore have involved *a priori* probabilities, i.e., primitive probabilities assigned to simple events on the basis of the theory of behavior of some phenomenon, such as the toss of a coin, the throw of a die, or the spin of a wheel. In introducing two more properties of probability, let us draw an hypothetical example for which the primitive probabilities have been assigned equally on the basis of observation, i.e., *a posteriori*. Our purpose in doing this is merely to point out that the properties of probability apply no matter what the source of our information concerning the behavior of the phenomenon in question.

Let us suppose that a builder enters a new area and proposes to erect residences which will meet the demands of his potential customers. At the outset he has no information at all concerning these potential

NUMBER OF HOUSES WITH STATED CHARACTERISTICS

Roof Style House Type	Asphalt Shingle (R_1)	Cedar Shingle (R_2)	Built-up (R_3)	Total
Frame House (H_1)	20	30	0	50
Brick House (H_2)	0	30	20	50
Total	20	60	20	100

Fig. 10.5.2

customers in terms of the kind of house which they might buy. Under the assumption that what has sold in the past will continue to be sold in the future, our builder surveys a number of neighborhoods, with the results shown in Fig. 10.5.2. His broad classifications consist of frame or brick houses, and three different roof styles. The survey was made by merely observing each of 100 houses and tallying each house according to the characteristics which it displayed.

The table indicates that the 100 houses surveyed are evenly divided between frame and brick, but that cedar shingles appear to be much more popular than either of the other types of roof. With this information, our builder is no longer operating in a decision situation characterized by uncertainty, but is now in a position to answer such questions as "How likely is it that any customer will want a frame house? A brick house? A house with cedar shingles? A frame house with built-up roof? Of all those people who want brick houses, how many are likely to want an asphalt shingle roof?"

A posteriori, we may now assign probabilities to some of these basic events, remembering our previous assumption about past and future performance of the house market. The universe consists of 100 houses; these 100 chance events (a customer might pick any house) are mutually exclusive, collectively exhaustive, and equally likely, by our assumption about the market. The event H_1, that a customer will want a frame house, can occur in 50 ways, since there were 50 frame houses in the survey out of a total of 100. The probability of H_1 is thus $\frac{1}{2}$, or 0.5; the same reasoning and result applies to the computation of the probability of H_2, that any customer will want a brick house. We have therefore constructed a new table, Fig. 10.5.3, in which we have not entered the number of elements in the set describing some event, but instead the probability of that event. In the right-

	R_1	R_2	R_3	Total
H_1	0.2	0.3	0	0.5
H_2	0	0.3	0.2	0.5
Total	0.2	0.6	0.2	1.0

Fig. 10.5.3

hand margin we enter the probabilities of H_1 and H_2; in a similar fashion we compute and enter the probabilities of R_1, R_2, and R_3 along the bottom margin of the table. In the body of the table we enter the various joint probabilities of the events described by the intersection of a row and a column. The entry in the first row and first column is the joint probability of the event that a customer will want a frame house with an asphalt roof, which we compute as before:

$$P(H_1, R_1) = \frac{n(H_1 \cap R_1)}{n(\Omega)} = \frac{20}{100} = 0.2.$$

The student should verify the computation of the remainder of the entries.

The probabilities of the various events shown in the margins are called the *marginal probabilities* of the associated events; we notice that the marginal probability of the event H_1, for instance, is the sum of the probabilities of the events which have the characteristic H_1:

$$P(H_1) = P(H_1, R_1) + P(H_1, R_2) + P(H_1, R_3) = 0.2 + 0.3 + 0 = 0.5.$$

The components of this sum are exactly the joint probabilities of the event that a customer will want a frame house with any of the roof styles; since the three roof styles are the only ones considered, the marginal probability of the event that the customer will want a frame house with *any* kind of roof is exactly the probability that he will want a frame house.

Definition 10.5.2: The *marginal probability* of an event is the sum of the joint probabilities of that event and all other events with which the event can occur.

The marginal probability of an event thus ignores one (or more) of the criteria of classification; if we seek the marginal probability of the event that a customer will want a built-up roof, $P(R_3)$, we ignore his desires as to the style of house on which it will be placed. When only two classification criteria are used, the marginal probabilities and joint probabilities may be read directly from the table.

Now suppose that we wished to know the probability of a somewhat different event, perhaps the probability of the event that a customer who wants a frame house will want a cedar shingle roof on it. This is not the same event as the event of wanting a frame house *with* a cedar shingle roof. In this case we seek the *conditional probability* that a customer will want a cedar shingle roof, *given* the fact that he wants a frame house. We may consider that he has already chosen the frame house, and we are now assessing the probability associated with the choice of a roof for it. The distinction between the joint probability of the two events and the conditional probability of one, given the other, obviously has something to do with the universe of possible events (simple events) in which the desired event will take place. The condition that the customer has already chosen a frame house, which previously was a chance event but is now known, restricts the outcome set to the universe of all frame houses, a set containing only 50 elements. There are 30 elements in the set of frame houses with cedar shingle roofs. The conditional probability of this event, written $P(R_2|H_1)$ and read "the probability of R_2 given H_1," can thus be computed according to the definition of probability, having made the proper adjustment in the relevant (non-empty) universe:

$$P(R_2|H_1) = \frac{n(R_2 \cap H_1)}{n(H_1)},$$

where H_1 is now the relevant universe. There are 30 elements (houses, or chance events) in the set $(R_2 \cap H_1)$; thus the probability of the event is $P(R_2|H_1) = \frac{30}{50} = 0.6$.

There is an easier method for finding the conditional probability of an event, which takes advantage of the fact that the joint and marginal probabilities are already known, and also provides us with a definition. Let us manipulate the formula used to find the conditional probability by dividing both numerator and denominator of the right-hand side by $n(\Omega)$:

$$P(R_2|H_1) = \frac{n(R_2 \cap H_1)}{n(H_1)} = \frac{n(R_2 \cap H_1)/n(\Omega)}{n(H_1)/n(\Omega)} = \frac{P(R_2, H_1)}{P(H_1)}.$$

The numerator of the resulting fraction, $P(R_2, H_1)$ is the joint probability of R_2 and H_1; the denominator is the marginal probability of H_1. Thus the conditional probability of R_2 and H_1 is equal to the ratio of the joint probability of R_2 and H_1 to the marginal probability of H_1. Let us formalize this as a definition.

Definition 10.5.3: The *conditional probability* of an event A, given that another chance event B has occurred, is the joint probability of A and B divided by the marginal probability of B:

$$P(A|B) = \frac{P(A, B)}{P(B)}.$$

We referred earlier to the concept of independent events, and we are now equipped to define what we mean by independence.

Definition 10.5.4: Two events A and B are said to be *stochastically independent*, that is, independent in the probability sense, if the conditional probability of A given B is equal to the probability of A:

$$P(A|B) = P(A).$$

We see that placing the condition on the probability of A that B has occurred does not change the probability of A, and thus A is independent of the condition imposed by B; thus the occurrence of B has no effect upon the probability of A.

10.5   Exercises

10.5.1   The following questions refer to the table of probabilities in Fig. 10.5.3.

(a) What is the probability that a family having decided to buy a brick house, will choose a cedar shingle roof?

(b) What is the probability that a family having decided to buy a frame house will choose a built-up roof?

(c) What is the probability that, having expressed a definite preference for an asphalt shingle roof, a buyer will order a frame house? a brick house?

10.5.2   The personnel department of the Butler Company has completed an interesting survey of the relationship of lost time due to illness and the sex of employees.   The survey covered 500 employees in the plant who were employed full time during 1961, the base period of the study.   The table shows the joint and marginal probabilities for various periods of absence of men and women.

Absences / Sex	0 Days	1 to 5 Days	6 to 10 Days	11 or More Days	Total
Men	0.3	0.2	0.1	0	0.6
Women	0.1	0.1	0.1	0.1	0.4
Total	0.4	0.3	0.2	0.1	1.0

(a) Based on this survey, what is the probability that a woman will be absent 11 or more days in a year? a man?

(b) What is the probability that a man will miss at least 1 day from work by a reason of illness? fewer than 6?

(c) If you know that a given employee missed 8 days during 1961 by reason of illness, what is the probability that the employee was a woman?

10.5.3   The safety engineer of the Karter Kook Kompany, believing that there was a definite relationship between a worker's age and the number of accidents which he had, conducted an analysis of the relative frequency of accidents by age group for the employees of the company's machine shop.   The table here summarizes his findings, showing the number of employees in each age group according to the number of accidents experienced by members of that group.

No. of Accidents Age Group	None	1	2	3 or more	Total
Under 25	8	20	10	12	50
25–34	16	16	10	8	50
35–44	24	12	10	4	50
45 and over	32	8	10	0	50
Total	80	56	40	24	200

(a) Assuming that the relative frequencies analyzed above are indicative of the performance of the machine shop to be expected in the future, develop a table of marginal and joint probabilities which can be used by the Safety Engineer for predicting accidents in the future.

(b) What is the probability that an employee who has had 2 accidents is in the 25–34 age group?   What is the probability that a 25-year-old employee will have 2 accidents?   Are these probabilities the same?   Explain.

(c) What is the probability that a 40-year-old employee will have more than 1 accident?   Less than 1?

(d) What is the probability that an employee older than 34 will have more than 2 accidents?

(e) Of what significance might this information be with regard to: (1) Company policies regarding the age of employees hired for the machine shop?   (2) Safety training programs in the machine shop?

10.5.4 Draw a tree diagram of a game played by tossing a single fair coin 4 times. Compute the joint probabilities of the possible outcomes.

(a) What is the joint probability of the event that the coin will turn up heads on all 4 tosses?

(b) What is the joint probability of the event that there will be an equal number of heads and tails?

(c) How does the sample space illustrated by your tree diagram differ from the sample space if the game were played by tossing 4 fair coins all at the same time? (*Hint: List* all of the possible outcomes.)

(d) Justify your answer in c on the basis of the definitions given.

10.5.5 The game of craps is played with two dice as follows: a player rolls both dice; if they turn up a combination of spots adding to the number 7 or the number 11, he wins the game. If they turn up 2, 3, or 12 he loses the game. If any other number should turn up, this number is called his "point," and he will continue to roll the dice until he makes his point by again rolling that number, or he shoots a 7, in which case he loses. Draw a tree diagram of the game of craps, i.e., through only one roll of the dice.

(a) What is the probability of losing the game on the first throw?

(b) What is the probability of winning the game on the first throw?

(c) What is the probability of making your point on the second throw if the result of your first throw was 8?

(d) What is the probability of making a 2 on the first throw? a 3? a 4? a 5? a 6? a 7? an 8? a 9? a 10? an 11? a 12? (*Hint:* Show first the number of ways in which each of these can occur: refer to tree diagram.)

(e) What is the joint probability of throwing a 7 on two successive tosses?

(f) What is the basis of all of the probabilities assigned above?

10.6 Permutations and combinations

As we have seen in some examples and exercises of the previous sections, calculating elemental *a posteriori* probabilities is a matter of tallying observations according to their characteristics, and then constructing a relative frequency for each marginal characteristic, and/or joint characteristic, according to our definitional formula of probability. We have used this simple device up to now in calculating *a priori* probabilities as well, at least in the respect that we have *counted* the elements in an event and in the outcome set.

In many instances, however, neither the number of elements in an event nor the number of points in the sample space can be determined easily by diagramming or listing, if only for reasons of size: the sheer number of these elements makes the job of counting extremely difficult. Fortunately, we have some help in such cases, in the form of methods for determining permutations and combinations. A *permutation* is an ordered set, sometimes called an arrangement, and a *combination* is an unordered set; our previous work in set theory thus provides us a useful tool in yet another area. By using certain formulas for determining the number of permutations or combinations for various sets of events, we can simplify the work of counting the elements in the sets with which we work.

Let us examine what we mean by a permutation and a combination with some examples. In a two-seater sports car there are two positions, left and right, which could be occupied by two people. Occupant A could sit on the right side while occupant B sat on the left, or vice versa. Each of these two arrangements is called a permutation: there are thus two permutations of the two occupants when we put them in the car together. We might write these permutations as two sets: $\{A, B\}$ and $\{B, A\}$; the left position in the set represents the left seat in the car, etc. However, there is only one combination of occupants A and B; by combination we mean only whether or not the occupants are in the car, and we do not care where they sit. In set terms, $\{A, B\}$ and $\{B, A\}$ are the same combination, because we do not care about the order of the elements in the set. There is thus only one combination of two things (occupants) taken two at a time (both in the car).

Let us digress for a moment and consider another problem. If we were considering a trip to three cities, X, Y, and Z, and we could travel by train T or bus B, among how many different alternatives of destination and mode of travel must we choose? We may travel to each of the three cities by each of two means, i.e., (X, T), (X, B), (Y, T), (Y, B), (Z, T), (Z, B). There are three ways to accomplish one of the ends and two ways to accomplish the other; the total number of ways to accomplish both ends is $3 \times 2 = 6$ ways.

Rule 10.6.1: *If we can do one thing in m ways and for each of these m ways we can do another thing in n ways, then the total number of ways in which we can do both things is m times n.*

Now consider the number of different ways in which we can permute (arrange) a set of say, four objects. The first object can be placed in any of the four positions; the second can be placed in any of the three remaining positions; the third in any of the two remaining positions; and the fourth must occupy the remaining position. We can thus place the first object in 4 ways, the second in 3 ways, the third in 2, and the last in 1. By Rule 10.6.1, the total number of ways in which we can do all these things (make these arrangements) is $4 \times 3 \times 2 \times 1 = 24$, which is thus the number of permutations of four objects. If n is the number of objects to be permuted, in this case 4, then we see that $4 \times 3 \times 2 \times 1$ is equivalent to $4(4 - 1)(4 - 2)(4 - 3)$. Such a product is called a *factorial*, written $n!$.

$$n! = n(n - 1)(n - 2) \cdots [n - (n - 1)]. \quad \text{Thus}$$

$$1! = 1$$

$$2! = 2 \times 1 = 2$$

$$3! = 3 \times 2 \times 1 = 6$$

$$4! = 4 \times 3 \times 2 \times 1 = 24$$

$$5! = 5 \times 4 \times 3 \times 2 \times 1 = 120, \text{ etc.}$$

By definition, $0! = 1$.

We see then that if we are asked to find the number of permutations of n objects, this number is $n!$. Another way to ask the same question makes use of set theory: for a set of n objects, how many different ordered sets can be made of these n objects? For example, given the set $\{A, B, C\}$, how many different ordered sets are there containing A, B, and C? We list them: $\{A, B, C\}$, $\{A, C, B\}$, $\{B, A, C\}$, $\{B, C, A\}$, $\{C, A, B\}$, $\{C, B, A\}$, and no others.

Our formula gives us the answer with a great deal less trouble: $n! = 3! = 3 \times 2 \times 1 = 6$.

Rule 10.6.2: *The number of permutations of n objects is $n!$.*

We recall that the elements of an ordinary set do not have to be in any special order, i.e., the six arrangements above are all permutations of the *same* set. Thus,

Rule 10.6.3: *The number of combinations of n objects is 1.*

The permutation or combination of n objects is but a special case of the general question, "How many permutations or combinations are there of n objects if we arrange them r at a time?" The number r is thus the number of elements in each of the subsets which we construct from the set of n elements.   In Rules 10.6.2 and 10.6.3 we assume that $n = r$, e.g., the rule tells us that the number of permutations of n things, *taken n at a time*, is $n!$.   The number r, of course, cannot logically be greater than the number n.   The number of permutations of n things taken r at a time is written nPr; the number of combinations of n things taken r at a time is written nCr.   The student should understand that these symbols stand for positive integers which indicate the number of subsets (permutations or combinations) of r elements which can be constructed from a set of n elements.

Now suppose that we had three people who wanted to ride in our sports car.   How many ways can we permute (arrange) three people among two seats?   For each pair of people there are two permutations, as we found previously.   But there are three pairs of people to arrange; thus the total number of permutations of three people two at a time, is six.   We notice that the number of combinations is only three, since, again, we do not care how the people are seated in the car.

Further, suppose that we now have four people to arrange in the car. There are still only two permutations of each pair, but there are now six pairs, or combinations, each of which is to be arranged in two ways; total, twelve permutations of four things taken two at a time.

Let us summarize:

(n) Number of People	(r) Seats	Combinations	Permutations
2	2	1	2
3	2	3	6
4	2	6	12
further: 5	2	10	20
6	2	15	30

The number of permutations can be calculated in each case as follows: The first seat in the car can be filled in any of n ways, the second seat in $(n - 1)$ ways; we have only two seats, and therefore $r = 2$.   Thus $nP2 = (n)(n - 1)$ by Rule 10.6.1.   If we wish to compute the number of permutations of four people in the automobile, then $4P2 = 4(4 - 1) = 4 \times 3 = 12$.   We may now state a rule for determining the number of permutations of n things taken r at a time:

Rule 10.6.4: *The number of permutations of n things taken r at a time is:*

$$nPr = \frac{n!}{(n - r)!}$$

Example: $4P2 = \dfrac{4!}{(4 - 2)!} = \dfrac{4 \times 3 \times 2 \times 1}{2 \times 1} = 4 \times 3 = 12.$

We noted previously that while there are $n!$ permutations of n things, there is but one combination of n things. The same is true for r things: $rPr = r!$, but $rCr = 1$. In loading our automobile, we noticed that as we increased the number of people (n) we wished to arrange in it, the number of possible arrangements increased because of an increase in the number of combinations (pairs) of people; r did not change. Thus $nPr = r! \times (nCr)$. Therefore,

$$nCr = \frac{nPr}{r!} = \frac{n!}{r!(n-r)!},$$

which we shall formalize as a rule:

Rule 10.6.5: The number of combinations of n things taken r at a time is:

$$nCr = \frac{n!}{r!(n-r)!}$$

Example: $\quad 4C2 = \dfrac{4!}{2!(4-2)!} = \dfrac{4 \times 3 \times 2 \times 1}{2 \times 1 \times 2 \times 1} = \dfrac{12}{2} = 6$

10.6 Exercises

10.6.1 Using the rule given for permutations find:

(a) nPn
(c) $5P5$
(e) $6P4$
(g) $2P0$

(b) $3P2$
(d) $4P3$
(f) $7P2$
(h) $3P5$.

10.6.2 Using the rule given for combinations find:

(a) nCn
(c) $5C5$
(e) $15C10$
(g) $5C0$

(b) $3C2$
(d) $10C5$
(f) $7C1$
(h) $2C3$.

10.6.3 Explain why, given the number of *permutations* of n things taken r at a time, the number of *combinations* of n things taken r at a time can be found by dividing the number of permutations by $r!$ That is:

$$nCr = \frac{nPr}{r!}.$$

10.6.4 As the personnel director of a firm, you are attempting to plan the company's vacation schedule. Your policy is to let employees select their own vacation periods, with the single restriction that not more than 3 employees may be on vacation at any one time. In analyzing the schedule for the month of July you discover that 5 employees have requested permission to begin their vacation July 1st. Show by tree diagram and set analysis:

(a) the number of possible combinations of employees (A, B, C, D, and E) which could be selected for the desired vacation period.

(b) the probability that any single employee among the 5 would be among the group given the desired vacation period. (Find this 2 ways.)

10.6.5 Five men work in an office. If the payroll clerk hands out their paychecks at random, what is the probability that everybody will get his own paycheck? that exactly 4 men get the right paycheck?

10.6.6 The Many Big Chiefs Company has 12 directors. At their annual meeting the Board elected a President, Vice President, Secretary and Treasurer. If we assume that any one of the directors was equally likely to be selected for any one of the offices:

(a) How many permutations of officers are possible?

(b) How many combinations?

(c) What is the probability that any given director would be elected President? to any one of the offices?

10.6.7 The letters of the word Colorado are scrambled, and then rearranged in random order:

(a) What is the probability that the word so formed will begin with the letter "o?"

(b) What is the probability that the 3 "o's" will be found in consecutive order?

(c) What is the conditional probability that the 3 "o's" will be consecutive, given that the first 3 letters are "l," "r," and "a?"

10.6.8 A baseball catcher can instruct his pitcher to deliver 1 of 4 pitches—a fast ball, a slider, a curve, or a change of pace. Answer the following questions, symbolizing these pitches by the letters A, B, C, and D respectively. Explain all work.

(a) If the catcher were told to call for these pitches in combinations of 3 different pitches, how many combinations could he "order" the pitcher to throw? how many combinations of 4 pitches? of 1 pitch?

(b) If this catcher were told by his coach to call for these 4 pitches in sequence without repetition, how many sequences of these 4 pitches considered 3 at a time, would he have to select from?

(c) What is the probability, assuming each pitch to be equally likely,

(1) of pitch A being the first pitch thrown in any sequence of 3 different pitches?

(2) of pitch B being the second pitch thrown in any sequence of 4 different pitches, if the first pitch thrown is unknown? if the first pitch was pitch A?

(3) of pitch B being the third pitch thrown in any sequence of 4 different pitches, if the first 2 pitches thrown were A and C? if the first 2 pitches thrown were A and B?

10.7 Expected value

When he is making decisions under conditions of certainty, the "rational" administrator will always choose the alternative with the highest return, or payoff. We note that this statement is more a definition of the world "rational" than an observable rule of economic behavior; yet it is basic to our further understanding of such behavior. Given rationality as a standard, we may then determine the conditions under which lack of rationality may be expected. If you were offered a choice between one dozen doughnuts and two dozen of the same doughnuts at the same total cost, you would be rational if you chose the greater amount. In such a circumstance, we notice that the facts and outcomes are known: same doughnuts, same cost, twice as many doughnuts for the money.

Under conditions of risk, however, the rule of rational behavior must be changed to account for the fact that the payoffs or facts are not known with certainty, and that choosing a given alternative *may* not result in the payoff hoped for. In this case we must make our decisions in terms of our *expectations* of the outcomes, and thus we define a new concept, *expected value*. The *expected value* of any event is the value of the payoff of the event times the probability of the event. There are, of course, many ways to determine the *value* of an event: in business, value is often measured in terms of dollars, although we might use some other measure such as level of employee morale, business reputation, etc. In government, the value of some event might be measured in terms of the greatest good for the greatest number. One can see, however, that such measurements all but beg the question, since it is difficult to quantify such things as morale, reputation, or social welfare. We shall deal with problems where value is assumed to be measured in terms of dollars or some other easily recognized standard, with the understanding that the determination of measurement of value is a knotty problem which we only assume solved for our current purposes. We may now define a rule for decision-making under risk: under conditions of risk, the "rational" decision maker will choose the alternative that results in the payoff with the highest expected value.

Matching "fair" pennies is a risky game, since we cannot know whether or not two coins will turn up the same sides on a single toss, although we feel that the probability of this event should be $\frac{1}{2}$. What is the expected value of this game? Let S be the event that the coins match, and $\tilde{S}$ the event that they do not. Generally, in this game the winner earns the other's coin, and therefore the payoff is 1 cent to the winner and -1 cent to the loser. The expected value of the game, which is the event $(S \cup \tilde{S})$, is therefore $E(S \cup \tilde{S}) = P(S) \times$ (winnings) $+ P(\tilde{S}) \times$ (loss) $= 0.5(1\cent) + 0.5(-1\cent) = 0$. Since the game has two possible outcomes, win or lose, the game itself is really a compound event, and we have calculated the expected value of two events, winning and losing. The expected value of winning the game is $\frac{1}{2}$ cent; the expected value of losing is *minus* $\frac{1}{2}$ cent. Over the long run we would expect to lose as much as we win, and therefore the expected value of the game is zero. Such a game is called a *fair game*.

We should notice that it seems silly to play any fair game, but then our decision model does not take into account any other motivation for playing the game but that value, or those values, assigned to the outcome or outcomes. Horse racing is not a fair game; the expenses of maintaining a track, paying off the owners of winning horses, etc., all must come out of the "handle," the amount of money bet on the races, before any bettor can be paid off. In other words, the expected value of the event that any given horse will win is always negative for the bettor. People bet on the horses, however. Why? Our model does not take into account the values associated with the act of betting or taking a chance itself, and many people value this more highly than the losses which they will sustain in the long run. Many businessmen do this also; for some reason the long shot which pays off may have a tendency to imply an unwarranted amount of business acumen or "sixth sense" on the part of the "bettor." Unfortunately, many of those who have succeeded on this basis are written up in the various newspapers and trade magazines as very shrewd operators; whereas they were only very lucky. Those who were not so lucky end up as a statistic in the "business failures" column of the same publications. Our model deals only with the economic value of the outcome, and not with any additional, subjective value which might accrue from having won the game itself.

Any gamble in which the payoffs and probabilities associated with them are made explicit is known as a *lottery*. Organized lotteries are generally illegal in the United States, although some foreign countries not only allow them, but operate them as state monopolies, e.g., the Irish Sweepstakes and the national lottery of Italy. We might distinguish between a *game* and a *lottery* by stating that the actual cost of the lottery is determined in advance, perhaps by the purchase of a ticket; the cost of playing a game is not determined until the game is completed. The cost of a game, then, is the loss sustained having played the game. This distinction is drawn because the determination of the expected value of a lottery can be simplified from the general statement of the expected value of any gamble, since the cost of taking the gamble is known *a priori*. It should be understood, however, that the more general rule applies to lotteries as well as to games, as distinguished above.

Consider a lottery of the following type: 1000 tickets are sold at $1 each, the drawing is random, and the prize is $100. The expected value of this lottery can be calculated by computing the expected value of winning (probability of winning times total winnings) minus the cost of the gamble:

$$E(\text{Lottery}) = \frac{1}{1000}\,(\$100) - \$1 = \$0.10 - \$1.00 = -\$0.90.$$

The expected value of this lottery is thus *negative* ninety cents. Let us show that the same result would have obtained had we used the previous rule:

$$E(L) = P(W) \times (\text{net winnings}) + P(\tilde{W}) \times (\text{net loss})$$

$$= \frac{1}{1000}\,(\$99) + \frac{999}{1000}\,(-\$1) = \$0.099 - \$0.999 = -\$0.90.$$

The difference is accounted for of course by the fact that previously we had assumed that we had paid our dollar to play, and thus this was a known "loss" of $1, and thus we compute our winnings as the gross amount won. In the latter case, we consider the actual net winnings and the actual net loss, since neither winning nor losing is determined until after the play. One may use either method to find the expected value of the lottery; caution must be used, however, in seeing that the proper payoffs are used in the computation. The administrative principle of *sunk cost* comes into play here: once we have irretrievably committed funds to some purpose, then for decision-making purposes the eventual payoff resulting from this commitment should consist of the total or gross return from the expenditure.

Suppose that you were required to choose between the lottery above and one with the following characteristics: 500 tickets are sold at $1.50 each and the prize is $500:

$$E(L) = \frac{1}{500}\,(\$500) - \$1.50 = \$1 - \$1.50 = -\$0.50.$$

Obviously the latter lottery has the higher value; although it is still negative, the expected loss is not so great. Our rule might then be restated to cover this circumstance specifically, by saying that the rational decision maker will choose the alternative which maximizes expected gain or minimizes expected loss. (The value problem itself occurs here; one might be more willing to risk $1 in the first lottery than $1.50 in the second, merely because of the amounts of money involved in the cost of buying the lottery.)

Let us apply the concept of expected value to the newsboy problem in Section 10.1, since he was left with his problem unsolved. Suppose that after 100 days of selling papers, he has found that on 40 days he had 11 customers; on 30 days, 12 customers; 20 days, 13 customers; 10 days, 14; and that he had never had 15 customers. Since he is guaranteed 10 customers every day, and assuming that he is rational under conditions of certainty, he will always stock at least 10 papers, and we shall omit this alternative from consideration.

In Fig. 10.7.1 we have redrawn Fig. 10.1.1, including the new informa-

Demand		Stock Alternatives				
Event	Prob.	11	12	13	14	15
11	.4	.220 / .55	.200 / .50	.180 / .45	.160 / .40	.140 / .35
12	.3	.165 / .55	.180 / .60	.165 / .55	.150 / .50	.135 / .45
13	.2	.110 / .55	.120 / .60	.130 / .65	.120 / .60	.110 / .55
14	.1	.055 / .55	.060 / .60	.065 / .65	.070 / .70	.065 / .65
15	0	0 / .55	0 / .60	0 / .65	0 / .70	0 / .75
Expected Value		.55	.56	.54	.50	.45

Fig. 10.7.1

tion available to the newsboy. Associated with each event, the number of papers sold in any day, is the probability of that event, calculated from the relative frequencies which he developed from his experience. The entry in the upper right hand corner of each cell of the matrix is the expected value, in dollars, of any stock alternative, given that the associated event occurs. When the newsboy makes his choice of a certain number of papers to stock, then one of the events 11, 12, 13, or 14 will occur; therefore the expected value of, for instance, the alternative to stock 11 papers is the sum of the expected values of the individual events which could occur, or

$$E(11) = (0.4)(0.55) + (0.3)(0.55) + (0.2)(0.55)$$
$$+ (0.1)(0.55) + (0)(0.55) = 0.55.$$

The expected value of choosing to stock 11 papers is thus $0.55. The expected value for each of the available alternatives is computed in the same manner. They are indicated in the bottom margin of Fig. 10.7.1. We are now ready to answer the newsboy's question: assuming that he is rational under conditions of risk, he should select the alternative with the highest *expected* value, which in this case is to stock 12 papers.

We may now state the rule for finding the expected value of any course of action, or alternative. This rule applies to any decision to be made under conditions of risk; we note that the purpose of determining the expected value of a game or lottery is to determine whether or not we should play the game, or buy the lottery.

Rule 10.7.1: *Let A be an alternative the choice of which leads to the realization of one of a set of n mutually exclusive and collectively exhaustive possible payoffs* $x_1, x_2, \ldots, x_n$, *where* x_i *is some measure of value. Associated with each payoff is its probability* $p_1, p_2, \ldots, p_n$.

The expected value of the alternative is then:

$$E(A) = p_1x_1 + p_2x_2 + \cdots + p_nx_n.$$

If one is faced with a number of alternatives under conditions of risk, then the rational decision maker will choose that alternative with the highest expected value.

10.7 Exercises

10.7.1 Two men, A and B, toss coins with the agreement that if A's coin matches B's, A wins both coins and if the coins do not match, B wins both coins. What is the expected value to A, and to B, if:

(a) A and B each use a silver dollar?

(b) A uses a penny and B a nickel?

(c) Why is a gambling game in which the sum of the expected values to each player is zero called a "fair game"?

10.7.2 If the rules of the game in Exercise 10.7.1 were changed so that A would win only if both coins came up heads, what is the expected value of the game to A, and to B, if:

(a) A and B each use a silver dollar?

(b) A uses a quarter and B a silver dollar?   Is this a "fair" game?

(c) In part a, how much must B pay to A on each toss to get him to play, if they are both rational?

10.7.3 One type of roulette wheel has 36 numbers, 1–36, on its perimeter, alternately colored red and black.   In addition, there is the number zero, colored green.   The payoff on red, black, odd, or even (excluding zero) is two for one.   The payoff for any given number, including zero, is thirty-six to one.

(a) What is the expected value of a $1 bet on black?

(b) What is the expected value of a $10 bet on odd?

(c) What is the expected value of a $1 bet on zero?

(d) How does the *amount* of money bet affect the relative payoff?

10.7.4 A firm is considering an insurance plan for a new plant, valued at $200,000.   The estimated probability of this plant's being destroyed by fire is 0.005, according to the local fire "mortality" rates.

(a) If the insurance premium is $2000 what is the expected value of the decision to insure?

(b) Even though the expected value computed in part a is negative, most firms would decide to buy the insurance.   Why?

10.7.5 A firm suffers an absenteeism rate due to illness of 25/1000 man days, and figures the net cost per day per employee at $27.   It is estimated that establishing a plant clinic with a resident doctor and nurse would reduce the time lost due to illness by 40 per cent.   If this firm has 2000 employees, how much could they spend on a plant clinic in a normal 21-working-day month, without net cost to the company?

10.7.6 A cement contractor takes a very risky job during a winter period.   If the weather is good he could earn $3000 on the job; if the weather is bad he could lose as much as $1000.   What is the expected value of the job:

(a) If the probability of good weather is 0.5?

(b) If the probability of good weather is 0.2?

10.8 Success and failure: Bernoulli trials

A very common situation in administrative decision-making arises when the payoff of some decision can be considered solely in terms of success or failure, not measured in degrees of relative success or relative failure, but absolutely: we either succeed or we fail. For instance, the quality control supervisor of an industrial plant is interested in the number of items rejected due to faults in the process, i.e., the number of items which fail to meet the requirements of some quality standard. We recall the story of the man sorting apples: good ones here and bad ones there. (He quit his job because he had to make too many decisions!)

If the probability of success on any one observation is known, then the probability of failure is also known, since these are the only admissible outcomes in such a situation. If p is the probability of success and q the probability of failure, then $p + q = 1.0$. Symbolically, if S is the set of all observations which are successful, and F is the set of all failures, then $S \cap F = \phi$ and $S \cup F = \Omega$. If $P(S) = p$ and $P(F) = q$, then $P(F \cap S) = 0$ and $P(S \cup F) = 1.0$. Since S and F are mutually exclusive and collectively exhaustive, $P(S \cup F) = P(S) + P(F) = p + q = 1.0$. If from a tallying of items inspected in the past, we found that 10 per cent of them were defective, then we could state the empirical probability of failure to be $q = 0.1$, and thus $p = 0.9$. With such information we could develop predictions such as, for instance, that 450 out of a batch of 500 items would be expected to pass inspection.

In many areas of administration such information, albeit useful, is hardly sufficient for optimal decision-making. More useful predictions might be derived from such questions as: "What is the probability that out of 100 items inspected, given the probability of failure to be 0.1, exactly 15 will be found to be defective? What is the probability that no more than 10 items will be defective? What is the probability that at least 95 items will pass inspection?"

In each case we ask for the *a priori* probability of some compound event, given the known probability associated with the outcome of each simple event (the inspection of each item). Suppose that we wished to find the probability of exactly 15 defectives, as in the first question above. The set of events which would satisfy our wish, i.e., $P(F = 15)$, where f symbolizes an item defective and s an item which passes, could be written $\{f_1, f_2, f_3, \ldots, f_{15}, s_{16}, \ldots, s_{100}\}$, indicating that the first 15 inspected failed, and the rest passed. This is of course only one of the ways in which the desired event can happen; in fact, the number of ways in which the event can happen is exactly the number of combinations of 100 things taken 15 at a time, or $100C15$. This is an important part of the determination of the required probability, but we recall that the probability of failure on each inspection is known and must be taken into account. Before we state how this is done, let us generalize this problem, and state some nomenclature.

Each inspection or event is called a *Bernoulli trial*, satisfying the requirements of mutual exclusion and collective exhaustion above, i.e., success *or* failure. A collection or sequence of such trials is called a *Bernoulli process* when the trials are stochastically independent, i.e., when the outcome of one trial has no effect upon the probability of the outcome of any other trial. For purposes of illustration, let us examine a problem of smaller scope before plunging into the problem outlined above. Suppose that we were to toss a fair coin 4 times, and wanted to know the *a priori* probability of getting heads on the first 2 tosses and tails on the last 2. Of all the events that could occur, we see that this event can occur in only one way: $\{H_1, H_2, T_3, T_4\}$. If we represent the probability of a head by p and the probability of a tail by q, then the probability P of the desired event is

$$P(H_1, H_2, T_3, T_4) = p_1 p_2 q_3 q_4 \text{ (by Definition 10.5.1)}$$

$$= \left(\frac{1}{2}\right)\left(\frac{1}{2}\right)\left(\frac{1}{2}\right)\left(\frac{1}{2}\right)$$

$$= \frac{1}{16}.$$

Thus to find the probability P of exactly r successes in n Bernoulli trials, given the *order* of successes and failures, we multiply the probability of success p for r outcomes times the probability of failure q for $n - r$ outcomes:

$$P_o(r) = \overbrace{p \times p \times p \times \cdots \times p}^{r} \times \overbrace{q \times q \times \cdots \times q}^{n-r} = p^r q^{n-r},$$

and we develop

$$Formula\ 10.8.1: \quad P_o(r) = p^r q^{n-r},$$

where $P_o(r)$ is the probability of exactly r successes *where the order is specified.*

For the inspection problem above, if we wished to know the probability that the first 15 items would be found defective and the next 85 not defective, then

$$P_o(r = 85) = (0.9)^{85}(0.1)^{15} = 1.18(10)^{-19} \text{ (Approx.)}.$$

More often than not, the *order* of success and failure is not important, as in the first statement of the inspection problem, where we considered merely a batch of items without regard for the order in which they were produced or inspected. Thus the event satisfying the conditions is any event containing 15 defects and 85 passing items, no matter in what order they occur. We have already stated this as the number of combinations of n things taken r at a time. We therefore apply Rule 10.6.5 to Formula 10.8.1 to develop the general formula for the probability P of exactly r successes in n Bernoulli trials, the order of occurrence of the successes being of no importance:

Formula 10.8.2: $P(r) = nCr(p)^r(q)^{n-r}.$

This formula is known as the *binomial probability* formula, since it can be developed as well from the rth term in the expansion of the binomial $(p + q)^n$.

Let us apply this formula to the coin tossing experiment outlined above, only now ask for the probability of getting exactly no heads, 1 head, 2 heads, ... , 4 heads in four tosses of the coin:

$$P(r = 0) = 4C0 \left(\frac{1}{2}\right)^0 \left(\frac{1}{2}\right)^4 = \frac{4!}{0!4!}(1)\left(\frac{1}{16}\right) = \frac{1}{16}$$

$$P(r = 1) = 4C1 \left(\frac{1}{2}\right)^1 \left(\frac{1}{2}\right)^3 = \frac{4!}{1!3!}\left(\frac{1}{2}\right)\left(\frac{1}{8}\right) = \frac{4}{16}$$

$$P(r = 2) = 4C2 \left(\frac{1}{2}\right)^2 \left(\frac{1}{2}\right)^2 = \frac{4!}{2!2!}\left(\frac{1}{4}\right)\left(\frac{1}{4}\right) = \frac{6}{16}$$

$$P(r = 3) = 4C3 \left(\frac{1}{2}\right)^3 \left(\frac{1}{2}\right)^1 = \frac{4!}{3!4!}\left(\frac{1}{8}\right)\left(\frac{1}{2}\right) = \frac{4}{16}$$

$$P(r = 4) = 4C4 \left(\frac{1}{2}\right)^4 \left(\frac{1}{2}\right)^0 = \frac{4!}{4!0!}\left(\frac{1}{16}\right)(1) = \frac{1}{16}$$

Thus for any Bernoulli process, given p and n, we can compute the probability of as many successes r as we wish; and having found the probability of success, we can find the probability of failure, since $q = 1 - p$. We note for the system above that the sum of the probabilities is 16/16, or 1.0, as we would expect, since the five events listed exhaust the possible outcomes of the experiment.

The list above comprises a *discrete probability density function*, or *probability distribution function*, i.e., $P = f(r)$. It is a discrete function because the function is defined only for the five isolated points in the sample space. The graph of such a function is called a *histogram*, as shown in Fig. 10.8.1. A histogram is drawn so that each event is represented by a segment of the horizontal axis, these segments being of equal, unit size. The height of each rectangle is the probability of the event which it represents, and thus the area of each rectangle is

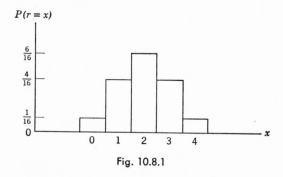

Fig. 10.8.1

also proportionate to the probability associated with the event represented. The sum of the areas of the rectangles must therefore equal 1.0.

So far we have answered only the first type of question asked concerning an exact number of successes or failures. Suppose we wished to know the probability of not more than 3 heads, i.e., at most 3 heads. This event is obviously the sum of the probability of no heads, the probability of 1 head, of 2 heads, and of 3 heads. We can write this probability as

$$P(r \leq 3) = P(r = 0) + P(r = 1) + P(r = 2) + P(r = 3),$$

because the outcomes are mutually exclusive. The density function described above gives us the values of the necessary probabilities:

$$P(r \leq 3) = \frac{1}{16} + \frac{4}{16} + \frac{6}{16} + \frac{4}{16} = \frac{15}{16}.$$

Now we may make a new list of the probabilities of the outcomes in terms of the "at most" criterion:

$$P(r = 0) = \frac{1}{16}$$

$$P(r \leq 1) = \frac{1}{16} + \frac{4}{16} = \frac{5}{16}$$

$$P(r \leq 2) = \frac{1}{16} + \frac{4}{16} + \frac{6}{16} = \frac{11}{16}$$

$$P(r \leq 3) = \frac{1}{16} + \frac{4}{16} + \frac{6}{16} + \frac{4}{16} = \frac{15}{16}$$

$$P(r \leq 4) = \frac{1}{16} + \frac{4}{16} + \frac{6}{16} + \frac{4}{16} + \frac{1}{16} = \frac{16}{16} = 1.0.$$

This function is called a discrete *cumulative* probability density function, or *cumulative* distribution. It is distinguished from the previous function by the fact that each point in the domain includes those other points of lesser order, i.e., an interval, as shown in the graph of this function in Fig. 10.8.2.

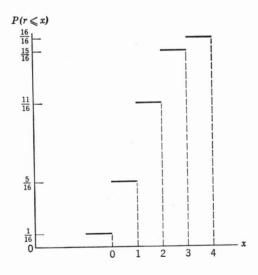

Fig. 10.8.2

The graph of the cumulative function does not consist of rectangles, as in the histogram, because the statement of a cumulative probability implies that the function is defined over intervals in the domain, rather than at isolated points in the domain. The result is the "step" function illustrated, the "height" of each step representing the cumulative probability of the associated events in the domain.

Since the determination of the probabilities for either of these functions becomes very tedious when n is large or p is carried to more than one place, tables have been constructed which state the desired probabilities for various values of p and n. Such tables are highly useful for control purposes in areas like quality control and acceptance sampling, subjects which are discussed further in the study of statistics.

10.8   Exercises

10.8.1   Given a Bernoulli process of 10 trials, with probability $p = 0.6$ of success on one trial, find the probability of

(a) exactly no successes   (b) exactly 1 success
(c) exactly 2 successes   (d) at most 3 successes
(e) at least 3 failures.

10.8.2   Below is the "top" part of "Pascal's Triangle":

$$
\begin{array}{ccccccccc}
 & & & & 1 & & & & \\
 & & & 1 & & 1 & & & \\
 & & 1 & & 2 & & 1 & & \\
 & 1 & & 3 & & 3 & & 1 & \\
1 & & 4 & & 6 & & 4 & & 1
\end{array}
$$

It is constructed by increasing the number of elements by 1 in each subsequent row, in such a way that the first and last elements are 1 and each interior term is the sum of the two terms immediately above it, as shown. Complete the triangle to 10 rows. What relationship do you observe between the triangle and Formula 10.8.2? (*Hint:* Expand the binomial $(p + q)^n$ using the formula, for $n = 0, 1, 2, 3, 4$. Compare your result with each row in the triangle.)

10.8.3   The output of an automatic machine at the Stroh Strong String Corp. has been analyzed and found to be a Bernoulli process for which the probability of failure is $q = 0.2$. In the analysis of a sample of 10 units produced by the machine, what is the probability of

(a) the first 4 units failing and the last 6 OK?
(b) the first 6 OK and the last 4 failing?

(c) the first OK and alternate failures thereafter ($\{s, f, s, f, s \ldots f\}$)?
(d) exactly 4 failures?
(e) exactly 5 failures?
(f) less than 5 failures?
(g) at most 5 failures?

Are you more likely to find no defectives than some defectives in the sample (some defectives = at least one)? What is the expected number of defectives in a sample of 10? Draw the histogram of the probability distribution for this problem. Draw the cumulative distribution.

Chapter 11

Non-Linear Functions

11.1 Non-linearity

Observation of the behavior of administrative phenomena in an attempt to find and define relationships among variables leads us to the conclusion that linear relations and functions provide only a limited, albeit useful, tool of analysis. For instance, in our study of breakeven analysis, we found that revenue could be described as a linear function of quantity sold, given some constant price. In Fig. 11.1.1 is graphed such a function : $y = f(x) = \$1x$ where the price of the commodity is \$1 per unit. Suppose we were to ask for the relationship between price and quantity, in a circumstance where the total revenue were fixed (constant), rather than the price? Such a request might have the form, "what combinations of price and quantity sold provide a revenue of \$100?" The relationship required is graphed in Fig. 11.1.2, this particular function being described by the equation $xy = \$100$. Let us write this function in the form used previously: $\{(x, y) | xy = k\}$, and recall that the statement in this form defines a set each of whose elements is an ordered pair of numbers (x, y) which make the equation $xy = k$ a true statement, where k is a constant. A function of this form is said to be *hyperbolic*, and the graph of the function (Fig. 11.1.2) is called a *hyperbola*.

The salient feature of the hyperbola and other non-linear functions is that the rate at which one of the variables changes relative to the other is not constant; as the values of the independent variable increase, for example, by a constant amount, the values of the dependent vari-

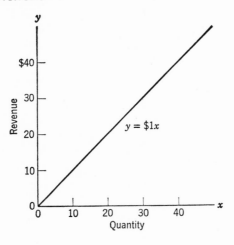

Fig. 11.1.1

able may grow smaller in such a way that the *differences* between successive values of the dependent variable diminish in value. Such behavior is evident in Fig. 11.1.2. Let us examine some of the ordered pairs describing this function, writing them in tabular form, as in Fig. 11.1.3, and noting the successive differences between the values. The symbol Δ, read "delta," means "change in," and Δx and Δy represent the difference between successive values of x and y, respectively

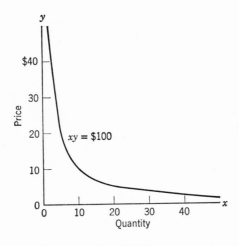

Fig. 11.1.2

x	y	Δx	Δy
0	(∞)		
		5	($-\infty$)
5	20		
		5	-10
10	10		
		5	$-3\frac{1}{3}$
15	$6\frac{1}{3}$		
		5	$-1\frac{1}{3}$
20	5		
		5	-1
25	4		

Fig. 11.1.3

We let x change by a constant amount, i.e., $\Delta x = 5$. The rate of change of y with respect to x is obviously not constant, but is diminishing. Also, since y decreases as x increases, y is said to be *decreasing* at a *decreasing rate*. On the other hand, the linear expression in Fig. 11.1.1 indicates that y increases as x increases, but the change in y relative to the change in x, which can be written $\Delta y / \Delta x$, is constant; y is said to be increasing at a constant rate.

There are thus two things with which we are concerned which relate the behavior of the dependent variable to the behavior of the independent variable: (1) *the direction of change* in y as x changes (increasing, constant, decreasing), and (2) *the direction of the rate of change* in y as x is allowed to change by equal increments, for example, *an increasing rate*, as in "increasing at an increasing rate." The differences Δx and Δy we shall call *first differences*.

The graph of the hyperbolic function in our example (note that we have examined only the first quadrant) is seen to decrease throughout its length with respect to y as x increases: such a function is said to be *monotonic decreasing*. Monotonicity refers to the consistency of direction taken by a function when we follow its graph from left to right over an interval. A curve that never "falls" as we trace it over an interval describes a function that is monotonic increasing in that interval. A curve that never "rises" describes a function that is monotonic decreasing. The case of a horizontal straight line is special: such a function is also monotonic, although it neither increases nor decreases. Thus there is the possibility that a curve may "rise" through part of the interval, become "flat" or horizontal, and then continue to rise again. Such a function would be monotonic increasing over the entire interval, although there might be a sub-interval in which it did not increase. A function which has no "flat" spots in a given interval is said to be *strictly* monotonic in that interval. Our hyperbola is therefore *strictly monotonic decreasing.*

It can be shown that the sign of the first differences of this hyperbola when drawn in the first quadrant will always be negative (except for an interval containing $x = 0$). The sign of the first difference provides a means of determining the monotonicity of a function over various intervals. As the values of x in the domain of the function are increased by small amounts, if the sign of the first differences of y remains non-positive in an interval, then the function is monotonic decreasing in that interval; if the sign is non-negative, then the function is monotonic increasing. Note that we allow for the first differences

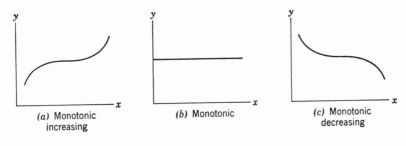

(a) Monotonic increasing (b) Monotonic (c) Monotonic decreasing

Fig. 11.1.4

of y to be zero, indicating a flat spot on the curve. If the first differences of y are *always* negative in an interval, then the function is strictly monotonic decreasing, etc. In Fig. 11.1.4 are the graphs of various functions with certain monotone characteristics; in Fig. 11.1.5 is a composite curve illustrating a function that is not monotonic over its entire length, but does exhibit monotonicity over certain intervals. (The student should perhaps review briefly the work on intervals in Section 6.3.)

Another common behavior pattern of economic phenomena can be described by the U-shaped curve illustrated in Fig. 11.1.6. Unit costs of production at various levels of plant capacity are usually assumed to behave in this fashion. With a plant of given size, the cost of producing each of the first few units is very high, since all of the costs of production including such things as rental of plant property must be distributed over very few items. As the level of production increases,

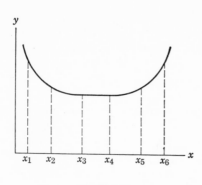

$\{x_1 \leq x \leq x_2\}$;
   strictly monotonic decreasing
$\{x_1 \leq x \leq x_3\}$;
   monotonic decreasing
$\{x_3 \leq x \leq x_4\}$;
   monotonic
$\{x_4 \leq x \leq x_5\}$;
   monotonic increasing
$\{x_5 \leq x \leq x_6\}$;
   strictly monotonic increasing.

Fig. 11.1.5

however, these unit costs can be expected to decrease since there are more units over which the total cost can be spread. At some point, however, a minimum cost per unit must be reached beyond which unit costs begin to rise, a phenomenon attributed to the necessity of spreading too thinly over each unit of a large output such things as supervision and management, not to mention the use of poorer and poorer resources, etc.

Next to the graph in Fig. 11.1.6 is a table of ordered pairs in the set $\{(x, y) | y = x^2 - 8x + 18\}$ and also the first differences of y with respect to the tabulated values of x. We notice that as x increases in equal increments, y decreases in the interval $\{-\infty < x < 4\}$; in the interval $\{4 < x < \infty\}$, y increases. At the point $(2, 4)$, the curve reaches a minimum; at this point the sign of the first differences of y changes from negative to positive. We shall demonstrate these latter statements subsequently in our study of calculus; it suffices for the moment to reflect upon the symmetry of this curve and to arrive at these conclusions by inspection. The equation

$$y = x^2 - 8x + 18$$

states that the unit cost of production (y) can be determined for various levels of output (x) by substituting a value for x in the right-hand side of the equation, as we have done in constructing the table in Fig. 11.1.6.

Although the example above is but an hypothetical illustration, it is implied that real-life circumstances may be expressed in such mathematical language, as indeed they have been expressed. The inquisitive student may well wonder how phenomena of the real world can be reduced to such relatively simple statements of behavioral relationship: such reduction is both possible and meaningful in terms of administrative decision-making.   In this example, which deals with the behavior of economic variables, we rely upon our understanding of economics to provide a basis for decisions.   The substantive scientist in economics is expected to be able to tell us those variables of concern in such a problem, and in addition to be able to describe their general behavior and relationship.   As an example of "behavior" of a variable, we note that a negative value for x (level of output) has no economic meaning; zero production is the minimum output.   We must therefore restrict the domain of x to the set of all non-negative real numbers.   As to the relationship between the variables, we might expect the scientist to tell us that over a certain interval the function relating unit cost and level of output is monotonic decreasing, the function reaches a minimum, and then over another interval it is monotonic increasing.   With this information we can then find a mathematical expression which behaves in the same fashion: the parabola described by the function above is one such function.   Fitting the mathematical function to the problem is often referred to as "curve-fitting," and there are various techniques for doing this, some of which we shall study subsequently.   The student may be ultimately neither economist nor mathematician; we assume, however, that he will eventually occupy a position as an administrator.   An understanding of these concepts will allow him immediate access to the abilities of these specialists in the solution of his problems.

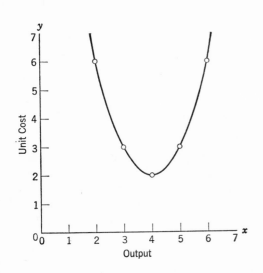

$$y = x^2 - 8x + 18$$

x	y	Δx	Δy
2	6		
		1	-3
3	3		
		1	-1
4	2		
		1	1
5	3		
		1	3
6	6		

Fig. 11.1.6

The purpose of this section has been to introduce the concept of non-linearity as a tool for the behavioral analysis of economic phenomena. It is important to realize that the functions described in this section and in those to come are highly useful to the administrator, because they set forth in a precise and powerful way the relationships that exist among variables, the values of which it is the responsibility of the administrator to determine, or perhaps to predict under various circumstances.

11.1 Exercises

For each of the following problems, determine a minimum of seven of the ordered pairs comprising the solution set, tabulating them in the form of Fig. 11.1.3. Choose the values of x so that Δx is measured in equal integral increments. Graph the function on $\frac{1}{4}$-inch graph paper. Describe the direction and monotonicity of each curve in terms of intervals in the domain. Unless otherwise specified, the range and domain is the set of all real numbers.

11.1.1 $\{(x, y) | (y = 3 - 2x) \wedge (-5 \leq x \leq 5)\}$

11.1.2 $\{(x, f(x)) | (f(x) = (0.38x)) \wedge (x \geq 0)\}$

11.1.3 $\{(x, y) | y^2 = 4 - x^2\}$ Range: set of positive real numbers.

11.1.4 $\{(x, y) | y = 100/x\}$

11.1.5 $\{(x, y) | y = x^2 - 8x + 18\}$

11.1.6 $\{(x, y) | (y = 6 + 2x - x^2) \wedge (0 \leq x \leq 4)\}$

11.1.7 $\{(x, y) | (y = x^2 - 4x + 4) \wedge (0 \leq x \leq 4)\}$

11.1.8 $\{(x, y) | y = 30 - x^2/60\}$.

11.2 Symmetry, limits, asymptotes, and continuity

In addition to the characteristic of monotonicity, many functions can be described by certain other behavior characteristics. These characteristics assist us both in graphing and in understanding what "happens" to the function at points, or in intervals, that cannot be graphed due to physical limitations. Although it was not shown on the graph of the function $xy = \$100$, because we had restricted the range and domain to positive numbers, the graph of this hyperbolic function of unrestricted range and domain appears in both the first and third quadrants. In Fig. 11.2.1 the function $xy = 1$ is graphed; some of the ordered pairs in the solution set of the statement $\{(x, y) | xy = 1\}$ are

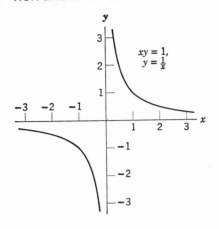

Quadrant I		Quadrant III	
x	y	x	y
⅓	3	-⅓	-3
½	2	-½	-2
1	1	-1	-1
2	½	-2	-½
3	⅓	-3	-⅓

Fig. 11.2.1

also tabulated.   For each point on the curve with coordinates (x_1, y_1) there is another point with coordinates $(-x_1, -y_1)$, e.g., the solution set contains both the point $(1, 1)$ and the point $(-1, -1)$.

Such a graph is said to be *symmetric with respect to the origin*.   If a pin were driven exactly through the origin of the graph, and the entire graph were rotated 180° (through half a circle), we would have the identical picture that we had before the rotation.

In Fig. 11.2.2 the function $yx^2 = 1$ is graphed.   The accompanying table indicates that for each point (x_1, y_1) there is a point $(-x_1, y_1)$, e.g., $(½, 4)$ and $(-½, 4)$.   Such a graph is said to be *symmetric with*

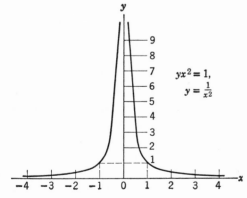

Quadrant I		Quadrant II	
x	y	x	y
⅓	9	-⅓	9
½	4	-½	4
1	1	-1	1
2	½	-2	½
3	⅑	-3	⅑

Fig. 11.2.2

respect to the range axis. (Range axis is another name for the y axis.) If we were to draw this graph in the first quadrant on a piece of transparent material, and then fold that quadrant across the range axis, as in turning the page of a book, we would find that our drawing would coincide exactly with the graph of the function in the second quadrant.

Therefore, when tabulating values of the variables x and y preparatory to graphing a function, one should examine for *each* (x_1, y_1) the point whose value in the domain is $-x_1$ to determine if its associated coordinate is y_1 or $-y_1$; in the former case, the graph of the function will be symmetric to the range axis; in the latter, symmetric to the origin.

The graph which appears in Fig. 11.1.6 is obviously symmetrical, although it is not symmetrical to the range axis, but to the vertical line passing through the point $(4, 2)$. A *translation*, or shift, of the range axis of four units to the right would result in this function's satisfying our definition of symmetry; if we substitute for each x the value $(x - 4) = h$, then our table now has the required characteristic that for each point (h, k) there is a point $(-h, k)$ in the solution set of the function. Recognition of the fact that a given function describes a symmetrical curve assists considerably in graphing and in further understanding the behavior of the function.

Another highly useful concept is that of a *limit*, which can be defined as the exact solution approached by a sequence of approximate solutions to a problem. As an example, we might ask "how long would a board become if we were to saw off half of it repeatedly?" If the board were originally x units long, then after the first cut it would be $\frac{1}{2}x$ units long; after the second, $\frac{1}{4}x$ units, etc. If x were one unit to start, then successive approximations of the length of the board would be $\frac{1}{2}$, $\frac{1}{4}$, $\frac{1}{8}$, $\frac{1}{16}$, ... (assuming that our saw blade does not reduce the length of the board which we are measuring). After a great many cuts, the remaining length of board would be very short indeed, although we could presumably continue to reduce this length indefinitely under the proper physical circumstances. We can define the ending point of this procedure, then, only in terms of its *limit*, which is that never-reached point when there is no more board to saw, i.e., the length of the board is zero units. After each cut, we will have a better approximation to the correct answer to our question, but the exact answer itself can only be defined in terms of the limit. We say: "in the limit, the board will have zero length." The function describing the length of the board $f(n)$ after each saw cut n can be stated explicitly as $f(n) = (\frac{1}{2})^n$, as illustrated in Fig. 11.2.3 by the table and the graph. (Note that the table lists a value of the function only for integral

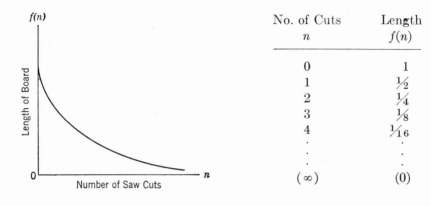

No. of Cuts	Length
n	$f(n)$
0	1
1	$\frac{1}{2}$
2	$\frac{1}{4}$
3	$\frac{1}{8}$
4	$\frac{1}{16}$
.	.
.	.
.	.
(∞)	(0)

Fig. 11.2.3. $f(n) = \left(\dfrac{1}{2}\right)^n$, $\displaystyle\lim_{n \to \infty} f(n) = \lim_{n \to \infty} \left(\dfrac{1}{2}\right)^n = 0$.

values of n, while the graph is drawn as a continuum of points; this problem will be discussed shortly.) The table indicates that after infinitely many saw cuts, the board will have zero length. Of course, infinity is not a number, and therefore cannot be used as a value in the domain of n. Thus the last pair of values in the table represent limiting values that cannot be reached in the real sense, but are nonetheless meaningful in analyzing the behavior of functions. To express these values, then, we write $\displaystyle\lim_{n \to \infty} f(n) = 0$, read "the limit of $f(n)$ as n approaches infinity is zero." Since $f(n) = (\frac{1}{2})^n$, we may also write $\displaystyle\lim_{n \to \infty} (\frac{1}{2})^n = 0$. The student should be able to reason intuitively that as n becomes larger and larger, $f(n)$ becomes smaller and smaller.

As another example, if we were to deposit one dollar in a savings bank which paid 4 per cent interest per year and computed this interest twice a year, then after the first six months our investment would be worth \$1.02. At the end of the next six months, assuming that we did not withdraw the previous interest, the investment would be worth \$1.0404; the increase in the total value of the investment is not constant at 2 per cent per period since interest also accrues on previously paid interest. If n is the number of periods over which interest is to be computed on our investment, and $f(n)$ is the value of the investment at the end of n periods, then $f(n)$ may be calculated by the formula $f(n) = P(1 + 0.02)^n$, where P is the amount originally invested. This formula is recognized as the standard compound interest formula. What happens to the value of our investment if we leave the original

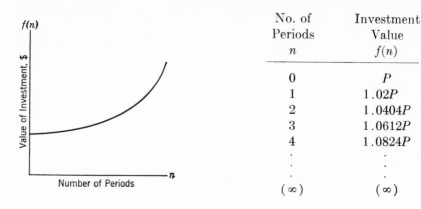

No. of Periods n	Investment Value $f(n)$
0	P
1	$1.02P$
2	$1.0404P$
3	$1.0612P$
4	$1.0824P$
.	.
.	.
.	.
(∞)	(∞)

Fig. 11.2.4. $f(n) = P(1 + 0.02)^n$, $\lim_{n \to \infty} f(n) = \lim_{n \to \infty} P(1 + 0.02)^n = \infty$.

deposit and all accrued interest in the bank for an indefinitely long period of time? Obviously it grows without bounds, but the exact amount cannot be calculated; we must again use the limit concept to explain the behavior of the value of the function when n is very large: $\lim_{n \to \infty} f(n) = \infty$. This function is illustrated by table and graph in Fig. 11.2.4.

In Fig. 11.2.3 the graph of the function decreases at a decreasing rate, always approaching the value $f(n) = 0$. Thus the domain axis represents a boundary or limit below which the function never falls, and, indeed, which it never reaches. The domain axis is said to be an *asymptote* of the function $f(n) = (\frac{1}{2})^n$, or, the function is asymptotic to the domain axis. Turning back to the function graphed in Fig. 11.2.1, we note that the function $y = f(x) = 1/x$ is asymptotic to both the range axis and the domain axis. On the other hand, our interest rate example, graphed in Fig. 11.2.4, does not display asymptotic behavior. Asymptotes are not limited to the range and domain axes; we shall study examples of functions having various kinds of asymptotes. In terms of the graph of a function, an asymptote is a straight line which the graph approaches, but never reaches. Because the functions with which we deal will most likely have either vertical or horizontal asymptotes (or both) we recognize that it is possible to state the equation of an asymptote itself. A vertical asymptote will have the form $x = a$, where a is a limiting value of the domain of the function; the horizontal asymptote will have the form $y = b$, where b is a limiting value of the range of the function. Thus the function illustrated in Fig. 11.2.1 is asymptotic to $x = 0$ and $y = 0$, as is the function illustrated in Fig. 11.2.2.

Our last general classification of the behavior of functions is that of *continuity*. Very simply, as we have said, a function is continuous if its graph can be drawn without lifting the pencil from the paper. Although this is a very unrigorous definition from a mathematical standpoint, it describes intuitively what is meant by this term. We are often concerned, however, about the continuity of a function at a given point, as well as its continuity over an interval. In fact, we say that a function is continuous over an interval only if it is continuous at every point in the interval. Thus if we should have to lift our pencil from the paper while graphing a function at any given point, then the function is discontinuous in any interval which includes that point. Let us examine those circumstances under which a function may be *discontinuous* at a point. Discontinuity can occur under three conditions; if a function is not discontinuous at a point for one of the following reasons, then it is continuous at the point.

(1) If for some value in the domain, no value in the range is specified by the function, then the function is discontinuous at that point. Fig. 11.2.3 obviously takes some liberties with the sense of the board-sawing problem, since the number of the saw cuts must necessarily be measured in terms of integers (one-half of a saw-cut doesn't "count"), and this function can only be properly described by a series of unconnected points on the graph rather than a line. This function is thus discontinuous at all values in the domain except for integers. Such a function is said to be *discrete*, and is illustrated in Fig. 11.2.5. In Fig. 11.2.6, we show another graph which is continuous except for a discontinuity in the interval $\{x_1 < x < x_2\}$; in this interval the function specifies no value in the range for the values in the domain.

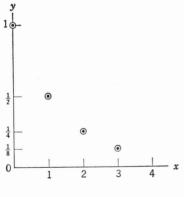

Fig. 11.2.5

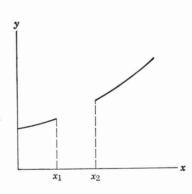

Fig. 11.2.6

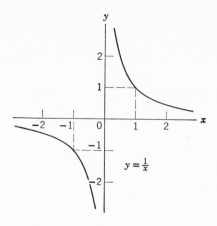

Fig. 11.2.7

(2) If the limit of a function at a point does not exist, then the function is discontinuous at that point. By "exist," we mean that the value selected in the range is a real number; since infinity is not a real number, if the limit of a function at a certain point selects infinity as the value in the range, then that limit is said not to exist for that value in the domain. The hyperbola in Fig. 11.2.7 displays this characteristic: $\lim_{x \to 0} f(x) = \lim_{x \to 0} 1/x = \pm \infty$. We note that it is not possible to graph these "values" ($\pm \infty$).

(3) If the limit of a function at a given value in the domain is not equal to the value of the function at that value, then the function is discontinuous at that value. In other words, a function is discontinuous at a (a value in the domain of the function) if $\lim_{x \to a} f(a) \neq f(a)$. This is the distinguishing characteristic of the so-called "step function," as illustrated in Figure 11.2.8, where the function "skips" an interval in the range. This is a very common representation of behavior

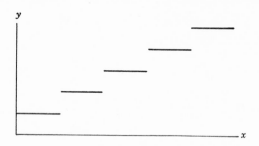

Fig. 11.2.8

encountered in administration; the phrase "cheaper by the dozen" is a manifestation of such behavior.

At this point it would undoubtedly be well to reconsider the concept of infinity, since it plays an important part in understanding limits. We usually consider that a solution to an administrative problem, solved by mathematical techniques, must be a real number, since in administration we deal with real quantities of things. Now if the limit of a function is infinitely large (or infinitely small), it is true that such information may be quite useful in terms of administration; yet this limit fails to exist in a mathematical sense, because the limit of a mathematical function must itself be a value in the range of the function. Infinity (∞) is not a number, and therefore cannot be in either the range or domain of a function. It should be understood as well that if the limit of a function is zero, this value exists in the mathematical sense, since it is a number which is usually a valid element of the range and domain of a function.

11.2 Exercises

11.2.1 Graph these functions, showing for each, if applicable: (1) conditions of symmetry; (2) intervals in the domain over which the curve is discontinuous; (3) asymptotes (4) direction of the curve (e.g., monotonic increasing).

(a) $y = \dfrac{4}{x}$

(b) $y = -\dfrac{4}{x}$

(c) $y = \dfrac{9}{x^2}$

(d) $y = -\dfrac{9}{x^2}$

(e) $y = x^2 - 4x + 4$

(f) $y = x^2 + 2x - 6$

(g) $y = 6x - 3x^2 + 4$

(h) $4y - 6 = x^2$

(i) $y - 3 = 4x - 2x^2$

(j) $y + 5 + 2x + 3x^2 = 0.$

11.2.2 The table below shows the United States postage required on

U.S. First Class Mail Rates

Weight (Oz.)	Postage (Cents)
x	y
$0 < x \leq 1$	4
$1 < x \leq 2$	8
$2 < x \leq 3$	12
$3 < x \leq 4$	16
$4 < x \leq 5$	20

first class mail by letter weight. State this relationship as a function, graph the function, and note discontinuities in the curve (if any), stating reasons for the discontinuities.

11.2.3 Find the following limits:

(a) $\lim\limits_{x \to \infty} 4/x$

(b) $\lim\limits_{x \to 0} 4/x$

(c) $\lim\limits_{x \to 0} 9/x^2$

(d) $\lim\limits_{x \to 1} 2x + 3$

(e) $\lim\limits_{x \to -2} x^2$

(f) $\lim\limits_{x \to \infty} -3x^2 + 2x - 7.$

11.2.4 Assume that you are a distributor of petroleum products and have a \$100 inventory of naptha on hand. Your storage conditions are such that each week enough naptha evaporates so that the inventory value of naptha decreases by one tenth. Prepare a table showing what happens to the inventory value of your naptha in the first six weeks of storage, graph the points tabulated, and find the function which describes the value of your inventory at any time. What is the limit of your function as the number of weeks approaches ∞? Discuss the continuity and direction of this curve giving reasons for your statements. (*Hint:* Consider board-sawing example.)

11.3 Analytic geometry

We recall from our study of linear systems in Chapter 7 that any function in two-space having the general form $y = a + bx$ is called a linear function, and the graph of such a function is a straight line. From the functional statement $y = f(x) = a + bx$ we learned to recognize some important things about the relationship between x and y without plotting the graph of the function, to wit: (1) the value of the constant a indicates where the graph crosses the range axis (the y-intercept) and (2) the value of the constant b specifies the *slope* of this graph, which is the rate of change in the values of the dependent variable relative to changes in the value of the independent variable.

By analyzing the statement of the functional relationship, we are more able to understand the behavior of the variables involved. We know that one way to determine this behavior is to find all of the ordered pairs in the solution set of the open sentence defining the function; this, however, is an impossible task if the function is defined over the entire set of real numbers. In the previous sections of this chapter, we have found a very few of these ordered pairs, or points, in order to sketch the graphs of certain functions. We have been forced to make some very broad assumptions about the behavior of the functions between the points selected, however; and most students have perhaps at one time or another guessed wrongly about this behavior, which is a very easy thing to do. Few students, however, should make a wrong guess about the behavior of a given linear function at this point; recognition of the fact that a function is linear and knowledge of the slope and intercept of the function provide all of the information necessary to describe it completely, either in words or in the graph. This pursuit is called *analytic geometry*. A number of functions, such as the linear function, display consistent characteristics which can be analyzed to provide clues to their behavior very rapidly, and thus clues to the manner in which they can be described by graphing. The characteristics of direction and monotonicity, of symmetry, limits, asymptotes, and continuity, are all means of describing the behavior of functions further. We shall use them in stating the general behavior characteristics of a number of important functions in solving administrative problems.

11.3 Exercises

11.3.1 Graph the linear functions having the following characteristics:

(a) $a = 3, b = -\frac{2}{3}$
(b) $a = -5, b = 3.6$
(c) $a = 0, b = 0$
(d) $\{-\infty < x \leq 2\}; a = 1, b = 1$
(e) $\{2 \leq x < \infty\}; a = 2, b = \frac{1}{2}$.

11.3.2 For each of the following exercises, draw a graph meeting the stated requirements:

(a) $\{-3 < x < 3\}$, strictly monotonic increasing, symmetric with respect to origin, asymptotic to $x = -3$, $x = 3$, continuous in the interval.
(b) $\{-4 \leq x \leq -2\}$, strictly monotonic decreasing; $\{2 \leq x \leq 4\}$, strictly monotonic increasing; continuous only in these intervals, symmetrical to the range axis.

11.4 The quadratic equation and conic sections

The equation

$$k_1 x^2 + k_2 xy + k_3 y^2 + k_4 x + k_5 y + k_6 = 0,$$

in which x and y are variables and the k_i are real number constants is

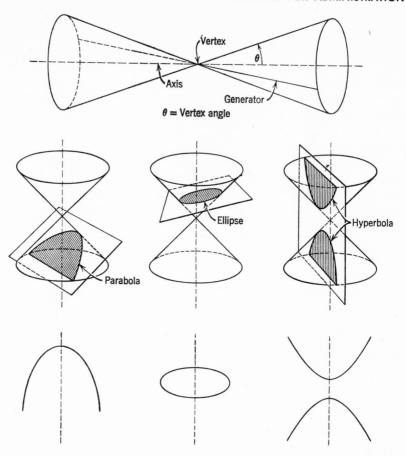

Fig. 11.4.1. At the top is illustrated a right circular cone, showing its *axis* and *vertex angle,* and the *generator,* which is a straight line passing through the vertex and revolved about the axis at the constant vertex angle θ. At the left we have intersected a cone with a plane parallel to the generator, the result of which is a parabola, as shown in the plan view of the plane. An ellipse is formed in the middle illustration; we note that if the plane were perpendicular to the axis of the cone, the intersection would describe a circle. To the right a plane is passed through the cone parallel to the axis of the cone; the intersection is a hyperbola.

called *the quadratic equation,* or sometimes the *general second-order equation.* This equation describes, depending upon the values of the constants, all of the possible curves or lines which result from the intersection of a right circular cone with a plane, as illustrated in Fig. 11.4.1. The physical result of this operation is called a *conic section,* the word section having the same connotation as that implied by taking a "cross-section" of some object, in order to see "inside" it. For instance, we might take a cross-section of a log to find the age of the tree it came from, by counting the rings. Analogous to the rings of a tree are the curves traced upon the plane by its intersection with the surface of the cone. Each of the curves described by a conic section has a name: a circle, an ellipse, a parabola, an hyperbola, a straight line, a point, or nothing. The last three "curves" represent special cases, although every conic section is in some respect unique.

Each of the conic sections is the graph of an equation formed from the quadratic equation by a proper selection of the values of the con-stants. For instance, $x^2 + y^2 = 4$ is the equation of a circle with its center at the origin and radius 2; this conic section is described by the quadratic equation in which

$$k_1 = k_3 = 1, k_2 = k_4 = k_5 = 0, \text{ and } k_6 = -4.$$

We note further that if $k_1 = k_2 = k_3 = 0$, the quadratic equation becomes the equation of a straight line.

We shall not deal further with the three-space concepts of cones or conic sections. The general purpose of this section has been to point out how the functions with which we shall deal can be interpreted in the general terms of the quadratic equation. It is important for the student to realize that each of these functions is a member of the same general family, and that the members of the family can be distinguished by the values assigned to the constants in the general statement of the quadratic form.

11.5   The parabolic function and the parabola

If in the quadratic equation we define

$$k_1 = -a \neq 0, k_2 = 0, k_3 = 0, k_4 = -b, k_5 = 1, \text{ and } k_6 = -c,$$

and rewrite the expression, $y = ax^2 + bx + c$, we have developed the conventional form of the *parabolic function*, whose graph is a *parabola*. In Fig. 11.5.1 are graphed various parabolas, showing us also the important nomenclature of this quadratic. Since most of our work deals with functions, it is important to realize that although the graph in Fig. 11.5.1c is a parabola, it is not the graph of a parabolic function, and cannot be represented by the expression given above for a parabolic function. (Why?)

Just as the values of the constants in the quadratic equation deter-

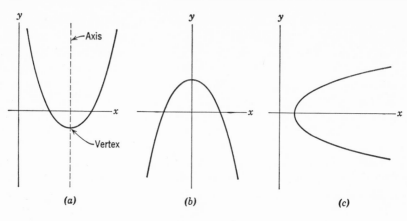

Fig. 11.5.1

mine the associated type of conic section, the values of a, b, and c will determine the characteristics of the parabolic function (henceforth simply called the parabola). Let us examine some of the things that are immediately evident concerning the function which graphs as a parabola. We notice that it is symmetrical with respect to the range axis, *if* the axis of the parabola coincides with the range axis. Otherwise the vertical line that is the axis of this parabola may be translated a certain number of units left or right until it does coincide with the range axis. The point where the graph of the parabola crosses the axis of the parabola is called the vertex, and is an important point since, as we shall see, it is where the graph changes its direction. The coordinates of the vertex of a parabola (x_v, y_v) can be computed by algebraic techniques using this set of formulas:

$$x_v = -\frac{b}{2a}; \quad y_v = c - \frac{b^2}{4a}.$$

It is obvious that the constant a can never be zero if we are to find the graph of a parabola, since both of the values above would be undefined if $a = 0$. But we know that the graph of every parabolic function has a vertex which can be located in terms of real number coordinates. As an example of finding the vertex of a parabolic function, let us find the vertex of $f(x) = x^2 - 8x + 18$. In this function $a = 1$, $b = -8$, and $c = 18$. Thus,

$$x_v = -\frac{(-8)}{2(1)} = \frac{8}{2} = 4; \quad y_v = (18) - \frac{(-8^2)}{4(1)} = 18 - 16 = 2,$$

and the vertex of the parabola is the point (4, 2), as illustrated in Fig. 11.1.6.

Knowing the vertex of the parabola, our next concern is whether the graph opens upward or downward, since if it is a parabolic function it must do one or the other. If the sign of a is positive, the graph opens upward; if it is negative, the graph opens downward. Another way of stating this is that the function reaches a minimum at the vertex if the sign of a is positive, and reaches a maximum at the vertex if the sign is negative. A little thought will indicate why this is so. For very large or very small (negative) values of x, the term (x^2) becomes very large, and "swamps" the other terms in the function. If the sign of the coefficient of x^2, i.e., a, is positive, then for large or small values of x this term will be positive, and will grow larger as x increases or decreases at a much greater rate than the increase or decrease in x. Therefore the value of the function at these extreme values must be positive. The same reasoning holds true when the sign of a is negative: no matter how large x^2 becomes, the term will always be negative, and eventually swamp the other terms in the function, so that the value of the function ultimately becomes very negative. In terms of limits, we may write:

$$\lim_{\substack{x \to \infty \\ \text{or} \quad x \to -\infty}} ax^2 + bx + c = \infty, \, a > 0, \text{ or}$$

$$\lim_{\substack{x \to \infty \\ \text{or} \quad x \to -\infty}} ax^2 + bx + c = -\infty, \, a < 0.$$

Finally, we can find by algebraic techniques those points where the graph crosses the domain axis (in the case of a parabola which crosses this axis; a parabola may not cross the domain axis, as in the figure referred to above). In this circumstance, we are searching for the values in the domain for which the function takes on the value zero, i.e., where $y = 0$. These values in the domain are called *zeroes* of the function. (We recall that $y = 0$ is the equation of the domain axis; our search is thus for the intersections of the function with the domain axis.) The problem reduces to that of finding the *roots* of the *equation* $ax^2 + bx + c = 0$, since $y = f(x) = 0$ where these roots will be found (if they exist). Note that the zeroes of a function are identical to the roots of its defining equation. To find these roots we use another formula, called the *quadratic formula:*

$$x = \frac{-b \pm \sqrt{b^2 - 4ac}}{2a}.$$

Let us find the zeroes of the function $f(x) = -x^2 + 4x$, in which

$a = -1$, $b = 4$, and $c = 0$.   Substituting in the quadratic formula:

$$x = \frac{-4 \pm \sqrt{(4)^2 - 4(-1)(0)}}{2(-1)} = \frac{-4 \pm \sqrt{16}}{-2} = \frac{-4 \pm 4}{-2},$$

$$x = \frac{0}{-2} = 0, \text{ and } x = \frac{-8}{-2} = 4.$$

The roots of the equation $-x^2 + 4x = 0$ are thus 0 and 4; the points where the function $f(x) = -x^2 + 4x$ crosses the domain axis have coordinates $(0, 0)$ and $(4, 0)$, as illustrated in Fig. 11.5.2.

It should be quite obvious that the problem of symmetry is easily solved when the vertex of the parabola is known, since a parabolic

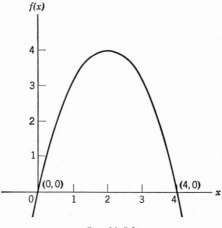

Fig. 11.5.2

relationship can be a function only when the axis of the parabola is a vertical line.   A parabolic function is symmetrical with respect to the range axis when the x-coordinate of the vertex is zero.   When the graph of a parabolic function is displaced from the range axis, this displacement can be measured in terms of the distance of the vertex from the range axis, which is exactly the value of the x-coordinate of the vertex.   We speak of a *translation* of axes, by which we mean the displacement of the axes; a graph whose vertex does not lie upon the range axis may be displaced by a translation to the range axis so that the symmetry condition can be applied.   In effect, we move the axis of the parabola right or left to coincide with the range axis, and therefore speak of a translation of the axis " ... 3.2 units to the left," or

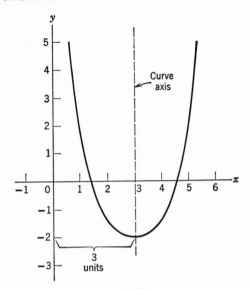

Fig. 11.5.3

" ... 10 units to the right." Thus, if $y = f(x) = x^2 - 6x + 7$, the vertex of the graph of this function is at $(3, -2)$. This function will be symmetrical to the range axis after a translation of the graph 3 units to the left, i.e., we must subtract 3 from the x-coordinate of the vertex to make it 0. These ideas are illustrated in Fig. 11.5.3.

Let us review what we have learned about parabolic functions, using the example $y = f(x) = -\frac{1}{2}x^2 + 2x + 3$. We note first that the right-hand side is properly a quadratic equation in x of the form $ax^2 + bx + c$, in which $a = -\frac{1}{2}$, $b = 2$, and $c = 3$. We shall first graph this function, and then draw some conclusions about the general behavior of parabolic functions from the graph. Since a is negative, the graph will open downward. The vertex is found by substituting in the proper formulas:

$$x_v = \frac{-b}{2a} = \frac{-2}{2(-\frac{1}{2})} = 2$$

$$y_v = c - \frac{b^2}{4a} = 3 - \frac{(2)^2}{4(-\frac{1}{2})} = 3 - \frac{4}{-2} = 5,$$

and is located at $(2, 5)$. The graph crosses the domain axis where $y = 0$, thus we determine two more points on this curve by finding the

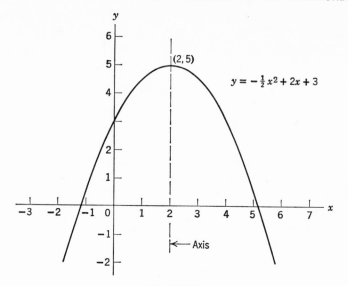

Fig. 11.5.4

roots of the equation using the quadratic formula:

$$x = \frac{-b \pm \sqrt{b^2 - 4ac}}{2a} = \frac{-2 \pm \sqrt{4 - 4(-\frac{1}{2})(3)}}{2(-\frac{1}{2})}$$

$$= \frac{-2 \pm \sqrt{10}}{-1}$$

$$= 2 \pm \sqrt{10},$$

or approximately 5.16 and -1.16; the graph crosses the domain axis at $(5.16, 0)$ and $(-1.16, 0)$. With this information we sketch the graph of this function in Fig. 11.5.4.

Assuming the domain of the function to be the set of all real numbers, let us state the general characteristics of the parabolic function in terms previously used:

(1) If the sign of the coefficient of x^2, i.e., a, is positive, then the graph opens upward. If the x-coordinate of the vertex is v, then in the interval $\{-\infty < x \leq v\}$, the graph is strictly monotonic decreasing; in the interval $\{v \leq x < \infty\}$, the curve is strictly monotonic increasing. If a is negative, then in the respective intervals above the direction of the graph is reversed, i.e., it opens downward.

(2) The graph of a parabola is always symmetrical with respect to its own axis, and is symmetrical with respect to the range axis after

translation of the axis if the axis of the parabola does not coincide with the range axis.

(3) The function has no asymptotes.

(4) The function is continuous in all intervals.

11.5   Exercises

11.5.1

(a) Graph the function defined by $y = x^2$.   Find the coordinates of the vertex.

(b) Graph the function defined by $y = x^2 + 2$.   Find the coordinates of the vertex.

(c) Graph the function defined by $y = (x - 3)^2$.   Find the coordinates of the vertex.

(d) Graph the function defined by $y - 2 = (x - 3)^2$.   Find the coordinates of the vertex.

(e) Express the last equation in the form $y = ax^2 + bx + c$.   What relation do you notice between the coordinates of the vertex and the form of the functional statement as expressed in d?   What conclusion can you draw about translation of axes, the vertex of the parabola, and the form in which the functional statement is expressed?

11.5.2   A newsboy on another corner who has been in the business for some time operates under conditions of certainty to the extent that he knows that his profit, a function of the number of papers he sells (x), can be determined by the functional statement $\pi = f(x) = -2450 + 100x - x^2$.   Sketch the graph of this function.

(a) How many papers should he sell to maximize profit on each paper sold?

(b) At what volume of papers does he break even $(\pi = 0)$?

(c) How does the assumption of continuity fit this problem?

11.5.3   The Picayune Pea-Packing Plant has a capacity of 200 pecks of packed peas per day.   The dollar cost C of each peck depends upon the number of pecks packed (x), and can be expressed by the statement $C = f(x) = 0.01x^2 - 2x + 300$.   Sketch the graph of this function.

(a) What is the minimum cost output level?

(b) To be economically meaningful, what restriction must be placed upon the mathematical statement given?   *Hint:* $(x < 0)$?; $(x > 200)$?

11.6   The hyperbolic function and the hyperbola

The parabola describes a useful function for relating the behavior of one variable to that of another when changes in the independent variable cause the values of the dependent variable to increase through an interval and then decrease, or vice versa.   Cost and profit relationships, for example, are assumed to behave in such fashion, as illustrated in the exercises of the previous section.   Another common behavior pattern is that of *inverse proportionality*, by which we mean that the values of the dependent variable are inversely proportional to the values of the independent variable.   Statements such as, "the higher the price, the fewer sold," "the longer the waiting line, the fewer the new customers," are examples of situations in which the values of the dependent variable (number sold, number of new customers) may be inversely proportional to the values of the independent variable (price, length of line).   Although there are many types of hyperbolic functions, the one having the form $xy = c$ expresses the concept of inverse proportionality of interest to us.   Functions of this sort are not new to us, since this chapter was introduced with one of them, which purported to explain the relationship between the price of a product and the quantity of the product sold, keeping total revenue from sales constant.

The graph of the function $xy = c$ or $y = c/x$ is illustrated in Fig. 11.6.1, from which we can draw the following conclusions:

(1) In the interval $\{-\infty < x < 0\}$, the function is strictly monotonic decreasing, and in the interval $\{0 < x < \infty\}$, the function is strictly monotonic decreasing.

(2) The function is symmetrical to the origin.

(3) The function is asymptotic to $x = 0$ and $y = 0$.

(4) The function is continuous in all intervals except those containing the *point $x = 0$*.

In Exercise 11.5.1 the form of the parabolic function $y = ax^2 + bx + c$ was found to be restatable as $(y - k) = (x - h)^2$, where (h, k) was uniquely the vertex of the parabola, and $k = c - (b^2/4a)$ and $h = -b/2a$.   Where the *vertex* is perhaps the characteristic of greatest interest in the analysis of parabolic functions, the asymptotes are perhaps the most important characteristic of the hyperbolic function, and fortunately we have a relatively simple means for determining the asymptotes.

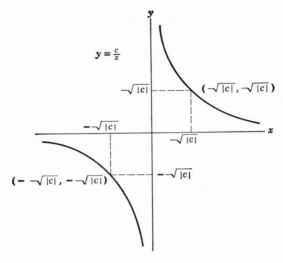

Fig. 11.6.1

One explicit hyperbolic function can be expressed as

$$y = f(x) = \frac{c}{x + h} - k.$$

When this function is expressed implicitly in what we shall call standard form, $(y + k)(x + h) = c$, then the asymptotes are found directly by setting each of the left-hand members equal to zero and solving each expression:

$$y + k = 0; y = -k \text{ (horizontal asymptote)};$$

$$x + h = 0; x = -h \text{ (vertical asymptote)}.$$

The right-hand side of the equation is the constant c, which can be either positive or negative. When the expression is put in standard form $(y + k)(x + h) = c$, the sign of c determines the quadrants of the rectangular coordinate system formed by the translated axes in which the branches of the hyperbola lie. If $c > 0$, the branches will be found in quadrants I and III after translation of the axes; if $c < 0$, the branches lie in quadrants II and IV after translation of the axes. The square root of the modulus (absolute value) of c tells us where the vertices of the hyperbolas will be found. If we measure the distance $\sqrt{|c|}$ in all directions along the *translated* axes from the *translated* origin, the vertices will lie at $(\sqrt{|c|}, \sqrt{|c|})$ and $(-\sqrt{|c|}, -\sqrt{|c|})$

in quadrants I and III respectively (see Fig. 11.6.1); if $c < 0$, the vertices in II and IV are found at $(-\sqrt{|c|}, \sqrt{|c|})$ and $(\sqrt{|c|}, -\sqrt{|c|})$.

Let us apply this analysis to the example $y = \dfrac{4}{x-2} + 2$. We write the function implicitly: $(y-2)(x-2) = 4$, and note immediately that the asymptotes are $y = 2$ and $x = 2$. The sign of c is positive, thus the branches lie in I and III. Since $\sqrt{c} = 2$, we find the vertices *relative to the translated origin* to be at $(2, 2)$ and $(-2, -2)$. Since the translated origin is at $(2, 2)$ (the intersection of the asymptotes), the vertices of the hyperbola lie at $(4, 4)$ and $(0, 0)$, as graphed in Fig. 11.6.2.

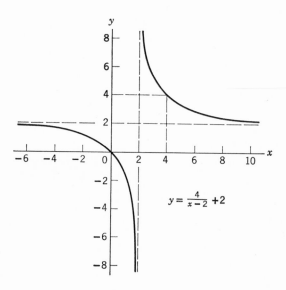

Fig. 11.6.2

Consider the general quadratic equation in which $k_1 = k_3 = 0$, $k_2 = 1$, $k_4 = k$, $k_5 = h$, and $k_6 = d$, where h, k, and d are real numbers. The result will be an implicit hyperbolic function having the form $kx + xy + hy + d = 0$. It can be shown that the value of c for the associated hyperbola is $c = hk - d$. The asymptotes can be determined by inspection of the implicit function, e.g., the coefficient of x provides the horizontal asymptote, $y = -k$, as before. (*Example:* $-4x + xy + 5y - 11 = 0$.) By inspection, $k = -4$, $h = 5$, $d = -11$. Therefore the asymptotes are $y = -k = -(-4) = 4$; $x = -h = -5$.

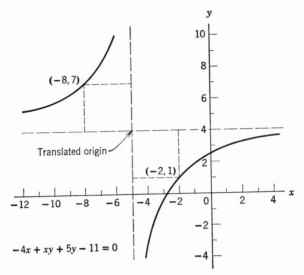

Fig. 11.6.3

And $c = hk - d = (5)(-4) - (-11) = -9$. The graph therefore appears in the second and fourth quadrants of the translated axes, and the vertices are found at $(-8, 7)$ and $(-2, 1)$ as in Fig. 11.6.3.

11.6 Exercises

11.6.1 Sketch the following hyperbolas. In each case specify the asymptotes, and locate the vertices.

(a) $(x + 3)(y + 2) = 6$
(b) $(x - 3)(y - 2) = 6$
(c) $xy - 2x = 4$
(d) $y = \dfrac{8}{(x - 2)} + 4$
(e) $(x - 4)(y + 2) = 10$, $x \geq 0$
(f) $y = 2x/(x - 1)$
(g) $xy + 2x + 3y - 6 = 0$
(h) $xy + 3x - 2y - 4 = 0$, $x \geq 0$, $y \geq 0$
(i) $(x - 30)(y - 20) = 180$, $0 \leq x \leq 30$, $y \leq 0$
(j) $xy - 20x - 10y + 100 = 0$, $x \geq 0$, $y \geq 0$.

11.7   Higher-order functions

The student is well aware at this point that the basic method used to find the value of a dependent variable, given some value of the independent variable, is to substitute that value of the domain into the equation of the function, and, after performing the required arithmetic manipulations of multiplication and addition, the associated value of the dependent variable is produced. Let us review some of the algebraic terminology involved in these operations, specifically, the expressions *monomial*, *binomial*, and *polynomial*, which are useful in the description of the form of a given function or equation. Examples of monomials are: x^2, $\frac{1}{2}x^3$, $-3x_2$, ax^n. A binomial is the sum of two such expressions: $x + 1$, $x^2 - \frac{1}{2}x^3$, $a(x + b)$, etc. A binomial is a special case of the polynomial, which describes any expression that is the sum of such monomials. A *polynomial function* in x may be written

$$f(x) = a_n x^n + a_{n-1} x^{n-1} + \cdots + a_2 x^2 + a_1 x + a_o,$$

where a_0, a_1, etc., are real numbers and $a_n \neq 0$, and n is a non-negative integer called the *degree* of the polynomial. Linear functions are said to be of degree one, or of the first *order;* the exponent of the variable in the general expression for the linear function $f(x) = a + bx$ is 1. A quadratic function is of degree two, or of the second order. A third-order function is called a cubic function; fourth-order, quartic, etc. We wish to examine the nature of these latter types of functions briefly.

The direction of a first-order (linear) function, when $b \neq 0$, we have found to be strictly monotonic increasing *or* strictly monotonic decreasing. The direction of the parabola, a second-order function, was found to be strictly monotonic increasing over an interval in the domain, then strictly monotonic decreasing through the balance of the domain, *or* vice versa. The first-order function has but one direction, which never changes; the second-order function changes its direction once at the most. The hyperbola is also a second-order function; we note that the graph of the hyperbolic function does not change its direction in the same manner as the parabola, but has a point of "extreme" discontinuity at the vertical asymptote. If we consider one branch of a hyperbola alone, then we note that it is either strictly monotonic increasing or strictly monotonic decreasing, like the linear function, i.e., the function does not change direction, although it is a second-order function. The third-order function may have as many as two changes of direction; the fourth- as many as three, etc.   We shall examine the nature of such functions more thoroughly later in the book, but at the moment there are certain intuitive ideas which may be expressed without the use of calculus.

Consider the polynomial function

$$f(x) = (x - 1)(x - 2)(x + 1).$$

If we expand the polynomial by multiplying the binomials, we develop the equivalent expression

$$f(x) = x^3 - 2x^2 - x + 2.$$

The highest power of x is 3; this function is therefore a cubic, or third-

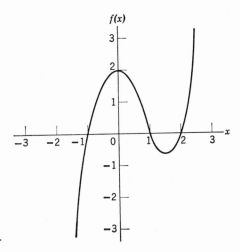

Fig. 11.7.1.
    $f(x) = (x - 1)(x - 2)(x + 1).$

order function.   We note that when x takes on the values 1, 2, and -1, the value of the function is zero.   In terms of the graph of this function: the curve crosses the domain axis at $x = 1$, $x = 2$, and $x = -1$, and not elsewhere.   This graph must necessarily change its direction twice in order to cross the x axis three times, as illustrated in Fig. 11.7.1.

As stated previously, the values of x for which $f(x)$ is zero are called zeroes of the function.   The zeroes of a polynomial function are readily determined by inspection if the function is stated as the product of binomials, as in the example above.   Finding the zeroes of a polynomial function expressed as the sum of monomial terms is possible by applying formulas (the quadratic formula is an example), but this is tedious for third- and fourth-order polynomials.   It has been proved, in addition, that no such formula exists for polynomials of degree greater than four. Our purpose in finding zeroes is to simplify graphing the function.

The quotient of two polynomial functions is called a *rational function*, e.g.,

$$f(x) = \frac{g(x)}{h(x)} = \frac{x - 1}{x + 1}.$$

If $g(x)$ is zero, then $f(x)$ is also zero, and thus the zeroes of a rational function are the zeroes of the function in the numerator. If $h(x)$ is zero, then $f(x)$ is not defined. The rational function above thus has one zero, $x = 1$, and is undefined at $x = -1$.

Functions of order higher than two are of generally limited use in the explanation of behavior of basic economic and administrative phenomena. Their important characteristic is the fact that they change direction a certain number of times. Although we certainly are interested in the direction which one variable takes relative to another, the unique limitations on the higher-order function, as well as their increasing complexity as the order increases, renders their use limited. In analysis, however, these higher-order functions may be developed as the result of the synthesis of a model of behavior, and for this reason the student should be able to recognize them as bona fide functions.

11.7 Exercises

Find the zeroes of the following polynomial and rational functions where possible; draw a sketch of each; find the *order* of each function (except 11.7.4 and 11.7.6).

11.7.1 $f(x) = (x - 2)(x - 1)(x)$

11.7.2 $f(x) = (1 - x)(1 + x)$

11.7.3 $f(x) = (x)(x^2 - 4x + 4)$

11.7.4 $f(x) = \dfrac{x^2 - 1}{x^2 + 1}$

11.7.5 $f(x) = (x^2 - 1)^2$

11.7.6 $f(x) = \dfrac{x^2 + 1}{x^2 - 1}.$

11.8   Some administrative applications

To this point we have studied the mathematics of some basic linear and non-linear relationships without paying a great deal of attention to the ultimate use of such a study.   In this section we shall attempt to illustrate, by some relatively simple examples from economic theory, how the concepts and methods may be used in administrative decision making.   For our present purposes, we shall assume that our illustrations are authoritative, i.e., that the functions do reflect some aspect of the real world.   How such functions are constructed will be left to Chapter 15, where techniques of *model building* are discussed.

In these times, when every man is a do-it-yourself economist, many terms such as demand, supply, market price, total cost, total revenue, and profit have come into common usage.   Each of these terms implies some basic economic idea, which can be represented by relationships among things, both real and abstract.   Mathematics provides perhaps the best means available for describing these relationships, and, more important, the only usefully powerful means for analyzing them.

Let us consider as an example the phenomenon of *market price*, knowledge of which is of inestimable value to the decision maker. Since the market price is the result of the two major forces in any free market, supply and demand, we shall examine these concepts first in order to arrive at the definition of market price, as well as the means for its determination.   The student should realize that we work with highly simplified economic "models," or mathematical relationships, in order to minimize the amount of explanation necessary to clarify the theory behind the models.   Since we are more interested in the mathematics of the models than in their economic conventionality, we shall express certain functions according to our previous explanation, rather than according to economic convention.

Let us insert an historical note.   Mathematical economists did not discriminate, in the early days of their science, between relations and functions as we do today.   For this reason, it was unimportant to them whether the independent variable were placed on the x axis or the y axis; unfortunately, they chose to place the independent variable on the y axis for their explanations of the behavior of market phenomena (supply and demand).   Although the market price solution is not affected by the selection of axes, the student is cautioned to recognize the difference between the presentation here and that found in standard economics textbooks.

There are two "sides" to a market: the buyer's side and the seller's side.   The behavior of buyers is explained by a *Demand Law*, which asserts that the higher the price of a product, the less of it will be demanded, and conversely.   We state that the quantity demanded is a function of price, or $D = f(P)$.   The behavior of sellers is explained by a *Supply Law*, which asserts that the higher the price of a product, the more of it will be supplied, and conversely.   We state that the quantity supplied is a function of price, or $S = g(P)$.   The demand function is thus considered to be a monotonic decreasing function of price, and the supply function a monotonic increasing function of price. The market price of a product is the price, determined in the market, at which the total amount of a product demanded by buyers is equal to the amount offered for sale by suppliers.   Such a market is said to be in *equilibrium*, since no buyer is left unsatisfied and no seller finds himself with a surplus.

Let us determine the market price in an hypothetical market where the demand and supply functions are given to be

$$Demand: \quad D = f(P) = 40 - 0.5P$$

$$Supply: \quad S = g(P) = 10 + P.$$

Both D and S are measured in terms of units of product, and P is the price in dollars.   Some of the ordered pairs in the sets satisfying these

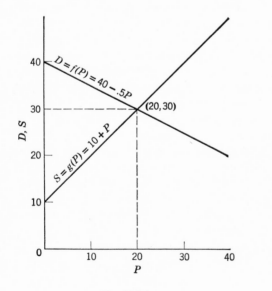

Demand Schedule		Supply Schedule	
P	D	P	S
0	40	0	10
10	35	10	20
20	30	20	30
30	25	30	40
40	20	40	50
$D = f(p)$		$S = g(P)$	

Fig. 11.8.1

functions are tabulated in Fig. 11.8.1; these tables are known as demand, and supply, *schedules*. Each of these functions is also graphed in Fig. 11.8.1. They are immediately recognized as linear functions; their graphs are straight lines. The market will be cleared of 30 units at a price of \$20, i.e., at the equilibrium point (20, 30) the quantity demanded is equal to the quantity supplied, and the market price is established at \$20. This point can also be found analytically as the solution set of the simultaneous system established by the demand and supply equations, since at equilibrium, $D = S$, and the system contains only two variables. A faster method in this case consists of setting the equations equal to each other and solving immediately for the market price:

$$D = S$$

$$40 - 0.5P = 10 + P$$

$$-1.5P = -30$$

$$P = 20.$$

We note that the range and domain of the functions is limited to the set of non-negative numbers, since negative price and negative quantity have no meaning in the economic example.

The linear functions used in the example above are abstractions from reality in the sense that we would be surprised to find a market the behavior of which could be described by a linear function over a significant range and domain. For instance, our linear demand schedule states that buyers will reduce the amounts that they are willing to buy at a *constant* rate even as the price becomes relatively high, whereas it is more reasonable to assume that this rate of change is not constant but variable. For some other reasons, too, which we do not have time to explore, the hyperbolic function provides a better theoretical representation of demand behavior. Let us examine another example in which such is the case:

$$Demand: \quad D = f(P) = \frac{36}{P - 5} + 5$$

$$Supply: \quad S = g(P) = -5 + P.$$

The range and domain of these functions is the set of all non-negative numbers. Converting the demand function to standard hyperbolic form, $(D - 5)(P - 5) = 36$, we find the equations of the asymptotes to be $D = 5$ and $P = 5$, and $c = 36$. The demand function is graphed in Fig. 11.8.2, along with the supply function, which is again linear.

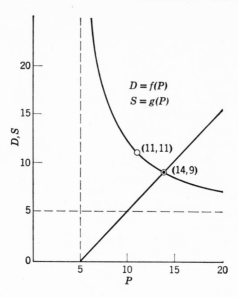

Fig. 11.8.2

Inspection of the graph shows the point of equilibrium to be (14, 9), which can be found analytically as before:

$$D = S$$

$$\frac{36}{P - 5} + 5 = -5 + P$$

$$36 + 5P - 25 = -5P + 25 + P^2 - 5P$$

$$0 = P^2 - 15P + 14.$$

This quadratic equation is solved for P by applying the quadratic formula, and finding $P = 14$ and $P = 1$. It would appear that two equilibrium points, (14, 9) and (1, −4) exist; however, the point (1, −4) is not within the range of the functions, and thus is not a solution to the problem.

Let us at this point be more specific in terms of administrative problems and introduce the term *decision variable*, by which we mean a variable over which we can exert some control, whose value we choose as the result of a decision. The value of this variable will be selected in such a way that some goal is attained as a result of the decision. As an example, if we are hungry, then our goal would be to satisfy our hunger by having something to eat. The decision variable might be the amount of food which we must eat to satisfy our hunger. If we can define the relationship between the level of goal attainment and the values of the decision variable, we are then in a position to find the value of the decision variable that maximizes the attainment of the goal.

Applying this idea to the administrator of a business enterprise, we find that one of his important goals is to maximize profit. We note that this idea is not new; in the study of linear programming we dealt with the maximization of objective profit functions. In our current study, however, we relax the assumption that the profit on an item is a linear function of the quantity of that item produced; the student will recall that in the linear programming model we assumed that a certain profit per item would hold no matter how many units of that item were produced or offered for sale. Although this is sometimes true in real life for certain levels of output, it is not generally true, and our purpose is to examine the behavior of profit relative to the decision variable, output.

Profit has already been defined as the difference between Total Revenue and Total Cost. If the difference $TR - TC$ is positive, the result is profit; if it is negative, the result is loss or negative profit. Note that profit, unlike the variables previously examined in this chapter, can take on both positive and negative values. Some of the characteristics of profit have already been studied in the work covering breakeven charts. Figure 11.8.3 is the breakeven chart for the circumstance where Total Revenue is defined by the function $TR = f(Q) = \$8Q$

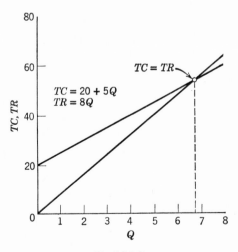

Fig. 11.8.3

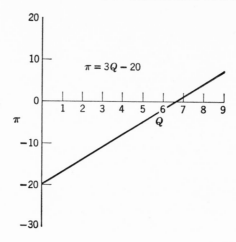

Fig. 11.8.4

where Q is the quantity sold, and $TC = f(Q) = \$20 + \$5Q$, where Q is the quantity produced (output). We assume that this decision maker will be able to sell at a price of \$8 as many units as he produces. The intersection of the two linear graphs is the breakeven point where $TR - TC = 0$. Algebraically, $\$8Q - \$20 - \$5Q = 0$ and solving for Q we find that the required output to break even is 6.67 units. Production of less than this amount will result in a loss; production of a greater amount will result in profit.

The profit function is thus $\pi = TR - TC = \$3Q - \$20$. If we wish to maximize profit, we must obviously make the right-hand side of the profit function as large as possible. However, this model implies that we can increase production forever, making Q larger and larger, and reaping greater and greater profits without bound. This is illustrated by Fig. 11.8.4 which plots this profit function; our decision variable is Q, output, and the larger Q becomes the greater our profit, presumably without limit. Of course, we are limited by the capacity of our production facilities, although we might continue to build plants so long as this profit function were a representation of reality.

Obviously, this is not generally true, or there would be many more millionaires in the world than we can find at present. It is likely that neither of the functions involved will be linear over the entire domain of real numbers. This is especially true of the revenue function, for as the market becomes saturated with our product, we cannot expect to continue to sell it at its original price. (Remember the "hula-hoop"?) So let us assume that the true revenue function is $TR = \$10Q - \$0.2Q^2$.

In Fig. 11.8.5 we reconstruct the breakeven chart using this new revenue function, which we observe to be parabolic. There are now two breakeven points, which we can determine by setting $TR - TC = 0$:

$$(10Q - 0.2Q^2) - (20 + 5Q) = 0$$

$$10Q - 0.2Q^2 - 20 - 5Q = 0$$

$$-0.2Q^2 + 5Q - 20 = 0.$$

The student should verify that the roots of this equation are 5 and 20, which are the output levels at which this process breaks even. This is borne out by the schedule of total cost, total revenue, and profit in Fig. 11.8.5.

The graph of the profit function defined by $\pi = TR - TC = -0.2Q^2 + 5Q - 20$ is drawn in Fig. 11.8.6, and from it we can now determine the value of the decision variable Q which maximizes profit: it is the value of the Q-coordinate of the vertex of the function, 12.5 units.

These rather simple models are only indicative of the scope of application of mathematical analysis to administrative problems, and serve to illustrate the analytical capabilities of the rather rudimentary tools developed so far. We shall soon develop some more powerful tools for further simplifying the analysis of decision models. Our purpose to

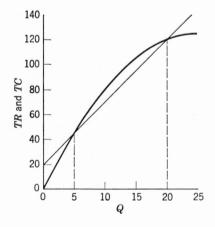

SCHEDULE OF REVENUE, COST, AND PROFIT

Q	TC	TR	π
0	20	0	-20
5	45	45	0
10	70	80	10
12.5	82.50	94.65	12.15
15	95	105	10
20	120	120	0
25	145	125	-20

Fig. 11.8.5

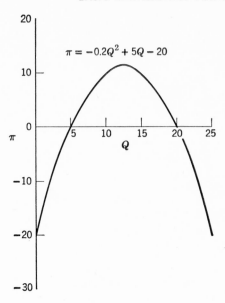

$$\pi = -0.2Q^2 + 5Q - 20$$

Fig. 11.8.6

this point has been to discuss the basic types of functions used to describe certain behavioral relationships. The student should by now have developed considerable familiarity with linear and non-linear functions.

11.8   Exercises

11.8.1   Draw the following demand and supply curves estimating the market equilibrium price from the graph. Check your graphic solutions by finding this point algebraically. (*Note:* Domain and range are each the set of all non-negative numbers.)

(a) demand: $D = f(P) = 12 - 5P$
     supply: $S = g(P) = 4 + 4P$
(b) demand: $D = f(P) = 6$
     supply: $S = g(P) = 3P - 3$
(c) demand: $D = f(P) = 15 - 2P$
     supply: $S = g(P) = 5$
(d) demand: $D = f(P) = 16 + P - P^2$
     supply: $S = g(P) = 4 + P$

(e) demand: $D = f(P) = 16/P$
  supply: $S = g(P) = 2 + P$
(f) demand: $D = f(P) = 18 - 2P - P^2$
  supply: $S = g(P) = P^2 - 2P.$

11.8.2 Graph the following total cost and total revenue functions. Note on your graph the breakeven points, solving algebraically for these points. Indicate the profit function, and graph this function below your graph of the related cost and revenue function (i.e., extend the range axis). Indicate the point of maximum profit on the graph and find algebraically the optimum output level and the maximum profit.

(a) $TR = f(Q) = -0.2Q^2 + 10Q$
  $TC = g(Q) = 40 + Q$
(b) $TR = f(Q) = 2Q - 0.1Q^2$
  $TC = g(Q) = 4.5 + 0.2Q$

11.8.3 Suppose that you are a government administrator in the department of Agriculture. Your research bureau has prepared the graph below showing the current behavior of the market for wheat. The vertical line represents the current level of the price $\bar{P}$ for wheat as set by your department under the price support program. What do you expect the result of this price decision to be?

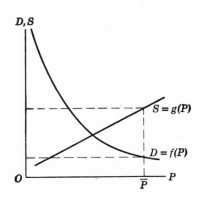

Progressions, Exponents, and Logarithms

Chapter 12

12.1 Number sequences and arithmetic progressions

One of the things with which all of us are intimately familiar in this age of credit transactions is *interest* on money. When we are paid interest on money deposited, for instance, in a savings account, we are literally paid for foregoing the current use of that money. Interest is therefore not only the payment made to us by the bank for the use of our money, but our payment for "waiting." When we withdraw our money for our own use, we will receive not only the *principal* amount deposited, but also the interest earned while the money was on deposit. Similarly, if we buy a television set or an automobile impatiently, borrowing the money from some source of credit, we can expect to pay back to the lending agency, over a period of time, not only the total amount of money borrowed, but interest for its use as well. In this case interest is the cost we suffer for not waiting until we could make the purchase from our accumulated savings.

Interest received or paid is conventionally determined by an interest rate which states the percentage of the principal earned or owing for a year's use of that principal. Thus, a 6 per cent loan is one which bears interest at 6 per cent per year; if the principal borrowed were \$200, then the interest accumulated at the end of a year would be \$12. The fine print in any contract where interest is involved should be carefully

228

examined, however, since the conventional charging of interest on a year's basis is not required by law although there are statutory limits on the amount of interest which may be charged in any year. The interval between interest payments is called the *interest period*, and this period is determined by contract between the borrower and lender. If the period is not stated, then it is assumed to be one year. If the period of a given contract should be shortened by half to six months, then the interest payable is usually halved as well; a bank loan to run a year at 6 per cent, if repaid in six months, would normally accrue only 3 per cent interest on the principal borrowed. Thus the total amount of interest due is a function of time, as we would expect, since it is payment for "waiting" over a period of time.

When interest is calculated upon the principal alone, regardless of the number of interest periods over which the loan extends, it is called *simple* interest. Suppose a person deposits $100 in a bank paying 3 per cent simple interest annually. At the end of the first year this person's account would be credited with $3 and his savings balance would be $103. At the end of the second year he would again receive $3; his balance would be $106. At the end of n periods, the balance in this person's account would consist of his original principal plus n times the interest earned in one period, as illustrated in Fig. 12.1.1.

The "Balance" column in Fig. 12.1.1 is a *sequence* of numbers: a sequence is an ordered set of numbers formed by some specific rule. In the illustration in Fig. 12.1.1, the rule is: "add three dollars to the previous account balance to find the next succeeding number in the set." Some examples of sequences are $\{1, 2, 3, 4, 5\}$, $\{1, 4, 16, 256, \ldots\}$, $\{2, 1, \frac{1}{2}, \frac{1}{4}\}$, $\{4, 2, 0, -2, -4, \ldots\}$. If the number of terms of a

Period	Principal	Interest	Balance	Term	Value
0	$100	$0	$100	1	$a + (0)d$
1	100	3	103	2	$a + (1)d$
2	100	3	106	3	$a + (2)d$
3	100	3	109	4	$a + (3)d$
.	.	.	.	.	.
.	.	.	.	.	.
.	.	.	.	.	.
n	100	3	$100 + 3n$	n	$a + (n - 1)d$

Fig. 12.1.1   Fig. 12.1.2

sequence is finite, it is called a *finite sequence*, as in the first and third examples. If the terms continue without end, the sequence is called an *infinite sequence*, as in the second and fourth examples.

A number sequence formed by adding some *fixed* number to the first term and to each successive term is called an *arithmetic progression*. The fixed number is called the *common difference* of the progression. If we denote the first term of an arithmetic progression ($A.P.$) by a and the common difference by d, an $A.P.$ will be formed as shown in Fig. 12.1.2. We note that the coefficient of d for a given term is one less than the number of the term. If we let z be the value of the *last* term of an $A.P.$ of n terms with common difference d, then z may be computed by:

$$z = a + (n - 1)d,$$

and we note that z is a linear function of n.

With a slight change in the definition of the variable n, we find this formula to be immediately applicable to the computation of the value of an amount of money invested at simple interest at any given time. In the example above, $a = \$100$, $d = \$3$; if we wished to compute the value of the investment after 5 years, we ask for the value of the sixth term in the $A.P.$:

$$z = \$100 + (6 - 1)\$3 = \$100 + (5)\$3 = \$115.$$

The difference between the *term* of an $A.P.$ and the *period* of an interest payment accounts for the apparent difference in the formulas used: for the first term in an $A.P.$, $n = 1$; but the corresponding element of the interest set, in terms of the period, is zero. Either formula is applicable, but one must be careful to understand the difference in terminology.

It is often useful to be able to compute the sum of the terms of an $A.P.$ It can, of course, be done by simple addition. If the number of terms is large, however, this can be a tedious operation. The sum S_n can be computed from the formula:

$$S_n = \frac{n}{2}(a + z);$$

careful examination of this formula shows that the sum is nothing more than the average of the first and last terms times the number of terms. For example, the sum of the finite $A.P.$ $\{0, 1, 2, 3, 4, 5, 6, 7, 8, 9\}$ is found as follows ($n = 10$, $a = 0$, $z = 9$):

$$S_{10} = \frac{10}{2}(0 + 9) = 5(9) = 45.$$

Five specific values are involved in any $A.P.$:

a, the first term,
z, the last term (or nth term),
n, the number of terms,
d, the common difference,
S_n, the sum of n terms.

Given the values of any three of these characteristics, the values of the remaining two may be found by using the two formulas developed:

$$Formula\ 12.1.1: \quad z = a + (n - 1)d$$

$$Formula\ 12.1.2: \quad S_n = \frac{n}{2}(a + z).$$

12.1 Exercises

12.1.1 Find the last term (z) of the following arithmetic progressions:

(a) $\{-1, 2, 5, \ldots\}$ to 8 terms   (b) $\{0, -2, -4, \ldots\}$ to 5 terms
(c) $\{7, 5, 3, \ldots\}$ to 10 terms   (d) $\{1, 4, 7, \ldots\}$ to 15 terms.

12.1.2 Find n for the following arithmetic progressions:

(a) $\{1, 2, 3, \ldots, 8\}$ (b) $\{2, 1, 0, \ldots, -5\}$
(c) $\{4, 7, 10, \ldots, 40\}$ (d) $\{6, 3, 0, \ldots, -21\}$.

12.1.3 Find a for the following arithmetic progressions:

(a) $z = 27, n = 15, d = -2$ (b) $z = 10, n = 7, d = -2$
(c) $z = 15, n = 15, d = 3$ (d) $z = 9, n = 10, d = 10$.

12.1.4 The 4th term of a certain arithmetic progression is 10, the 7th term is 19. Find a and d.

12.1.5 Find the sum of the following arithmetic progressions:

(a) $a = 1, d = 2, z = 21$ (b) $a = 7, d = -1, n = 15$
(c) $a = 4, d = 3, n = 10$ (d) $d = -2, n = 10, z = 10$
(e) $d = 1, n = 15, z = 20$ (f) $a = 2, n = 10, z = 40$.

12.1.6 Find the sum of all positive even integers less than 100.

12.1.7 Find the sum of all positive integers less than 100.

12.1.8 Find the sum of all integers between 10 and 100 whose last digit is 5.

12.1.9   Find the interest and total value (T) of $300 deposited at simple interest:

(a) After 5 years with interest at 5 per cent per annum,
(b) After 10 years with interest at 4 per cent per annum.

12.1.10   What is the rate of simple interest if $500 has a total value (T) of $575 after 3 years?

12.2   Geometric progressions

We would be hard pressed today to find a financial institution that calculated interest according to the simple interest formula on loans extending beyond one interest period. Indeed, the concept of simple interest applies more naturally to a situation of short-term borrowing or lending, such as a contract for $50 payable in 60 days at 1 per cent simple interest. Certain types of mutual investment programs allow for the withdrawal of dividends as they are paid, or provide the option to leave any accrued dividends in the program, representing a new, additional investment. When such dividends, which are much like interest, are withdrawn, the result is the same as if the investment holder were being paid simple interest. On the other hand, if he should elect to have his dividends credited to his investment balance, in future periods his "interest" would be calculated on the basis of this new, higher balance. Such a situation reflects the concept of *compound interest*.

A transaction involving the use of money over time that provides for the calculation of interest upon the balance of the principal *and* of any interest accruing from previous periods is said to bear compound interest, i.e., interest is paid on interest (as well as on principal). Let us consider the case of the depositor with $100 who elects to save his money at a bank paying 3 per cent interest compounded annually. The growth of this deposit, with interest compounded annually, is illustrated in Fig. 12.2.1. At the end of the first year, the amount of interest earned is $3, which is then added to the account balance, and which becomes an additional part of the principal deposited. In the next period interest is computed on the "new" principal of $103: the amount of interest is now $3.09, which again is added to the principal. Compare the balance of the account with interest computed in this fashion with the similar situation of simple interest in Fig. 12.1.1. We note that after five periods the value of the account is almost $1 greater

Compound Interest Table $100 at 3 Per Cent Annually				Geometric Progression Table	
Period	Principal	Interest	Balance	Term	Value
0	$100.00	—	$100.00	1	ar^0
1	100.00	$3.00	103.00	2	ar^1
2	103.00	3.09	106.09	3	ar^2
3	106.09	3.18	109.27	4	ar^3
4	109.27	3.28	112.55	5	ar^4
5	112.55	3.38	115.93	·	·
·	·	·	·	·	·
·	·	·	·	·	·
·	·	·	·	n	ar^{n-1}

Fig. 12.2.1   Fig. 12.2.2

when interest is compounded. In addition, we notice by inspection that this difference is increasing at an increasing rate.

The values appearing in the "Balance" column in Fig. 12.2.1 comprise a *geometric progression*, a sequence of numbers (an ordered set) such that every term after the first term is found by multiplying the preceding term by a constant, called the *common ratio*. If we denote the first term of a geometric progression (*G.P.*) by a and the common ratio by r, then any geometric progression will be formed as in Fig. 12.2.2. We note that the exponent of r for the nth term is $(n - 1)$. If z is the last term in a *G.P.*, then

$$z = ar^{n-1}.$$

In the compound interest problem above, if we wished to find the value of the investment during the sixth year, we would substitute in this formula the values of a, r, and n: $z = \$100(1.03)^{6-1} = \$100(1.03)^5 = \$100 (1.1593) = \$115.93$. The student should verify that the value of r is indeed 1.03.

Adding up the terms of a *G.P.* is just as tedious as summing the terms of an *A.P.*, when the number of terms is large. A short-cut formula is available to find the sum:

$$S_n = \frac{a - ar^n}{1 - r}.$$

For example, if we wished to find the sum of the first five terms of the

G.P. $\{1, 2, 4, \ldots\}$, substituting $a = 1$, $r = 2$, and $n = 5$,

$$S_5 = \frac{1 - 1(2)^5}{1 - 2} = \frac{1 - 32}{-1} = 31.$$

There are five specific values involved in any *G.P.*:

a, the first term,
z, the last term,
n, the number of terms,
r, the common ratio,
S_n, the sum of n terms.

When any three of these are known then the other two may be found by using the formulas:

Formula 12.2.1: $z = ar^{n-1}$

Formula 12.2.2: $S_n = \dfrac{a - ar^n}{1 - r}.$

If the terms of a geometric progression are linked together by plus signs, the result is called a *geometric series:*

$$4 + 2 + 1 + \tfrac{1}{2} + \tfrac{1}{4} \text{ or } 1 + 3 + 9 + 27 + \cdots.$$

The former example is a *finite geometric series* because there is a finite number of terms in the series; the latter is an *infinite geometric series.* Under certain conditions, a formula for the sum of an infinite geometric series (i.e., $n \to \infty$) can be found as the result of the following argument:

$$S_n = \frac{a - ar^n}{1 - r} = \frac{a}{1 - r} - \frac{ar^n}{1 - r}.$$

When the absolute value of r is less than 1, i.e., $|r| < 1$, then the numerator of the expression $\dfrac{ar^n}{1 - r}$ approaches zero as n approaches infinity.

In terms of limits,

$$S = \lim_{n \to \infty} S_n = \lim_{n \to \infty} \frac{a}{1 - r} - \frac{ar^n}{1 - r} = \frac{a}{1 - r} - \frac{0}{1 - r} = \frac{a}{1 - r}.$$

For example, let us find the sum of the infinite geometric series

$1 + \frac{1}{3} + \frac{1}{9} + \frac{1}{27} + \cdots$, for which $a = 1$, $r = \frac{1}{3}$, and $n \to \infty$:

$$S = \lim_{n \to \infty} S_n = \frac{1}{1 - (\frac{1}{3})} - \frac{1(\frac{1}{3})^n}{1 - (\frac{1}{3})} = \frac{1}{\frac{2}{3}} - \frac{0}{\frac{2}{3}} = \frac{3}{2}.$$

If $|r| > 1$, then r^n as $n \to \infty$ either becomes infinitely large or infinitely small (large negative) as we would expect from examination of the infinite geometric series: $1 + 3 + 9 + 27 + \cdots$, for which $r = 3$. An infinite geometric series in which $|r| < 1$ is said to *converge* to the sum as computed above. When $|r| > 1$, the series is said to *diverge*. Note that the notation for the sum of an infinite geometric series which converges, i.e., $|r| < 1$, is S, written without subscript.

12.2   Exercises

12.2.1   Find the last term for the following geometric progressions:

(a) 2, 1, $\frac{1}{2}$, $\frac{1}{4}$, ... to 8 terms
(b) 1, (1.03), (1.03)^2 ... to 6 terms
(c) 9, -3, 1, $-\frac{1}{3}$ ... to 6 terms
(d) 1, 3, 9 ... to 8 terms.

12.2.2   Find S_n for each of the geometric progressions given in 12.2.1.

12.2.3   For each of the geometric progressions given below find the quantities designated:

(a) $a = 3$, $n = 10$, $r = -\frac{1}{2}$.   Find z and S_n.
(b) $n = 7$, $r = 4$, $z = 4096$.   Find a and S_n.
(c) $r = \frac{1}{2}$, $z = \frac{1}{64}$, $S_n = 3(\frac{63}{64})$.   Find a and n.
(d) $a = 2$, $z = -64$, $S_n = -42$.   Find r and n.

12.2.4   How much would an employer have to pay an employee on the last day of the month if he entered into an employment contract agreeing to pay the employee one cent on the first day, two cents the second day, four cents the third day, etc.?   Assume the employee works every day of a 30 day month.

12.2.5   A man deposits $100 at the beginning of a year in a bank which pays 4 per cent interest compounded annually.   If he makes no additions or withdrawals:

(a) How much *interest* would he receive after the fifth year?
(b) What is the total value of his deposit after the interest for the fifth year is added to his account?

12.2.6 Find the sum of each of the following infinite geometric series.

(a) $4, 2, 1 \ldots$
(b) $1, \frac{1}{2}, \frac{1}{4} \ldots$
(c) $1, 2, 4 \ldots$
(d) $2, -1, \frac{1}{2}, -\frac{1}{4} \ldots$.

12.3 Exponents

In this section we shall review the algebra of exponents preparatory to examining the characteristics of another class of functions called *exponential functions*. In the expression x^n, n is called the *exponent* of x, and the expression is read "the nth *power* of x." Placing a number in the position of the exponent implies that a certain operation is to be performed, just as writing one number over another with a bar between them means that the operation of division is to be performed. When the exponent is a positive integer, the operation consists of raising the number to the power specified by the integer which we do by multiplying the number by itself that number of times (n). If the exponent is a negative integer, the result of the operation is the reciprocal of raising the number to the positive power. If the exponent is a fraction whose numerator is 1, then the operation indicated is to find another number, which when raised to the power indicated by the denominator of the exponent, results in the original number. Such a number is called a *root;* the expression $x^{(1/n)}$ implies that we are to find the nth root of x. The number z will be the nth root of x if $z^n = x$. Thus one of the equal factors of a power is the root of the power: z is the nth root of x, and x is the nth power of z. The operation of extracting (finding) a root is sometimes indicated by the use of the *radical* symbol "$\sqrt{\ }$." The nth root of x may be called for by the symbol $\sqrt[n]{x}$, where n is called the *index* of the radical and x is called the *radicand*. We note that $\sqrt[n]{x} = x^{(1/n)}$, or, more generally, $\sqrt[n]{x^m} = x^{(m/n)}$. The second root of a number is called the square root of the number; the third root is called the cube root. The index (2) is conventionally omitted from the radical when the operation to be performed is the extraction of the square root.

The following rules of exponents are given without proof, although the proof of each follows rather directly from the definitions given above. With the exceptions stated within the set of laws, the laws hold for positive and negative, integral and fractional exponents.

Rule 12.3.1: $x^n = (x)(x)(x) \ldots (x)$. ($x$ multiplied by itself n times)

Examples: $3^2 = (3)(3) = 9$;

$(1/2)^3 = (1/2)(1/2)(1/2) = 1/8$.

Rule 12.3.2: $(x^m)(x^n) = x^{m+n}$

Examples: $(2^2)(2^3) = 2^5 = 32$;

$(1/2)(1/2)^3(1/2)^2(1/2)^5 = (1/2)^{11}$.

Rule 12.3.3: $(x^m)^n = x^{mn}$

Examples: $(2^2)^4 = 2^8$; $[(1/2)^4]^3 = (1/2)^{12}$.

Rule 12.3.4: $x^n/y^n = (x/y)^n$, $y \neq 0$

Example: $3^2/8^2 = (3/8)^2$.

Rule 12.3.5: $x^{-n} = 1/x^n$, $x \neq 0$

Examples: $2^{-2} = 1/2^2 = 1/4$; $1/3^{-2} = 3^2 = 9$.

Rule 12.3.6: $x^m/x^n = x^{m-n}$

Examples: $2^2/2 = 2^{2-1} = 2$; $3^2/3^3 = 3^{2-3} = 3^{-1} = 1/3$.

Rule 12.3.7: $(xyz)^n = x^n y^n z^n$

Example: $(2 \times 3 \times 4)^2 = (2^2)(3^2)(4^2) = (4)(9)(16) = 576 = (24)^2$.

Rule 12.3.8: $x^0 = 1$ (*Note:* 0^0 is not defined.)

Examples: $2^0 = 1$; $1/2^0 = 1$.

One immediate use of exponents is in the representation of numbers which are very large in absolute magnitude or very close to zero, by expressing them in terms of some exponent of 10. The number 2000 can be written $2(10)^3$; 2,000,000 can be written $2(10)^6$. The fraction 0.002 can be represented similarly: $0.002 = 2/1000 = 2/(10)^3 = 2(10)^{-3}$. Likewise, $0.000000075 = 7.5(10)^{-8}$. This representation of numbers is called *scientific notation,* and the significant digits in the number so represented are conventionally expressed with one digit to the left of the decimal point.

12.3   Exercises

12.3.1   Simplify each of the following expressions:

(a) $x^4 x^2$ (b) $5^7 \times 5^{-4}$

(c) $2^{-1} \times 2^{-1}$ (d) $3^3/3^2$

(e) $3^3/3^{-2}$ (f) $(5^2)^2$

(g) $(x^2)^{-3}$ (h) $(\frac{4}{9})^{\frac{1}{2}}$

(i) $(\frac{9}{4})^{-\frac{1}{2}}$ (j) $(5^2)(4^2)(3^2)$

(k) 3^0 (l) $(a + b + c)^0$

(m) $(8)^{\frac{1}{3}}$ (n) $(0.49)^{\frac{1}{2}}$

(o) $(\frac{1}{8})^{-\frac{1}{3}}$ (p) $(\frac{16}{9})^{-\frac{1}{2}}$

(q) $2x^3/x^{-2}$ (r) $(4x^4)^{-\frac{1}{2}}$

(s) $(x^{-2} + x^{-1} + 1)(x^{-1})(x^0)$.

12.3.2   Transform each of the following into scientific notation:

(a) $71,000,000,000,000$ (b) $(325,000)(2,000,000)$

(c) $-67,400$ (d) 0.000000475

(e) 0.001001 (f) $\dfrac{-25}{1,000,000}$.

12.4   Logarithms

In high school everyone is exposed to logarithms, as an almost magical device for simplifying the calculation of products or quotients of large or otherwise intractable numbers. In this section we shall review the nature of logarithms from a strictly practical point of view, and in the next section attempt to show "how they got that way." At present we merely wish to review quite technically, by what we hope is an illuminating method, what logarithms are, and how a scheme for calculation can be constructed from them.

Consider the number 387. In the last section we learned how to represent numbers in terms of powers of ten, and we note that $387 = 3.87(10)^2$ in scientific notation, i.e., the decimal point in the given number is moved so that there is one digit to the left of it, and the result is multiplied by the power of 10 that preserves the identity. Let us assume that there is a number x such that $10^x = 3.87$. If we could find such a number, then we could write

$$387 = (10^x)(10)^2 = 10^{2+x},$$

by Rule 12.3.2. In Appendix I is a table of logarithms, which is but a list of the value of this exponent x for any given number N. The value of x to four places can be found immediately for numbers of three or fewer digits; for numbers having more than three digits, interpolation, which will be explained shortly, is necessary. Let us find the value of x for the number 387. We read down the left-hand column of the table to the number 38, and then across to the column headed 7; the number found at the intersection, 0.5877, is x, such that $10^{0.5877} = 3.87$. Note that we put a decimal point before the number, and that obviously there is some error in the result of this "table look-up": 0.5877 is a good approximation of the desired exponent, but it is not exact. At this point we should emphasize this important fact: the logarithm of a number is an exponent! Let us complete the problem posed above, where we found $387 = 10^{2+x}$. Since $x = 0.5877$, we may now write

$$387 = 10^{2+0.5877} = 10^{2.5877}.$$

The exponent of 10, which is 2.5877, is called the *base* 10 or *common logarithm* of the number 387, and we see that the common logarithm of a number is the power to which 10 must be raised in order to get the number. We write down these identical representations of the number:

$$387 = 3.87(10)^2 = (10)^{0.5877}(10)^2 = 10^{2.5877}.$$

Let us consider the number 7.375 in the same fashion. The first step is to represent the number in standard notation: $7.375 = 7.375(10)^0$. We ask then for x such that $10^x = 7.375$, and referring to the table in Appendix I, we find that 7.375 is not tabulated. Therefore we must interpolate: the value of x, i.e., the logarithm of 7.37 is found to be 0.8675; the logarithm of 7.38 is 0.8681. Since 7.375 is half-way between 7.37 and 7.38, and the difference between 0.8675 and 0.8681 is 0.0006, we *assume* that the logarithm of 7.375 is half-way between the logarithm of 7.37 and the logarithm of 7.38, or $0.8675 + 0.0003 = 0.8678$. Therefore we write:

$$7.375 = 7.375(10)^0 = (10^{0.8678})(10^0) = 10^{0.8678+0} = 10^{0.8678}.$$

Let us finally consider the number 0.0008532:

$$0.0008532 = 8.532(10)^{-4} = (10)^{0.9310}(10^{-4}) = 10^{0.9310-4}.$$

The student should verify that $0.9310 = \log 8.532$ since interpolation was necessary to find the logarithm. Notice also that 10^{-4} was indicated by showing the -4 at the end of the logarithm. We do this so that the exponent is not represented by a negative number, i.e., we *could* represent our number as

$$10^{-4+0.9320} = 10^{-3.0680}.$$

However, the logarithm table is not set up to handle negative logarithms, and thus we cannot further manipulate a logarithm in this form, but must convert it as shown above. Using our standard exponent form this convention should cause no confusion.

The process, which we have described above, of converting some number into a power of 10 is reversible: given 10^x where x is known, we may then find the number N such that $N = 10^x$ by working the logarithm table backwards, and writing the identical expressions in reverse order. For instance, we might ask for the number N such that $N = 10^{4.7832}$. We write:

$$10^{4.7832} = (10)^{0.7832}(10)^4 = 6.07(10)^4 = 60,700.$$

We enter the table with the value 0.7832, which is a logarithm, and find the associated value of N to be 607, which we write, in standard notation, 6.07. The number 6.07, is called the *antilogarithm* of 0.7832, or, antilog 0.7832 = 6.07. Note that we find the *logarithm* of a *number*, and the *antilogarithm* of a *logarithm*.

It is often necessary to interpolate in the tables to find the antilogarithm. This process is similar to the one we have already discussed. For example, find antilog 0.1882 − 3, i.e., $N = 10^{0.1882-3}$. We find that 0.1882 lies between 0.1875 and 0.1903. The difference between 0.1875 and 0.1903 is 0.0028. The number we seek thus lies $7/28$ of the distance from 1.54 to 1.55, so that the number associated with the logarithm 0.1882 is 1.5425, which we round off to 1.543. We write:

$$10^{0.1882-3} = (10)^{0.1882}(10)^{-3} = 1.543(10)^{-3} = 0.001543.$$

Since the process of interpolation is a means of estimating the value of an unknown number, we must consider the problem of accuracy, especially with regard to rounding. Generally, we should carry an operation to no more significant digits than there are in the least significant term involved in the operation. Since our logarithm table reports logarithms for three-digit numbers to four decimal places, the logarithm of a number of more than three digits should carry no more than four decimal places either. Thus, the logarithm found by interpolation should be rounded to four decimal places. We follow the usual rounding convention of increasing the least significant digit in our answer by 1 if the digit to its right is greater than 4. When finding an antilogarithm, we may approximate a fourth digit, as above, by rounding the number 1.5425 to 4 places, i.e., to 1.543. The fact that the resulting number is not accurate in the least significant digit forces us to observe the rule stated above for operating with such numbers. Otherwise we would imply an unwarranted accuracy in our results.

Now we are ready to use our system of calculation. Suppose that we wish to multiply 387 by 0.0008532. Since we have already found the identical representations of these numbers as powers of 10, we realize that this product can be represented as:

$$(10)^{2.5877}(10)^{0.9310-4} = 10^{2.5877+0.9310-4} = 10^{0.5187-1}$$
$$= (10)^{0.5187}(10)^{-1} = 3.302(10)^{-1} = 0.330.$$

In interpolating for the antilogarithm of 0.5187, we develop the fraction $\frac{2}{13}$, which we have rounded off to 0.2.

In the answer we report only 3 significant digits, i.e., 0.330, because the multiplicand 387 contained only this many significant digits. The exact answer to this multiplication, i.e., the product of two numbers without regard to significance, is 0.3301884, as can be determined by multiplying the original numbers. The difference arises from the fact that with only a four place logarithm table, and arguments N of only three significant digits, our approximations of the logarithms are grossly imprecise. It should be realized, however, that even had we used a ten place, twenty place, or n-place table (n a large number) our answer, arrived at by logarithms, would still contain some error. By using a sufficiently large logarithm table we can reduce the error in using logarithms, and in fact render it negligible. However, the error inherent in using logarithms will always exist, except when eliminated coincidentally by mutually offsetting rounding errors.

The example above demonstrates our first rule for the use of logarithms:

Rule 12.4.1: *The logarithm of a product is equal to the sum of the logarithms of the factors:*
$$\log (MN) = \log M + \log N.$$

Thus to find the product of two numbers, we find the antilogarithm of the sum of the logarithms of the numbers. Note that this rule follows directly from Rule 12.3.2. Since Rule 12.3.6 is concerned with division, it seems reasonable to assume that a logarithmic rule should follow from it as well, and that is the case:

Rule 12.4.2: *The logarithm of a quotient is equal to the logarithm of the dividend (numerator) minus the logarithm of the divisor (denominator):*
$$\log (M/N) = \log M - \log N.$$

As an example, let us divide:

$$\frac{5.74}{.347} = \frac{10^{0.7589}}{10^{0.5403-1}} = 10^{0.7589-(0.5403-1)} = 10^{0.2186+1}$$
$$= (10)^{0.2186}(10)^1 = 1.654(10)^1 = 16.54.$$

Since raising a number to a power is tantamount to multiplying the number by itself the number of times indicated by the exponent, we should not be surprised to find the last rule for operating with logarithms to be:

Rule 12.4.3: *The logarithm of the nth power of a number is n times the logarithm of the number:*

$$\log N^n = n \log N.$$

This rule follows from Rule 12.3.3. Let us illustrate this rule with a simple example:

$$4^2 = [4.0(10)^0]^2 = [(10)^{0.6021}(10)^0]^2 = (10)^{1.2042}(10)^0$$
$$= (10)^{0.2042}(10)^1 = 1.600(10)^1 = 16.00.$$

Since n may be negative as well as positive, let us examine this case, which requires a small trick, although the procedure is straightforward. Find 142^{-3}:

$$142^{-3} = [1.42(10)^2]^{-3} = [(10)^{0.1523}(10)^2]^{-3} = [(10)^{-0.4569}(10)^{-6}].$$

We notice at this point that we have developed a negative exponent for the first term, and recall that the table contains no negative exponents. Here is the trick: we multiply the last expression by $(10)^1(10)^{-1}$, which does not change its value, and collect terms:

$$[(10)^{-0.4569}(10)^{-6}(10)^1(10)^{-1}] = [(10)^{-0.4569}(10)^1][(10)^{-6}(10)^{-1}]$$
$$= [(10)^{0.5431}(10)^{-7}] = 3.492(10)^{-7} = 0.0000003492.$$

Whenever a negative exponent turns up in the course of the computation, it can be handled in this way.

When performing computations with negative numbers, we may still use logarithms to develop the numerical answer, but we must work only with the absolute value of the numbers involved in the calculation. The problem is examined to determine the sign of the answer; the absolute value of the answer is found according to the techniques described above; and the sign is then attached to this result.

At this point we shall name the parts of a logarithm. We did not name them previously because the names were not necessary to the methods employed. The logarithm of a number consists of two parts: the *mantissa*, which is the power of 10 of the number in scientific notation, and the *characteristic*, which indicates how far out of scientific notation position the number is. Thus the mantissa deals only with the numerical aspects of a number without regard to the decimal point, and the characteristic deals only with the position of the decimal point.

In our exponential notation, for instance, we find these two elements immediately:

$$574 = (10)^{0.7589}(10)^2; \log 574 = 2.7589,$$

where 2 is the characteristic and 0.7589 is the mantissa. A table of logarithms is thus a list of the mantissas of numbers in scientific notation.

12.4   Exercises

12.4.1   Complete the table below, following the format developed in Section 12.4.

(a) 0.00342	$= 10$	$\times$	$= 10$	$\times 10$	$= 10$
(b) 6.745	$= 10$	$\times$	$= 10$	$\times 10$	$= 10$
(c) 575.4	$= 10$	$\times$	$= 10$	$\times 10$	$= 10$
(d) 42.57	$= 10$	$\times$	$= 10$	$\times 10$	$= 10$
(e) 4,695,000	$= 10$	$\times$	$= 10$	$\times 10$	$= 10$
(f)	$= 10^{-4}$	$\times 1.23$	$= 10$	$\times 10$	$= 10$
(g)	$= 10^{10}$	$\times 9.762$	$= 10$	$\times 10$	$= 10$
(h)	$= 10$	$\times$	$= 10^2$	$\times 10^{0.1055}$	$= 10$
(i)	$= 10$	$\times$	$= 10^{-2}$	$\times 10^{0.8341}$	$= 10$
(j)	$= 10$	$\times$	$= 10$	$\times 10$	$= 10^{0.9386-6}$
(k)	$= 10$	$\times$	$= 10$	$\times 10$	$= 10^{3.3418}.$

12.4.2   Perform the indicated operations on the numbers below, using common logarithms to develop your answers.

(a) $(0.00342)(4,695,000)$

(b) $(575.4)(-127.5)$

(c) $\dfrac{2197}{0.06825}$

(d) $\dfrac{0.00492}{-6.745}$

(e) $(42.57)^{-5}$

(f) $(0.00921)^7$

(g) $(575.4)^{\frac{1}{4}}$

(h) $(4,695,000)^{\frac{1}{5}}.$

12.4.3   Find the antilogarithms of the following common logarithms.

(a) 3.4914

(b) $0.9085 - 4$

(c) 10.7324

(d) $0.8751 - 1$

(e) $0.9268 - 6$

(f) 0.8603.

12.5   Exponential and logarithmic functions

A function of the form $f(x) = x^n$ is called a *power function*. We
have dealt with power functions previously; for instance, the power
function $y = f(x) = x^2$ we recognize as a parabolic function. Of interest to us at this point is a function in which the independent variable is
an exponent. Such a function is called an *exponential function* and has
the form $y = f(x) = b^x$, where b is any constant, called the *base* of the
function.

Let us examine such a function, $y = f(x) = 2^x$. Some of the ordered
pairs in the solution set of this function are tabulated in Fig. 12.5.1, for
integral values in the domain of x in the interval $\{-9 \leq x \leq 9\}$. We
note the interesting feature of this function: the values of x form an
arithmetic progression with common difference 1, while the associated
values $f(x)$ form a geometric progression with common ratio 2, the base
of the function. An exponential function is a useful tool for describing
the relative behavior of two phenomena when the elements in one set
can be ordered as an arithmetic progression and the associated elements

x	$f(x) = 2^x$
-9	0.001953125
-8	0.00390625
-7	0.0078125
-6	0.015625
-5	0.03125
-4	0.0625
-3	0.125
-2	0.25
-1	0.5
0	1.0
1	2.0
2	4.0
3	8.0
4	16.0
5	32.0
6	64.0
7	128.0
8	256.0
9	512.0

Fig. 12.5.1

of the other form a geometric progression. An immediate example is the growth behavior of a sum of money placed at compound interest, such that the sum deposited increases geometrically with time: $A = P(1 + i)^n$. The value of the amount A is thus a function of time n: $A = f(n)$. Another exponential function of time was illustrated in Exercise 11.2.4, where the distributor's naptha inventory evaporated at the rate of 10 per cent per month of the remaining amount. This function can be written $I_n = I_o(0.9)^n$, where I_n is the amount remaining in inventory at time n, and I_o is the original inventory.

Let us examine the form of an exponential function more closely. If $y = 10^x$, then from the previous section we know that x is the logarithm of y, i.e., the power to which 10 must be raised to produce y. More generally, if $y = b^x$, then x is the logarithm of y *to the base b*, i.e., x is the power to which b must be raised to produce y. We write:

$$x = \log_b y.$$

Conventionally, omission of the base (b) means that we are dealing with base 10, or *common* or *Brigg's* logarithms. It is clear that any number greater than zero (except 1) can be used as the base of a logarithm, although as a matter of practice, we consider only two kinds of logarithms: the base 10 logarithm, which we write *log*, and another kind to be discussed shortly, called the natural logarithm, written *ln*.

Any exponential function whose base is greater than zero, and not equal to 1, thus has an associated logarithmic function; the functions are said to be the *inverse* of each other. Note then in Fig. 12.5.1 that the column headed x in effect constitutes logarithms to the base 2 of the numbers to the right. We could use this system of logarithms for computation as well as the common logarithms used in the previous section; for instance:

$$(16)(0.0625) = (2)^4(2)^{-4} = 2^0 = 1.$$

However, tables of logarithms to the base 2 are not commonly available, and their use is thus impractical. In addition, our decimal number system itself is based upon multiples of the number 10, and the base 10 logarithm fits neatly into it, i.e., $10^{-3} = 0.001$; $10^{-2} = 0.01$; $10^{-1} = 0.1$; $10^0 = 1.0$; $10^1 = 10$; $10^2 = 100$; etc.

The most common exponential function is the one whose base is the number e: $y = e^x$. This type of function is so widely used that it is known as *the* exponential function, and is written simply *exp*. For instance, the function $f(x) = \exp (x - 3)$ means $f(x) = e^{x-3}$. Since we shall deal only with relatively simple forms of the exponential function, we shall use the former notation. The value of the number e can be approximated by increasing n in the following expression to attain the desired accuracy:

$$\lim_{n \to \infty} \left(1 + \frac{1}{n}\right)^n = e = 2.7182818285 \text{ (to ten places)}.$$

The function $f(x) = e^x$ is graphed in Fig. 12.5.2; note some of the characteristics of the function. It is strictly monotonic increasing throughout its length, continuous in all intervals, and asymptotic to the domain axis.

If $y = e^x$, then $x = \log_e y = \ln y$; we write $\log_e$ as ln, called the *natural* or *Naperian* logarithm. Thus the natural logarithm function is the inverse function of the exponential function, and the logarithmic function $y = g(x) = \ln x$ is graphed in Fig. 12.5.3. If the graph of $f(x) = e^x$ is reflected across a line which bisects the first quadrant ($y = x$), then the result is the inverse of $f(x)$, or $g(x) = \ln x$. The fact

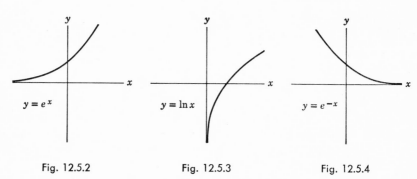

| Fig. 12.5.2 | Fig. 12.5.3 | Fig. 12.5.4 |

that the inverse of $f(x)$ is itself a function is important, since not all inverses are functions (try $y = x^2$; is the inverse a function?). An important variation of the exponential function is the negative exponential, $h(x) = e^{-x}$, which is graphed in Fig. 12.5.4.

An application of the exponential function to banking will illustrate its usefulness. We have already noted that banks make money by charging interest on money lent, and that a bank thus depends upon some source of loanable funds. A primary source for many banks is the savings deposited by the public. As a result, banks compete for these savings, but are restricted by law to only a very few means of competition. One of these is the manner in which they compute and pay interest. Many savings banks which compound interest semiannually only pay interest semiannually as well. To make a bank more attractive, its management may decide to pay accrued interest at any time, by compounding interest daily and paying any accrued interest upon funds withdrawn on any day. Thus the compound interest formula $A = P(1 + i)^n$, where i is the interest rate for each period of n periods, is changed to $A = P\left(1 + \dfrac{i}{c}\right)^{cn}$, where c is the number of times in one interest period that interest is compounded. As an example, consider the bank which has previously paid 3 per cent per year compounded annually, and which now wishes to compute interest on a daily basis. To compute the amount A to which a deposit P will grow in n years, the bank could use $A = P\left(1 + \dfrac{0.03}{360}\right)^{360n}$. An approximation to the amount A, making use of the exponential function, assumes that the number of times interest is compounded in any period becomes infinite, i.e. we find $\lim\limits_{c \to \infty}\left(1 + \dfrac{i}{c}\right)^c = e^i$. It can be shown that if i is the interest to be charged in any period n, and interest is to be compounded continuously, $A = Pe^{in}$ will give the value of A at any time n. With a table of natural logarithms, this calculation is somewhat simpler than the previous one, since

$$\ln A = \ln P + (in)\ln e = \ln P + in;$$

we note that $\ln e = 1$, since $e^1 = e$.

Our purpose in this section has been to expose the student to a class of functions and their characteristics which can be very useful in analysis. We have contented ourselves in merely describing these functions, leaving their analysis to the following exercises and work in subsequent chapters.

12.5 Exercises

12.5.1 Make a table similar to the one in Fig. 12.5.1 for the exponential function $y = 5^x$, over the interval $\{-4 \leq x \leq 4\}$. Compute $(\frac{1}{125})(625)$ using $\log_5$.

12.5.2 Construct a similar table for $y = (\frac{1}{2})^x$. Compute $(16)(0.0625)$ using $\log_{\frac{1}{2}}$.

12.5.3 Show by a similar table why the number 1 cannot be used as the base of a logarithmic system.

12.5.4 By reasoning from the definition of a logarithm and an exponential function, show why the logarithmic base cannot be negative.

12.5.5 Show by using the tables in Fig. 12.5.1 and Exercise 12.5.1 that $\log_b a = \dfrac{1}{\log_a b}$.

12.5.6 Let $b = 10$ and $a = 2$; show that $\log_a x = \dfrac{\log_b x}{\log_b a}$. (Note that this expression indicates how a logarithm to one base can be changed to an equivalent logarithm to another base; to change from natural to common logarithms, for instance, we notice that $\log x = \dfrac{\ln x}{\ln 10} = \dfrac{\ln x}{2.30} = 0.43 \ln x.$)

12.5.7 Semi-logarithmic paper is graph paper ruled arithmetically along the horizontal axis and logarithmically along the vertical axis; it is available at bookstores. From a sheet of 3-cycle semi-logarithmic paper, cut two strips approximately 1 inch wide, making the cuts parallel to the vertical axis. Label each strip as shown in the illustration. By placing the strips side by side, show how the product of two numbers can be found by "adding" lengths. This illustrates the principle of the *slide rule;* what rule in this text provides the justification for the operation of such an instrument?

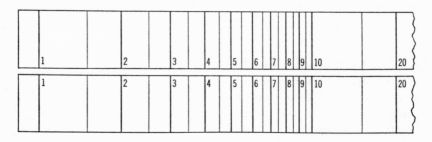

12.5.8 On another sheet of semi-logarithmic paper, plot the graph of the function $y = f(x) = 2^x$. How do you account for the unique characteristic displayed? (*Hint:* Arithmetic vs. geometric progressions?)

12.6 Annuities

Throughout history man has been concerned about the security of his future. In these times of high standards of living and longer life spans, security has become one of most important motivations of personal behavior. Probable illness, eventual retirement, and the education of our children have all become important future events, which require planning and decision-making. For example, consider the father who contemplates his son's entrance into college 10 years hence, and who realizes that the cost of 4 years of college will be at least \$5000. Suppose the father decides to start financing this program now, to have \$5000 available 10 years in the future. One way to hatch such a nest egg is to establish an *annuity* in the *amount* of \$5000, to mature in 10 years. This is accomplished by depositing equal amounts of money to the annuity fund over equal intervals of time. If \$500 is put under the mattress every year for 10 years, then the desired amount will be available. This is uneconomic, however, since money saved institutionally in banks or savings associations, etc., can be put to work to earn more money. If the \$500 were deposited regularly in a savings program, at the end of the first period the first deposit will have earned interest, which will be added to the total amount saved. If interest is paid at 4 per cent per annum, then we can construct a schedule showing how much each of the 10 deposits of \$500 is worth on the maturity date of the annuity:

$$
\begin{aligned}
\text{Value of 1st deposit on date of 10th dep.} &= \$500(1.04)^9 = \$\ 711.65 \\
\text{Value of 2nd deposit on date of 10th dep.} &= \$500(1.04)^8 = 684.30 \\
\text{Value of 3rd deposit on date of 10th dep.} &= \$500(1.04)^7 = 657.95 \\
\text{Value of 4th deposit on date of 10th dep.} &= \$500(1.04)^6 = 632.65 \\
\text{Value of 5th deposit on date of 10th dep.} &= \$500(1.04)^5 = 608.35 \\
\text{Value of 6th deposit on date of 10th dep.} &= \$500(1.04)^4 = 584.95 \\
\text{Value of 7th deposit on date of 10th dep.} &= \$500(1.04)^3 = 562.45 \\
\text{Value of 8th deposit on date of 10th dep.} &= \$500(1.04)^2 = 540.80 \\
\text{Value of 9th deposit on date of 10th dep.} &= \$500(1.04)^1 = 520.00 \\
\text{Value of 10th deposit on date of 10th dep.} &= \$500(1.04)^0 = \underline{500.00} \\
& \$6003.10
\end{aligned}
$$

The *amount* of the annuity is the sum of the values of the payments at the maturity of the annuity, or \$6003.10, and the difference between putting the money under the mattress and depositing it in the annuity fund is \$1003.10. Any annuity has the characteristics displayed in the schedule above: it is a set of equal payments made at equal intervals. If the father's goal is to realize exactly \$5000, then it is obvious that his payments will be something less than \$500 per period, and his problem is to determine what these equal deposits should be.

Let us adopt some notation for the variables in this problem as follows:

R is the amount of each of the equal payments,
i is the interest rate per annum,
n is the number of payments,
A is the amount of the annuity.

For this problem, then, $A = \$5000$, $i = 4$ per cent, and $n = 10$. We wish to find R. We could of course try to find R by trial and error, by substituting values for R into the schedule above until we found the value that caused the sum of the values in the right hand column to be equal to A. This would be extremely tedious, so we shall look for a relationship among the variables that will provide a more direct means to the solution. Let us add up the values of each payment by using the equivalent values listed, starting from the bottom:

$$A = \$500(1.04)^0 + \$500(1.04)^1 + \$500(1.04)^2 + \cdots + \$500(1.04)^9$$
$$= \$500[1 + 1.04 + (1.04)^2 + \cdots + (1.04)^9].$$

The expression in brackets in the last equation should be recognized as a finite geometric series, in which the first term (a) is R, the sum (S_n) is A, the common ratio (r) is $(1 + i)$, and the number of terms (n) is n. We see that if

$$S_n = \frac{a - ar^n}{1 - r} = a\,\frac{1 - r^n}{1 - r},$$

then

$$A = R\,\frac{1 - (1 + i)^n}{1 - (1 + i)},$$

which reduces to

$$Formula\ 12.6.1: \quad A = R\,\frac{(1 + i)^n - 1}{i}.$$

This expression relates all of the variables concerned in the problem, and we may now find the amount of the payment required in the problem given:

$$\$5000 = R\,\frac{(1 + 0.04)^{10} - 1}{0.04} = R\,\frac{(1.04)^{10} - 1}{0.04}.$$

The expedient way to find the value of $(1.04)^{10}$ is by logarithms (in the absence of tabulated values):

$$\log (1.04)^{10} = 10 \log 1.04$$
$$= 10\,(0.0170) = 0.170$$
$$\text{antilog } 0.170 = 1.48 \text{ (approximately).}$$

Substituting this value into the formula above:

$$\$5000 = R\,\frac{1.48 - 1}{0.04} = R\,\frac{0.48}{0.04}$$

$$R = \frac{(0.04)(\$5000)}{0.48} = \$416.67.$$

Thus, ten payments of \$416.67 each year for ten years at 4 per cent will amount to \$5000. The last payment will be less than the others, since inaccuracies were introduced by the small logarithm table used.

Another type of annuity arises in installment buying, by which we may purchase cars, homes, television sets, trips to Europe, etc., now, and pay later. The significant feature of loans to finance such expenditures is that they are repaid in equal installments over a fixed number of intervals of time, at some stipulated interest rate. The process of repayment is called *amortization*, and the problem of computing the value of each payment is complicated by the fact that as each payment is made, the balance owing is reduced, and thus the total amount of interest charged on each succeeding payment will be effectively reduced. We note the similarity between this annuity and the previous type, but in this case we are interested in the present value of a set of payments to be made over intervals in the future, during which time the unpaid balance is accruing interest.

The term *present value* perhaps need some explaining. When we use the term, we mean the value at the present time of an amount of money to be realized some time in the future. For instance, if we deposit \$1 at 6 per cent for a year, at the end of the year our original deposit has grown to \$1.06. We then say that the present value of \$1.06 at 6 per cent one year from now, is \$1.00. The compound interest formula $A = P(1 + i)^n$ tells us the value of an amount P placed at interest i for n periods. If we ask how much should be placed at interest i for n periods in order to accumulate an amount A, then we are in effect asking for the present value of A, which is of course P in the compound interest formula. Thus the formula for the present value P of an amount A is

$$P = \frac{A}{(1 + i)^n} = A(1 + i)^{-n}.$$

The term $(1 + i)^{-n}$ is called the *discount factor*. Present value is often spoken of in terms of the discounted value of an amount to be received or paid in the future.

The present value of a debt before we have made any payments to amortize it is therefore the amount of the debt. If we let V stand for the present value of an annuity, and V_n be the present value of the nth payment, then

$$V_n = R(1 + i)^{-n}.$$

For instance, the value of the first payment before any payments are made is $V_1 = R(1 + i)^{-1}$; the amount R paid in the first period is discounted by the interest due in that term. Not all of R is used to repay the principal, since we must pay interest for the use of V for one period. The present value of the second payment before making any payments is $V_2 = R(1 + i)^{-2}$; we note that R is discounted for the two periods over which we have used the money borrowed. The present value V of the annuity is the sum of the present value of each payment, before any payment is made, i.e.,

$$V = R(1 + i)^{-1} + R(1 + i)^{-2} + \cdots + R(1 + i)^{-n}.$$

We note that this expression is also a finite geometric series, and thus may develop a formula for the present value of an annuity by the method used previously, with the result that:

$$\text{Formula 12.6.2:} \quad V = R\frac{1 - (1 + i)^{-n}}{i}.$$

As an example, suppose we were to borrow \$800 from the I.M. Friendly Loan Company, agreeing to repay the loan in 12 monthly installments, paying interest at the rate of 1 per cent per month on the unpaid balance. The present value of the annuity is the \$800, which we owe before making any payments, and we wish to find the amount R, which will amortize the debt in 12 months. Using Formula 12.6.2:

$$\$800 = R\frac{1 - (1.01)^{-12}}{0.01}.$$

Using logarithms to evaluate $(1.01)^{-12}$:

$$\log (1.01)^{-12} = -12 \log (1.01)$$

$$= -12 (0.0043) = -0.0516$$

$$= 0.9484 - 1$$

$$\text{antilog } 0.9484 - 1 = 0.888$$

$$\$800 = R\frac{1 - 0.888}{0.01} = R\frac{0.112}{0.01}$$

$$\$800 = R(11.20)$$

$$R = \$71.43.$$

This formula is also useful for determining the present value of an item when it is offered for sale on "terms." The careful buyer will compute the present value to determine whether or not the real cost of the item is out of line.

An annuity through which equal payments are received at a stated interval for an indefinite period of time is called a *perpetuity*. For instance, one may buy "perpetual care" for a cemetery lot by making one payment, the interest from which is sufficient to pay for the upkeep of the lot each year, without reducing the amount earning the interest. The present value of a perpetuity is derived from Formula 12.6.2; we let n approach infinity since the number of payments is indefinitely large, and thus the term $(1 + i)^{-n}$ approaches zero. If we let V be the present value of a perpetuity, then

$$Formula\ 12.6.3: \quad V = R\frac{1}{i}.$$

This formula states the amount of money V which must be invested at interest rate i to return equal payments R at the end of each interest period indefinitely.

As an example, suppose that a family wishes to establish a memorial for the public library to provide $100 each year. If the return on the investment is known to be 5 per cent per year, then

$$V = \frac{\$100}{0.05} = \$2000.$$

At the end of the first year, and every year thereafter, an original investment of $2000 at 5 per cent will provide the required $100 memorial. In business, this formula is often used to establish the "value" of a going concern in terms of the amount of income which it generates. The rate of interest i, known as the *capitalization rate*, to be used in this calculation varies with the type of business, and is generally considered to be the "normal" *rate of return* expected for a given type of business, based on average income statistics. The riskier the business, the higher the rate of return necessary to attract investment. Thus utilities, which are very stable businesses, have a lower "normal" rate of return than, say, restaurants. If the capitalization rate for a certain type of business is established to be 15 per cent and a given business of that type earns an average of $30,000 profit per year, then the present value, or "worth," of the business is

$$V = \frac{\$30,000}{0.15} = \$200,000.$$

Suppose that instead of paying out the accumulated interest on the investment each period, the interest is allowed to accrue over, say, 5 periods, before it is paid. For example, how much must a conservative city council set aside at 3 per cent compounded annually in order to provide \$2000 every 5 years to paint the interior of the city hall? The formula for this type of problem is:

$$\textit{Formula } 12.6.4: \quad V_k = \frac{R}{(1 + i)^k - 1},$$

where k is the number of interest periods over which interest is allowed to accumulate before R is paid. Note that when $k = 1$, which implies that R will be paid at the end of each period, the formula is identical to Formula 12.6.3. To solve the problem above, for which $R = \$2000$, $i = 0.03$, and $k = 5$,

$$V_5 = \frac{\$2000}{(1.03)^5 - 1} = \frac{\$2000}{1.1593 - 1} = \frac{\$2000}{0.1593} = \$12,555.55.$$

Thus a perpetuity in the amount of \$12,555.55 would provide the desired maintenance funds indefinitely.

The last important use of the present value concept that we shall discuss is the computation of the *capitalized cost* of an asset. By capitalized cost, we mean the total cost burden we must assume if we purchase an asset, including repairs and replacements. The reason for considering these costs beyond the original cost of the asset is that we commit ourselves to the future expense of maintaining the asset once it is purchased, so that the present value of the cost of the asset, before it is purchased, must take into account the fact that these future costs will be incurred. If the cost of each replacement and the useful life of the asset can be determined, a perpetuity may be established to provide the payments necessary to make the replacement. Where an asset has an indefinitely long life, but must be repaired periodically, then the same thinking applies to the cost of each repair and the length of the period before which the repair or maintenance must be performed. The capitalized cost of an asset can therefore be found by

$$\textit{Formula } 12.6.5: \quad C_C = C_O + C_{Vk},$$

where C_C symbolizes the capitalized cost (present value of the proposed purchase), C_O is the original cost of the asset, and C_{Vk} is the present value of the perpetuity formed by the indefinite series of replacement or repair costs, when replacement or repair occurs each k periods.

Since the determination of future repair or replacement costs is difficult, not to mention determining the value of a dollar in terms of what it will buy, the capitalized cost of an asset can be only an estimate. However, the concept is still extremely useful when comparing alternative assets. Annuity calculations are also very useful in choosing between the alternatives of making or buying a product, or leasing or buying an asset. As an example of the latter case, the automobile rental agencies can show that leasing a fleet of cars is more economical for a company than buying cars and maintaining a motor pool, mostly because of tax advantages. But in order to make this decision we must consider the capitalized cost of an owned pool; if we were to consider only the original cost, then the decision would most likely be incorrect.

We have considered only a few of the many kinds of annuities useful to administrative decision-making. Other types, and their application to decision problems, can be explored with the help of a financial analyst in a bank or accounting firm. In addition, tables have been constructed for finding values of the variables involved, and they greatly simplify the calculations. Our purpose has been to expose the student simultaneously to some uses of logarithms and some useful tools of administration.

12.6 Exercises

12.6.1 Find the amount of an annuity having payments of $200 at the end of every 3 months for 6 years, interest at 1 per cent per quarter, compounded quarterly.

12.6.2 How much has been borrowed if the amount is to be paid off in $200 installments at the end of every 3 months for 6 years, interest at 1 per cent per quarter, compounded quarterly?

12.6.3 How much money must be paid into an annuity to accumulate $1500 after 5 years, if payments are made semiannually and the investment earns 6 per cent *per annum* compounded *semiannually?* (*Note:* Six per cent per annum is converted to $6\%/2 = 3$ per cent semiannually when computed semiannually.)

12.6.4 A home is purchased for $20,000, with a down payment of $2000 and an agreement to pay the balance in equal *monthly* payments over a period of 120 months. Find the amount of each monthly payment if the payment includes both interest and principal, and interest is figured at 7.2 per cent per annum converted monthly.

12.6.5 Find the rate of interest charged by the Smiling Shark Loan Company for each of the following loan repayments:

(a) $500 repaid in 24 monthly payments of $25 each.
(b) $100 repaid in 12 quarterly payments of $10 each.
(c) $50 repaid in 3 semiannual payments of $18 each.

12.6.6 What is the present value of a business whose average net income over the past 10 years has been $15,000, if the average return on that type of business is 11.5 per cent?

12.6.7 A widow claims her husband died from overwork, and seeks a court judgment from his former employers to set up an annuity to pay her $8000 per year indefinitely. How large an amount must be invested in such an annuity if long run investments earn 5 per cent?

12.6.8 What is the capitalized cost of the following assets?

(a) Original cost $10,000, replacement every 5 years, with interest at 5 per cent per annum compounded annually.

(b) Original cost $500, replacement every 10 years, with interest at 4 per cent per annum compounded semiannually.

12.6.9 A firm is considering the installation of one of two available machines. Machine A has an original cost of $30,000 and must be replaced every 10 years. Machine B has an original cost of $50,000 but needs replacement only every 25 years. If the cost of money is 4 per cent per annum, which is the less expensive machine?

12.6.10 A washing machine costs $200 and must be replaced at a net cost of $150 every 5 years. What is the capitalized cost of the washer if money is worth 6 per cent? If a family averaged $5 per month in machine fees at a laundromat washing their clothes, what is the present value of the perpetuity which would provide them $5 a month forever, if money is worth 6 per cent? Would it be less expensive to buy a washer or to use the commercial clothes washing facilities?

Chapter 13 — Introduction to Differential Calculus

13.1 Decision-making at the margin

One of the most common and important decision problems faced by an administrator is that of whether or not changing the scope or size of an activity would allow his organization to attain its goals more easily. Such decisions take the form of alternatives to increase or decrease an operation by adding a unit of input to it or subtracting a unit of input from it. Such alternatives may be spelled out in practice in the form of adding another machine to a plant's production capacity, adding an additional salesman to the sales force, reducing advertising outlay by not running one ad, or adding a unit to inventory. Assuming the objective of a firm to be only the maximization of total profit, the new machine should be added only if total earnings derived from its use exceed the total cost of using it, and it thus contributes to profit; he should add the salesman only if the total income the firm derives from his activity exceeds the cost of maintaining him as a salesman; etc. Thus these decisions must be made in terms of their effect upon the *total* objective function, i.e., whether the change results in improved performance as measured by a change in goal attainment. Analyzing decision problems from this point of view is called *marginal analysis,* the word marginal referring to changes in the total function. Thus we

INPUT	PRODUCTION OUTPUT		
Units of Power	Total	Average	Marginal
x	y	y/x	$\Delta y/\Delta x$
0	0	—	
			100
1	100	100	
			160
2	260	130	
			190
3	450	150	
			150
4	600	150	
			100
5	700	140	
			80
6	780	130	
			60
7	840	120	
			−40
8	800	100	

Fig. 13.1.1

speak of decision-making at the margin; we shall develop the tools for this important activity in this and subsequent chapters.

As a simple example, let us consider the problem of lighting an office or shop. Obviously, if no power is applied to the lighting fixtures, we shall expect no output. As the amount of power is increased, we expect our employees to do a better job since they can see more clearly what they are doing. If the lighting should become too bright, however, then our employees may suffer eyestrain or other annoyance, which will decrease productivity. If we measure amount of lighting in terms of power used for this purpose, and output in terms of useful product (non-defective items or accurate work), and consider no other inputs, or conditions upon the productive process, then we can state that production is a function of power input, or $y = f(x)$, where y is total production in units and x is power input in units. Such a functional relationship is called a *production function*. We have indicated some of the ordered pairs in the solution set of the function by the table shown in Fig. 13.1.1, which shows for given amounts of power the resulting total productivity, or output.

The table includes two additional columns: *average* output and *marginal* output. The average output for a given number of units of input is the ratio of the total output realized from employment of that many units to that number of units of input, i.e., average output $= y/x$. If we employ 3 units of power to produce 450 units of output, then the average output per unit of input is $450/3 = 150$ units. Marginal productivity or output is the *change* in total output caused by a change in input, and we represent a change in total output by Δy and the corresponding change in input by Δx. Thus marginal output $= \Delta y/\Delta x$. The marginal productivity of the fourth unit, for instance, is the change in total productivity caused by adding or subtracting the fourth unit of input, or $150/1 = 150$ units. Since this change takes place as we increase input from 3 to 4 units, we record the resulting change in output *between* the rows of the table. We note here that the sum of the marginal outputs is equal to the total output, which we expect to be true, because the marginals represent increments to the total.

Our production function is graphed in Fig. 13.1.2. Note that the function is represented by a continuous curve, under the assumption that our inputs can be changed by very small amounts, i.e., that we can adjust power and therefore lighting by very small amounts. With this graph we can illustrate the concepts of average and marginal output geometrically. Let the point $(2, 260)$ be represented by a, and the point $(3, 450)$ be represented by b. Then average output for 2 units of input is measured by the slope of the straight line segment from the

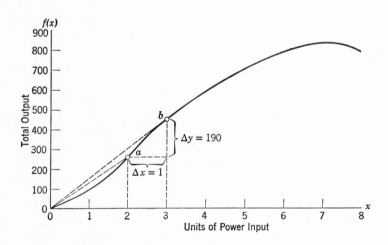

Fig. 13.1.2

origin to a, or $0a$. Likewise, average output for 3 units is the slope of the line segment $0b$. Thus the average output for any input x is measured by the slope of a line from the origin to the point $(x, f(x))$. Marginal output, on the other hand, is measured by the slope of the line *between the points* on the curve. For instance, the marginal output of the third unit of input is measured by the slope of the line from a to b.

From an analysis of the data tabulated in Fig. 13.1.1 and graphed in Fig. 13.1.2 we observe the truth of the following important generalizations about the relationship between total, average, and marginal figures:

(1) When the marginal is greater than the average, the average is increasing.

(2) When the marginal is less than the average, the average is decreasing.

(3) When the marginal is equal to the average, the average is unchanging.

(4) The total is the sum of the marginals.

These relationships hold for the analysis of any "total" curve. It is also important to realize that in the study of administrative decision-making we often analyze only the average and marginal figures in detail (e.g., average and marginal cost, average and marginal revenue), but when such is the case the relationships noted above still apply in the same fashion.

At this point the student should realize the vital difference between average and marginal information in making decisions. For example, in deciding whether or not to employ another unit of power we must answer the question, "Will the unit added produce *at least* as much as it costs?" If the direct expense of adding any unit of power is $10, and the value added in the shop to each unit of output is $0.15, then the first power unit costs $10 and produces a product value of $(100 \times \$0.15) = \$15$. The decision to employ the first unit is clear cut, but the decision to add the seventh or eighth unit is not so obvious. With 7 power units employed we have a total production of 840 units, with a total product value of $126, and an average production of 120 units with an average product value of $18 per power unit employed. We can easily afford the seventh power unit based on a comparison of average costs and income from the application of 7 units. However, if we look at the marginal production of the seventh unit of power, which is 60 units, we see that the value of the marginal product is $60 \times \$0.15 = \$9$, indicating that the use of the seventh power unit actually reduces shop income by $1. Similarly, in analyzing the application of the eighth unit of power we see that on the basis of average figures the employment seems reasonable; however, the eighth power unit has a marginal product of −40 units with a marginal value product of −$6. The use of the eighth unit would reduce shop income by a total of $16.

It is extremely unfortunate that most accounting information available today is presented in the form of total and average data, with few systems set up to identify marginal values. Although marginals may be difficult to develop with existing data collection and reduction systems, they could easily be developed if the existing systems were properly modified. It does no good to argue that the easily developed average figures are "practical" and that marginal figures may depend upon estimates or guesses of the unknown, for the decision at the margin is the decision that determines the attainment of the established goal. As was illustrated above, a decision based on averages may produce economically feasible outcomes, but they are not sufficient to determine optimum outcomes. Thus the rate at which a variable changes, i.e., its marginal value, is the sensitive element of decision-making.

13.1 Exercises

13.1.1 The Olsen-Utter Sales Company has hired a new sales manager in an attempt to improve a deteriorating profit performance. Knowing that the firm has committed large amounts of money to promotion and advertising of its products, the new man wishes to know the effect of such advertising on sales. His first request for information is therefore a summary of unit sales and marketing expenditures for the past 10 years. These data are presented in the accompanying table.

Year	Marketing Expenditures	Sales
1952	1	2.8
1953	3	7.2
1954	4	8.8
1955	2	5.2
1956	6	10.8
1957	8	11.2
1958	7	11.2
1959	5	10.0
1960	9	10.8
1961	10	10.0

Marketing expenditures are given in units of dollar expense, and sales in hundreds of thousands of dollars.

(a) Plot the data, letting x = marketing expenditures and y = unit sales.

(b) Develop a table similar to that found in Fig. 13.1.1, listing the units of marketing expense in numerical order.

(c) On the basis of the information developed in the table, what recommendations should the sales manager make concerning marketing expenditures? Distinguish between the concepts of average sales and marginal sales as decision criteria.

13.1.2 Ignoring other costs of production, if each unit of marketing expenditure cost $100,000, and each unit of sales grossed $100,000 as before, at what level of marketing expense would you recommend the curtailment of further marketing expenditures? Why? (Consider only whole units.)

13.1.3 If the production cost of the product were $0.25 per unit and the selling price were $1.00 per unit, and we were still required to expend our marketing budget in units of $100,000, how many units of marketing expenditure would you recommend? Why? (*Hint:* Construct a new table including production cost, remembering that x is measured in 100,000 units. Total cost will then be the sum of production expense plus marketing expense.)

13.2 Rate of change

Assume that we are driving an automobile down a "through" street, and notice that another driver is approaching the next intersection, which is marked with a sign indicating that he is to stop. In such a circumstance, we are not much concerned with his *position* relative to ours; we are concerned with his *speed* at the moment, for we expect it to be approaching zero. Out of the corner of our eye we see him slow down, i.e., decrease his speed, and we expect that he will indeed stop. In a dynamic environment, i.e., an environment where things are moving, we may not be nearly so interested in the position of something at any moment of time as we are interested in the direction and rate at which the thing is moving to some other position. The speedometer of an automobile provides us with such information: it is a device which measures the rate of change of position relative to time. The fact that there are speed laws is in recognition of the importance of rate of change: the policeman does not care that you are racing to a movie which started five minutes ago, but only in the fact that you are doing 50 miles per hour in a 30 mile per hour zone. Moving from one place to another is not unlawful, nor is it the concern of many save those who do the moving. How fast it is done, however, is a matter of social discrimination, since high rates of speed imply lack of control of a vehicle.

The control of an organization which is continually striving toward some goal or goals should also be considered in the light of rates of change in goal attainment. Our federal government, for instance, is concerned with the maintenance of a steady upward improvement in living standards as measured by Gross National Product. Aberrations in the desired steady upward trend are caused by recessions in the economy (the word "depression" having been outlawed, it seems), and the true path of economic progress follows what are called business cycles. Our administrators in Washington continuously take steps to smooth out wide fluctuations in the economy through various control measures. The concern of the decision maker who would take steps to correct a bad condition is to determine how fast the condition is worsening (or perhaps improving), because the rate of change in the condition may dictate the speed with which he should act and the magnitude of the corrections he should try to effect. This is precisely the problem of making decisions at the margin; analysis of the problem requires further understanding of the concept of rate of change.

In Section 11.1 we introduced the concept of the first differences of a function, and we recognize this to be exactly the same thing discussed in Section 13.1, then called marginals. These values represent the change in the total resulting from a unit change in the number of inputs employed, or, mathematically, the change in the value of the function caused by a unit change in the independent variable. For any given change in the independent variable, then, the marginal tells us how fast the function is changing. Referring to Fig. 13.1.1, we note that adding the sixth unit, for instance, causes total product to increase by 80 units; the rate of change in the function over this interval of the domain is thus 80 units per unit input. This figure is of course the slope of the line from $(5, 700)$ to $(6, 780)$ in Fig. 13.1.2, and is symbolized by $\Delta y/\Delta x$, where $\Delta y = 780 - 700$ and $\Delta x = 6 - 5$, so that $\Delta y/\Delta x = {}^{80}\!/_1 = 80$. This marginal we call the *average rate of change* over the interval $\{5 \leq x \leq 6\}$. If the domain of the variable consisted only of integers, then this interval would of course be empty save for the two end points, and we would have developed the best information obtainable for making a decision at the margin. We note that the average rate of change idea can be extended to cover any interval.

For instance, we could ask for the average rate of change over the interval $\{6 \leq x \leq 8\}$:

$$\frac{\Delta y}{\Delta x} = \frac{800 - 780}{8 - 6} = 10.$$

The implication of this information is that by increasing the number of inputs by 2 units from 6 to 8, we can increase output by 10 units per unit of input, which is true. However, we have overlooked the behavior of the function in the middle of the interval (the criticism of the average concept made in the previous section). Thus, we must exercise care in identifying the true marginal of importance to decision-making. The average rate of change is a measure of this marginal only if the average is taken over the interval associated with the added unit of input.

We have arrived at the problem posed by the continuous function, which implies that the size of changes in inputs is infinitely small, and that the average rate of change at the margin must be measured over an infinitely small interval.

Most of our analysis has been in terms of the relationship of one phenomenon to another at some given point: given the value of the independent variable, find the value of the dependent variable. Now we wish to examine the behavioral relationships of phenomena in terms of change: if the independent variable changes a certain amount, what will be the resulting change in the dependent variable? This change is measured by a *rate* (recall the word *ratio*), and we speak of the rate at which one variable changes relative to another variable. Speed is measured in miles per hour, and is the rate at which distance is covered relative to time. A wage rate states how much money will be paid relative to time worked, or to number of units produced, etc. Gross National Product is the rate at which all final goods and services are being produced in the United States, measured in dollars per year. The next question might be, what is the rate of change, not *between* any two points but *at* a given point? This question seems all but ludicrous, since a point has no dimension, and we cannot measure its "length." Yet we see that the straight lines connecting points on the graph of a function are not accurate representations of the rate of change at the points they connect. To solve this problem, we introduce the concept of *instantaneous* rate of change, by which we mean the rate of change of a function at a given point.

Since the average rate of change is measured by the slope of a line, it seems reasonable that the instantaneous rate of change should be

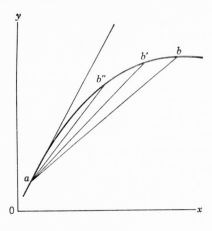

Fig. 13.2.1

measured similarly.   We therefore introduce the concept of a *tangent* to a curve.   We may define the line tangent to a curve by referring to Fig. 13.2.1.   The straight line ab is called a *secant* of the curve; if the secant is drawn successively smaller, i.e., ab', ab'', etc., then the limiting position of point b is point $a: b \to a$.   In this limiting position, the secant is said to be tangent to the curve at point a.   The instantaneous rate of change is then measured by the slope of the line tangent to the function at the point where we wish to measure this rate of change.

Certain functions may behave in such a way that it is not possible to measure the instantaneous rate of change at every point.   This is obviously true if the function is discontinuous in some interval, for, if the function is not defined for some value of the domain, there can be no point at which a line may be tangent!   On the other hand, continuity is no guarantee that we can find a unique tangent line.   Consider the function drawn in Fig. 13.2.2; at the points where the graph of the function has sharp peaks and valleys we obviously cannot find a unique tangent.   There are two lines tangent to the function at each point of peakedness, p and q; but we are hardly well off when the rate of change we seek can have more than one value.   In such a circumstance we say that the function is not *differentiable* at that point.   This word arises from the name of the process which we shall use to find the slope of the tangent line, called *differentiation*.   The student should realize that when we speak of the slope of a line tangent to a non-linear function we are interested only in the point of tangency and its immedi-

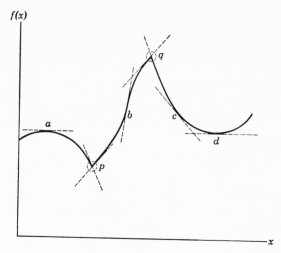

Fig. 13.2.2

ate "neighborhood." The fact that a tangent line might somewhere *cross* the function is of little concern so long as it is truly tangent at the point at which we wish to measure the slope of the function. At points a, b, c, and d in Fig. 13.2.2 we have drawn unique tangent lines as indicated by the dotted line segments.

13.2 Exercises

For each of the first three exercises, graph the function, compute the required average rates of change, and show on the graph the lines whose slopes represent these average rates of change.

13.2.1 Given the function $y = f(x) = 4 + x - x^2$, find the average rate of change in the intervals $\{0 \leq x \leq 4\}$ and $\{-4 \leq x \leq 2\}$. What is the meaning of the sign of the average rate of change?

13.2.2 Given the function $y = f(x) = 4 - x + x^2$. Find the average rate of change in the interval $\{0 \leq x \leq 4\}$.

13.2.3 Given the function $y = f(x) = 6 + 4x - x^2/2$. Find the average rate of change in the intervals $\{0 \leq x \leq 4\}$, $\{0 \leq x \leq 8\}$, $\{0 \leq x \leq 12\}$, $\{4 \leq x \leq 8\}$, $\{8 \leq x \leq 12\}$.

13.2.4 Which of the following measures or is a measure of an instantaneous rate of change, and which measures or is a measure of the average rate of change? Why?

(a) The speedometer on a car.
(b) The number of units produced in the last hour.
(c) The average number of units produced per day since the plant opened.
(d) The opening and closing quotations for a stock on the New York Stock Exchange.
(e) The change over time in a company's accident rate.

13.3 The difference quotient and the first derivative

Our problem is to find the slope of the line tangent to a curve at any point on the curve where such a tangent may uniquely exist. As indicated in previous illustrations, this slope has various values, which depend on the point at which we wish to measure the instantaneous rate of change, i.e., the slope of a non-linear function is not constant, but is itself a function of the independent variable. The solution to our problem will thus be a function, and we note that for various values in the domain of the original function, we shall be able to find the slope of the function.

Let us now see how we might find the slope of the function graphed in Fig. 13.3.1 at some point $(x, f(x))$. An approximation to the slope

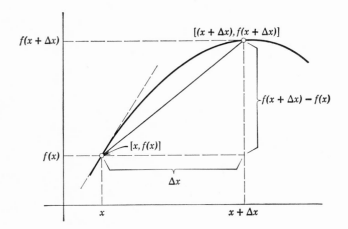

Fig. 13.3.1

at this point is given by the average rate of change between this point and another "near" point on the curve, say $[(x + \Delta x), f(x + \Delta x)]$. We move along the domain axis a distance Δx, to the value in the domain $(x + \Delta x)$, where the associated value of the function is $f(x + \Delta x)$. To find the average rate of change in the function between these two values in the domain, we must find Δy, which is the change in y associated with the change, Δx, in x. We see that

$$\Delta y = f(x + \Delta x) - f(x),$$

and thus that

$$\frac{\Delta y}{\Delta x} = \frac{f(x + \Delta x) - f(x)}{\Delta x}.$$

This expression is called the *difference quotient*, and represents a first approximation to the slope of the tangent line we seek. We now notice that if Δx is allowed to get smaller and smaller, the average rate of change $\Delta y / \Delta x$ becomes a better approximation to the slope of the line tangent at $(x, f(x))$. In fact, if Δx becomes infinitesimally small, then $\Delta y / \Delta x$ will approximate the desired slope with only an infinitesimally small error! Since $\Delta y / \Delta x$ is the difference quotient, we then say that the slope of the tangent is the *limit of the difference quotient as* Δx *becomes infinitesimally small*, i.e., as $\Delta x \to 0$. The result of this operation is called the *first derivative* of the function $f(x)$, and represents the solution to our problem. Note that the first derivative of the variable y with respect to the variable x is the value in the limit (as $\Delta x \to 0$) of the marginal change in y. We shall represent the first derivative with the notation dy/dx, read "the derivative of y with respect to x," and thus

$$\frac{dy}{dx} = \lim_{\Delta x \to 0} \frac{f(x + \Delta x) - f(x)}{\Delta x}.$$

A function is differentiable at a point if it has a unique tangent at the point. The slope at any point of any differentiable function can be found by using this formula. Let us apply it to an example: find the first derivative of the function $y = f(x) = x^2$:

$$\frac{\Delta y}{\Delta x} = \frac{f(x + \Delta x) - f(x)}{\Delta x} = \frac{(x + \Delta x)^2 - x^2}{\Delta x}$$

$$= \frac{(x^2 + 2x\,\Delta x + \Delta x^2) - x^2}{\Delta x} = \frac{2x\,\Delta x + \Delta x^2}{\Delta x}$$

$$= 2x + \Delta x.$$

Now we let $\Delta x \to 0$:

$$\frac{dy}{dx} = \lim_{\Delta x \to 0} (2x + \Delta x) = 2x.$$

Although we shall use dy/dx to indicate the first derivative of y with respect to x because it is the most commonly used notation in the literature of administrative analysis, the student should be aware of other suitable notations. One of these is the notation $f'(x)$, indicating the first derivative of $f(x)$; this notation is very useful because it recognizes the fact that the first derivative of a function is also a function, and we shall use it interchangeably with the notation dy/dx. Recent literature in mathematics makes use of other notation, notably $D_x y$, and even the symbol D alone. Whatever the notation, we must realize that the symbol calls for the performance of some operation upon a function: the operation of differentiation. If we wish to differentiate the function $y = f(x)$, we may call for this operation by writing either $(d/dx)f(x)$ or dy/dx. For instance, if $f(x) = x^2 - 3$, we may call for the differentiation of this function by writing $(d/dx)(x^2 - 3)$ or $f'(x)$.

The differentiation of a function is relatively simple as long as we remember what we are looking for. We must keep in mind that we are looking for the slope of the line tangent to the function at any point $(x, f(x))$. When we have found $f'(x)$ we have found, in addition to the slope of the tangent, the instantaneous rate of change of the function for any value in the domain, since that rate of change is measured by the slope of the tangent. Thus, if we are given $f(x) = x^2$, then $f'(x) = 2x$. To find the instantaneous rate of change of the function when x is 4, for example, we write $f'(4) = 2(4) = 8$. The interpretation of this result is that the value of the function is increasing 8 times as fast as the value of the independent variable when the value of the independent variable is 4.

Since the first derivative of a function is also a function, we should be able to graph $f'(x)$ as well as the function itself. As an illustration we have graphed the function $f(x) = x^2$ in Fig. 13.3.2. Immediately below it appears the graph of the first derivative of the function $f'(x) = 2x$, which is a linear function of x. With these two graphs, we can not only estimate quickly the value of the function for some given value in the domain, but also find the instantaneous rate of change in the function for that value, by referring to the lower graph. For instance, when $x = 3$, $f(x) = 9$. We might then ask, "What is the rate of change of the function at the point $(3, 9)$?" Since the domain axes of each of the functions are drawn to correspond, we drop a

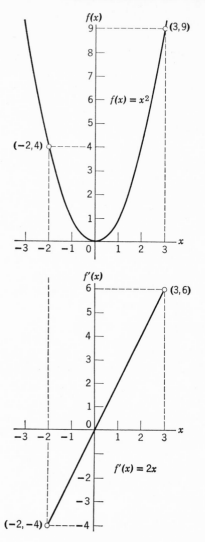

Fig. 13.3.2

perpendicular from $(3, 9)$ to the domain axis of the graph of the function $f'(x)$. Where this perpendicular intersects the graph of the function $f'(x)$, we find the associated rate of change, 6, which is a value in the range of $f'(x)$. Therefore, at $(3, 9)$, $f(x)$ is increasing 6 times as fast as x. Similarly, we find $f'(x)$ for $x = -2$ to be -4; the slope of the function $f(x)$ at $(-2, 4)$ is -4.

13.3 Exercises

13.3.1 Graph the following functions, find the first derivative of each by the difference quotient method, and graph the first derivative beneath the graph of the function.

(a) $f(x) = x^2 + 5$ (b) $f(x) = 5x - 5$
(c) $f(x) = x^2 - 3x + 2$ (d) $f(x) = x^3$.

13.3.2 What is the instantaneous rate of change of each of the functions in 13.3.1 when $x = 1$, $x = 4$, $x = -2$, $x = 0$?

13.3.3 If the cost of production of a certain firm is given by the expression $TC = 4 + 2Q - Q^2/2$, and $\{0 \leq Q \leq 10\}$, graph the cost function and find:

(a) The average rate of change over the interval $\{0 \leq Q \leq 10\}$
(b) The average rate of change over the interval $\{9 \leq Q \leq 10\}$
(c) The first derivative of the function
(d) The instantaneous rate of change when $x = 2$, $x = 6$, $x = 9$, $x = 10$.

13.3.4 Given the function $y = f(x) = 4 + 2x - x^2/2$, $\{-4 \leq x \leq 4\}$, graph the function, and find and graph the first derivative.

(a) What is the average rate of change over the interval $\{2 \leq x \leq 4\}$?
(b) What is the instantaneous rate of change when $x = 3$?
(c) Explain the relationship between the answers which you found to a and b, by referring to the graph.
(d) What is the average rate of change of the function over the interval $\{1 \leq x \leq 3\}$?
(e) What is the instantaneous rate of change of the function when $x = 1$, $x = 2$, $x = 3$?
(f) Compare your answer in d to your answers in e. What is the relationship among them?

13.4 Differentiation of various functions

Finding the first derivative of a function is called differentiation; differential calculus is thus the set of *rules* and *concepts* by which we determine the derivative(s) of a given function. To differentiate *with respect to* a certain variable merely means to find the rate of change of one variable with respect to that certain variable. Usually we differentiate with respect to the independent variable; although a function in implicit form does not discriminate between the independent and dependent variables (e.g., $xy = 4$), we may still differentiate the function with respect to either of the variables by putting the defining equation in some other form (e.g., $y = 4x^{-1}$) or by another process to be described later. In any event, it is important to realize that the instantaneous rate of change is a ratio, and thus that we must compare change in one variable with change in another, the latter being the variable which we "differentiate with respect to . . . ."

It is quite obvious that the process of applying the difference quotient to a function in order to determine the first derivative is laborious at best. It is our good fortune that this work has been simplified by the construction of simple formulas for the differentiation of any of the functions with which we shall come in contact. A word of warning, however: a formula is non-intuitive as far as giving some clue to the nature of the beast with which we work. Therefore, the student should understand that each of the formulas given is deduced from the basic operation of differential calculus, i.e., from taking the limit of the difference quotient, and, as a result, finding the slope of a tangent to the graph of a function. The purpose, once again, is to find the instantaneous rate of change of a function at any given point.

We assume that each of the following formulas and concepts is to be applied to a differentiable function, i.e., we assume that a unique tangent does exist at every point on the function which we are differentiating. We shall not attempt to show the derivation of any of the formulas, although the student should apply the difference quotient method to the first three formulas to see how they are derived.

Formula 13.4.1:   *The Derivative of a Constant*

If $f(x) = C$,

then $f'(x) = 0$;

or $\dfrac{d}{dx} C = 0$.

Example: $f(x) = 5; f'(x) = 0$.

Since the graph of a constant function is a horizontal straight line, it is clear that no matter what the change in x, the change in $f(x)$ is zero, and thus the instantaneous rate of change in the function is zero for all values of x.

Formula 13.4.2:   *The Derivative of a Linear Function*

If $f(x) = a + bx$,

then $f'(x) = b$;

or $\dfrac{d}{dx}(a + bx) = b$.

Examples: $f(x) = 4 + 9x$; $f'(x) = 9$

$f(x) = -13x$; $f'(x) = -13$

$y = -4 + \tfrac{1}{2}x$; $\dfrac{dy}{dx} = \tfrac{1}{2}$.

The linear function states that as x changes by one unit, y changes by b units, and thus the instantaneous rate of change must be the constant b for any value of x.

Formula 13.4.3: *The Derivative of a Power Function*

If $f(x) = bx^n$,

then $f'(x) = nbx^{n-1}$;

or $\dfrac{d}{dx}(bx^n) = nbx^{n-1}$.

Examples: $f(x) = 4x^3$; $f'(x) = 12x^2$

$f(x) = x^{\frac{1}{2}}$; $f'(x) = \tfrac{1}{2}x^{\frac{1}{2}-1} = \tfrac{1}{2}x^{-\frac{1}{2}}$

$y = x^{-2}$; $\dfrac{dy}{dx} = -2x^{-3}$.

Formula 13.4.4: *The Derivative of a Polynomial Function*

If $f(x) = g(x) + h(x) + \cdots + k(x)$,

then $f'(x) = g'(x) + h'(x) + \cdots + k'(x)$.

Examples: $f(x) = 2x^4 + 3x^2$; $f'(x) = 8x^3 + 6x$

$y = 3x^2 + 2x - 7$; $\dfrac{dy}{dx} = 6x + 2$.

Thus the derivative of a polynomial function in x is the sum of the derivatives of the terms of the polynomial with respect to x.

Formula 13.4.5: *The Product Rule*

If $f(x) = g(x)h(x)$,

then $f'(x) = g(x)h'(x) + h(x)g'(x)$.

Example: $f(x) = (x^2 - 1)(3 - x^4)$;

Let $g(x) = x^2 - 1$, then $g'(x) = 2x$.

Let $h(x) = 3 - x^4$, then $h'(x) = -4x^3$.

$$f'(x) = (x^2 - 1)(-4x^3) + (3 - x^4)(2x)$$

$$= -4x^5 + 4x^3 + 6x - 2x^5 = -6x^5 + 4x^3 + 6x.$$

The derivative of the product of two functions is the sum of the product of the first function times the derivative of the second and the product of the second function times the derivative of the first.

Differentiation of our example would have been simplified by expanding the given function and applying Formula 13.4.4; however, this is not always possible. For instance, the function $f(x) = (x^2) \log x$ cannot be simplified, but must be differentiated by the product rule as it stands. As a corollary to this formula we note that the derivative of a constant times a function is the constant times the derivative of the function, or $\dfrac{d}{dx} [cf(x)] = c \dfrac{d}{dx} f(x)$. (Apply the product rule to prove this.)

Formula 13.4.6: *The Quotient Rule*

If $f(x) = \dfrac{h(x)}{g(x)}$,

then $f'(x) = \dfrac{g(x)h'(x) - h(x)g'(x)}{[g(x)]^2}$.

Example: $f(x) = \dfrac{x - 1}{x^2}$

$$h(x) = x - 1, \quad h'(x) = 1$$

$$g(x) = x^2, \quad g'(x) = 2x$$

$$f'(x) = \frac{(x^2)(1) - (x - 1)(2x)}{(x^2)^2}$$

$$= \frac{x^2 - 2x^2 + 2x}{x^4} = \frac{x(2 - x)}{x^4} = \frac{2 - x}{x^3}$$

We note that neither the rational function nor its derivative is defined at the zeroes of the denominator of the function. This derivative might also have been found by expressing the function as a product: $f(x) = (x - 1)x^{-2}$ and using Formula 13.4.5, or simplifying further to

$f(x) = x^{-1} - x^{-2}$, applying Formula 13.4.4. The student should check these possibilities and verify that the resulting derivatives are all the same.

Formula 13.4.7: *The Chain Rule (Function of a Function)*

If $y = f(u)$ and $u = g(x)$,

then $y = f[g(x)]$

and $\dfrac{dy}{dx} = f'(u)g'(x) = \dfrac{dy}{du}\dfrac{du}{dx}.$

Example: $y = (x^2 - 1)^2$. Let $u = x^2 - 1; \dfrac{du}{dx} = 2x,$

$$y = (u)^2; \quad \frac{dy}{du} = 2u$$

$$\frac{dy}{dx} = (2u)(2x) = 4x(u) = 4x(x^2 - 1) = 4x^3 - 4x.$$

The chain rule is perhaps the most useful formula in differentiation, because it indicates how more complicated functions can be differentiated. Sometimes called the Function of a Function Rule, it applies when a function is specified that is a combination of functions. For instance, $y = (x^2 + 1)^2$ is a function of a function: the second power function of a polynomial function. Likewise, $y = (\ln x)^{\frac{1}{2}}$ is the second root function of the natural logarithm function. To differentiate, the functions are set up in such a way that the chain rule may be applied.

Formula 13.4.8: *The Derivative of an Exponential Function*

If $f(x) = ab^{cx}$,

then $f'(x) = cab^{cx} \ln b.$

Example: $f(x) = 3(2)^{\frac{1}{2}x}$, $f'(x) = \frac{3}{2}(2)^{\frac{1}{2}x} \ln 2.$

Consider the special case of the above formula when $b = e$, and $c = 1$:

If $f(x) = ae^x$,

then $f'(x) = ae^x \ln e = ae^x.$

The first derivative of the exponential function is the exponential function! Or, in practical terms, the instantaneous rate of change of the exponential function for any x is the value of the function itself, and therefore the importance of this function in analysis.

Formula 13.4.9:   *The Derivative of a Logarithmic Function*

If $f(x) = a \log_b (cx)$,

then $f'(x) = \dfrac{a}{x} \log_b e$.

Example: $f(x) = 2 \log 3x$,

then $f'(x) = \dfrac{2}{x} \log e$.

Consider the special case when the function is the natural logarithm function (base e):

If $f(x) = a \ln cx$,

then $f'(x) = \dfrac{a}{x} \ln e = \dfrac{a}{x}$.

The formulas given above provide the tools necessary to differentiate most of the functions we shall encounter. Although the student is charged with the responsibility for developing reasonable skill in their application, the really important purpose of finding the instantaneous rate of change of a function should not be forgotten in the midst of his algebraic gyrations. While it might be well to memorize some of the simpler formulas, if not all of those given, the student should realize that they are available from many sources and that he will do well not to trust his memory, as it may be faulty. If the principle of rate of change is well understood, then the differentiation formulas follow directly.

13.4   Exercises

13.4.1   For each of the following functions, find $f'(x)$, and find $f'(-1)$, $f'(0)$, $f'(\frac{1}{2})$, and $f'(3)$.

(a) $f(x) = -2$ (b) $f(x) = x + 3$

(c) $f(x) = 934x$ (d) $f(x) = \dfrac{x^5}{25}$

(e) $f(x) = 2\sqrt{x^3}$ (f) $f(x) = 3x^2 + 6x + 2$

(g) $f(x) = ax^2 + bx + c$ (h) $f(x) = (x + 1)(x - 1)$

(i) $f(x) = (1 - x^2)(1 - x^2)$ (j) $f(x) = \dfrac{9x}{1 - x}$

(k) $f(x) = 39 \log 3x$ (l) $f(x) = 6 \ln 5x$

(m) $f(x) = x$ (n) $f(x) = 3.4176x$

(o) $f(x) = 934x^2$ (p) $f(x) = 3 \sqrt[3]{x}$

(q) $f(x) = \dfrac{1}{x}$ (r) $f(x) = (x)(x^2 + 1)$

(s) $f(x) = \dfrac{x}{x + 1}$ (t) $f(x) = (17 \ln 17x)(x^2)$

(u) $f(x) = 23e^{4x}$ (v) $f(x) = 7^x(x - 1)$

(w) $f(x) = 7 \log_2 x - e^{2x}$

(x) If $y = f(u) = \ln u$, and $u = g(x) = 2x - 3x^2$, find dy/dx.   Find $f'(2)$ and $f'(-2)$.

(y) If $f(x) = \ln e^x$, find $f'(x)$.

13.5   Maxima, minima, and points of inflection

Many previous exercises have pointed out that the criterion of rational decision-making in a theoretical sense is the maximization (minimization) of some desirable (undesirable) thing, the usefulness of which can be measured.   We wish to maximize the amount of profit which can be realized from a given situation; on the other hand, we wish to minimize costs since they are undesirable, although of course necessary.   When such things can be expressed mathematically as functions of some controllable variable, i.e., such a decision variable as level of production, then our problem is to find that value of the decision variable associated with the desired outcome, maximum or minimum.   In dealing with linear systems (linear programming) and quadratic functions, our functions were sufficiently simple for the determination of such maxima or minima to be accomplished with relatively simple techniques.   Some analytic statements of functional relationships, however, are much too complicated to be dealt with by graphing or simple analysis, and this is where differential calculus comes to the rescue.

In Fig. 13.5.1 is the graph of an hypothetical function defined over the interval in the domain $\{x_1 \le x \le x_{15}\}$.   Certainly the analytic statement of such a function would be a very complicated thing (in fact, it would be at least of order seven), and would require the computation of a great many ordered pairs of numbers satisfying it if one were to try to analyze such a given function by graphing it.   Our problem is

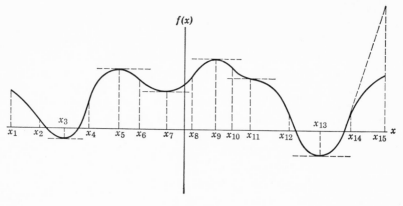

Fig. 13.5.1

complicated by the fact that there is no unique or absolute maximum or minimum.   There are two *relative* maxima and three *relative* minima, and two *boundary points*, i.e., points whose x-coordinates are the ends of the interval over which we have defined the function.   By *relative* maximum (or minimum) we mean that the value of the function at a point is greater than (or less than) the value of the function at any point in the immediate neighborhood of the point where the relative maximum (minimum) occurs.   If we can show that at a certain point in an interval the function takes on a value greater than its value at *any* other point in that interval, then we call such a maximum an *absolute* maximum in that interval, or *maximum maximorum* in the language of the economist, and similarly for the *absolute* minimum, or *minimum minimorum*.   We notice this important fact, however: for a differentiable function, wherever there is a maximum or a minimum at an interior point of the interval over which the function is defined, the slope of the function is zero.   Since the slope of the function is by definition the first derivative of the function, then a maximum or minimum may exist where the first derivative of the function is zero.   (We say "may exist" since zero slope may indicate another possibility, visible from the graph, which will be discussed later.)   Therefore, if we can find the first derivative of a function and set it equal to zero, i.e., $f'(x) = 0$, then a maximum or minimum of the original function may exist at those values of x which are elements of the solution set of $f'(x) = 0$.

Example: if $y = f(x) = \dfrac{x^3}{3} - x$, then $f'(x) = x^2 - 1$.

Setting $f'(x) = 0$ and solving for $x: x^2 - 1 = 0; x^2 = 1; x = 1, x = -1$. Thus when x is 1 or -1, the slope of the function is zero, and we suspect that a relative maximum or relative minimum will be found (by substituting these values in the original function) at $(1, -\frac{2}{3})$ and $(-1, \frac{2}{3})$.

The next question is, "maximum or minimum?" Let us draw the graph of this function for purposes of illustration, keeping in mind that we are developing the means for analyzing a function *without* having to draw its picture. From Fig. 13.5.2 we see that this function has indeed one maximum and one minimum. Below the graph of the function is the graph of the first derivative of the function; where the first derivative is zero, the function takes on its maximum and minimum. We note that the first derivative, however, does not state explicitly whether these values are associated with a maximum or minimum, but just that this is a possibility.

Below the first derivative is graphed the second derivative, $f''(x) = 2x$. We note that in the "neighborhood" where the function reaches a maximum, the second derivative is negative; where the function has a minimum, the second derivative is positive. Although this is rather flimsy evidence, it is not a coincidence, and illustrates the following rule:

If the second derivative is negative where the first derivative is zero, then the function takes on a maximum at that point; if the second derivative is positive where the first derivative is zero, then the function takes on a minimum at that point.

We have left out a possible alternative for the second derivative, for we notice that the second derivative might be zero as well as positive or negative. What if the second derivative is zero where the first derivative is zero? This case is illustrated in Fig. 13.5.3 for the function $f(x) = x^3$. The first derivative is parabolic: $f'(x) = 3x^2$; setting this equal to zero, we find the slope of $f(x)$ to be zero when $x = 0$; $f'(0) = 0$. Now $f''(x) = 6x$, so that when $x = 0$, the second derivative is also zero: $f''(0) = 0$. What is happening to the function when $x = 0$? We note that the slope of the function is zero (from the graph), but at this point the function takes on neither maximum nor minimum but merely appears to have paused in its upward climb. The point at which this pause occurs is called a *point of inflection*, and represents the mysterious possibility alluded to previously. There are thus three kinds of critical points of behavior of a function with respect to rate of change: maxima, minima, and points of inflection.

The example graphed in Fig. 13.5.3 is rather a special kind of inflection point, indicating that a point of inflection may exist where the

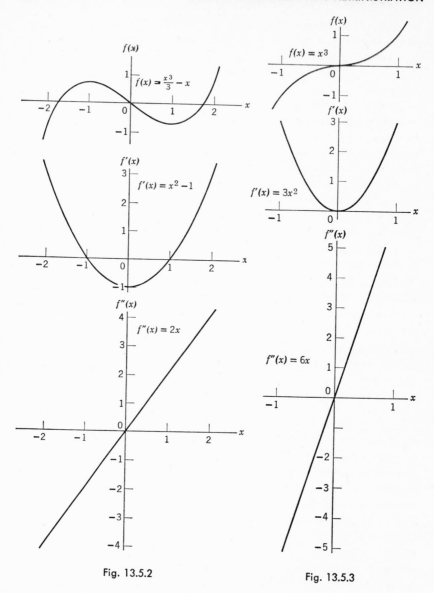

Fig. 13.5.2   Fig. 13.5.3

second derivative is zero.   The graph of $f'(x)$ is always positive except at $(0, 0)$, and thus the function is *strictly* monotonic increasing in all intervals except those containing the point $(0, 0)$; it is monotonic increasing throughout.   Where the second derivative is negative, the slope of the function is decreasing; where the second derivative is positive, the slope of the function is increasing; and where the second derivative is zero, the slope of the function is neither increasing nor decreasing. Therefore this function increases $[f'(x) > 0]$ at a decreasing rate $[f''(x) < 0]$ in the interval $\{-\infty < x < 0\}$; it pauses at $(0, 0)$, the inflection point $[f''(x) = 0]$; it increases $[f'(x) > 0]$ at an increasing rate $[f''(x) > 0]$ in the interval $\{0 < x < \infty\}$. Thus we see how the second derivative measures the rate of change of the rate of change. Over intervals in which the second derivative is negative, then, the slope of $f(x)$ is changing at a decreasing rate; where it is positive, the slope of $f(x)$ is changing at an increasing rate; and when it is zero, the rate of change of the change in the function is zero, or, as in certain higher-order functions, the function is at a maximum or minimum point. We should recall that the second derivative is the slope of the first derivative and is related to the slope of the function itself in that it measures the rate of change of the slope of the function. The conclusions above may not hold for certain higher-order functions, but they are sufficient for the analysis of the functions with which we shall commonly deal. When higher-order functions are encountered the student can refine his analysis of such functions by a similar interpretation of the third, fourth, fifth, etc., derivatives of the function.

Equipped with these tools, we may now analyze a function such as that illustrated in Fig. 13.5.1. The first derivative of the function tells us all the values of x for which the slope of the function is zero, and thus indicates where we should look for maxima or minima. For each of the values of x for which the slope is zero, i.e., for which $f'(x) = 0$, we examine the value of the second derivative. At x_5 and x_9 we would find $f''(x)$ to be negative and at x_3, x_7, and x_{13} we would find $f''(x)$ to be positive. At x_2, x_4, x_6, x_8, x_{10}, x_{11}, x_{12}, and x_{14} the second derivative would be zero, since these are all inflection points.

A very simple way to set up the analysis of such a function is to make a table, such as that shown in Fig. 13.5.4, which indicates all of the points of interest and the behavior at those points of the function graphed in Fig. 13.5.1. Note that we are interested generally only in those "critical" points for which the first or second or both derivatives are zero. Points such as x_1 and x_{15} are of interest only because they are on the "boundary" of the interval in the domain in which we have defined our function. Any other point in the interval is of little concern, since it cannot qualify as one of the things for which we seek, and is analogous to the interior points in the feasible solution space of a linear programming problem. Having narrowed the important points in the domain down to those associated with maxima, minima, or inflection points, we need only "plug" these values into the original function to determine which of the values provides the best solution to

x	$f'(x)$	$f''(x)$	Behavior
x_1	$-$	$+$	boundary
x_2	$-$	0	inflection
x_3	0	$+$	minimum
x_4	$+$	0	inflection
x_5	0	$-$	maximum
x_6	$-$	0	inflection
x_7	0	$+$	minimum
x_8	$+$	0	inflection
x_9	0	$-$	maximum
x_{10}	$-$	0	inflection
x_{11}	0	0	inflection
x_{12}	$-$	0	inflection
x_{13}	0	$+$	minimum
x_{14}	$+$	0	inflection
x_{15}	$+$	$-$	boundary

Fig. 13.5.4

our decision problem. Notice that this entire analysis depends not upon values of the function, but merely upon whether the values of the derivatives are positive, negative, or zero. By taking the first and second derivatives of the function, and analyzing them for sign or zero, we can learn all that is necessary to find maxima, minima, and inflection points of the continuous, differentiable, and otherwise "well-behaved" functions with which we usually deal in administration.

We shall analyze one additional function to illustrate the tabular procedure more precisely. Given the function $f(x) = x^4 - 8x^2$, then $f'(x) = 4x^3 - 16x$ and $f''(x) = 12x^2 - 16$. To identify the maximum and minimum points we set $f'(x) = 0$ and solve for x as follows. When $f'(x) = 0$, then

$$4x^3 - 16x = 0; \; 4x(x^2 - 4) = 0; \; x = 0, \; x = 2, \; x = -2.$$

We enter these three critical points, where the slope of the function is zero, into the table in Fig. 13.5.5. We note the associated values for $f(x)$ and $f''(x)$, and by inspection identify these as maximum or minimum points.

In seeking the inflection points we take the second derivative of the function, set it equal to zero, and solve for the solution values of x.

TABLE OF CRITICAL POINTS: $f(x) = x^4 - 8x^2$

x	$f(x)$	$f'(x)$	$f''(x)$	Behavior
-3	$+\ 9$	-60	$+92$	boundary maximum
-2	-16	0	$+32$	relative minimum
-1.15	$-\ 8.89$	$+16.88$	0	inflection
0	0	0	-16	relative maximum
1.15	$-\ 8.89$	-16.88	0	inflection
2	-16	0	$+32$	relative minimum
3	$+\ 9$	$+60$	$+92$	boundary maximum

Fig. 13.5.5

If $f''(x) = 0$, then

$$12x^2 - 16 = 0; x^2 = \frac{16}{12}; x = \pm \sqrt{\frac{16}{12}} = \pm 1.15 \text{ (approx.)}$$

These points, $x = 1.15$ and $x = -1.15$, give us two more critical points which we enter into the table in Fig. 13.5.5, and solve for the associated values of $f(x)$ and $f'(x)$. If the function is defined only over the interval $\{-3 \leq x \leq 3\}$, then we evaluate $f(x)$ at these values in the domain to find the value of the function at the boundaries: $f(3) = 9$, $f(-3) = 9$.

Differential calculus is useful in selecting decision alternatives which *optimize* an objective. However, a word of caution is in order regarding the analysis of maximum and minimum points as outlined above. It should be realized that a function may have two or more maximum (minimum) points identified by the methods of differential calculus. Which of these *relative* maximum (minimum) points optimizes our decision objective is not defined by the techniques of differential calculus, but can only be determined by specific comparison of the values of the function at the identified points. Also of importance is the fact that a point or set of points may exist that have functional values "greater than" those of the identified maximum points, or "less than" those of the identified minimum points, as in the case where the values of the function continue to increase or decrease indefinitely; again, the techniques of differential calculus would not identify these points as maxima or minima. Of course they are not maxima or minima as defined by differential calculus, but in terms of decision alternatives they may provide feasible solutions better than those discovered where the first derivative is zero.   In Fig. 13.5.1 we see that the *maximax* (i.e., maximum maximorum) is $[x_9, f(x_9)]$ and the *minimin* (i.e., minimum minimorum) is $[x_{13}, f(x_{13})]$.   We do not know or care what happens to the function outside of the stated domain, but it is of course necessary to examine the values of the function at x_1 and x_{15} to make sure that these are not better than the optima found above, even though the function does not take on maxima or minima, as these terms are used above.   The dotted line at the right in Fig. 13.5.1 illustrates this idea: if the function followed the dotted line, then the maximax would be at x_{15}.

13.5   Exercises

By taking derivatives and using the tabular method, analyze the following functions for maxima, minima, and points of inflection. After setting up the table, *sketch* the graphs of the function and the first and second derivatives.

13.5.1 $f(x) = x^2 + x - 12$

13.5.2 $f(x) = \dfrac{x^3}{3} - \dfrac{3x^2}{2} + 2x$

13.5.3 $f(x) = \dfrac{x^4}{2} + \dfrac{2x^3}{3} - x^2.$

13.6   Differentiation of implicit functions

From time to time we have run across a relationship in which the association among the variables has been expressed in such a way that the dependent and independent variables have not been identified as such explicitly.   This was particularly true in linear systems, where a functional relationship might have been written, for example, $3x_1 + 14x_2 + 2.3x_3 = 0$.   Although there is obviously a dependency relationship among x_1, x_2, and x_3, this function does not state explicitly the system of relationship which exists.   No matter how the relationship is expressed, however, we are still interested in rates of change, and must therefore provide some means for differentiating such a function.   It turns out that the method of differentiating such functions is little different from the methods applied heretofore.

Let us consider the function $y + 3x - 2 = 0$, which is a linear function written in implicit form. We differentiate each term in accordance with the polynomial rule with respect to x:

$$\frac{dy}{dx} + \frac{d}{dx}\,(3x) - \frac{d}{dx}\,(2) = \frac{d}{dx}\,(0)$$

$$\frac{dy}{dx} + 3 - 0 = 0$$

$$\frac{dy}{dx} = -3,$$

which is the answer we would have arrived at had the function been written in the explicit form $y = 2 - 3x$. Now suppose we were to differentiate the function $xy = 1$ with respect to x; the product rule applies since this implicit function is the product of two functions:

$$x\left(\frac{dy}{dx}\right) + y\left(\frac{dx}{dx}\right) = 0$$

$$x\left(\frac{dy}{dx}\right) = -y$$

$$\frac{dy}{dx} = -\frac{y}{x}.$$

Had we started with the explicit function $y = 1/x = x^{-1}$, we could have found $dy/dx = -x^{-2}$, which does not appear to be the same derivative as $dy/dx = -y/x$. They are the same, however, since $y = 1/x$, $-y/x = (-1/x)(1/x) = -1/x^2 = -x^{-2}$.

All functions are not so easily manipulated as these two examples. Although here we were able to solve our implicit function for y and differentiate with respect to x, many implicit functions do not have simple solutions in terms of one of the variables. As an example, consider the function $x^2 + xy + y = 0$; differentiating with respect to x, we get:

$$2x + x\left(\frac{dy}{dx}\right) + y + \frac{dy}{dx} = 0$$

$$\frac{dy}{dx}(x + 1) = -2x - y;\ \text{thus}$$

$$\frac{dy}{dx} = \frac{-2x - y}{x + 1}.$$

Note carefully that dy/dx becomes a part of the algebraic calculation itself and that the result of the differentiation of an implicit function is (usually) an implicit function.

13.6 Exercises

Differentiate the following implicit functions with respect to x; check by differentiating the associated explicit function, when possible.

13.6.1 $3x^2 + y = 4$
13.6.2 $x^2y = 16$
13.6.3 $ax^2 + bx + c - y = 0$
13.6.4 $x^3 + x^2y + xy = 0$.

13.7 Partial differentiation

Very seldom in the analysis of administrative phenomena do we find that one variable is a function of only one other variable. When we say, "profit is a function of the level of output," or, "revenue is a function of quantity sold," or "cost is a function of accuracy," etc., we are of course oversimplifying the true state of nature in order to develop an understanding of the relationship of the two variables under consideration, regardless of any other variables which might affect the dependent variable. This is the so-called *ceteris paribus* assumption of the economic theorist, meaning "all other things being equal." We know of course that profit depends on many variables, not all of them even quantifiable or capable of measurement. It is often possible, however, to express relationships among more than two variables analytically, as we have seen in linear programming. In linear programming, the geometric result of a system of linear equations in two variables is a set of straight lines; in three variables, the result is a system of planes; in n-space, a system of hyper-planes. The same general geometric interpretation holds for non-linear equations. Up to this point we have dealt only with relationships between two variables, the geometric result being the non-linear graph of a function in two space. The geometric interpretation of a functional relationship among three variables is a *surface* in three-space, which has the appearance of a topographical relief map. In the mountainous parts of Colorado, it is obvious that our height above sea level is a function of our longitude and latitude at any time. At the top of Mt. Elbert, we reach a maximum height (in fact, an absolute or maximum maximorum for Colorado); low spots on the various valley floors represent relative minima (the absolute minimum for the state, however, is a point near Holly, Colorado, near the Kansas *boundary*).

If we were to proceed west from Denver along a parallel of latitude, we would undoubtedly traverse many relative maxima and minima, but very seldom find ourselves at an absolute maximum or minimum; most often we would be standing on the *side* of a hill. If we aim to reach the top of a hill, i.e., maximize height, then we must find a point from which a step (a change) in any direction would decrease our height. Another way of stating this criterion for having attained a relative maximum is to say that the slope of the hill at the point is zero in all directions, which we could show by placing a flat board horizontally on the top of the hill and noting that the hill touches the board in only the one point, our relative maximum. A necessary condition for the maximum is thus that the slope of the hill at our point be zero in the north-south and simultaneously in the east-west directions (as well as for all other points of the compass). Let us assume that these are the *only* tests we need apply, mainly because the sufficient tests for a maximum are quite complicated and beyond our present purpose, which is to introduce the student to the elementary operation and use of partial derivatives.

Let us consider a profit maximization problem, which is directly analogous to the hill-climbing problem above. We are given a profit function as a function of two variables, where Q is the level of output and S is the amount spent to promote the sale of the product, such that

$$\pi = f(Q, S) = -5 - Q^2 + 8Q - 2S^2 + 12S - 2QS.$$

If we were to make a "map" of this function, we would find that each point on the surface of the map would have three coordinates: (π, Q, S). In order to find the maximum point on the surface, that is, that point where the profit coordinate is maximized, we must apply our north–south and east–west tests, by the process of *partial differentiation*. This process is exactly the same as that studied previously, except that we must make an adjustment for the added variable. Since for the N–S test we are not interested in the E–W variable, *we treat it as constant*, differentiating the function with respect to the N–S variable and treating the other variable as if it were any other constant. If we let Q be the N–S variable, and S the E–W variable, then we would differentiate the function first with respect to Q, the result being called the *partial derivative* with respect to Q, the symbol for which is $\partial \pi / \partial Q$.

Thus

$$\frac{\partial \pi}{\partial Q} = \frac{\partial}{\partial Q} (-5 - Q^2 + 8Q - 2S^2 + 12S - 2QS)$$

$$= \frac{\partial}{\partial Q} (-5) + \frac{\partial}{\partial Q} (-Q^2) + \frac{\partial}{\partial Q} (8Q) + \frac{\partial}{\partial Q} (-2S^2) + \frac{\partial}{\partial Q} (12S)$$

$$+ \frac{\partial}{\partial Q} (-2QS)$$

$$= (0) + (-2Q) + (8) + (0) + (0) + (-2S)$$

$$= -2Q + 8 - 2S.$$

Likewise,

$$\frac{\partial \pi}{\partial S} = \frac{\partial}{\partial S} (-5) + \frac{\partial}{\partial S} (-Q^2) + \frac{\partial}{\partial S} (8Q) + \frac{\partial}{\partial S} (-2S^2) + \frac{\partial}{\partial S} (12S)$$

$$+ \frac{\partial}{\partial S} (-2QS)$$

$$= (0) + (0) + (0) + (-4S) + (12) + (-2Q)$$

$$= -4S + 12 - 2Q.$$

Each of these expressions represents the slope of the function in its respective direction, and when the slope is zero, one may find a maximum, a minimum, or a point of inflection. To find the maximum of our surface, however, both derivatives must have zero slope simultaneously. Therefore, if we set each partial derivative equal to zero, and solve the resulting set of equations simultaneously, we shall find the values of Q and S for which the function is maximized, recalling our simplifying assumptions:

$$\frac{\partial \pi}{\partial Q} = -2Q + 8 - 2S = 0 \qquad \frac{\partial \pi}{\partial S} = -4S + 12 - 2Q = 0$$

$$2Q + 2S = 8 \qquad\qquad 4S + 2Q = 12$$

$$
\begin{array}{r}
2Q + 2S = 8 \\
(\text{Subtract}) \quad 2Q + 4S = 12 \\
\hline
-2S = -4 \\
S = 2 \\
2Q + 2(2) = 8 \\
2Q = 4 \\
Q = 2.
\end{array}
$$

At a level of production of 2 units and promotion cost of 2 units, our profit function is maximum, and we find the maximum value of profit by substituting these values into the original profit function:

$$\pi = f(Q, S) = f(2, 2) = -5 - (2)^2 + 8(2) - 2(2)^2 + 12(2) - 2(2)(2)$$

$$= -5 - 4 + 16 - 8 + 24 - 8$$

$$= 15 \text{ (units of profit)}.$$

We have assumed this point to be a maximum; in practice one would want to examine second derivatives to make sure that this were true. It does not suffice any longer, however, to examine only second derivatives in the same way as in the past, because there are other conditions that may apply in the three-space problem. Suffice it to say that we *should* do this; at the moment we are only interested in the basic concept and the applicability of calculus in the solution of this type of problem. It should be noted that this method, like the linear programming method, can be extended to cover any number of variables, although the determination of the second derivative behavior becomes increasingly complicated.

13.7 Exercises

13.7.1 Differentiate with respect to each of the independent variables:

$$z = f(x, y) = 3x^4 - 4x^3y - 5x^2y^2 - 6xy^3 - 7y^4 - 8x - 9y - 10.$$

13.7.2 Differentiate with respect to each of the independent variables:

$$z = f(x, y) = x^2 \ln y + y^2 \ln x - 3e^{xy}.$$

13.7.3 Suppose that you are production superintendent of the Kleckner Korkskrew Kompany and are charged with minimizing production costs. Only two inputs are used, man-hours and chrome steel, and the cost function is known to be

$$TC = \frac{736}{9} + x^2 - 4x + y^2 - 8y - xy,$$

where x is the number of man-hours and y is the number of pounds of steel for one production run. How much of each input should be used to minimize the cost of one production run? (Assume that the given function has a minimum.) What is this minimum cost if TC is measured in tens of dollars? Does this problem make economic sense when only one of the inputs is used?

Chapter 14 —— Introduction to Integral Calculus

14.1 The antiderivative and the indefinite integral

It is interesting to note that most of the algebraic operations which we have studied have "reverse" operations. For instance, subtraction is the reverse of addition, division the reverse of multiplication. Certain matrices have inverses, and we have noted the inverse relationship between the logarithmic and the exponential functions. In differential calculus we defined a function, called the derivative, which was the result of performing an operation, called differentiation, upon another function. Now it seems reasonable that we should be able to put the process of differentiation into "reverse" as well. This process is called *antidifferentiation*, or *integration*. In symbols, if we are given a function $f(x)$, we should like to find another function, $F(x)$, such that $F'(x) = f(x)$, where $F'(x)$ is the first derivative of $F(x)$. As for most operations, we have a symbol which calls for the operation to be performed: $\int$, read *integral*. Knowing the basic rules of differentiation, it is usually an easy operation to find an antiderivative of a simple function. For instance, suppose we are to find an antiderivative of $f(x) = x$. We write the antiderivative as $\int x \, dx$, where dx can be considered a part of the integral symbol for the moment. Now $\int x \, dx = F(x)$, some function whose first derivative is x. We know that

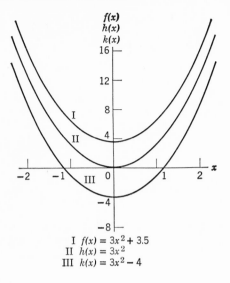

I $f(x) = 3x^2 + 3.5$
II $h(x) = 3x^2$
III $k(x) = 3x^2 - 4$

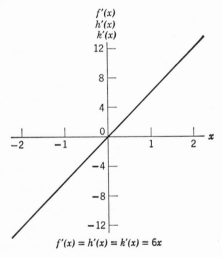

$f'(x) = h'(x) = k'(x) = 6x$

Fig. 14.1.1

$\dfrac{d}{dx}(x^2) = 2x$, so that if $F(x) = \dfrac{x^2}{2}$, then $\dfrac{d}{dx}\left(\dfrac{x^2}{2}\right) = \dfrac{2x}{2} = x$. Thus $F(x) = \displaystyle\int x\,dx = \dfrac{x^2}{2}$ is an antiderivative of $f(x) = x$.

Notice that we have said *an* antiderivative, rather than using the definite article *the*.   This is because the process of integration produces not one function, but a whole "family" of functions, each called an antiderivative of the function integrated.   Let us see why: if we differentiate the function $f(x) = 3x^2 - 4$, we get $f'(x) = 6x$.   In differentiating the constant 4, it becomes 0.   Likewise, if $g(x) = 3x^2 + C$, where C is any constant, $g'(x) = 6x$.   Therefore, $\int 6x \, dx = 3x^2 + C$. The result is called the *indefinite integral* of $g(x)$, because no particular function of the family of functions $G(x)$ is specified.   The reason for this is illustrated in Fig. 14.1.1.   In the upper graph are shown the functions $f(x) = 3x^2 + 3.5$, $h(x) = 3x^2$, and $k(x) = 3x^2 - 4$, and below is graphed *the* first derivative of these functions: $f'(x) = h'(x) = k'(x) = 6x$.   A little thought thus shows why the indefinite integral will always be some function plus the constant C: the first derivative tells us the slope of the function for any value in the domain, and any function may be translated upward or downward from the origin merely by adding a constant to it, without changing the slope of the function for a given value in the domain.

In the exercises below, the student is requested to find the indefinite integral of various functions, i.e., to integrate, purely by trial and error. Formulas for integration are published, of course, similar to the formulas for differentiation given in Section 13.4, but at this point the student will improve his understanding of integration by "groping" for the result, rather than by looking it up in a table.

14.1   Exercises

Find the required indefinite integrals, and check your answers by differentiation.

14.4.1 $\int 2x \, dx$

14.4.2 $\int x^2 \, dx$

14.4.3 $\int x^{\frac{1}{2}} \, dx$

14.4.4 $\int 3x^{\frac{2}{3}} \, dx$

14.4.5 $\displaystyle\int \frac{1}{x} \, dx$

14.4.6 $\int (x^2 - 3) \, dx$

14.4.7 $\displaystyle\int \left(\frac{1}{x} - x \right) dx$

14.4.8 $\int e^x \, dx$

14.4.9 $\int C \, dx.$

14.2   Applications of the indefinite integral

The economic interpretation of the relationship between a function
and its first derivative has already been explained in terms of total and
marginal analysis: given a function representing the behavior of some
total, say total cost, the first derivative of the function describes the
behavior of *changes* in the total; this function is called the marginal
cost function.   If we know the marginal behavior of some phenomenon,
then the indefinite integral of the marginal function provides a means
for finding the total function, and the definite integral of the marginal
function tells us the value of the total for some given value of the independent variable.

As a further example of the economic application of the integral
calculus to decision-making, let us consider the following simplified
problem, which relates the integral and differential calculus in terms
of *marginal physical productivity*, by which we mean the increments in
output realized by adding units of input.   Suppose that we are in the
excavating business and have a contract to dig a hole preparatory to
the erection of a large building.   In the time allowed to finish the contract, we know that one power shovel can move a certain quantity of
earth, but with the addition of more shovels the average amount of
work done by each shovel decreases as the work area becomes cluttered
with machinery.   This information can be expressed as the marginal
physical productivity function $f(x) = a - 0.4x$, where a is some starting value, and each additional shovel is 40 per cent unproductive.   In
order to find a, we need some more information, so let us suppose that
we know that one shovel can move 1.8 units of earth.   At this point,
let us reconsider the decision problem of how many shovels to use,
assuming that we shall use as many as are economically feasible.   (The
person for whom we are digging the hole will supply the shovels at no
cost to us.)

The marginal physical productivity function is the first derivative
of the total physical productivity function, which we shall call $F(x)$.
Therefore $F(x) = \int f(x)\,dx$, and since $f(x) = a - 0.4x$, we find

$$\int f(x)\,dx = \int (a - 0.4x)\,dx$$
$$= \int a\,dx - \int 0.4x\,dx$$
$$F(x) = ax - 0.2x^2 + C.$$

When $x = 0$, i.e., when no shovels are used, then $F(x)$, total output, will also be zero, and thus C will be zero, leaving

$$F(x) = ax - 0.2x^2,$$

and we must find a. Since we know that total output $F(x)$ will be 1.8 units when we use one shovel, we substitute this information into the expression above:

$$1.8 = a(1) - 0.2(1)^2$$

$$1.8 = a - 0.2$$

$$a = 2.0.$$

Therefore we know that $f(x) = 2 - 0.4x$, and $F(x) = 2x - 0.2x^2$.

These two functions are graphed in Fig. 14.2.1, which clearly shows that the decision should be to use five shovels. This decision should be obvious from either graph, for total physical productivity (output) is maximized when $x = 5$ as shown by the maximum of the parabola;

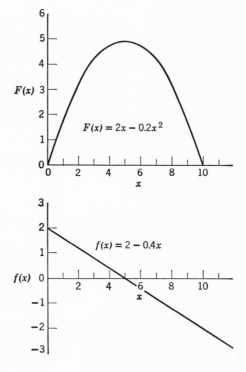

Fig. 14.2.1

or by examination of the marginal function, addition of shovels beyond five results in negative increments of work. Each additional shovel up to and including five adds more to total physical product, but each additional shovel beyond that number not only does not produce anything, but gets in the way of the other shovels so that their production is decreased. If we should choose to use ten shovels, we would accomplish no work at all, possibly because all of the equipment is sitting atop the earth to be excavated, unable to move!

Notice that no cost was associated with the previous example, which is unrealistic since inputs are usually not free. If we had known the marginal cost of additional shovels, it would have been possible to construct this problem as a cost minimization problem, although we shall not do so. Making some assumptions about the value of the product, we can see that our decision rule would be to increase the number of shovels so long as the value of the marginal increment to product exceeds the marginal cost incurred.

The student should realize that there are endless ways in which the analysis above might apply, and for which the facts as given in the problem may very well be available. Without the proper tools of analysis, these decision problems can become intractable at best, and unsolvable at worst. Since *marginal analysis* is one of the most important tools of the administrator, let us review the concepts of marginal cost and marginal revenue developed in Section 13.1 in terms of the indefinite integral. Marginal revenue is the increase or decrease in revenue realized from the sale of the last unit sold, and thus reflects the change in the total revenue over all units sold. As the rate of change of the total revenue function, it is also the first derivative of the total revenue function. Thus, if we know the total revenue function, we can determine the change in this function for any level of sales. Suppose that we do not have available the function specifying the behavior of total revenue, but we do know how much additional revenue is realized from additional increments of sales. To find the total revenue function, we need only find the indefinite integral of the marginal function, and then determine the value of C to find the specific total revenue function which applies. For instance, if we know our marginal revenue function to be

$$f(Q) = 500 - 0.16Q,$$

then we can find the total revenue function:

$$F(Q) = TR = \int (500 - 0.16Q)\, dQ$$
$$= \int 500\, dQ - \int 0.16Q\, dQ$$
$$= 500Q - 0.08Q^2 + C.$$

Since we realize no revenue when sales are zero (thus, $(0, 0)$ is a point on the total revenue function), we substitute these values into the function to find C:

$$0 = 500(0) - 0.08(0)^2 + C$$
$$C = 0.$$

The total revenue function is, therefore,

$$TR = 500Q - 0.08Q^2.$$

Since $TR = P \times Q = Q(500 - 0.08Q)$, the demand function can be easily derived:

$$P = 500 - 0.08Q, \text{ and thus, } Q = 6250 - 12.5P,$$

where P is the price per unit and Q is the quantity sold.

The total cost function can be derived from a known marginal cost function in the same manner, since marginal cost is the rate of change in the total cost function. If we are given the information that each additional unit of production costs \$100, then the marginal cost function

$$g(Q) = MC = 100.$$

(The assumption of constant marginal cost is not unreasonable; it is the same assumption made in the linear programming model.) To find the total cost function, we integrate this expression:

$$G(Q) = TC = \int 100 \, dQ$$
$$= 100Q + C.$$

If our fixed costs are \$375,000, then we incur these costs even when we produce no output, or

$$375,000 = 100(0) + C$$
$$C = 375,000$$
$$TC = 375,000 + 100Q.$$

Having developed these functions, we are now in a position to find the level of output (Q) that will maximize profit (π), which we know to be that value of Q such that the first derivative of the profit function is

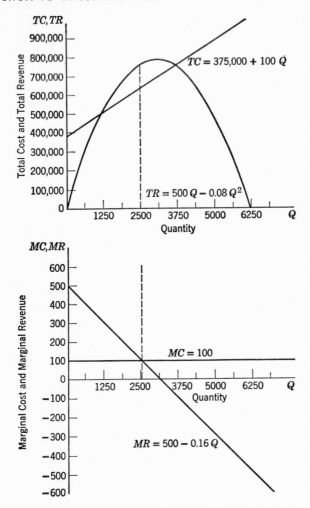

Fig. 14.2.2

zero, or

$$\pi = TR - TC = F(Q) - G(Q)$$

$$\frac{d\pi}{DQ} = \frac{d}{dQ} [F(Q) - G(Q)] = 0$$

$$0 = F'(Q) - G'(Q)$$

$$F'(Q) = G'(Q)$$

$$MR = MC.$$

Follow carefully each step of this last development. From it we deduce that maximum profit will be realized at that level of production Q for which marginal revenue equals marginal cost. In our problem

$$MR = MC$$

$$500 - 0.16Q = 100$$

$$0.16Q = 400$$

$$Q = 2500 \text{ (units).}$$

At this level of production, we can show that $TR = \$750,000$ and $TC = \$625,000$; thus profit is $\$125,000$. The total and marginal functions are graphed in Fig. 14.2.2 in order to show the relationships discussed above. Note that equating MR and MC implies the intersection of the two graphs; as Q is increased from zero, additional units of output add more to revenue than to cost, up to the point where the graphs intersect. Beyond this value of Q, each additional unit costs more than it contributes to revenue. Therefore the general decision rule of production: produce additional units so long as marginal revenue exceeds marginal cost. Note carefully that if the rule were to produce as long as *total* revenue exceeded *total* cost, we would not enjoy maximum profit from the operation.

14.2   Exercises

14.2.1 Given the marginal revenue function $MR = 4 - 0.4Q$, find the total revenue function, and graph both functions as in Fig. 14.2.1.

14.2.2 Given the marginal revenue function $MR = 5 - 0.5Q$, find the total revenue function and graph as above.

14.2.3 Given the marginal cost function $MC = 2$, and the information that fixed cost is 1, i.e., total cost is 1 when output is 0, find the total cost function and graph both functions.

14.2.4 Given the marginal cost function $MC = Q - 1$, and the information that fixed cost is 4, find the total cost function and graph both functions.

14.2.5 Combine the information developed in 14.2.1 and 14.2.3 above and indicate the desired level of operation to maximize profit. Graph all of the functions, i.e., MR, MC, TR, TC, on one graph, and indicate the relationship of MR and MC at the maximizing level of output.

14.2.6 Repeat Exercise 14.2.5 using the information in 14.2.2 and 14.2.4.

14.3 Area under the curve: the definite integral

We have examined integration in terms of the antiderivative of a function, using the concept to find an unknown function whose rate of change is known. Another useful application of integral calculus is in the determination of areas, specifically areas "under the curve." We shall use a simple example to illustrate this concept.

Suppose that we are given the function $y = x^2$ and asked to find the area between the graph of the function and the domain axis, over a distance from the origin of x units measured along the domain axis, as shown in Fig. 14.3.1. An approximation of this area is given by the area of the triangle whose base is x and whose height is x^2, and by the formula for the area of a right triangle, this approximate area is $\frac{1}{2}x^3$. This is obviously an overestimation of the area; let us try a different approach. If we divide the distance x into 4 equal segments and construct a rectangle over each segment as in Fig. 14.3.2, the sum of the areas of these rectangles will also give us an approximation of the area,

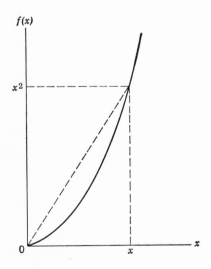

Fig. 14.3.1

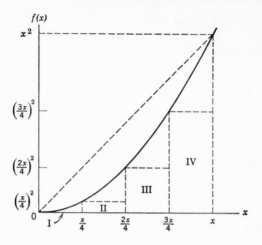

Fig. 14.3.2

this time underestimated, but closer to the true area. Let us find this approximate area. We shall first number the rectangles, as shown, and indicate each area by $A(\text{I})$, $A(\text{II})$, etc. In each case the base of the rectangle is $x/4$; only the height is different.

The height of each rectangle is measured by the distance from the domain axis to a point on the curve, i.e., $f(x)$. The height of rectangle I is 0, since $f(0) = 0$. Thus $A(\text{I}) = (x/4)(0) = 0$. The height of rectangle II is $f(x/4) = (x/4)^2$; $A(\text{II}) = (x/4)(x/4)^2$, which we shall leave in that form for the moment. Likewise we find $A(\text{III})$ and $A(\text{IV})$, and add them all up:

$$A = A(\text{I}) + A(\text{II}) + A(\text{III}) + A(\text{IV})$$

$$= \frac{x}{4}(0) + \frac{x}{4}\left(\frac{x}{4}\right)^2 + \frac{x}{4}\left(\frac{2x}{4}\right)^2 + \frac{x}{4}\left(\frac{3x}{4}\right)^2$$

$$= \frac{x}{4}\left[\left(\frac{x}{4}\right)^2 + 2^2\left(\frac{x}{4}\right)^2 + 3^2\left(\frac{x}{4}\right)^2\right]$$

$$= \left(\frac{x}{4}\right)\left(\frac{x}{4}\right)^2(1^2 + 2^2 + 3^2)$$

$$= \frac{x^3}{64}(1 + 4 + 9) = \frac{7}{32}x^3 = 0.2187x^3 \text{ (approx.)}.$$

The true area is underestimated by the area not included in the rectangles. We see that a better approximation could be found by dividing x into 8 parts; the result of adding the areas of the 7 resulting rectangles can be shown to be $^{140}\!\!/_{512}x^3$ or approximately $0.2734x^3$. No matter how small we make the segments, we see that the sum of the resulting rectangles will be some fraction times x^3, and it can be shown that as the number of segments n approaches ∞, the fraction will approach $\frac{1}{3}$, so that the area under the curve is $A = x^3/3$. If we let S_n be the sum of the areas of n rectangles under the curve, i.e., the graph of the function $f(x) = x^2$, then

$$\lim_{n \to \infty} S_n = \frac{x^3}{3}.$$

Now here is the interesting part: if we differentiate $x^3/3$, we get $3x^2/3 = x^2$, but $f(x) = x^2$ is our original function! If we let $F(x) = x^3/3$, then $F'(x) = f(x)$, so that by our original definition of the integral, $F(x)$ is the integral of $f(x)$:

$$\int f(x)\, dx = F(x)$$

$$\int_0^x x^2\, dx = \frac{x^3}{3}.$$

Note that now the integral symbol carries the characters 0 and x, indicating that we have summed the areas of rectangles over the interval in the domain from 0 to x, and this sum is exactly $x^3/3$. Such an integral is called a *definite integral*, and we read "the definite integral of $x^2\, dx$ from 0 to x," which is exactly the area under the curve over the interval 0 to x.

We observe two interesting things in passing, which may help the student from a rather intuitive standpoint. First, the integral symbol looks something like the letter S, from which it probably developed as the limit of the sum S_n as n approaches infinity. Second, the expression $f(x)\, dx$ looks like the product of $f(x)$ and dx; if $f(x)$ were the height of a rectangle and dx were the base of the rectangle, then $f(x)\, dx$ would be the area of the rectangle. If dx were the base of infinitely many rectangles in the interval $\{a \le x \le b\}$ under the curve $f(x)$, for each of which there is a varying height $f(x)$, then the sum of all of these rectangles, indicated by $\int_a^b f(x)\,dx$ would indicate the area under the curve from a to b.

Although we have illustrated the concept of the area under the curve using an example, the results indicated above can be applied for any of the continuous functions with which we shall be concerned.

We have one chore left, and that is concerned with *evaluating* an integral, by which we mean finding the numerical value of the area required. To do this we apply the *fundamental theorem of calculus*, so called because it is the connection between differential and integral calculus: if $f(x)$ is continuous in the interval $\{a \le x \le b\}$, and $F(x)$ is any antiderivative of $f(x)$, then:

$$\int_a^b f(x)\,dx = F(x)\,\Big|_a^b = F(b) - F(a).$$

The vertical bar in the middle expression indicates the limits over which the function $F(x)$ is to be evaluated, and the right-hand expression indicates how this is done. For example, suppose we are to find the area under the graph of the function $f(x) = x^2 - 6x + 11$, over the interval $\{1 \le x \le 5\}$. This area is indicated in Fig. 14.3.3.

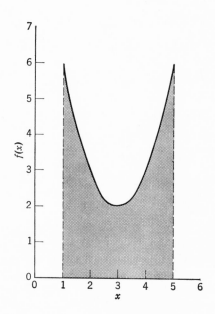

Fig. 14.3.3

$$\int f(x)\, dx = F(x) = \int (x^2 - 6x + 11)\, dx$$

$$= \int x^2\, dx - \int 6x\, dx + \int 11\, dx$$

$$= \frac{x^3}{3} - 3x^2 + 11x$$

$$F(x)\ \Big|_1^5 = F(5) - F(1)$$

$$= \left[\frac{(5)^3}{3} - 3(5)^2 + 11(5) \right] - \left[\frac{(1)^3}{3} - 3(1)^2 + 11(1) \right]$$

$$= [125\tfrac{2}{3} - 75 + 55] - [\tfrac{1}{3} - 3 + 11]$$

$$= 40\tfrac{2}{3} = 13.33. \quad \text{(Approx.)}$$

The area required is thus 13.33, but 13.33 what? The student will realize of course that areas must be expressed in some kind of units, such as square feet or acres. In this case we have measured x and $f(x)$ in units of some unspecified measure, and thus the result will be 13.33 square units. Suppose that $f(x)$ is a continuous average unit cost function, reflecting the fact that as x (units produced) increases, unit costs decrease over an interval and then increase. Since the number of units produced times the cost per unit in dollars is the total cost, our result would be \$13.33, since $\dfrac{\text{cost}}{\text{unit}} \times \text{units} = \text{cost}$.

The following properties of the definite integral are handy in the simplification of the process of integration:

Property 14.3.1: The integral of a constant times a function is the constant times the integral of the function. If k is a real number constant, then:

$$\int_a^b kf(x)\, dx = k \int_a^b f(x)\, dx.$$

Property 14.3.2: The integral of the sum of two functions is the sum of the integrals of the functions. Thus,

$$\int_a^b [f(x) + g(x)]\, dx = \int_a^b f(x)\, dx + \int_a^b g(x)\, dx.$$

Property 14.3.3: If p is some number in the interval $\{a \le x \le b\}$,

$$\int_a^b f(x)\, dx = \int_a^p f(x)\, dx + \int_p^b f(x)\, dx.$$

The last property indicates the method for finding the area "under" a curve that crosses the domain axis. Obviously the word "under" is poorly chosen, since in effect what we are looking for is the area

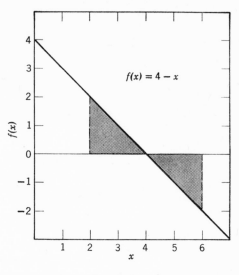

Fig. 14.3.4

between the curve and the domain axis. In Fig. 14.3.4 is the graph of the function $f(x) = 4 - x$; suppose we wish to find the shaded area "under" the curve over the interval $\{2 \leq x \leq 6\}$.

$$F(x) = \int (4 - x)\, dx$$

$$= \int 4\, dx - \int x\, dx$$

$$= 4x - \frac{x^2}{2}$$

$$F(x)\Big|_2^6 = F(6) - F(2)$$

$$= \left[4(6) - \frac{6^2}{2} \right] - \left[4(2) - \frac{2^2}{2} \right]$$

$$= [24 - 18] - [8 - 2] = 6 - 6$$

$$= 0.$$

Integrating over the given integral produces an answer of zero, which does not appear to be correct since we can see that the desired area does in fact exist as shaded on the graph. But we recall that the area is computed by summing rectangles, the heights of which are determined by the function. Over the interval $\{4 \leq x \leq 6\}$, the values of $f(x)$ are negative, and thus the area of each rectangle in this interval will have a negative sign. The two triangles in question are congruent, and thus the sum of their areas is zero, since the area of the triangle below the domain axis has a negative sign.

In the physical terms of area as a measure of space, negative area has no real meaning. However, there are many instances in which the total sum of the products of two variables might be negative, for instance, total profit. If we integrate such a function we should not be surprised to develop a negative quantity for the definite integral, i.e., the area under the curve, since a negative total may have just as much meaning as a positive total.

If we wish to find the absolute area indicated by the shaded part in Fig. 14.3.4, then it is necessary to split the problem into two parts, in one part integrating over the intervals in which the function is positive, and in the other, integrating over the intervals in which the function is negative. The latter integral will have a negative sign; since we are interested only in the absolute value of the areas, we sum the integrals without regard to sign. Let us find the absolute area between the curve and the domain axis shaded in Fig. 14.3.4. The function is positive in $\{2 \leq x \leq 4\}$ and negative in $\{4 \leq x \leq 6\}$. Integrating over the first interval:

$$F(x) \Big|_{2}^{4} = \left[4(4) - \frac{(4)^2}{2} \right] - \left[4(2) - \frac{(2)^2}{2} \right]$$

$$= [16 - 8] - [8 - 2] = 8 - 6$$

$$= 2 \text{ (square units)}.$$

Integrating over the second interval:

$$F(x) \Big|_{4}^{6} = \left[4(6) - \frac{(6)^2}{2} \right] - \left[4(4) - \frac{(4)^2}{2} \right]$$

$$= [24 - 18] - [16 - 8] = 6 - 8$$

$$= -2 \text{ (square units)}.$$

We ignore the sign of the last result, and see that the sum of the two absolute areas is 4 square units.

To summarize, let us examine the function $f(x)$ whose graph appears in Fig. 14.3.5. We note that the curve crosses the axis at x_2, x_3, x_4, and x_5, i.e., each of these values is a zero of the function $f(x)$. If we wish to find the "net" area under the curve in $\{x_1 \leq x \leq x_6\}$, then we merely evaluate $F(x) \Big|_{x_1}^{x_6}$. If we wish to find the absolute area between the curve and the domain axis, then we must evaluate

$$F(x) \Big|_{x_1}^{x_2} + F(x) \Big|_{x_3}^{x_4} + F(x) \Big|_{x_5}^{x_6},$$

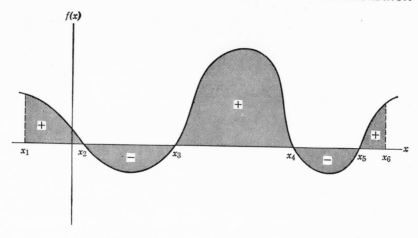

Fig. 14.3.5

and add to this sum the absolute value of

$$F(x)\;\Big|_{x_2}^{x_3} + F(x)\;\Big|_{x_4}^{x_5}.$$

14.3 Exercises

Integrate the given functions over the stated intervals. Sketch the function and indicate by shading the area determined.

14.3.1 $f(x) = 4$, $\{-4 \le x \le 4\}$
14.3.2 $f(x) = 4x - 4$, $\{0 \le x \le 2\}$
14.3.3 $f(x) = 2x - x^2$, $\{-1 \le x \le 3\}$
14.3.4 $f(x) = e^x$, $\{-1 \le x \le 1\}$

14.3.5 $f(x) = \dfrac{1}{x}$, $\{1 \le x \le 2\}$ *(Note:* $\ln 2 = 0.6931$.)

14.3.6 Given the function $f(x) = x^3 - 4x$, sketch the graph of this function and integrate over $\{-3 \le x \le 3\}$. Find the absolute area between the function and the domain axis.

14.4 Continuous probability distributions

An important application of the definite integral is found in the application of *continuous* probability distributions to the solution of administrative decision problems. In Section 10.8 we explored the nature of discrete distributions, or density functions, which specify for

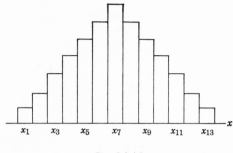

Fig. 14.4.1

an event the probability of the event. The binomial distribution specifies the probability of events which are the outcomes of Bernoulli trials, and since this distribution is a function of the number of trials, n, which must be a positive integer, the resulting density function is discrete. When graphed, such a function may take the form of a histogram, a set of rectangles of unit width and varying height, as indicated in Fig. 14.4.1. Since the set of possible events is mutually exclusive and collectively exhaustive, the sum of the probabilities of the events must be 1.0, and since the area of each rectangle is exactly the probability of the associated event, the sum of the areas of the rectangles must also be 1.0. Now if we let the number of trials become infinitely large, then the number of possible events becomes infinitely large, and if we are to draw a picture of the function, the width of the rectangles must become infinitely small, with the result that the graph is a bell-shaped continuous curve, as shown in Fig. 14.4.2. We remember that the probabilities associated with an event were represented in the original histogram by areas, the sum of which was 1.0. The same is true of a continuous density function: the area under the curve is 1.0

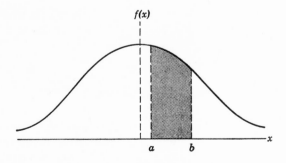

Fig. 14.4.2

If the function described by the curve is $f(x)$, then this area can be represented by the definite integral of the function over its entire interval, which is the set of all real numbers:

$$A = \int_{-\infty}^{\infty} f(x)\ dx = 1.0.$$

Likewise, the probability that an event will fall within an interval $\{a < x < b\}$ is found by

$$P(a < x < b) = \int_{a}^{b} f(x)\ dx.$$

The area under a part of the density function will obviously be determined by the shape of the function, and there are a number of functions used for this purpose. The most common function is that described by the *normal curve*, and called the *normal distribution*. The mathematical expression for this function is

$$f(x) = \frac{1}{\sqrt{2\pi}\ \sigma}\ e^{-(\mu-x)^2/2\sigma^2},$$

where μ (the Greek letter "mu") is the *mean* of the distribution, or the value of x on each side of which is found half of the area under the normal curve, and σ (the Greek letter "sigma") is the *standard deviation*, which is a measure of dispersion of the values about the mean. In the study of statistics we learn to compute the value of the mean and standard deviation of a given set of observations, and thus, if the phenomenon observed behaves in such a way that it can be described by the normal distribution, we may then compute the probability that it lies between any two values of x. To evaluate the integral of this function would certainly be extremely tedious, but fortunately this work has been simplified by construction of a table giving the areas under the normal curve, available in most statistics texts.

We shall leave the mechanics of this subject to the study of statistics, but point out its use by a brief example. Suppose that our vocation is retailing fine furniture. Being tired of the hustle and bustle of the large city where our business is now located, we should like to choose a smaller town in which to do business. Our business is such, however, that our merchandise does not appeal to lower-income families, and we estimate that the town which we choose must have at least 1000 families with income greater than $10,000 per year. We shall assume that the family incomes in the city we are considering are distributed normally, i.e., there are few families with no income and few families with very great income, and most families enjoy an income not too

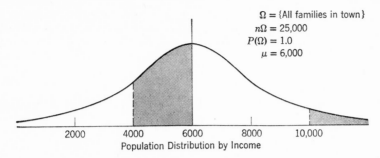

Ω = {All families in town}
nΩ = 25,000
P(Ω) = 1.0
μ = 6,000

2000   4000   6000   8000   10,000
Population Distribution by Income

Fig. 14.4.3

different from the incomes of their neighbors. Consider Fig. 14.4.3, which shows the distribution of income for our hypothetical town of 25,000 families. The area under the curve for any given interval in the domain (income) may thus be considered the percentage of the 25,000 families in town who have incomes within the limits stated by the interval. For instance, if the area shaded in the middle of the illustration is the area under the curve resulting from integrating the function from $4000 to $6000, and the result of the integration is 0.42, then the probability that any family chosen at random will have an income between $4000 and $6000 is 0.42. We may go further, and estimate that there are $(0.42)(25,000) = 10,500$ families in the town within these income limits, since 100 per cent of the families equals 25,000 families.

The question which must be answered before we can make a decision on locating our store in this town is whether or not 4 per cent of the families, i.e., 1000/25,000, have incomes over $10,000. Since our function is asymptotic to the domain axis, i.e., $(-\infty < x < \infty)$, we obviously cannot integrate from $10,000 upward; but since 50 per cent of the area lies to the right of the mean income ($6000), we may integrate over the interval $\{\$6000 < x < \$10,000\}$, subtract the result from 0.50, and if the result is less than 0.04, then we should reject the town as too limited a market for our merchandise. If our goal is to find the smallest town meeting these qualifications, then we need investigate the same data for a number of towns until we find the smallest town, or, perhaps, any small town, satisfying the given criteria, i.e., 1000 families with $10,000 minimum income. These data, by the way, are generally available from census figures, and this type of study is common among large real estate firms dealing in relocation of businesses.

As mentioned previously, given the mean and standard deviation of a distribution *assumed* to be normal, we may find the required probabilities by referring to a table of areas under the normal curve. It is important to realize the difference between discrete and continuous distributions: in the former we may ask for the probability of a specific event, and find its associated rectangle. In the latter, however, we may only find the probability of an event in terms of an interval, i.e., the height of the density function at some given value in the domain cannot be used for the probability of that value.

14.4   Exercises

14.4.1   Given a continuous function $f(x)$, show that the area under the curve at a point is zero. (*Hint:* Evaluate $\int_a^a f(x)\,dx$.)

14.4.2   List five phenomena of any type whose behavior must be represented by a discrete distribution.

14.4.3   List five phenomena of any type whose behavior must be represented by a continuous distribution.

14.4.4   State the difference between a discrete and continuous distribution.

Chapter 15 ———— Model Building and Analysis

15.1 Models

Everyone has at one time or another suffered the outrage of having his personal deficiencies emphasized by comparison with the set of "perfect" elements which comprise someone's idea of the *model* boy, wife, student, teacher, girlfriend, etc.   To insist that such a *model* does not exist is to no avail, for the person who has conceived the model has abstracted from real life the characteristics he or she embodies in the model, and those characteristics do represent real life to that person. All of us, in similar fashion, create models by abstraction from real life to represent to ourselves and others our ideas of life.

A model is a representation, usually simplified, of the real world; an abstraction from reality.   As such, the concept is one we deal with daily.   We are familiar with the type of hobby kit with which we could build a model of, for instance, the *H.M.S. Bounty*.   In the miniature ship fabricated by the hobbyist, an attempt is made to duplicate the *essential* features of the real life item.   In this sense the model ship is a copy of real life, but it still is an abstraction from real life because it is not the *H.M.S. Bounty* and (for obvious reasons) is not complete.

While the hobbyist builds his model of the *H.M.S. Bounty* to satisfy certain leisure time desires, ship designers and naval engineers construct quite similar models of ships for quite different reasons. Such models are designed so that characteristics of the actual ship can be analyzed before it is built. If the model is sufficiently representative of the real-life ship, then it has many important uses, common to all models, the most important of which are:

(1) The model may be analyzed to *identify*, *measure*, and *observe* the performance characteristics of critical components (variables), and of the total unit. As an example, the ship designer would be interested in determining the model's center of gravity, and observing the effect on the model's stability as the center of gravity was changed.

(2) The operations of the model under varying conditions may be analyzed to *predict* how the real-life counterpart would operate under similar conditions. Naval engineers, for example, might place a ship model in a "wave pond" to analyze the riding characteristics of the model as calm to heavy seas were simulated, in order that they might predict how the actual ship would react under varying sea conditions.

(3) The critical components of the model may be varied to *determine the influence* a change in one variable will have on other variables and on the operating characteristics of the model. A ship designer might be interested in studying the impact on other variables (i.e., center of gravity) and total ship operation, of a change in the material used in the model's main deck. Such studies are basic to design decisions.

(4) A model may be built and analyzed to *test an hypothesis*. For example, a designer may believe a newly proposed stabilizing fin would provide too much water drag (with undesirable effects on speed) to be practical. If he constructs the proper model he can test this hypothesis in a wave pond.

(5) Certain characteristics of the model *may be tested feasibly*, where it would not be feasible to test the real-life counterpart. "Life-testing" is a good example: we might fill our model ship with water until it sank, thereby determining its maximum flooding capacity. It would certainly be foolish to try this on the ship after it was built.

(6) Many models *have practical applications* beyond those suggested above. The "Link Trainer," for instance, is a device to simulate flight, used in the training of aircraft pilots. The cost of failure or mistake in the air is extremely high in terms of men and machines; the simulation model accomplishes the desired goal with virtually no cost incurred through operator error or failure. Another type of simulation model is of interest to the student of administration: the so-called "management game," which simulates the operations of a firm. The "player" must make decisions that will lead the firm to the attainment

of its goals, but once again, the cost of failure, at least in terms of real dollars, is zero.

The six uses outlined above have been illustrated primarily with examples drawn from physical models.   However, as we shall see, the concept of models is not limited to physical replicas of real life, and all models (regardless of the form they take) can be similarly used.   Our interest in models springs from the fact that they provide a powerful tool for analyzing real life.   Now life is, of course, extremely complicated, and we do well when we understand even isolated segments of either our physical environment or our cultural environment.

One way that man has achieved some understanding of the world and the people and things in it is by specialization: one man understands the making of shoes, another the tanning of leather, another the merchandising of footwear, another the logistics of supplying an army with boots, another the process by which armies are created and ultimately used, etc.   In effect, modern civilized man has simplified the task of organizing society, by distributing labor according to the amount of understanding that a single man is able to command over the things the knowledge of which is relevant to the society.   Of course, few men are satisfied with their limited understanding even of their own specialties, but without the simplification of total knowledge, no man would have sufficient command over a given subject to be socially useful in a modern society.   As Alfred North Whitehead has said, "Seek simplicity, and distrust it."   This is exactly what we do in model building: we represent in as simple and understandable terms as possible the behavioral relationships among phenomena, and, having developed some knowledge of the thing studied, proceed to complicate the model until it includes more and more of life's substance.

The form a model may take is limited only by our ability to make and understand an abstraction from real life.   As a matter of fact we might classify models by their degree of abstraction.   Under such a system of classification our ship model and all models which are designed to bear a physical resemblance to their real life counterparts are classified as *iconic* models.   Iconic models are pictorial or visual representations of real life; they may be physical miniatures as in our ship model, pictorial as in a map or photograph, graphic as in the chart of an organization, schematic as in the work flow diagram of an assembly line, etc.   The nature of iconic models limits their application to two- or three-dimensional phenomena.

Sometimes it is advantageous to construct a model utilizing one set of properties to represent another set we desire to analyze.   As an example consider the typical relief map, where colors are used to represent land and sea gradients. The map maker in developing his model has represented reality by drawing an *analogy* between colors and iso-altitude areas. Such models are called *analog* models, and although they may be more abstract than iconic models, they offer a much greater range of flexibility in model building because the concept is limited only by our ability to comprehend and use the analogies developed. Thus we can use colors to represent altitude on a map and solid lines to represent paved roads, dotted lines on an organization chart to represent lines of communication, and *symbols in a system of equations to represent the variable behavior of related phenomena.*

A *symbolic* model, where real-life phenomena are represented by symbols, is the most abstract of analog models. Although a symbolic model may seem difficult to conceive because it does not look like the real phenomena it represents, it is much more flexible in use than an iconic model. For example, symbolic models of n-dimension form may be developed, their shape being limited only by our ability to conceive and apply relationships. Symbolic models are also common to all of us; as an example, a language is a symbolic model for expressing reality.

Throughout this book we have analyzed symbolic models, calling them sets, equations, inequations, functions, etc. In each case we have used numbers or other symbols to represent phenomena. Such *mathematical* models are extremely useful in representing complex economic and social phenomena, and they provide the system by which the relationships between such phenomena can be examined and ultimately understood.

15.1 Exercise

Give an example of an iconic model and an analog model, showing for each its use and application, where possible, as illustrated by the six items in the text.

15.2 Model building

Much of our previous work has centered around the analysis of simplified mathematical models in which the relationships among certain economic phenomena were assumed correct as given. We have used both linear and non-linear models of profit ($\pi = TR - TC$), revenue [$TR = f(Q)$], costs [$TC = g(Q)$], etc., to illustrate the application of various mathematical techniques. We are thus already familiar with what is meant by a mathematical economic model. Before we take a close look at the development and techniques of analysis applicable to certain specific economic models, we shall cover briefly a general system by which reality can be analyzed to develop such models.

Anyone with proper training in mathematics can perform the required mathematical operations on a given set of functions, equations, inequations, etc., which comprise an economic model. It takes a quite different and very important skill, and a real understanding of the segment of reality being analyzed, to develop a meaningful model by identifying, measuring, and relating the phenomena incorporated in it. The skill necessary to develop useful economic models is one of the most powerful tools an administrator may possess.

Economic models are designed to facilitate the handling of two general types of problems:

(1) problems concerning the relationship between variables in a system and the *outcome* or *state* of the system, and
(2) problems involving the variation of established control or decision variables to optimize a given objective.

The first type of economic model is the most common and generally the easiest to understand. Consider the problem of a cost accountant who has to find the cost of producing a certain product. The model he would use to solve this problem might be:

$$TC = C_1X_1 + C_2X_2 + \cdots + C_nX_n,$$

where TC symbolizes the unknown cost of product P, and C_1X_1, C_2X_2, etc. represent the known costs of inputs required to produce P. The solution to this type of model is relatively simple, and consists merely of finding the value of the unknown variable (or variables) when the values of other variables are given.

The second type of model, designed to facilitate the choice of an optimizing solution to a problem, is of greater interest to us. Such models require that the system of variables being analyzed be expressed in terms of some *measure of effectiveness*, which is to be maximized or minimized. We have worked with a number of such systems, expressed as cost functions, which we minimized, and profit functions, which we maximized. We should recall the application of differential calculus and linear programming techniques to the determination of optimal solutions.

In the development of either type of model, the following system of analysis is recommended. To facilitate understanding of the model building process, an *a priori* inventory cost problem will be used to illustrate the operational steps in model building.

(1) *Establish the purpose for which the model is to be built.* Is the model to be designed to solve a problem of the first type, or to assist in the development of an optimizing decision? The problem must be identified and the objective of the model must be expressed as some measure of effectiveness (e.g., maximum profit).

An administrator is concerned about the size and working capital costs of his inventory. He wants to know the inventory necessary to carry on his business, yet minimize the cost of the inventory. Because inability to supply a customer involves a cost associated with being out of stock (i.e., loss of sale, loss of goodwill, etc.), we can see that the administrator really seeks to minimize two costs: the cost of having too much inventory, and the cost of having too little. Therefore he wants to build an optimizing model, and its purpose is to assist in the development of a decision which *minimizes total inventory costs*.

(2) *Define the area to be analyzed, in order to provide specific limits to the information to be considered.*

The administrator is interested only in those costs associated with stock procurement and storage, and with being unable to supply orders.

(3) *Identify all of the elements which have an impact in the area of consideration.*

The administrator must determine the costs associated with:
Stock procurement costs (e.g., item purchase costs, freight, clerical costs of processing orders);
Carrying costs (e.g., warehouse costs, inventory insurance, obsolescence, interest on inventory); and
Out-of-stock costs (e.g., loss of sales, loss of goodwill).

(4) *Determine which of these elements have a vital effect on the problem being considered, i.e., which variables define and control the operation of the system.* This is perhaps the critical point in the development of a model, for here we analyze the system by which the variables are related. We must know if our system of relationships is based on a *definition*, such as

$$\text{Total Revenue} = \text{Price} \times \text{Quantity Sold},$$

or if the system is governed by a *law*, such as

$$\text{Demand} = f(\text{Price}).$$

If our model is based upon a definition, then it must of course agree with the definition. Choosing and combining the proper definitions is, of course, the essence of the *deductive* process for this type of model. If, on the other hand, the relationship is established originally by hunch, or if some general law appears to be controlling it, then the model must necessarily be tested to determine whether it does represent reality; this is the essence of the *inductive* process, to be explained in the next section.

Having determined the vital elements and their system of relationship, we can proceed to note those elements which are known or unknown, constant or variable, and controllable or uncontrollable.

Since our administrator seeks to minimize total inventory cost he would conclude that stock procurement, carrying, and out-of-stock costs were all vital. Each of these costs is, by *definition*, a function of the quantity of inventory, and thus the optimum cost would be determined by some inventory quantity (called the *economic lot quantity*). Procurement costs and carrying costs are usually known; out-of-stock costs on the other hand are difficult to determine, if not completely unknown. Certain of the cost elements are constant (warehousing, for example) and some are variable (freight costs, for example), and these considerations must be included in the explicit descriptions of each of the cost functions. Finally, each of these cost elements is controllable to some extent, and the essence of the model is the determination of some optimum quantity of inventory which in turn determines the level of each of the costs.

(5) *For each vital element define an appropriate symbol.*

The following symbols might be assigned in our example:

$$TC = \text{Total cost}$$

$$Q = \text{Inventory quantity}$$

$$C_s = \text{Cost of procurement}$$

$$C_1 = \text{Carrying cost}$$

$$C_2 = \text{Out-of-stock cost.}$$

(6) *Synthesize the relevant elements into a model consisting of a set of equations relating the elements.*

Analyzing the previously developed relationships the administrator establishes the following mathematical model:

$$C_s = g(Q); C_1 = h(Q); C_2 = k(Q):$$
$$TC = f(C_s, C_1, C_2) = g(Q) + h(Q) + k(Q).$$

(7) *Apply a decision rule.* The decision rule might be to maximize or minimize some objective function, or to find some satisfactory level of performance.

Since he wishes to minimize inventory costs, our administrator will apply the proper mathematical techniques to the total cost function, finding the value of Q which minimizes TC.

Economic models may be developed inductively (*a posteriori*) by a model builder who reviews his experience with a set of phenomena, and, knowing how things have happened in the past, abstracts the vital elements from this empirical evidence to construct an analytical model. Models may also be developed deductively (*a priori*) before the fact. In this sense a model describes the structural relationship between phenomena in terms of a theoretical statement that defines the system by which the elements are related. As a matter of fact, the analytical model developed from a theory is usually the vehicle by which the theory is tested.

In considering the actual development of decision models a number of model building precautions come to mind. First of all, with all of our emphasis on quantitative techniques, it must be realized that not all phenomena can be related in a quantitative model—some elements defy quantification. However, this does not destroy the basic idea of model analysis for non-quantitative relationships, for a great deal can be learned from qualitative models. After a qualitative model has been developed (often the logical first step in any case) it may be that a system of quantification will be discovered. Second, great care must be exercised in selecting the vital elements of the model, to eliminate unimportant items and to assure that no important variables are omitted. Third, a model—for reasons of cost, ease of understanding, and simplicity of operations—should be kept as simple as possible. The model builder must balance this need for simplicity against the loss of realism which may develop as detail is eliminated from a model. Finally, a model does not make decisions; it is only an aid to the decision maker. The effectiveness of a model will be determined by the accuracy with which it represents reality, and the wisdom with which it is applied.

15.2 Exercises

15.2.1 Following the steps outlined in the text, construct a model to explain:

(a) the determination of a contractor's cost in digging a basement
(b) the determination of the optimum number of gasoline stations in a town of 25,000 people.

15.3 Inductive modeling

As indicated previously, we mean by inductive modeling the determination of behavioral relationships through observation. Many scientists will not accept any theoretical model unless it can stand up under rigorous empirical testing of the relationships described in the model to prove that they are representations of reality. This is probably an extreme and unwarranted position in many instances, especially in those where measurement is difficult or impossible. Such a model may be very useful as a first approximation of the desired relationship. Arriving at an impasse in finding a proper relationship, and proving that no such model *can* exist, is as important an advance as discovering a practical model! In such a circumstance, other workers in the area may spend their time in more fruitful pursuits.

The inductive modeling process consists of observing the simultaneous behavior of two or more variables, and then drawing a conclusion or inference about the ways in which they are related. Let us illustrate this process by an example. Suppose there are seven houses along one side of a city street, and, in the early spring, the front lawns are each in the same condition. The homeowners make decisions at this time to fertilize their respective lawns, and each decides to apply a different quantity of the same fertilizer to his lawn. In the middle of the summer, we observe the condition of the lawns in terms of the color of the grass, and develop the following set of observations, the first item in each ordered pair being the number of pounds of fertilizer applied, and the second item being the color of the lawn, for each homeowner: {(0, brown), (1, yellow), (2, pale green), (3, forest green), (4, yellow green), (5, tan), (6, brown)}. We contemplate this information, concluding that if we apply too little or too much fertilizer, we can expect something other than a forest green lawn, which we presume to be the desired objective. Note carefully that this process was not purely inductive, for we started with the premise that fertilizer and color were related. In effect, we are building a model to test an hypothesis. More often than not, data collection without some prior expectation or assumption about behavior is an idle pursuit.

The set of observations above may be represented more clearly by graphing them, as in Fig. 15.3.1. The vertical axis represents a certain part of the color spectrum. Note that we have described a function, which you may have noticed from the set notation originally used. Each ordered pair represents a simultaneous observation of the behavior of the variables; the graph implies that the optimum application of fertilizer is three pounds. The next question might be, "What

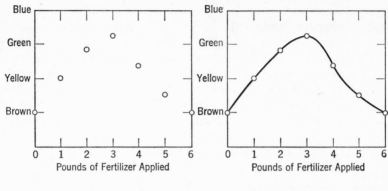

Fig. 15.3.1   Fig. 15.3.2

happens when $2\frac{1}{2}$ pounds of fertilizer are applied?". We have no such observation in our given set, yet it seems reasonable that the result of such an application should be somewhere between pale green and forest green. But where? One method of estimating the unknown color is to fit a curve to the data by inspection: assuming that there is some regularity in the behavior of these two variables, we might choose a parabolic function, as indicated in Fig. 15.3.2. Note that the result of this inductive process is an *analog* model which could be useful to the lawn fancier. We cannot state the entire relationship in mathematical form, because it is not very practical to attempt to quantify color. (We say *practical*, because such would be perfectly *feasible*: color can be quantified in terms of wavelength.) It suffices to state the function in general form: Color = f(quantity of fertilizer applied). We have excluded from this model any other variables, such as water and sunlight, which would have to be included in a complete set of instructions to the homeowner.

A more "exact" method, in the mathematical sense, of finding an explicit mathematical function describing the relationship is called *curve fitting*. The mechanics of this process will be left to your study of statistics; suffice it to say that formulas have been developed by which the original observations themselves are manipulated to produce an equation having the mathematical quality of fitting the data better (in a statistical sense) than any other equation of its particular type. In other words, if we think that a straight line fits the data well enough, then we can find the equation of the best-fitting linear function, and likewise for a parabola or any other function. Recalling one of the rules of model building, we always try to keep the model as simple as possible, not only for the sake of manipulation, but also because a high-order or otherwise exotic function may behave so erratically near the limits over which it is defined as to be a very unrealistic representation of the real world. The methods for fitting lines are very amenable to computerization, and thus the administrator who understands the concept need only use his computer facility to have his observations reduced to a usable function.

15.3   Exercise

Construct a set of ten hypothetical simultaneous observations of any reasonable pair of phenomena. Graph them, fit a line to the points graphed, and critically analyze the meaning of the function. (Don't try to find the values of the constants in your function, however.)

15.4   Simulation models

The development of the high-speed computer has opened a door to the analysis of many decision problems, a door that had remained closed because of the impractical length of time required for the computation involved in relatively simple models. Perhaps the most sensitive variable in administrative decision-making is *time*, because it is completely uncontrollable and inexorable. More often than not, the urgency of a situation will require immediate action, which precludes the accurate appraisal of alternatives offered by the circumstances, as well as of the outcomes of choosing any given alternative. In the absence of planning, each decision is a crisis decision, and one poor decision can precipitate a chain reaction of poorly advised expedients which result in further chaos. The enlightened decision maker will spend some of his time PLANNING AHEAD, considering possible states of nature in the future, and laying plans to turn any possible development to his own profit.

Now the vast number of possible states of nature for even a small problem can render the task of planning very difficult, if not impossible, especially if a great deal of computing or information gathering is necessary, because by the time we have completed our study, the event may have already occurred. The classic example in the recent past is the development and marketing of the Edsel automobile: implementing decisions to go ahead with the automobile required some three years to complete, and a reasonable decision at the time it was made became a fiasco by the time the payoff could be realized. In the interim period, the American car buyer's taste had changed from the large, powerful, middle-priced car to the compact car.   Where analytical techniques can be computerized, we can reduce the amount of time between fact gathering and decision.   Thus many analytical techniques have become feasible in practice and are no longer the province of the academician who is not pressured into a decision by the exigencies of time.

Although simulation models do not depend upon computers to provide useful results, their very nature lends itself to high-speed computation, where many facts can be rapidly analyzed.   By simulation we mean the duplication of an environment by a model in such a way that we can change the model environment at will to test the outcome of imposing certain actions or conditions on it.   The Link Trainer mentioned in Section 15.1 is sometimes called a flight *simulator*, for it duplicates the environment of the pilot, who can change the attitude and speed of the aircraft to simulate a stall or spin, for instance.   If we could simulate the entire operation of a business firm, then we could test certain decisions in the simulator at relatively low cost.   Obviously, the more sophisticated the simulator, the higher the degree of confidence that we may place in the results obtained from it.

In much of our work we have assumed that we operate under conditions of certainty, i.e., that facts and states of nature are known.   In simulation, we reintroduce the idea of risk.   A simulator is admirably suited to the testing of various hypotheses about the nature of a given environment.   Let us illustrate a practical simulation model, and show a powerful use of probability theory in decision-making.   Suppose that we are the managers of a supermarket in a highly competitive area, and in the remodeling of our store to match or exceed the facilities offered by our competition, we must decide how many checkout stands to install.   Obviously, we must have at least 1 checkout stand, but if we should decide to install only 1, then in periods of high volume we must expect to infuriate (if not completely alienate) many customers who must stand in line, waiting to have their purchases checked out.   If our competitors guarantee that no one will stand in their checkout line for more than 3 minutes, then we must do as well.   The length of the waiting line, or *queue*, is determined by the number of checkout stands available, the rate at which customers are serviced at each stand (called the service rate), and the rate at which customers join the queue to be checked out (called the arrival rate).   Consider first this simplification of the problem: 5 customers arrive simultaneously every 3 minutes, and the service rate is exactly 3 minutes per customer.   With 5 stands we could handle these customers with no queue and no idle time of the checkers. Suppose now that the 5 customers arrive every 2 minutes; what happens to the queue? Obviously, it begins to grow without bound. Thus in any queueing situation, if the service rate is less than the arrival rate, the queue tends to increase infinitely. If the service rate is greater than the arrival rate, then we expect to have idle time for the service facilities. Our decision as to the number of stands rests then upon balancing the costs of providing service and the costs of having a queue.

For relatively simple queueing problems, the analytical theory of queues, based upon probability distributions of arrivals and service, may provide the information necessary for a decision, in terms of expected queue length and waiting time. For more complicated problems, we turn to simulation and a particular method called *Monte Carlo*, in which we simulate the number of customers arriving in a given time interval, and the number of customers serviced in the time interval, and any other conditions upon the problem that make the model a better representation of the true state of nature. Let us see how this might be done, by examining a simplification of our supermarket problem. Suppose the fixed cost of a fancy checkout stand is $5 per hour, the average cost of checking out an order is $0.15, and the cost of having a customer wait is $0.50 per customer. We write the *total expected cost* of the checkout operation as the sum of these costs:

$$TEC = \$5x_1 + \$0.15x_2 + \$0.50x_3,$$

where x_1 is the number of stands used, x_2 is the number of customers who could be serviced with x_1 stands in a given time interval, and x_3 is the number of customers forced to wait in the time interval. The number of stands, x_1, is our decision variable, and we are constrained to have at least 1 stand. Now we need to know how many customers we will have, and how many customers we will be able to service with a given number of stands.

We recall the histogram, which describes the probability of certain events in terms of the area of a rectangle. Suppose we make a traffic count in our store between the hours of 10 A.M. and 11 A.M., and in each 5 minute interval tally the number of arrivals at the checkout stands and the number of people checked through the stands. We could then construct histograms for each distribution, each rectangle representing an event, such as the event that exactly 4 people arrived, or exactly 2 people were serviced. The area of each rectangle would represent the relative frequency of the associated event. Suppose that instead of constructing a histogram we represent the areas as pie-shaped pieces of a wheel. The total area of the wheel represents the universe of all

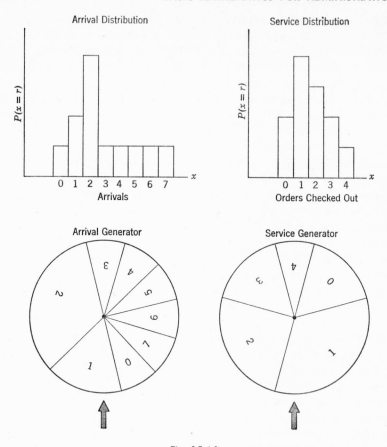

Fig. 15.4.1

people tallied, and the area of each wedge is the frequency with which its associated event occurs. In Fig. 15.4.1 are drawn the hypothetical distributions resulting from the tallies made above, showing the histograms of arrivals and services and the resulting wheels. If each wheel is perfectly balanced so that when we spin it, it is as likely to stop at one place as at any other place, then it is what we call a *random number generator*, and if the generator is spun many times and we tally each of the outcomes, we should find that the resulting distribution of outcomes does not differ significantly from the original distribution. Thus the name "Monte Carlo"; we shall simulate arrivals and people serviced by spinning the generators. Each spin represents a 5 minute interval; we spin both wheels for each interval, to find out how many people

arrive and how many are serviced in the interval.   If these numbers
are not the same, then either the queue grows longer or we have idle
checkout capacity.   We are now ready to simulate the checkout operation, to determine the cost of each of the alternatives available to us
in terms of the number of stands to install.

In Fig. 15.4.2 is a table showing how the analysis proceeds.   In
Column I are listed the time periods, each of which is of 5 minutes
duration, for one hour.   We spin the wheels for the first period; the
arrival generator indicates 2, meaning that 2 people arrive at the
stand, and we enter this number in Column II.   Column III is the
number of people waiting for service, which is the number of arrivals
plus the number already waiting in line (previous entry in Column V).
The service generator stops at 3, indicating that 3 people can be
checked out in period 1.   Since no one was waiting at the beginning,
there is still no one waiting at the end of the period, but 1 unit of checking capacity is idle.   We therefore enter 0 in Column V and 1 in
Column VI.

We go on to period 2, and spin both generators again.   The result is
1 arrival and 1 person checked.   No one was in line, and therefore the
queue is still empty at the end of the period.   In period 3 we find 7
arrivals, the first of whom has a great many groceries, and thus is the
only one capable of being serviced in the period.   The rest of the
arrivals are still waiting in line at the end of the period.   The table is
completed in the above fashion, and we notice that at the end of the
hour, there are 16 people waiting in line, and the line is growing.   We
serviced 20 people, and could have serviced 1 more; therefore $x_2 = 21$.
In the hour there were a total of 78 waiting units, and thus $x_3 = 78$.
Since $x_1 = 1$, we find the cost of this alternative to be

$$TEC(x_1 = 1) = \$5(1) + \$0.15(21) + \$0.50(78)$$

$$= \$5 + \$3.15 + \$39$$

$$= \$47.15.$$

We repeat the operation for 2 stands, using the same numbers
generated for the alternative above, since we wish to simulate what
would have happened under the same conditions had we had 2 stands
instead of 1.   So we use the same pattern of arrivals, and the same
pattern of service, except that our service capacity has doubled and
therefore we shall double each number generated.   Whether or not
the assumption is valid that service capacity is exactly doubled with
the addition of a second stand depends upon a number of factors,
including *queue discipline*.   By queue discipline we mean the rule by

	Time Period I	Number of Arrivals II	Number to Checkout III	Checkout Capacity IV	Queue Length V	Idle Units VI
	1	2	2	3	0	1
	2	1	1	1	0	0
1	3	7	7	1	6	0
	4	3	9	4	5	0
S	5	0	5	2	3	0
T	6	2	5	0	5	0
A	7	2	7	2	5	0
N	8	4	9	0	9	0
D	9	1	10	3	7	0
	10	5	12	1	11	0
	11	2	13	2	11	0
	12	6	17	1	16	0
		35		20	78	1
	1	2	2	6	0	4
	2	1	1	2	0	1
2	3	7	7	2	5	0
	4	3	8	8	0	0
S	5	0	0	4	0	4
T	6	2	2	0	2	0
A	7	2	4	4	0	0
N	8	4	4	0	4	0
D	9	1	5	6	0	1
S	10	5	5	2	3	0
	11	2	5	4	1	0
	12	6	7	2	5	0
		35		40	20	10
	1	2	2	9	0	7
	2	1	1	3	0	2
3	3	7	7	3	4	0
	4	3	7	12	0	5
S	5	0	0	6	0	6
T	6	2	2	0	2	0
A	7	2	4	6	0	2
N	8	4	4	0	4	0
D	9	1	5	9	0	4
S	10	5	5	3	2	0
	11	2	4	6	0	2
	12	6	6	3	3	0
		35		60	15	28

Fig. 15.4.2

which the members of the queue are serviced, such as first come, first served. Our assumption would imply that once a customer has lined up behind a counter, he will not change "lanes," which is true of most people unless they are extremely provoked. Thus the queues for both stands are independent, i.e., the length of one does not affect the length of the other. This is of course only an assumption, and a more realistic model would allow for the people who change lanes. In any event, we determine the number of units incurring service cost to be 40 checked plus 10 idle, or $x_2 = 50$. The number of units waiting has been reduced considerably to $x_3 = 20$. Therefore, total expected cost for two stands is

$$TEC(x_1 = 2) = \$5(2) + \$0.15(50) + \$0.50(20)$$

$$= \$10 + \$7.50 + \$10$$

$$= \$27.50.$$

The total cost of the operation is reduced by almost \$20 by adding the second stand. To see if we might realize a further reduction in cost by adding a third stand, we repeat the process again, this time tripling our original service capacity, under the assumption made previously. We determine $x_2 = 88$, $x_3 = 15$, and, of course, $x_1 = 3$. Thus

$$TEC(x_1 = 3) = \$5(3) + \$0.15(88) + \$0.50(15)$$

$$= \$15 + \$13.20 + \$7.50$$

$$= \$35.70.$$

We see that further increases in the number of stands will only increase cost, and thus our decision, since we are cost minimizers, should be to install 2 stands.

Since traffic patterns change for different hours of the day, we would sophisticate this model by extending it over a longer period of time, perhaps a day's operation, or even one as long as a week, to "iron out" different demand patterns due to different weekday and weekend shopping habits. Nor would we be satisfied with only one *iteration* of a given pattern of random numbers. We would make sufficient iterations to develop sets of observed costs, perhaps using the average cost of the set as the outcome of a given decision for x_1, and comparing these average total costs to determine the least cost alternative. Certainly there are many other changes and additions which could be made in and to this model; the student will be asked to consider some of them in the exercises. Although such refinements increase the tedium of working out each iteration of the simulation, it should be remembered that this type of model is admirably suited to computerization: the work done above could be accomplished on a medium-sized computer in a few seconds!

Although the Monte Carlo technique appears to be a gimmick, it is in fact a serious and defensible means of analysis when probabilities can be determined (and even when they must be guessed at), and a more straightforward analytical technique cannot be applied. In practice, the method has been used to develop understanding of such processes as the arrival and service of ships in San Francisco and airplanes at La Guardia Field, of inventory changes at service supply depots, and sequential production processes of all sorts of manufactured goods. Monte Carlo is only one example, of course, of a growing number of simulation techniques. When we consider that a total manufacturing plant has been simulated using a large scale computer, the scope and power of the method is readily apparent.

15.4   Exercises

15.4.1 Using the data of the illustration above, find the total expected cost of 4 checkout stands.

15.4.2 If the cost of waiting were assumed to be zero, what decision should be made in the illustration given? (*Hint:* Look at the total cost function.) Obviously, no supermarket would arrive at this decision. On the other hand, do you suppose that a supermarket manager knows this cost of waiting? (Ask one!) How would you go about telling a supermarket manager what his cost of waiting is, knowing what his decision was about the number of checkout stands?

15.4.3 If the cost of waiting were assumed to be infinite, i.e., so great that we would never allow a customer to wait in line, how many check stands would be needed in the example above? (*Hint:* Consider the arrival wheel.) Find the total cost of adopting this alternative using the data given.

15.4.4 Show how to develop the least cost alternative if the cost of each stand is $25 instead of $5, the other costs being as indicated in the illustration.

15.4.5 Show how to develop the least cost alternative if the cost of waiting is $5 per unit waiting instead of $0.50, the other costs being as given originally.

15.4.6 Make a list of any five applications that would be amenable to Monte Carlo analysis. In each case, state generally the relationship among the costs involved.

Four-Place Logarithm Table

Appendix I

No.	0	1	2	3	4	5	6	7	8	9
10	0000	0043	0086	0128	0170	0212	0253	0294	0334	0374
11	0414	0453	0492	0531	0569	0607	0645	0682	0719	0755
12	0792	0828	0864	0899	0934	0969	1004	1038	1072	1106
13	1139	1173	1206	1239	1271	1303	1335	1367	1399	1430
14	1461	1492	1523	1553	1584	1614	1644	1673	1703	1732
15	1761	1790	1818	1847	1875	1903	1931	1959	1987	2014
16	2041	2068	2095	2122	2148	2175	2201	2227	2253	2279
17	2304	2330	2355	2380	2405	2430	2455	2480	2504	2529
18	2553	2577	2601	2625	2648	2672	2695	2718	2742	2765
19	2788	2810	2833	2856	2878	2900	2923	2945	2967	2989
20	3010	3032	3054	3075	3096	3118	3139	3160	3181	3201
21	3222	3243	3263	3284	3304	3324	3345	3365	3385	3404
22	3424	3444	3464	3483	3502	3522	3541	3560	3579	3598
23	3617	3636	3655	3674	3692	3711	3729	3747	3766	3784
24	3802	3820	3838	3856	3874	3892	3909	3927	3945	3962
25	3979	3997	4014	4031	4048	4065	4082	4099	4116	4133
26	4150	4166	4183	4200	4216	4232	4249	4265	4281	4298
27	4314	4330	4346	4362	4378	4393	4409	4425	4440	4456
28	4472	4487	4502	4518	4533	4548	4564	4579	4594	4609
29	4624	4639	4654	4669	4683	4698	4713	4728	4742	4757
30	4771	4786	4800	4814	4829	4843	4857	4871	4886	4900
31	4914	4928	4942	4955	4969	4983	4997	5011	5024	5038
32	5051	5065	5079	5092	5105	5119	5132	5145	5159	5172
33	5185	5198	5211	5224	5237	5250	5263	5276	5289	5302
34	5315	5328	5340	5353	5366	5378	5391	5403	5416	5428
35	5441	5453	5465	5478	5490	5502	5514	5527	5539	5551
36	5563	5575	5587	5599	5611	5623	5635	5647	5658	5670
37	5682	5694	5705	5717	5729	5740	5752	5763	5775	5786
38	5798	5809	5821	5832	5843	5855	5866	5877	5888	5899
39	5911	5922	5933	5944	5955	5966	5977	5988	5999	6010
40	6021	6031	6042	6053	6064	6075	6085	6096	6107	6117
41	6128	6138	6149	6160	6170	6180	6191	6201	6212	6222
42	6232	6243	6253	6263	6274	6284	6294	6304	6314	6325
43	6335	6345	6355	6365	6375	6385	6395	6405	6415	6425
44	6435	6444	6454	6464	6474	6484	6493	6503	6513	6522
45	6532	6542	6551	6561	6571	6580	6590	6599	6609	6618
46	6628	6637	6646	6656	6665	6675	6684	6693	6702	6712
47	6721	6730	6739	6749	6758	6767	6776	6785	6794	6803
48	6812	6821	6830	6839	6848	6857	6866	6875	6884	6893
49	6902	6911	6920	6928	6937	6946	6955	6964	6972	6981
50	6990	6998	7007	7016	7024	7033	7042	7050	7059	7067
51	7076	7084	7093	7101	7110	7118	7126	7135	7143	7152
52	7160	7168	7177	7185	7193	7202	7210	7218	7226	7235
53	7243	7251	7259	7267	7275	7284	7292	7300	7308	7316
54	7324	7332	7340	7348	7356	7364	7372	7380	7388	7396
No.	0	1	2	3	4	5	6	7	8	9

No.	0	1	2	3	4	5	6	7	8	9
55	7404	7412	7419	7427	7435	7443	7451	7459	7466	7474
56	7482	7490	7497	7505	7513	7520	7528	7536	7543	7551
57	7559	7566	7574	7582	7589	7597	7604	7612	7619	7627
58	7634	7642	7649	7657	7664	7672	7679	7686	7694	7701
59	7709	7716	7723	7731	7738	7745	7752	7760	7767	7774
60	7782	7789	7796	7803	7810	7818	7825	7832	7839	7846
61	7853	7860	7868	7875	7882	7889	7896	7903	7910	7917
62	7924	7931	7938	7945	7952	7959	7966	7973	7980	7987
63	7993	8000	8007	8014	8021	8028	8035	8041	8048	8055
64	8062	8069	8075	8082	8089	8096	8102	8109	8116	8122
65	8129	8136	8142	8149	8156	8162	8169	8176	8182	8189
66	8195	8202	8209	8215	8222	8228	8235	8241	8248	8254
67	8261	8267	8274	8280	8287	8293	8299	8306	8312	8319
68	8325	8331	8338	8344	8351	8357	8363	8370	8376	8382
69	8388	8395	8401	8407	8414	8420	8426	8432	8439	8445
70	8451	8457	8463	8470	8476	8482	8488	8494	8500	8506
71	8513	8519	8525	8531	8537	8543	8549	8555	8561	8567
72	8573	8579	8585	8591	8597	8603	8609	8615	8621	8627
73	8633	8639	8645	8651	8657	8663	8669	8675	8681	8686
74	8692	8698	8704	8710	8716	8722	8727	8733	8739	8745
75	8751	8756	8762	8768	8774	8779	8785	8791	8797	8802
76	8808	8814	8820	8825	8831	8837	8842	8848	8854	8859
77	8865	8871	8876	8882	8887	8893	8899	8904	8910	8915
78	8921	8927	8932	8938	8943	8949	8954	8960	8965	8971
79	8976	8982	8987	8993	8998	9004	9009	9015	9020	9025
80	9031	9036	9042	9047	9053	9058	9063	9069	9074	9079
81	9085	9090	9096	9101	9106	9112	9117	9122	9128	9133
82	9138	9143	9149	9154	9159	9165	9170	9175	9180	9186
83	9191	9196	9201	9206	9212	9217	9222	9227	9232	9238
84	9243	9248	9253	9258	9263	9269	9274	9279	9284	9289
85	9294	9299	9304	9309	9315	9320	9325	9330	9335	9340
86	9345	9350	9355	9360	9365	9370	9375	9380	9385	9390
87	9395	9400	9405	9410	9415	9420	9425	9430	9435	9440
88	9445	9450	9455	9460	9465	9469	9474	9479	9484	9489
89	9494	9499	9504	9509	9513	9518	9523	9528	9533	9538
90	9542	9547	9552	9557	9562	9566	9571	9576	9581	9586
91	9590	9595	9600	9605	9609	9614	9619	9624	9628	9633
92	9638	9643	9647	9652	9657	9661	9666	9671	9675	9680
93	9685	9689	9694	9699	9703	9708	9713	9717	9722	9727
94	9731	9736	9741	9745	9750	9754	9759	9763	9768	9773
95	9777	9782	9786	9791	9795	9800	9805	9809	9814	9818
96	9823	9827	9832	9836	9841	9845	9850	9854	9859	9863
97	9868	9872	9877	9881	9886	9890	9894	9899	9903	9908
98	9912	9917	9921	9926	9930	9934	9939	9943	9948	9952
99	9956	9961	9965	9969	9974	9978	9983	9987	9991	9996
No.	0	1	2	3	4	5	6	7	8	9

Index